Chuck + Pat Humphreys
1531 West Boulder
Colorado Springs, Co
80904
Phone: 634-2700
19 October 1970

youth and the church

youth
and the church

a survey
of
the church's ministry
to youth

Edited by ROY G. IRVING
ROY B. ZUCK

MOODY PRESS ● CHICAGO

Library of Congress Catalog Card Number: 67-14388

Second Printing, 1968

foreword

FUTURE CHURCH HISTORIANS looking back upon the state of religion in America during the middle decades of this twentieth century will have to reckon with the present educational revival among evangelicals. For since World War II there has been in this segment of Protestantism a quickening of concern for the spiritual nurture of youth. Moreover, this concern has been steadily translated into action. New agencies for the evangelization of youth and their training in the Scriptures and in Christian living have arisen, older agencies such as the Sunday school have been reinvigorated, additional Christian elementary and secondary schools as well as higher educational institutions (Bible institutes and Bible colleges, liberal arts colleges and seminaries) have been founded, older institutions have been strengthened, and the number of accredited schools and colleges has been augmented. Even more significant, because a carefully reasoned position is essential to effective action, is the growing awareness of leaders in evangelical education that they must articulate a thoroughgoing philosophy and apply it to the whole of the teaching process. That evangelicals are indeed developing such a philosophy based on the biblical world view and thus making their distinctive contribution to contemporary educational thought is one of the hopeful developments of recent years.

Supreme Court decisions on prayer and Bible reading in the public schools have brought into sharp relief the crucial responsibility of parents and churches for the Christian nurture of youth. For if the faith is to be effectively communicated to the younger generation, then the churches, working side by side with parents, with Christian schools (although these reach only a minority of youth), and with various independent Christian agencies, must improve and amplify their educational programs. And in order for this to be done by evangelicals, they must have help in understanding and coping with the great opportunities before them.

Such help is provided by *Youth and the Church*. In this multifaceted volume, the editors, Roy G. Irving and Roy B. Zuck, have made available to pastors, Sunday school teachers and youth leaders of all kinds a compendium of pertinent information. The book is firmly based on biblically and theologically conservative presuppositions. Although a formal philosophy of Christian education is not elaborated, the specialists who contribute the twenty-eight chapters that make up the book are manifestly united in taking the Bible and the evangelical faith as their frame of reference. Objectives for the different aspects of Christian education are specifically stated, methods of preparation and teaching carefully presented, statistical data included when required, and useful bibliographies appended to each chapter.

Now that this helpful resource book for those who are engaged in the various kinds of evangelical education has been published, it might well be matched by a work that, somewhat on the analogy of James Bryant Conant's notable study *The Education of American Teachers,* would deal with the special training of committed Christian teachers for service in all types of schools, public as well as Christian; for evangelicals cannot stand aloof from their responsibility for witness to the whole of the educational enterprise. And if *Youth and the Church* serves as a catalyst for the production of such work, it will have the distinction of fulfilling a purpose quite beyond its inherent value in its own important field.

FRANK E. GAEBELEIN

contents

7

PART V   WORKING WITH YOUTH

PART I

youth education in perspective

Youth is the morning of life, and if the Sun of Righteousness does not chase away the moral fog and smog before noon, the whole life may remain overcast and gloomy.

TED W. ENGSTROM

1

the challenge of today's youth

IT IS AN INESCAPABLE FACT that "tomorrow belongs to today's youth." Little can be done to change this fact, but we can change the youth to whom we are leaving the world. The men of our generation are fighting wars, but the peace we gain with our blood will be left to young men now in their middle teens.

Our generation has produced scientists who invented television and spaceships. But in days ahead, youth will decide what programs will be shown on TV and where the spaceships will fly. Our generation has produced statesmen who have raised the standard of living in the United States and fought Communist inroads. But youth will decide in the future if the legislation is to be repealed or followed through, and if the fight against atheistic Communism is to be finally won or lost.

Many men and women of our generation have devoted their lives to making the world a better place in which to live. But if youth are unconcerned and unchallenged, the world could conceivably slip into a moral morass.

TED W. ENGSTROM, D.D., formerly President of Youth For Christ International, is Executive Vice-President of World Vision, Inc.

Dedicated Christians in our generation have devoted the best years of their lives to reaching men and women for Christ, building churches, sending out missionaries. But young people will help determine the answer to the question, "When the Son of man cometh, shall he find faith on the earth?" (Luke 18:8). Unless we win youth for the Lord we "labour in vain" (Ps. 127:1).

ADOLESCENCE—A TIME OF RESPONSE TO EVANGELISM

The thirteen years of adolescence—from ages 12 through 24—are a comparatively small portion of the 71-year life expectancy of the average American. But within that 13-year period many are won to the Lord. In fact, a number of surveys verify the fact that most Christians accepted Christ as Saviour during or before their teen years.

Evangelist Tom Rees of England found in his meetings that of all the Christians in England, 75 percent came to Christ before the age of 14, 20 percent between 14 and 21, and only 5 percent were saved after they had passed the age of 21.[1]

Lionel A. Hunt gives these statistics on conversions in the United States:

1 percent were converted when under 4 years old

85 percent were converted between ages 4 and 15

10 percent were converted between ages 15 and 30

4 percent were converted when over 30 years old.[2]

George W. Truett, famed Baptist minister, took a census of more than 1,200 men and found that

3 were converted when over 45 years of age

13 were converted between the ages of 40 and 45

less than 30 were converted when over 30 years of age

and 1,100 were converted when under 21.[3]

A survey of 5,000 Christian students in six Christian schools revealed the interesting facts that "the junior-age children from Christian homes and the high-school-age youngsters from non-Christian homes respond more readily to the gospel than any other age-groups" and that "one-half of those from non-Christian homes found Christ during the short and stormy period, ages 12 to 17, with 16 as the peak age."[4]

---

[1]Lionel A. Hunt, *Handbook of Children's Evangelism* (Chicago: Moody Press, 1960), p. 38.

[2]*Ibid.*

[3]*Ibid.*, p. 42.

[4]J. Robertson McQuilken, "Born of the Spirit," *Christian Life*, XVI:26 (March, 1954). The six schools were Biola Bible College, Bob Jones University, Columbia Bible College, Prairie Bible Institute, Providence Bible Institute, and Wheaton College.

The response of college-age youth to the gospel is evidenced by the successful evangelistic efforts of a number of campus groups, such as Campus Crusade for Christ, Inter-Varsity Christian Fellowship, and The Navigators.[5]

ADOLESCENCE—A TIME OF RELIGIOUS INTEREST

Contrary to common belief, the early teen-age years are years of an awakening interest in religious and spiritual matters. This growing religiosity is reflected in the large numbers of young people "who are found in attendance at religious assemblies, church camps, and other church meetings of youth groups."[6] J. Hudson Taylor, founder of the China Inland Mission (now the Overseas Missionary Fellowship), wrote, "If we think that boys or girls in their teens are too young for soul-experiences, we are indeed mistaken. At no time in life is there a greater capacity for devotion, if the heart's deepest springs are open to the love of Christ."[7]

Browning states that "youth, in every socioeconomic situation, are much more serious about their quest for a faith than we may have assumed," and that "our expectations concerning the basic seriousness of youth are much too low."[8] Lawton discovered that many of the questions to which teen-agers said they had tried to find a satisfactory answer but had failed, pertain to religious or moral issues.[9] Another writer points out that "youth are more aware of the gravity of their sins, more eager to be saved, more ready to accept help, more anxious for a right relationship with the Lord" than many adults recognize.[10]

But what accounts for this openness and sensitivity to spiritual things? Cole answers that adolescents investigate religion because they are looking for a possible source of emotional and intellectual stimulation and satisfaction.[11]

And Koonce observes that religion can give teens, who naturally tend to feel insecure, a feeling of security. Young people look for something that

---

[5]See chapter 20, "Reaching Youth in College."

[6]Ray F. Koonce, *Understanding Your Teen-agers* (Nashville: Broadman Press, 1965), p. 83.

[7]Dr. and Mrs. Howard Taylor, *Hudson Taylor's Spiritual Secret* (Philadelphia: China Inland Mission, 1935), p. 15.

[8]Robert L. Browning, "The Church's Youth Ministry," *An Introduction to Christian Education*, Marvin J. Taylor, ed. (Nashville: Abingdon Press, 1966), p. 187.

[9]G. Lawton, "A Preliminary Study of Questions Which Adolescents Find Unanswerable," quoted in Luella Cole, *Psychology of Adolescence* (New York: Rinehart & Co., Inc., 1948), pp. 407-8.

[10]Richard L. Harbour, "Adolescence," *The Westminster Dictionary of Christian Education*, Kendig Brubaker Cully, ed. (Philadelphia: Westminster Press, 1963), pp. 7-8.

[11]Cole, p. 367.

will help them establish a set of values and life-directing goals. They want high standards that will challenge them to be and do their best. They want that which will help them with social and moral problems.[12]

Adolescent religiosity challenges us to minister to youth in their spiritually sensitive years. The fact that young people are *not* essentially irreligious suggests that we give teens opportunity for more serious study of the Bible, for greater service for Christ and the church, for open discussion of their problems and questions about Christianity. Other chapters in this book will suggest ways by which this can be done most effectively.

Though youth are interested in spiritual matters, many young people go through a period of religious doubt. As they grow older, their knowledge increases, their experience broadens, their mental capacities expand. Therefore they begin to question and examine their beliefs. The older the teen, the greater may be the number and the intensity of his doubts.[13]

Young people may sense conflicts between their own beliefs and the information they gain in school or hear from teen or adult friends with different beliefs. Teens' increased ability for independent thinking may make them critical of beliefs taught in childhood, especially if those beliefs have been taught in an authoritarian, unnatural or bigoted manner. Doubting is an indication that one is maturing. Doubting can be healthy, for it can lead youth to come to a personal firsthand acceptance of truths. "For most adolescents, the period of doubt does lead to a revision of some of his religious beliefs. The change is often in the direction of a more carefully thought-out and a more tenable faith."[14] Horrocks confirms this by noting that changes in attitudes toward religion do occur during adolescence but that the changes are not particularly radical.[15]

This aspect of adolescent development challenges youth workers to help guide youth through this turbulent period with an attitude of loving acceptance and understanding. This period of religious muddle suggests that youth be given opportunity to engage in discussion (with individual leaders and groups) in a permissive atmosphere. A dogmatic "we don't discuss such things" attitude may squelch a teen's honest search for adequate *reasons* for believing what he does. Here is another reason youth work is challenging—it gives opportunity to minister to people in a period of life when they are in the throes of spiritual development.[16]

---

[12]Koonce, pp. 84-85.

[13]John E. Horrocks, *The Psychology of Adolescence* (2d ed.; Boston: Houghton Mifflin Co., 1962) , pp. 619-21.

[14]Koonce, p. 92.

[15]Horrocks, p. 624.

[16]For further information on adolescent religiosity see the section entitled "Confrontation Between the Church and the Tense Generation" in chapter 5, "The Sociological Context of Teen-age Behavior."

ADOLESCENCE—A TIME FOR DECISION-MAKING

In the junior high, senior high, and college-career years, major decisions are made by many youth. When vocational and career opportunities are discussed, many young people respond with intense interest. Christian young people are seriously concerned about how to find the will of God for their future life's work. This keen interest suggests that youth leaders challenge youth with church-related careers and give help in how to discern God's will.[17]

Other important decisions often made in teen years include *conversion* (as discussed earlier), *college* (which one to attend and what major to choose), and the choice of a life *companion*. Youth workers are privileged to have a part in influencing young people in godly directions.

ADOLESCENCE—A TIME OF ABILITY

The Scriptures include a number of examples of young people with spiritual stamina and ability.

Joseph is believed to have been about 17 years old when his brothers sold him into slavery in Egypt. Though a teen-ager, he manifested moral courage and right principles when tempted (Gen. 39:7-19).

David was so young when the Prophet Samuel came seeking the Lord's anointed that no one thought to bring him to Samuel. Instead Jesse brought his other seven sons to Samuel. But Samuel asked, "Are these all your sons?" Then Jesse called for his youngest. He was but a youth, perhaps a teen-ager, yet already the foundation of his character had been laid, and he was chosen of the Lord to be the king of Israel.

When Daniel was captured and brought to Babylon, the Scriptures speak of him as a "boy" (Dan. 1:4, Berkeley). He may well have been a teen-ager. He was old enough to take his stand for the right, refusing to drink the king's wine (Dan. 1:8).

Mary, the mother of Jesus, may have been about 15 when the Lord was born (though she is often pictured by artists as older). Two thousand years ago many Jewish girls were betrothed at 14, and Mary had been betrothed to Joseph. Most of the Jewish girls became mothers by the time they were 15 or 16. Mary, probably only a teen-age girl, was chosen for the most divine mission ever given a woman.

Secular history, too, is replete with illustrations of men who, in their youth, showed great ability and potential.

For example, Benjamin Franklin, American statesman and writer, wrote

---

[17]See chapter 27, "Counseling Youth for Their Future."

his first newspaper articles, called the "Do Good Papers," between the ages of 12 and 17. The first musical compositions of Ludwig van Beethoven, well-known German composer, were published when he was 13. William Cullen Bryant, outstanding American poet and journalist, wrote "Thanatopsis," one of the most comforting poems on the subject of death, when he was 18. Dwight L. Moody, outstanding evangelist of the late nineteenth century, built a church from the Sunday school he gathered from the streets when he was 21.

In every age of recorded history we see that youth is the spring of life. What is done in it will determine the glory of summer, the abundance of autumn, and the provision of winter. Youth is the morning of life, and if the Sun of Righteousness does not chase away the moral fog and smog before noon, the whole life may remain overcast and gloomy. Youth is the time of seed-sowing, and "whatsoever a man soweth, that shall he also reap" (Gal. 6:7).

Many Christian leaders received their call to full-time Christian service in their teen years. In a survey of 709 missionaries conducted by J. O. Percy, former general secretary of the Interdenominational Foreign Mission Association, 16.3 percent said they received their call to Christian service when they were children, *45.6 percent received their call in their teen-age years,* and 38.1 percent responded to the challenge of missions when they were adults.[18]

Young people are capable of more leadership ability than they are often given credit for. The church that utilizes its young people in service projects,[19] missionary outreach,[20] program planning,[21] and evangelistic efforts,[22] realizes something of the abilities of teens.

THE CHALLENGE OF DELINQUENT YOUTH

In one year more than a million young people appear in juvenile courts in our country, and more than 1,750,000 are arrested by the police. It is expected that in the next ten years the yearly figure will increase to between three and four million juvenile offenders coming before the courts. In other words, one out of every five children born is expected to become a delinquent.

---

[18]J. O. Percy, "Where Are the Recruits?" *Missions Annual, 1959* (Ridgefield Park, N.J.: Interdenominational Foreign Mission Association, 1959), p. 33.

[19]See chapter 17, "Youth Serving the Church."

[20]See chapter 16, "Missionary Education of Youth."

[21]See chapter 13, "Sunday Evening Youth Programs," and chapter 14, "Weekday Clubs."

[22]See chapter 10, "Evangelism of Youth."

Juvenile delinquency has been steadily rising in the post-World War II years, not only in number but also in the violence and brutality of the offenses. In 1963, youngsters under 18 accounted for 46 per cent of all arrests. In the suburbs, where many parents say they have moved "for the sake of their children," the rate was 51 percent. Teen-agers accounted for 63 percent of all auto-theft arrests.

Youth's predilection to crime is costly to the citizens of the United States. The cost of keeping a teen-ager in a state reformatory is approximately $4,000 a year. A conservative estimate puts the financial outlay for public services to delinquents at 200 million dollars annually. This does not take into consideration the talents frittered away, the life which becomes a doormat to hell.

Teen-age drinking and drug addiction are urgent problems in many communities. Teen-age sexual behavior is becoming more and more reckless and is resulting in numerous pregnancies among high school and even junior high school girls. The number of unwed mothers has increased by 120 percent in the last twenty years. And this does *not* count the estimated 35 to 40 percent of the teen-age brides who are pregnant on their wedding day. "Of the approximately 276,000 illegitimate births in 1964, 110,400—or 40 percent—were born to girls 15 to 19 years of age."[23]

The cure for juvenile delinquency lies in the hands of Christian parents and church workers.[24] As Harvey L. Long, executive secretary of the Illinois Youth Commission, said, "It is easy to tell . . . from where juvenile delinquents do *not* come. They do not come from families where [Christian] faith is practiced within the home."[25]

It has been well said:

Youth with his dream went forth.
"I must conquer the world," he said;
Held in his hand a sword.
Soon youth and his dream lay dead.

Youth with his dream went forth.
"Christ must rule o'er the world," he said;
Held in his hand a Cross,
And followed where'er the dream led.

AUTHOR UNKNOWN

23"Illegitimacy in U.S.—It's on the Rise," *U.S. News and World Report*, LXI:87 (July 18, 1966).

24For books and articles with specific suggestions on what churches can do about delinquency, see "For Further Reading" at the end of this chapter and at the end of chapter 5, "The Sociological Context of Teen-age Behavior."

25Harvey Long, "The Church's Mission and Delinquents," *Federal Probation*, XXVII: 26 (December, 1963).

A form of juvenile delinquency which is more formidable than the average run of crime is mob violence.[26]

In 1964, resorts from Seaside, Oregon, to Hampton Beach, New Hampshire, were the scenes of wild juvenile disorder.

At Seaside, Oregon, National Guardsmen had to be summoned on a Labor Day weekend to quell riots caused by two thousand rampaging youths. For two nights, the sweatshirt-clad fellows jeered and threw rocks and sand-filled beer cans at the police and guardsmen. Ninety-five teens were arrested.

In Monterey Bay, California, three hundred black-jacketed motorcyclists indulged in an orgy of rape, robbery, and fighting.

At Lake George, New York, sixty youths were arrested for disorderly conduct and drinking on the streets.

In Orchard Beach, New York, policemen were called to stop a fight in which fifty youths were engaged. Thirty-two teen-agers were arrested.

In Hampton Beach, New Hampshire, for the fourth consecutive year, youth rioted. Between 7,000 and 10,000 youths swarmed from the beach and elsewhere into the center of town, chanting obscenities. They ran through the streets, breaking windows, setting fires, hurling rocks, beer cans and garbage. More than one thousand gathered in front of the Hampton Beach Casino and the police station, screaming, "Kill the cops." State and local police held them off with billy clubs, police dogs, a fire hose, and shotguns loaded with bird shot and rock salt. The rioting started about 8:30 P.M. and continued until almost dawn.

No doubt these rioters have hard-core delinquents as ringleaders, but the followers are numerous and susceptible. It may take the minority to start the riot, but why are the majority more than willing to join in the epidemic of destruction?

Psychologists were asked to state what they believed to be the reason for this outburst on the part of youth. Jerome S. Brunner, professor of psychology at Harvard University, stated that in some measure these outbursts no doubt reflected an attempt to disengage themselves from society and its modern-day complexities. Professor Brunner felt these eruptions mirrored a desire in the demonstrators to give vent to a sense of mastery over their own destinies.

Presuming the psychologists are correct in their estimation, youthful violence, more than ever, is a challenge to the church. Young people need to be taught to let Jesus Christ control their lives and realize that "none of us liveth to himself" (Rom. 14:7). Delinquency among youth

---

[26]Also see chapter 5, "The Sociological Context of Teen-age Behavior."

challenges local churches to help teens see that the only truly satisfying life is that of discipleship to Christ.

Teens involved in rioting and destruction are usually in the full vigor of health. Therefore it takes a program of terrific challenge to appeal to them. Nothing short of a message which proposes that they receive Christ as Saviour and then live in total discipleship to Him will appeal to them. No average program of a mild meeting followed by refreshments of punch and cookies will counterbalance the "pleasure" of rebellious violence. When young people are busy preparing to give account to God (Rom. 14:12), they will not be busy giving account of themselves in the police courts.

THE APPEAL OF COMMUNISM TO YOUTH

Atheistic Communism is making one of the world's greatest efforts to win youth to its cause.

Communism has slowly but steadily taken over much of the world. Moscow claims that there are 40 million Communist party members throughout the world. The Federal Bureau of Investigation estimates that in the United States there are 25,000 Communists plus ten fellow travelers for every party member.

This is "growth by capture," revealed by the fact that many people have risked their lives to escape *from* Communism. During the Communist-sponsored 1962 World Youth Festival in Finland, 50 Communist delegates defected to the West. And to West Germany has come a flood of four million refugees from the East since 1945, with a rate sometimes as high as 400 a day.

The Communists are eager to have the United States under their domination. They prey on the inexperience of youth. J. Edgar Hoover, director of the Federal Bureau of Investigation, has said that Gus Hall, general secretary of the Communist Party in the United States, has launched an all-out effort to win youth to Communism. Hall said, "In October [1963] Communist party delegates met in Chicago, Illinois, to lay the groundwork for a new national youth organization aimed at exploitation of what the party describes as a drift toward the left among young people."[27] Mr. Hall stipulated that the youth movement "should avoid the appearance of a Soviet-style organization. However it should not tolerate anti-Soviet or anti-party thinking."[28]

---

[27]Quoted by J. Edgar Hoover, "World Newsgrams," *The King's Business;* LV:36 (June, 1964).

[28]*Ibid.*

One way the Communists attract youth is by their efforts to get Communist speakers on college campuses. In 1963 at least ninety party members spoke in colleges. This was twice the number in 1962. These party members gain entrance to lecture halls under the protective cloak of academic freedom and the right to free speech. Then with twisted facts and phrases, they influence gullible youth.

In many countries where Communism is agitating with riots and other revolutionary actions it is the young people, more than adults, who are easily influenced to take part.

But why does Communism appeal to youth? Because this godless system gives young people something to live and die for, it presents a goal to work for, and it demands full dedication and allegiance.

Surely Christianity offers as great a challenge—and greater—to young people!

ADOLESCENCE—A CHALLENGE TO THE CHURCH

When churches are challenged with their responsibility to youth, some church people react by saying, "What about the home? Aren't parents responsible for their young people?"

Indeed, each parent is responsible for the physical, mental, moral and spiritual upbringing of his child. The home has an immeasurable influence—for good or bad—on the child. Up to his teen years, the child spends much of his time at home. *But* when he becomes a teen, many other outside interests call for his loyalties and time. In his craving for adult independence, he may rebel against his parents. Young people may doubt what in previous years they accepted from their parents without question.

And school has a great influence on the lives of teens. But it is obvious that Christians cannot leave the spiritual training of teens to the public schools. If teens are to be prepared for the best of life in this world and the next, the *church* must reach and challenge them.

The church program can provide much that teens cannot get elsewhere: Bible instruction in Sunday school; worship in church services; training in youth programs; instruction and expression in vacation Bible school and weekday clubs; fellowship, worship and instruction in camps. Missionary education, service project opportunities, socials and recreation, evangelism—all these and many more church-related activities can contribute to the upbuilding of teens spiritually.

Unless churches enlarge, and, if necessary, revamp their educational programs to reach and train young people, they are missing one of the greatest challenges and needs of the day.

It is estimated by the U.S. Census Bureau that the number of teenagers in America increased by more than 25 percent in the decade between 1950 and 1960, that it will increase by 50 percent in the decade ahead, and another 10 percent beyond that figure by 1975. Therefore unless Sunday school enrollment and participation in youth programs have increased by 25 percent in the last decade and are geared to increase by 50 percent in the ten years ahead, the church is not keeping pace with the population growth.

Most people can remember admonitions, commandments, orders and suggestions made by their parents. Some of the things people do all their lives are the result of childhood training. The presence or absence of courtesy, moral standards and ambitions frequently stem from one's childhood.

In addition to pointing up the responsibility of parents, the Bible indicates that God will hold *teens* responsible for what they do. The Scriptures tell young people that if they forget God, sorrow will follow.

"Be mindful of your Creator in the days of your youth before the troubling days come and the years draw near when you will say, 'I do not enjoy them' " (Eccles. 12:1, Berkeley).

"Take pleasure, young man, in your youth and let your heart cheer you in your youthful days; follow the ways of your heart and the sight of your eyes, but be aware that for all these God will call you to account. Banish grief from your mind and keep pain from your body, for youth and the dawn (of life) are transitory" (Eccles. 11:9-10, Berkeley).

The Bible informs teens of the only answer to their problem of sin: Christ "died for the ungodly" (Rom. 5:6) so that "whosoever believeth in him should not perish, but have everlasting life" (John 3:16). The only answer to delinquency, teen violence, Communism, youth boredom and guilt is Jesus Christ. The Bible challenges teens to recognize their sin (Rom. 3:23; Eccles. 7:20) and to receive Christ as Saviour (Acts 16:31). Only then can teens have abundant life (John 10:10).

After a teen becomes a Christian, he should heed the challenges of God's Word, full of advice, suggestions, admonitions for his spiritual benefit, "How can a young man cleanse his way? By living in agreement with thy word" (Ps. 119:9, Berkeley).

SUMMARY

Our task as workers with youth is to win teens to Christ and then help them live in accordance with His Word. The church is to "urge the younger [people] . . to behave prudently" (Titus 2:6, Berkeley), to be an "example of the believers" (I Tim. 4:12) and to be "fervent in spirit, serving the Lord" (Rom. 12:11).

Youth workers should pray earnestly and work diligently so that, in time, they can say to their young people, "You are vigorous, God's message stays in your hearts, and you have overcome the evil one" (I John 2:14, Berkeley).

May God by His Spirit help us rise to the challenge of reaching today's teens for Jesus Christ!

FOR FURTHER READING

BELL, L. NELSON. "Don't Sell Them Short" *Christianity Today,* VI:24 (February 2, 1962).

CRAWFORD, PAUL L. *Working with Teen-age Groups.* New York: City Welfare Council of New York, 1950.

DAILY, STARR. *God's Answer to Juvenile Delinquency.* St. Paul: Macalester Park Publishing Co., 1953.

DALY, MAURREEN. *Profile of Youth.* Philadelphia: J. B. Lippincott Co., 1951.

DONAHUE, JOHN K. *Baffling Eyes of Youth,* New York: Association Press, 1957.

DUVALL, EVELYN MILLS. *Today's Teen-agers.* New York: Association Press, 1966.

EVANS, DAVID M. *Shaping the Church's Ministry with Youth,* Valley Forge, Pa.: Judson Press, 1965.

GRAHAM, BILLY. "The 'In' Generation," *Decision,* VIII: 1, 13, 14 (April, 1967).

HAYES, EDWARD L., "The Church's Uneasiness About Young People," *The Sunday School Times,* CIV:1, 6-7 (September 22, 1962).

HOYLES, J. ARTHUR. *The Treatment of the Young Delinquent.* London: Epworth Press, 1952.

HORROCKS, JOHN E. *The Psychology of Adolescence.* Second Edition. Boston: Houghton Mifflin Co., 1962.

JELLEMA, DIRK. "The Great Silent Shrug." *Christianity Today,* V:9-11 (May 23, 1960).

KOONCE, RAY F. *Understanding Your Teen-agers.* Nashville: Broadman Press, 1965.

MCCANN, RICHARD VINCENT. *Delinquency: Sickness or Sin?* New York: Harper & Row, 1957.

MILLER, HASKELL M. *Understanding and Preventing Juvenile Delinquency.* New York: Abingdon Press, 1958.

PERSON, PETER P. *An Introduction to Christian Education.* Grand Rapids: Baker Book House, 1958. Chapter 8, "Christian Education of Youth."

———. *The Church and Modern Youth.* Grand Rapids: Zondervan Publishing House, 1963.

REINER, BEATRICE SIMCOX. *Character Disorders in Parents of Delinquents.* New York: Family Service Association of America, 1959.

RISCHE, HENRY. *American Youth in Trouble.* Westwood, N. J.: Fleming H. Revell, 1956.

WILKERSON, DAVID, and SHERRILL, JOHN and ELIZABETH. *The Cross and the Switchblade.* New York: B. Geis Associates, 1963.

WINTER, DAVID. *Old Faith, Young World.* London: Hodder & Stoughton, 1965.

Because the Bible is the only Sourcebook of truth about God and about man's relation to Him, a solid foundation in God's written Word provides the proper framework for any Christian approach to working with young people.

KENNETH O. GANGEL

2

the biblical basis of youth work

SCRIPTURE REVEALS the truth about God, the truth about man, and the truth about the relationship between the two. The truth about God, of course, is that He is holy, infinite, eternal and loving. The truth about man is that he is sinful, finite, temporal and very much distant from real love in his natural state. The glorious crown of biblical truth is the story of redemption, telling us how the holy God can sustain a relationship with sinful man. Of course the whole plan of salvation with all of its wonderful aspects and eternal glories is God's pattern for this relationship.

But what does this have to do with working with young people? Our whole teaching and guiding ministry must be based on truth and must seek to lead teens into right relationships with God and others. Therefore because the Bible is the only Sourcebook of truth about God and about man's relation to Him, a solid foundation in God's written Word provides the proper framework for any Christian approach to working with young people. Certainly youth workers can gain much from psychology, educa-

KENNETH O. GANGEL, M.A., B.D., S.T.M., is Academic Dean and Assistant Professor of Christian Education, Calvary Bible College, Kansas City, Missouri.

tion and sociology. These can enhance one's knowledge of youth and youth work. But evangelicals seek to evaluate these principles in the light of God's Word.

But there are differing viewpoints in our day regarding the nature of the Bible. What in essence is the evangelical position on which youth work is to be based? Perhaps it can best be summarized by four words.

The first word is *revelation*. This pertains to the divine message itself. The self-communicating God chose to allow man to know something about His nature and His work. The Bible is God's written revelation to man.[1] The second word, *inspiration,* focuses our attention on the written form of the revelation. Peter wrote, "No prophecy ever resulted from human design; instead, holy men from God spoke as they were carried along by the Holy Spirit" (II Peter 1:20-21, Berkeley). God was concerned not only with the origin of the message but also with the way it was recorded. Paul wrote to young Timothy, "Every Scripture is God-breathed, and is profitable for teaching, for conviction, for improvement, for training with respect to righteousness, in order that the man of God may be complete, fitted out for every good work" (II Tim. 3:16-17, *Expanded New Testament* by K. S. Wuest).

The third word which relates to our position on the Bible is the word *preservation*. A game sometimes played at parties is the one in which one person originates a story, whispers it to the person next to him, and so on around the room. By the time the story reaches the last person in the line, it is grossly perverted and the end result is nothing like the original version. This is exactly what could have happened to Scripture if God had not superintended the transmission of His written Word down through the ages. No book on earth has been more often translated, more abused and rejected, confiscated and burned, and yet exists today in a form which adequately gives the originally written message, God has preserved His Word.

The fourth word, *illumination,* is related to the reader of the message. As a believer studies the Word of God, the Holy Spirit works in his mind and heart to enable him to understand and live out God's truth. Apart from the ministry of the Holy Spirit, we would be unable by our natural minds to understand the Bible. God has not left Himself without a witness; in this confused world He has provided a solid foundation for our service for Jesus Christ. That foundation is the Bible, God's truth *revealed, inspired, preserved* and *illuminated* by the Holy Spirit.

---

[1]The Bible is more than an instrument of or witness to or record of revelation; it *is* revelation. See James I. Packer, "Contemporary Views of Revelation," *Revelation and the Bible,* ed. Carl F. H. Henry (Grand Rapids: Baker Book House, 1958), pp. 89-104; and Robert Preus, "The Doctrine of Revelation in Contemporary Theology," *Bulletin of the Evangelical Theological Society,* IX: 111-23 (Summer, 1966).

THE BIBLE AND THEOLOGY IN CHRISTIAN EDUCATION

A young pastor, candidating at a small rural church, met with the deacons to ask and answer questions. The conversation turned to a discussion of the type of preaching the young man would engage in if he were to come; and one of the brethren indicated his preference by saying, "Well, don't give us any theology; just preach the Bible!" Unfortunately many Christians share the view of this gentleman though they might not word it so bluntly.

Some people have the false notion that there is a "great gulf fixed" between the Bible and theology, and that the latter is relatively undesirable. However, one cannot give consideration to the things of God without dealing in the realm of theology. Theology simply has to do with the truth about God; and as soon as a person says, "Christ died for our sins" or "Ye must be born again," he is speaking theologically.

Christian education, if it is to be true *Christian* education, must have a solid theological basis. Actually, the two cannot be severed. What one believes about theology affects what he does in Christian education— including youth work. Therefore an adequate program of youth work in the church must be based on a solid foundation of biblical theology. Three reasons justify this statement.

Theology Determines Objectives

Perhaps the most basic question that can be asked of any educational institution is whether or not it is fulfilling its stated objectives.[2] This question also has great importance for any church or for any part of its educational program. It is imperative that every youth group have objectives that are "brief enough to be remembered . . . clear enough to be written down . . . [and] specific enough to be achieved."[3] Such objectives can spell out what one expects to achieve in his group.

For the Christian, the determining factor in the formulation of objectives is his relationship to God through His eternal Word. For example, if a youth worker says, "We want our youth group to be evangelistic so that other teen-agers will find Christ through the witness of our own young people," he is suggesting that evangelism is one of the objectives for which a youth group exists. He has verbalized a concept which has many theological ramifications: (1) People are in need of salvation. (2) This salvation is obtainable. (3) Christian young people should communicate these facts to others. Another church which is not evangelical in its theology

---

[2]See chapter 4, "Objectives and Standards for Youth Work."
[3]Findley B. Edge, *Teaching for Results*, (Nashville: Broadman Press, 1956), pp. 92-93.

might state its objectives in terms of social fitness or relationship to the church as an organization rather than in terms of regeneration and commitment to Jesus Christ. The most important factor, therefore, in determining objectives for youth work is one's view of theology and his relation to the Word of God.

Theology Determines Philosophy

J. Oliver Buswell, Jr. wrote:

> Our generation needs an orderly system of thought related to the factual realities which surround us. It is my conviction that Christian philosophy has the answer, and that it will not be impossible to present this answer in terms of our current problems and in the language of our contemporaries. . . . The Christian philosophy of being begins with the Eternal Being of God. It then includes the objective reality of the created world and of created man in unique relationship with God . . . . It can be shown that every philosophy of ethics . . . which leaves God out of consideration, leads to a contradiction; and that the holy character of God, revealed by His will, is the only consistent criterion of good and evil, and right and wrong.[4]

These sentences make it plain that the Christian cannot divorce his theology from his philosophy of life. One's outlook on life will be determined by his understanding of God, His Word and His world. But what does philosophy have to do with planning interesting lessons and meetings for youth?

In a very real sense it has everything to do with youth work—not only in the matter of planning activities but also in evaluating why the group exists, what it is doing, and what effect it is having on the lives of its members. The questions most commonly asked today by young people of high school and college age have to do with the matter of being. Many of these questions are philosophical in nature: "Who am I?" "Why am I here?" "What should I be doing with my life?"[5] It is to these philosophical questions that the Christian faith can speak with clarity. Indeed, only when young people see temporal life in the wider perspective of eternal life will the reality and meaning of their existence come into focus. Is not this focus exactly what leaders should seek to help youth achieve? The leaders' purpose is—or should be—to help young people lead lives that are in proper relationship to God, His Son Jesus Christ and the Holy Spirit.

One's approach to leadership development, program planning, selection of curriculum materials, social events, and service activities will be determined by his views of God's Word. When a youth group and its leaders

---

[4]J. Oliver Buswell, Jr., "Why We Need a Christian Philosophy," *Eternity*, XII:35 (November, 1961) .

[5]Compare chapter 8, "The Nature and Needs of College-age Youth."

begin to see the group's relationship to theology, they will test the songs and choruses they sing to see if these meet the standards of sound Bible doctrine.

Theology Determines Authority

In all education someone or something is considered the ultimate source or authority for what is believed, taught and practiced. The question of authority is not unique to Christian education; it is faced by all educational organizations on all levels. Zuck has reminded us that "much of what happens in teaching situations is determined by the teacher's concept of the final authority in Christian education. Lesson aims or objectives, classroom atmosphere, student activities, teaching materials, lesson approaches and subject matter are influenced by the teacher's outlook on this problem."[6]

Some say that the church is the ultimate authority and that the counsels and traditions which have been transmitted through the years of church history must be the determining factor for what is believed and taught. Others suggest teachers as their authority, or perhaps their or others' religious experiences. (Many cults have set up extrabiblical revelation and human prophets as the authority for their practices and beliefs.) Some would argue that educational, not religious, experience is the authoritative sun around which the solar system of education revolves.

In our day, absolutes are frowned on by many people, and those who look to an immutable source for authority are considered old-fashioned, narrowminded and bigoted. Yet, since the days of the early church, evangelical Christians have accepted and insisted on the Bible as their authoritative Guide for faith and conduct. This is the testimony that Scripture gives of itself (Matt. 5:18; John 10:35; Acts 20:35; Rom. 15:4; I Cor. 10:11; II Tim. 3:16; II Peter 3:2; I John 1:1-5; Rev. 22:18-19). The Christian's absolute authority is that special written revelation which we call the Bible.

After examining a number of possible authorities for Christian education, Zuck concludes that "education that bypasses the central authority of God's Word is not evangelical Christian education."[7] The implications of this for the Christian education of youth are many, but they all boil down to one simple statement: Biblical theology is the basis on which all evangelical youth work must be founded. The written Word of God is the authority for our educational work with young people.

---

[6]Roy B. Zuck, "The Problem of Authority in Christian Education," *Bibliotheca Sacra*, CXIX:54 (January-March, 1962).

[7]*Ibid.*, CXIX:63.

THE BIBLE AND EDUCATION-RELATED DISCIPLINES

The preceding section is not meant to imply that information from education, psychology, sociology and other related disciplines of study are not beneficial. Indeed they are! The Scriptures can be said to have at least a twofold relationship to these disciplines.

First, the Bible provides a means of evaluating insights to be gained from other sources. If principles in other areas contradict Bible truth, then the evangelical youth worker feels obligated, because of his commitment to the final authority of Scripture, to accept the latter rather than the former. For example, some psychologists maintain man's nature is basically and inherently good, not evil. Because this is at variance with divine revelation, it is untenable for evangelicals. Or if psychology or education books teach that man is no more than animal, that he has no spiritual nature, this too is rejected by evangelicals because it does not corroborate scriptural authority. Or if sociology teaches that improving one's environment is the chief means of bettering the world, this does not correlate with the biblical teaching on man's sinful condition and his need of regeneration. Certain learning theories advocated in education and psychology should be analyzed in the light of a Christian theory of learning, based on a careful study of what scriptural statements and examples suggest with regard to the nature and process of learning.

Byrne summarizes this point by saying that "claims to truth from other areas should be tested and evaluated by the philosophical and theological truths of the Word of God."[8] And Zuck writes:

> Secular educational principles are often built on unscriptural philo-
> sophical bases such as pragmatism, empiricism, and naturalism. When
> there is conflict or variance in principles, Christian educators need to
> go back to their divine source to be sure that the principles they have
> formulated are drawn from or are consistent with Scripture.[9]

Second, the Bible provides the basis for a Christian perspective or frame of reference in which to view these other disciplines. In other words, the Scriptures enable one to see psychology, sociology, education from a *Christian* point of view. The wise youth leader seeks to relate the insights from the psychology of adolescence, the sociology of adolescence, and the education of adolescence to the Bible, and to integrate the Bible to these areas of study. For example, he asks how the fact of puberty in adolescence affects the content and activities to be included in the *Christian* education of youth. Or he asks how the changes in today's

---

[8]Herbert W. Byrne, *A Christian Approach to Education* (Grand Rapids: Zondervan Publishing House, 1961), p. 67.

[9]Zuck, *The Holy Spirit in Your Teaching* (Wheaton, Ill.: Scripture Press Publications, Inc., 1963), p. 100.

society as faced by college-age youth relate to the *Christian* education of that age-group. What does the Bible suggest with regard to the ways and means whereby teachers may best teach and learners may best learn? The wise youth leader lets the Bible have a directing and formative influence on his approach to various subjects. Byrne also speaks on this point:

> Through the Bible the interrelatedness of all other subjects and truths is made possible and clear. This means that all other subjects and truths have their first point of reference in the Word of God, draw their materials from the Bible wherever possible, and return to the Bible with their accumulation of facts for interpretation and practical application.[10]

The following statements suggest some of the areas of correlation between Scripture and education-related disciplines. Perhaps they may serve as the basis for further thought and study in this area.

1. The Scriptures teach that every person is a sinner, depraved and distant from God, and therefore in need of regeneration; but psychology points up how this degeneracy may be revealed in adolescent behavior, and observes the growing awareness of personal guilt of sin in the early teen years.

2. The Scriptures challenge Christian youth to be committed to the Lord and to serve Him; but education and psychology may suggest ways in which teens' growing interest in service opportunities may be channeled.

3. The Scriptures indicate that Christian educators have Bible truths to transmit; but education can help us learn *how to* communicate that content.

4. The Bible stresses that an intellectual grasp of Christianity is insufficient; and psychology and education can help the youth worker see how to take young people beyond this mere mental assent into a personal life-transforming relationship to Christ.

5. The Scriptures indicate that Christianity is timeless and always relevant to people's needs; psychology and sociology can call to the attention of youth workers some of the needs teens face in today's society, thus helping youth workers point up the relevance of Scripture.

6. The Bible teaches that the illuminating, teaching ministry of the Holy Spirit is necessary if one is to apprehend and appropriate Bible truth; but education can point up essential principles of teaching and learning through which the Holy Spirit seeks to teach.[11]

7. The Bible indicates something of youth's "spiritual potential." According to the Scriptures young people need God and are capable of

[10]Byrne, *op. cit.,* pp. 66-67.
[11]Zuck, *op. cit.* chaps. 13-14.

knowing God. Psychology studies the specific expressions of this spiritual potential or religiosity among adolescents.[12]

8. The Bible challenges teens to a high standard of moral, Christ-honoring living.[13] Christian adolescents are not excluded from the Lord's call to holy, Spirit-filled living. Sociology can acquaint the youth worker with some of the problems in today's society which make it difficult for Christian youth to maintain purity of mind and body.[14]

9. The Bible stresses the need for knowing, being concerned for and fostering the welfare of other believers. Psychology and education can enable Christian leaders to grasp something of the nature and needs of adolescents,[15] and how to counsel personally with youth.[16]

THE BIBLE AND THE YOUTH LEADER

A youth program stands or falls depending, to a great extent, on the adult leadership responsible for the group. It is the adult leader who can help promote enthusiasm, give guidance to the group, insure progress in the work, find and train other leaders and, above all, be an example of Christian maturity. All these tasks (particularly the latter) demonstrate the necessity for competent Bible knowledge on the part of the youth leader.

Knowledge of the Scriptures

There are many ingredients of sound leadership. For the Christian, a proper attitude toward and understanding of God's Word is high on the list. Joshua, for example, was a man whom God called to a place of leadership. Joshua had been preparing for many years as "Moses' minister." He depended on Jehovah, and he was filled with courage for the task that lay ahead. These qualities were insufficient without the saturation in the Word which Jehovah demanded of His human leader: "This book of the law shall not depart out of thy mouth; but thou shalt meditate therein day and night, that thou mayest observe to do according to all that is written therein, for then thou shalt make thy way prosperous, and then thou shalt have good success" (Joshua 1:8a).

The Christian may be ignorant in many fields of knowledge and still render acceptable service to Jesus Christ. But a knowledge of the Bible is not one of those fields. Of course God never makes any demands on His servants which they cannot fulfill with His help. Therefore for one to say, "I cannot work with young people because I don't know the Bible

---

[12]For example, see chapter 1, "The Challenge of Today's Youth."
[13]See, e.g., I Timothy 4:12.
[14]See chapter 5, "The Sociological Context of Teen-age Behavior."
[15]See chapters 6-8.
[16]See chapters 26-28.

well enough" is to state a self-indictment which should be promptly remedied. A Christian need not be a professional theologian to possess and use a working knowledge of Scripture.

A knowledge of the Bible is important for several reasons. First, spiritual growth comes through the Word. Every Christian, especially one who holds a position of leadership, should be growing in the grace and knowledge of Jesus Christ (II Peter 3:18). This growth depends entirely on the supernatural power of the Word applied to the life by the Holy Spirit. Jesus prayed that the disciples would be sanctified through the Father's truth. And then He added, "Thy word is truth" (John 17:17). The Christian life is a process of progress toward being like the Saviour Himself, and a necessary instrument or agent in this process is the Bible.

Second, a knowledge of the Scriptures helps the leader know his young people. Many of the desires and actions of young people strike adults as strange and unnatural. But actually many of those desires and actions fit perfectly into the pattern of natural, or carnal, living described in the Word of God. The Bible teaches what an unregenerate person is like and why he thinks and acts as he does. His condition is described as "lost," "blind," "ungodly" and "dead." A proper understanding of the biblical doctrines of anthropology (the doctrine of man) and hamartiology (the doctrine of sin) will enable the youth leader to understand and even anticipate behavior on the part of both Christian and nonchrisitian young people.

Third, a knowledge of God's Word equips youth leaders to help their young people. The process of guiding young people is not a ministry of solving their problems as much as it is giving them the tools and the techniques whereby they may solve their own problems through God's Word. If the youth leader has a growing knowledge of the Bible, he is better equipped to direct his young people to passages of Scripture which are needed in their lives. And he will be able to teach them principles of Bible study which they can then use in feeding themselves spiritually.

Fourth, the Scriptures give motivation to the youth leader. Working with young people can be discouraging at times, but the worker who is acquainted with the Scriptures will find encouragement. He will see that God rewards faithfulness (Matt. 25:20-23; I Cor. 4:2), that He encourages the worker to be steadfast in view of the fact that our work for Him is not in vain (I Cor. 15:58), that difficulties are to draw us to greater dependence on Him (II Cor. 9:8; 12:9-10), that rewards will be given to faithful laborers (I Peter 5:2-4).

Knowing a subject does not automatically mean that one can communicate that subject. Many people have known great scholars who had full knowledge and understanding of a certain subject but who, when standing before a class, could not communicate that knowledge. Likewise youth leaders must not only *know* *t*he Bible but be able to *use* it in teaching, counseling and leading youth.[17]

One of the greatest problems in working with young people is knowing how to apply eternal truth to everyday living. It is foolish to think that simply referring a teen to a few selected passages will automatically cause him to realize that all the Bible is relevant to his life. Some teachers, preachers and youth leaders in evangelical churches have the false idea that young people will automatically see how biblical truths relate to teen living.

Through the Scriptures youth leaders learn of the motivating forces of the love of Christ (II Cor. 5:14) and coming judgment (II Cor. 5:11*a*). These urge them on to continue reaching and ministering to young people.

THE BIBLE AND THE YOUNG PERSON

The youth leader is responsible to help the young person understand the Word of God and how it relates to him. But the young person is responsible to act on that understanding and bring his life into conformity with eternal truth. In a real sense, the Christian life is the process of coming to see all of life in *divine* perspective. Christian growth is learning, and learning includes seeing relationships.

Every aspect of the Christian life is based on some kind of a relationship between the believer and the Son of God. The initial relationship is one of sinner to Saviour. The continuing relationship is one of disciple to Lord, or commissioned to commissioner. It is the task of youth workers to help youth develop a biblical philosophy of life and to see their relationships to the Lord and others in a biblical frame of reference.

The Young Person's Relationship to the Lord Must Be Based on the Word

The life of Peter presents a checkered but very informative lesson in relationships between disciple and Lord. John 6 records Christ's sermon on the bread of life and the results which followed as many so-called disciples left Him at that time. Jesus turned to the twelve and said, "Will ye also go away?" Simon Peter answered Him, "Lord, to whom shall we go? Thou hast the words of eternal life. And we believe and are sure that thou art that Christ, the Son of the living God" (John 6:67-69).

Here Peter indentified himself with the One whom he called "Lord," "Christ," and "the Son of the living God." Through this experience Peter learned (and through him *we* learn) that discipleship is not merely an

---

[17]See chapter 11, "Youth in Bible Study." Also see Lois E. LeBar, *Education That Is Christian,* chapter 5, "The Use of the Bible in Teaching" (Westwood, N.J.: Fleming H. Revell, 1958).

outward form of following but rather that which demands absolute adherence to the truth. In other words, a young person's relationship to his Lord, like that of Peter, must be based not on what he thinks about truth but on what Jesus Christ Himself insists is God's truth.

Both verbs in the first part of verse 69 indicate, in the Greek, a past event with a continuing condition or result. Peter's relationship was one of faith and assurance which had its roots in a past commitment of his life to this One to whom he spoke. The results of that commitment were continuing even to the time when he was speaking. This Lordship-discipleship contact based on the assurance of eternal truth is the key to victorious Christian living.

The Young Person's Relationship to the Church Must Be Based on the Word

The word *church* has various meanings. It describes a building or a denomination; but neither of these uses is ever found in Scripture. The Greek word *ekklesia*, from which the word *church* is derived, meant one of two things in the New Testament: (1) the universal body of believers who belong to Christ through regeneration, or (2) any specific geographical representation of that body in any place at any time (a local church).

The Christian young person needs to realize that because he is a part of the church, the body of Christ, he has obligations and responsibilities to his local church. He is as much a part of the local church as any member of the official local church board. When the Christian teen-ager begins to see himself in this biblical perspective, his whole outlook on church attendance, support of and participation in church activities, and personal witness may be revolutionized.

The Young Person's Relationship to the World Must Be Based on the Word

Probably most youth directors or pastors face at some time or other the problem of worldliness in their young people. There are a number of controversial ramifications of this whole issue, and youth groups spend hours every year discussing and debating what a Christian "should" or "should not" do. Yet when one puts these various issues under the scrutiny of God's Word, there surely is no uncertain sound to the trumpet on basic principles of godly living. Note again the words of John the Apostle:

> Do not set your hearts on the godless world or anything in it. Anyone who loves the world is a stranger to the Father's love. Everything the world affords, all that panders to the appetites, or entices the eyes, all the glamour of its life, springs not from the Father but from the godless world. And that world is passing away with all its allurements, but he

who does God's will stands forever more (I John 2:15-17, The New
English Bible).

This is not an isolated text but a permeating principle of the entire
Bible regarding the Christian's behavior. One of the reasons we have
difficulty instructing and convincing our young people in the matter of
holy Christian living may be that we have not based our arguments for
such living on a careful analysis and full understanding of the Word of
God. Young people need to replace the shaky reasons such as "My church
says I should do this" or "My pastor wouldn't like it" with solid Bible-
based convictions that God has spoken and that our duty as Christians
is to obey.

But a young person's relationship to the "world" is broader than the
matter of separation from questionable practices. It includes the positive
aspects of Christlike living in all relationships—to one's parents, siblings,
schoolmates, teachers, Christian and nonchristian friends, employers, neigh-
bors, people in need in one's neighborhood, city, country, and to lost
millions in foreign lands. Because the Bible provides specific directives for
standards to be followed in each of these areas, it is important that youth
workers seek to help youth know—and live out—the Word.

The Young Person's Relationship to the Future Must Be Based on the Word

In John 21, Peter's future as a disciple was at stake. He was the recipient
of a question, a prophecy and a command. The question "Lovest thou me
more than these?" immediately removed Peter's decision of life vocation
from the realm of the natural and placed it in the realm of the supernatural. His relation to God's will for his life was not to be based on
the rationale of man but on his love for the Saviour.

Christ's prophecy regarding Peter's coming imprisonment and martyrdom
showed the dynamic apostle that he was not entering a debatable situation but was like a soldier receiving marching orders from the general
of the army. Peter was learning in this brief dialogue in John 21 the
very things Thomas had learned just a few days earlier when he responded
to the authority of Jesus Christ over his life with the form of address
"my Lord and my God."

After positing a genuine love relationship for Peter's Christian service
and warning him that the road ahead would not be an easy one, the Lord
gave the simple but engaging command "Follow me." Christ was not
interested in Peter's comparing his life with God's plan for another. The
relationship of the other disciple to the Lord was a matter between
those two and was not to be the concern of Peter. His only task was to
follow wherever the will of God and the lordship of Christ should lead him.

This is precisely the kind of future we wish for our young people. It might be a future in vocational Christian service or it might be an active lay witness, but in any case it is to be a genuine discipleship, a discipleship which tolerates no reservations or concern for one's own life. This kind of complete commitment should be the guideline for the future of every Christian young person; but until he sees his life in the light of the teaching of God's Word regarding discipleship, he probably will not make this kind of commitment.

THE BIBLE AND THE YOUTH PROGRAM

Any youth activity must have a *purpose;* it should include a maximum of *participation* on the part of the young people; there ought to be adequate *preparation* and effective *publicity;* and certainly the whole operation ought to be backed with fervent *prayer.* Stated in another way, every youth program and learning experience for teens must include at least three basic elements: objectives, content, and methods.

The Objectives of Youth Programs Must Be Based on the Bible

Earlier we discussed the relationship of theology to objectives in Christian education. However here we are considering more specifically those goals or aims which the youth leader and his young people will set for a particular program or series of programs, or the aims of a Sunday school teacher for a unit of study or a single lesson. The Bible and the needs of young people are to be kept in mind as one considers such aims.

The Content of Youth Activities Must Be Permeated with the Bible

Lessons and youth programs must be dynamic in the sense that they relate to the life experiences of the young people, and they must also be biblical. Having a "biblical curriculum" means more than just attaching some Scripture text to whatever lesson or program has been planned. Lois E. LeBar has stated:

> Experience with the Word cannot be left to chance. It will not automatically proceed from the written Word. Teachers must make definite provision for including experience in the curriculum. . . . As the divine and human teachers stimulate interaction between the Word and the pupil, both written and living Word gradually or suddenly penetrate to the interior of the pupil.[18]

A Bible-based theology indicates that education of youth includes the

---

[18]LeBar, *op. cit.,* pp. 205-6.

transmission of subject matter but goes beyond it toward the shaping of character.

The Methods Used in Youth Programs Must Be Consistent with the Bible

Methods in youth work are the ways by which leaders seek to help teens learn. Our choice of teaching methods are to be controlled by our educational objectives and by biblical content. Methods are not ends in themselves, but rather means to achieve the learning and the life-change which we hope to see in our young people. Edge reminds us that "method is concerned with the following questions which the teacher must answer in preparing to teach: (1) How can I help my class develop an interest in this study? (2) How can I help my class develop a purpose for this study? (3) How can I help my class to see meaning in this study?"[19]

Keeping methods consistent with Scripture may involve several things. It might, for example, cause us to study more carefully the life of Christ, noticing how He taught. This kind of study would immediately reveal the necessity for variety in methods and interaction on the part of those being taught. Another implication is that of avoiding those elements in our youth programming that are in poor taste when compared with the holiness of God reflected in His Word.

The principle of scriptural consistency when carried to its logical conclusions will affect the songs sung, the way the youth work is financed, the type of personnel used in the meetings, and the attitudes we seek to develop in young people regarding their programs.

A church may have the finest study materials, the best-equipped plant, the most adequately trained leaders and a group of intelligent, dynamic young people. But it can accomplish little of lasting, eternal value if its entire operation is not based solidly on the immutable, infallible Word of the living God.

FOR FURTHER READING

BOWMAN, CLARICE. *Ways Youth Learn.* New York: Harper & Bros., 1953.

BRUNK, ADA Z., AND METZLER, ETHEL Y. *The Christian Nurture of Youth.* Scottdale, Pa.: Herald Press, 1960.

HAKES, J. EDWARD (ed). *An Introduction to Evangelical Christian Education.* Chicago: Moody Press, 1964. Chapters 1, 3.

HARNER, NEVIN C. *Youth Work in the Church.* Nashville: Abingdon-Cokesbury, 1942. Chapters 1-3.

---

[19]Findley B. Edge, *Helping the Teacher* (Nashville: Broadman Press, 1956), p. 72.

LeBar, Lois E. *Education That Is Christian*. Westwood, N. J.: Fleming H. Revell, 1958.

Mason, Harold C. *Abiding Values in Christian Education*. Westwood, N.J.: Fleming H. Revell, 1955. Chapters 3-4.

Miller, Randolph Crump. *Education for Christian Living*. Englewood Cliffs, N.J.: Prentice-Hall, 1956. Chapters 3-5.

Zuck, Roy B. *The Holy Spirit in Your Teaching*. Wheaton, Ill.: Scripture Press Publications, Inc., 1963.

The major task of the church is to help its youth in the process of becoming spiritually independent and responsible Christian persons. If teachers and workers aim their lesson, unit and program objectives in this direction and consistently uphold Christian standards in their work, they can rely on God's faithfulness to bring about His will in the lives of youth as they respond to His Holy Spirit.

EDWIN J. POTTS

3

objectives and standards for youth work

NATURE AND IMPORTANCE OF OBJECTIVES

What Are Objectives?

OBJECTIVES ARE GOALS or desired ends toward which some action is directed. In addition to this simple and precise definition, educators find it necessary to distinguish between the various types of objectives. Individual lesson objectives are related to class objectives. And the objectives of each part of the classroom program together contribute to the achievement of total school objectives. Objectives are both ends as well as means toward further ends.

Often the terms "immediate and ultimate aims," "specific and general aims," or "subordinate and inclusive aims" are used to distinguish between aims that are means toward further ends and those that are final ends in themselves. Some educators use the term "aim" to indicate "that with which the educator starts," and "objective" as "the place of arrival."[1]

---

[1]Herbert W. Byrne, *A Christian Approach to Education* (Grand Rapids: Zondervan Publishing House, 1961), p. 89.

EDWIN J. POTTS, Th.D., formerly Chairman of the Department of Christian Education, Northwestern College, Minneapolis, is now Minister of Christian Education, Grosse Pointe Baptist Church, Grosse Pointe Woods, Michigan.

Other educators use the terms "aim," "objective," goal," and "purpose" interchangeably and distinguish between levels of objectives which lead into one another like links in a chain, and together achieve ultimate purposes. The following levels are generally accepted:

> *lesson objectives* (for one class session)
> *unit objectives* (for a quarter's work)
> *course objectives* (for a year's work)
> *departmental objectives* (for two to three years' work)
> *divisional objectives* (for children, youth and adults)
> *overall objectives* (ultimate desired outcomes)

Age-level objectives (such as those for departments and divisions) are generally based on averages. Thus they gloss over important individual differences, and imply uniform starting points. But there is some question as to whether age-level objectives are genuinely useful catagories. New people enter church programs at every age level without fulfilling any "prerequisite requirements," and after entering may advance at vastly different rates. This greatly magnifies existing individual differences.

One way of looking at objectives is to state them as means by which to involve pupils in the nurturing process at each stage of overall development. Besides avoiding the dangers of overly close age grading, this broadens the perspective to include both divine and human tasks—and distinguishes between them.

The overall objective of becoming like Christ through a growing, experiential knowledge of God guides the entire nurturing process. Both God and man are involved in this goal.

God's part includes: (1) revelation,[2] (2) spiritual illumination, (3) transformation. Christian educators may formulate objectives which include these, but must realize that these are not humanly attainable and are not controlled by the teacher. The human instrument cooperates with God and is controlled by Him to accomplish His purposes, not vice versa. The difficulty of stating objectives as desired behavior changes is that it puts the educator in the position of attempting to use or control God to accomplish human purposes. It also implies that educational conditioning in good habits is the means of building Christian character.

Man's part includes: (1) student experiences of God's revelation, (2) preparing the heart for spiritual illumination, (3) responding to God in

---

[2]Evangelicals view special revelation as the work of God by which He discloses Himself and truth about Himself. God reveals Himself today through the Scriptures, which were recorded without error by human authors whose writings were inspired by the Holy Spirit. Illumination, on the other hand, is that supernatural work of the Holy Spirit whereby He enables man to apprehend and appropriate God's written Word. See Roy B. Zuck, *The Holy Spirit in Your Teaching* (Wheaton, Ill.: Scripture Press Publications, Inc., 1963), pp. 23, 35-50.

ways that lead toward spiritual transformation. Also important are teaching techniques that lead the student to undertake and complete his tasks successfully.

This approach is age-related. Designed student tasks must correspond to his abilities. The student's response to God will stem from his ability to relate God's truth to his experience, and will lead to a modification of that experience. Students at the same age level tend to experience much in common. Spiritual development often parallels other areas in the growth of the total person.

In this chapter youth objectives are viewed in relation to *experiences* youth should undergo as means of encouraging spiritual growth. Lesson, unit and course aims must be developed which will lead toward these "youth objectives." These must be formulated in harmony with curriculum materials used.

Why have objectives?

The saying, "Aim at nothing and you are sure to hit it" wraps a kernel of truth in a husk of falsehood. People *are* constantly learning something— even if it is nothing more than that they don't like church!

1. *Good objectives will help teacher and student know how to submit cooperatively to God's work in and through them.*

2. *Objectives are meant to give direction for the entire nurturing process, and to provide a general basis for the development of curriculum materials.*

3. *Objectives are meant to serve as guides to help student and teacher take successive steps in the desired direction.* Learning is progressive and cumulative. Care must be taken that objectives are not stated or followed so strictly that they become straitjackets that restrict spiritual growth.

4. *Objectives serve as guards against slipping into inappropriate or meaningless activity.* Good aims can help prevent a teacher from becoming so involved in incidental details that he misses the main points. Aims must not be permitted, however, to limit individual freedom to search out and act on the truth.

5. *Objectives provide limitations to group experiences within bounds that a teacher can handle.* Only frustration and failure will result from attempts to reach ultimate goals immediately. An overambitious teacher may attempt to cover too much ground, and in the process may fail to cover anything effectively. However, aims must not limit so much that they hinder effort to meet the genuine needs of individuals.

6. *Objectives express purposes common to both teacher and student.* They are useful aids in stimulating motivation, cooperation, and participation. However a teacher must always avoid any tendency to force his aims on others or to manipulate rather than educate.

7. *Objectives provide good bases for evaluation of teaching.* They must therefore be broader than merely "content to be learned" but not so general that they provide little or no help in measuring spiritual growth.

DETERMINING YOUTH OBJECTIVES

Objectives and development

Spiritual goals must be determined in relation to the total development and changing needs of persons. Past physical, intellectual, social, emotional, and spiritual development determines one's readiness for further spiritual growth. There is developmental sequence involved in spiritual growth just as there is in psychophysical maturation. Spiritual maturation is inevitably related to areas of development other than the spiritual. This is true because a person develops as a functional whole. Each new task builds on tasks previously completed and prepares for successful completion of future tasks.[3]

Objectives and the Bible and human experience

Christian nurture is a cooperative effort between God and man. When God uses man to accomplish His spiritual purposes, it is through His Word.[4] Objectives must be formulated to help a person interact with God's Word meaningfully.

The Old Testament prophets did not merely quote the law to God's erring people.[5] They pointed up how God's Word relates to human experience. Christ expounded Scripture in terms of current situation.[6] The variety of material in the epistles is due not only to different areas of divine truth touched but to varying situations and different needs of people.

---

[3]Jenkins, Bauer, and Schacter identify seven developmental tasks for adolescent persons: (1) to acquire a set of values, (2) to learn social skills, (3) to accept oneself as boy or girl, (4) to understand and accept one's body and its changes, (5) to learn to get along with family members, (6) to decide upon and prepare for lifework, and (7) to learn to become a responsible citizen. Gladys Gardner Jenkins, W. W. Bauer, and Helen S. Schacter, *Teen-agers* (New York: Scott, Forseman and Co., 1954). Clarice Bowman summarizes these and adds spiritual tasks to the list. *Op. cit.*, pp. 49-50. Havighurst lists ten tasks for adolescents. Robert J. Havighurst, *Developmental Task and Education* (New York: David McKay Co., Inc., 1952), pp. 33-71.

[4]For instance note the experiences of Moses and Aaron (Exodus 4:28,30; 19:7), Joshua (Joshua 3:9; 8:34-35), Samuel (I Samuel 3:21—4:1), Ezra (Neh. 8:5-8), various prophets (I Kings 12:22; 18:1; 22:19; II Kings 19:21; 20:16), Christ (John 14:24), and the apostles (Acts 4:29,31; 8:4,25; 10:44; 11:1; 13:5,44; 15:35).

[5]See, e.g., Hosea 4; Amos 3—4; Malachi, 1—3.

[6]*Cf.* Matthew 9:13; 12:7; 13:14-15; 15:7-9; 18:16; 19:4-8; 21:13,16; 22:32.

Thus, youth objectives must be stated in terms of the relevance of God's truth to the lives of youth.

Objectives and mental processes

An indispensable but often missing link between hearing the Word of God and responding to it is *thinking* on it. The Scriptures often speak of thinking as meditation or remembering. Thinking has a long and distinguished history as an important facet (if not the most important part) of education of all types. However the necessity of thought is often too casually treated, and sometimes neglected or omitted from educational discussion. Church educational programs have aimed at many good things, but thinking as a goal has not been prominent.

When a Christian person truly thinks on God's Word, is open to its meanings, and exerts himself mentally with its implications to his life, this enables the Holy Spirit to do His work of illumination and transformation most fruitfully.

The following considerations, then, must be involved in the formulation of youth objectives: (1) Objectives must be formulated during youth years as steps of maturing which are consistent with youth ability, which build on preceding growth, which are related to present experience and needs, and which prepare for future growth. (2) Objectives must include helping the young person relate God's truth to his present situation and experiences. (3) Youth objectives must include involvement in mental activity and meditation beyond merely recognizing, memorizing, or remembering facts and ideas. The Word of God must be contemplated in depth and in relation to life as it is.

OBJECTIVES OF YOUTH WORK

To lead youth to Christ for salvation and then into responsible spiritual maturity, and to help them retain and utilize their abundant youthful resources under the lordship of Christ is the primary challenge of youth workers. This over-arching objective is expressed by Paul in Ephesians 4:13: "That the whole Body might be built up until the time comes when, in the unity of common faith and common knowledge of the Son of God, we arrive at real maturity—that measure of development which is meant by the fullness of Christ" (Phillips Translation).

Overall objectives may be stated in various ways. The Baptist Sunday School Board of the Southern Baptist Convention has pinpointed seven broad areas for objectives for any age level:

1. Christian conversion—to lead each person to a genuine experience of the saving grace of God through Jesus Christ.

2. Church membership—to guide each Christian into intelligent, active, and devoted membership in a New Testament church.

3. Christian worship—to help each person make Christian worship a vital and constant part of his expanding experience.

4. Christian knowledge and conviction—to help each person grow toward mature Christian knowledge, understanding, and conviction.

5. Christian attitude and appreciations—to assist each person in developing such Christian attitudes and appreciations that he will have a Christian approach to all of life.

6. Christian living—to guide each person in developing habits and skills which promote spiritual growth and in applying Christian standards of conduct in every area of life.

7. Christian service—to lead each person to invest his talents and skills in Christian service.[7]

Sometimes overall objectives are stated in terms of relationships—the pupil and his relationship to (1) God, (2) Christ, (3) the Holy Spirit, (4) the Bible, (5) the church, (6) himself, and (7) others.

Schreyer suggests several aims for junior highs, several for senior highs, and still others for older youth.[8]

Roy Zuck has suggested some excellent overall objectives of youth work:

A. To lead youth to
  1. Accept Christ as Saviour.
  2. Commit their lives to Christ as their Lord and Master.
  3. Be sensitive to the guidance and power of the Holy Spirit.
  4. Become church members and loyal Christian disciples.
  5. Participate in Christian ministries and world missions.
  6. Witness for Christ, thus directing others to Him.
  7. Be faithful stewards of their time, talents and money.
  8. Use their leisure time constructively.

B. To help youth to
  1. Genuinely worship the Lord.
  2. Grow in their knowledge and understanding of Bible truths.
  3. Apply Christian principles in every area and relationship of life.
  4. Develop habits of personal Bible study and devotions.
  5. Recognize and respond to the will of God in all decisions.

---

[7]John T. Sisemore, (ed.), *Vital Principles in Religious Education* (Nashville: Broadman Press, 1966), pp. 20-21.

[8]George M. Schreyer, *Christian Education in Theological Focus* (Philadelphia: Christian Education Press, 1962), pp. 120-22.

The following aims[9] are broader statements encompassing many of the above. They are objectives for which every teacher, leader or sponsor of youth groups should strive.

To lead youth to a personal relationship to Jesus Christ by their receiving Him as Saviour

This is the first overall goal-concern of evangelical educators. As Gaebelein has stated, "The first aim of Christian education must be defined in terms of evangelism."[10] Of course this is not the sole aim, but it is certainly the initial aim. Genuine spiritual nurture of young people is impossible unless they have first received spiritual life through regeneration.

This suggests that the plan of salvation—including the fact of personal sin, God's gracious provision of Christ as Saviour, and the necessity of personal acknowledgment of sin and a by-faith acceptance of Christ as Saviour—be made explicitly clear to young people.

A young person's lack of interest in spiritual things may be due to several factors, and one of these factors in the case of some teens is lack of a genuine spiritual conversion experience. Being brought up in an evangelical church and a Christian home is no substitute for personal salvation. Nor is confirmation for young people completing junior high school, as practiced by some evangelical churches, to be considered a substitute for regeneration.

Methods by which youth may be evangelized—and by which Christian youth may be engaged in evangelizing unsaved youth—are discussed in another chapter of this book.[11]

To confront youth with the biblical message in meaningful relation to their own experience

Two approaches to youth work have predominated in the past as either-or alternatives: (1) the Bible could be the starting point and its truth expounded and applied to life, or (2) problems of youth could serve as starting points toward biblical answers. Both approaches have dangers and problems.

---

[9]Objectives listed here are "Youth Objectives" in the widest sense. They are not categorized into junior high, senior high, and young people's levels. By the end of adolescence (about 24 years of age), some objectives should have been attained. Others are lifelong tasks. In general the junior higher is beginning, the high schooler proceeding toward, and the college-age person is achieving them. More specific objectives than these tend to be individual rather than departmental.

[10]Frank E. Gaebelein, *Christian Education in a Democracy* (New York; Oxford University Press, 1951), p. 30.

[11]Chapter 10, "Evangelism of Youth."

There is the danger that the first approach might not meet the genuine needs and questions of youth. There are the problems of establishing meaningful contact and maintaining interest. The second approach might hinder the Scriptures from speaking their genuine message by reducing the biblical message to a set of psychological gimmicks and predetermined answers. Even though specific youth problems may be raised, this approach does little to overcome biblical illiteracy or to enable the young person to use the Bible for himself.

Some kind of synthesis of these two is desirable. Problems of twentieth-century youth grow out of cultural settings so diverse from those of the Bible that much biblical understanding is necessary before any genuine relationship between problem and answer can be established. Earlier educational experience in the church may have provided some help in enabling youth to feel at home in Bible cultures. Not specifically twentieth century problems, but deeper problems which were prevalent in biblical times as well as now provide good starting points. To understand—at ever deepening levels—God's love, His noncondemning acceptance, and His gifts which relate to youth's deepest needs and experiences are the most vital Christian insights youth can gain. Broader scriptural knowledge must build upon these ever deepening understandings.

Ideas apart from biblical contexts are not enough. The understandings suggested above should result from group and personal study of the Scriptures. Young people must see how the Word relates to their present needs and experiences. Sufficient depth of meaning is usually attained through receiving the Word in a variety of ways, through many senses, and in differing contexts. "Clusters of experiences" or many related teaching procedures will most like be necessary.[12] Which comes first—the Scripture meaning in context, or personal experience and need—is a matter of pedagogical expediency. Ultimately both are essential for effective nurture.

To help youth think seriously and constructively concerning the deep implications of the Word of God

The old saying that "the teacher has not taught unless the pupil has learned" is especially applicable to Christian education. Learning at depth levels involves painful, mind-stretching thought. Christian thought should include not only critical thinking but also faith in action involving submission of the mind to Christ. A short time of concentrated thought can do more to cooperate with God's Spirit toward change than many hours

---

[12]For a discussion of such approaches for youth see chapter 24. Also see Eleanor Shelton Morrison and Virgil E. Foster, *Creative Teaching in the Church* (Englewood Cliffs, N.J.: Prentice-Hall, Inc., 1963) , pp. 69-77, 123-49.

of skipping from pat answer to pat answer, or of skimming along the surface of biblical truth.

Thoughts such as the following would provide meaningful content for youth's meditation:

How does my love differ from God's love in kind rather than quantity? Where could I most likely begin to express God's kind of love?

Do I exercise and exhibit other Christ-honoring virtues such as patience, self-control, gentleness, peace, joy?

Have I ever accepted anyone completely without any condemnation, as God has accepted me? Could I? Am I willing, as God is, to pay the necessary price?

What of God's gifts and blessings could I share with others?

Could I forgive and forget? Could I help someone else feel important even if I lost some status in the process? Could I give my life to bring the gospel to a strange people?

Are my activities and rationalizations free from self-interest?

Am I a responsible person? Do my requests from God reflect a responsible attitude? Could all Christians reasonably expect as much as I request? If all Christians lived as I do, would God be magnified? What activities or attitudes in my life need to be omitted, added or altered, to help me become more pleasing to the Lord?

To equip youth to study the Bible with zest and to interact with its basic issues independently

The young person, who is gaining more and more independence, must be prepared to be responsibly dependent on God and His Word. He must be led to know that the Bible is not a magical lodestar, a set of rules to be followed blindly, or merely a list of propositions to be believed. He should accept it as God's means of revealing Himself through both the record of His actions in relation to man and the inspired words which interpret His actions. He must be helped to realize that his responses of faith, worship and obedience to God will enable him to mature as a Christian. He can learn to grow in his knowledge of God through studying God's dealings with people in foreign cultures and other times, but understand that the never changing God is still active and real in his own times and experience. He can live in realization of God's present activities and will, and can actively obey His will in reliance on the Spirit's power which God provides.

Young people need to realize the important place meditation on the Word of God plays in the Christian life. In a cultural climate where quietness and thoughtfulness are not popular he must choose to be independently different and provide the mental field where the Holy Spirit can work effectively.

Youth years are ideal times to become acquainted with methods and tools of Bible study. Leaders must lead youth to develop and sharpen their study skills and to find satisfaction through personal discoveries in God's Word.

To lead youth through experiences which will enable them to test and evaluate their Christian insights and develop a Christ-centered view of life

One of the features of Christ's ministry was His reliance on more than hortatory words alone to accomplish His purposes. Many incidents in the gospels illustrate experiences through which He led the disciples in order to test their understandings. The Christian faith is built around interpersonal relationships. Youth years are years of growing understanding of oneself and of self in relation to God and others.

Varied worship experiences, for example, enable youth to evaluate their relationship with God. A variety of social experiences give opportunities to test their relationships with others. Frank and honest appraisals of these experiences through individual counseling and group discussions enhance their value greatly.

Confronting youth through personal experience with life as it is and affording them opportunities to serve in areas of special need will provide occasions to consider such questions as "Who am I?" "What do I want out of life?" "In what way can God use my life?" "What do I want to become?" "What does God want me to do?" "How can my life glorify the Lord?"

To help youth face honestly and openly issues pertaining to the relation of faith and reason

Children believe what they are told by people whom they trust. Young people have many doubts and desire reasonable explanations for what they believe. Doubting is a healthy youth experience. Without honest doubt and questioning, answers may be little more than clichés.

All doubts cannot be resolved by reasoning. Revelation must be received by faith. Reason is employed by devout persons to *interpret* revelation, but reason cannot *test* the validity of revealed truth. Youth need help in understanding the legitimate functions of reason and to develop discrimination in understanding the pronouncements of churches, theologians, ministers and teachers. Lest youth be trapped by the glitter of contemporary rationalistic systems of thought, they need help to understand the limitations of reason and the possibility of its distortion by sin and self-interest.

Interest in discussions between scientists and theologians should not be avoided but used as a means of clarifying issues for youth and of helping them avoid spiritual shipwreck and intellectual dishonesty by knowing what truths they hold unreservedly and what interpretations they hold tentatively. Youth should be encouraged to dedicate their minds to their Lord as fully as they dedicate their other talents and energies.

When teens are given a learning climate where they may test their beliefs, refine them, and relate them to wider experiences of life, they tend to develop a firsthand rather than a "hand-me-down" faith in God and His Word.

YOUTH DEPARTMENT STANDARDS

A standard is a statement of a norm which exemplifies desirable characteristics of a program. Standards may be formulated in areas such as classification of pupils, curriculum, methods of instruction, qualities of leadership, and organization.

Since nurture is primarily the engagement of *persons* in processes which provide conditions in which God can work in lives, personal standards are of chief importance. Of secondary importance are standards which relate to organizational framework and program content.

Personal standards

The attitude church workers take toward pupils is very important to successful youth work. Young people in the church should be motivated, not manipulated. They should be persuaded, not propagandized; served, not used; viewed as persons, not things; and supported, not babied.

Meaningful involvement through many different types of free participation is essential if youth goals are to be achieved. Excessive pressure to conform to adult standards or to change in ways adults desire will not achieve Christian results in the nurture of youth. Freedom to choose either good or bad, and awareness of spiritual rather than human pressures are essential if youth are to mature.

This maturing will take place not in a rigid, condemning atmosphere, but in an atmosphere of love, acceptance and freedom. This leads to standards for youth workers whose relationships with youth contribute significantly to this needed growth environment.

Youth workers should not be mere purveyors of precepts. They should be sympathetic, responsive human beings who respect youth for what they are and can be. They should be able and willing to face youth's problems with them. And rather than criticize the ways young people handle their problems, youth workers should be willing to counsel—to exhibit the kind of life youth can safely follow.

The youth worker should be well adjusted and responsible. The challenge of available untouched spiritual resources to be used under the lordship of Christ should fire him with the kind of enthusiasm which youth can catch and fan into flame as they draw closer to Christ.[13]

Organizational standards

The basic standard underlying youth organization is that youth should be so classified, arranged and organized that independence and responsi-bility are fostered and promoted in a safe and supportive framework. An adult-dominated organization or a totally unguided organization must be avoided. The purpose of adult guidance is not so much to keep youth from making mistakes as it is to help youth learn from them.

If youth are guided and inspired they are capable of organizing and developing programs that are efficient, functional and spiritual. Goals such as exhibiting the love of Christ, developing good personal relationships, and using time effectively should guide youth in organizing themselves in the church.[14]

Program standards

General standards underlying the program include the following. Maintain a good balance between preparing young people to serve Christ in the future and meeting present needs and problems. Develop a program which will lead youth to conform to Christian ideals, and to reject unchristian standards. Help them remain open to the Holy Spirit. Emphasize throughout the program the indispensability of God's grace and power to do anything which will please Him, and encourage youth to submit their wills to God.

The general pinciple is that program and lesson content should consist of that which is most essential and most appropriate for the spiritual nurture of youth.

Continually measuring each aspect of youth work in the local church by these standards can help workers gauge the effectiveness and quality of their ministry to young people.

SUMMARY

Clear youth department objectives and standards are essential for achieving ultimate purposes in a truly Christian way. Since it is God who is working in youth to enable them to will and do His pleasure, youth objectives should be stated as ways of helping young persons meet God in His Word and respond to Him. The youth worker as Christ's minister

---

[13]For more on personal qualifications of workers with youth, see chapter 18.

[14]For more on organization, see chapter 9.

should desire to help youth face personally and responsibly the genuine message of God's Word.

The major task of the church is to help its youth in the process of becoming spiritually independent and responsible Christian persons. If teachers and workers aim their lesson, unit and program objectives in this direction and consistently uphold Christian standards in their work, they can rely on God's faithfulness to bring about His will in the lives of youth as they respond to His Holy Spirit.

Questions such as the following should be considered by church leaders with reference to youth aims and standards:

Should church aims touch all areas of youth needs or be restricted to spiritual nurture aims? Has the "whole person" concept been overemphasized to the place of diluting the spiritual aims of the church? Should the church use its limited resources to attempt programs which other agencies are already doing well, or can the church use educational experiences outside the church so that they contribute to spiritual nurture? Can the church make its aims so vital to youth that they themselves can use non-church provided experiences as means for achieving these goals?

Can the educational goals of the church and its missionary aims be separated, or must the church be fulfilling its mission to the world in a context of education and nurture? Should not a responsible Christian be noted for involvement in the church's mission? Are young people not challenged by the church because the church program is centered primarily in self-service rather than in missionary outreach?

Are youth programs structured to foster direct allegiance to the lordship of Christ in whatever way He will lead, or are leaders just as concerned that youth feel free to think and work only within the traditional forms which have guided them? Are leaders afraid to lead youth to question their beliefs and practices, or are they willing to trust the Holy Spirit and the Word of God to lead youth as they were led? Is the church willing to expose youth while they are secure within the Christian community to all possible answers to the great questions of life, or must it protect them from all but "orthodox" views? What best prepares youth to cope with life's problems successfully?

Honesty in facing and answering these questions will help leaders to think beyond and build on the suggestions of this chapter.

FOR FURTHER READING

BARUCH, DOROTHY W. *How to Live with Your Teen-ager.* New York: McGraw-Hill Book Co., Inc., 1953.

BOWMAN, LOCKE. *How to Teach Senior Highs.* Philadelphia: Westminster Press, 1963.

Brunk, Ada Z., and Metzler, Ethel Y. *The Christian Nurture of Youth.* Scottdale, Pa.: Herald Press, 1960.

Cummings, Oliver DeWolf. *The Youth Fellowship.* Philadelphia: Judson Press, 1960.

Garrison, Karl C. *Before You Teach Teen-Agers.* Philadelphia: Lutheran Church Press, 1962.

Harner, Nevin C. *Youth Work in the Church.* Nashville: Abingdon-Cokesbury Press, 1952.

Hechinger, Grace and Fred M. *Teen-age Tyranny.* New York: Wm. Morrow & Co., Inc., 1963.

Jenkins, Gladys Gardner, Bauer, W.W., and Schacter, Helen S. *Teen-Agers.* New York: Scott, Foresman & Co., 1954.

Morrison, Eleanor Shelton, and Foster, Virgil E. *Creative Teaching in the Church.* Englewood Cliffs, N.J.: Prentice-Hall, Inc., 1963.

Vieth, Paul Herman. *Objectives in Religious Education.* New York: Harper & Bros. Publishers, 1930.

Wittenberg, Rudolph M. *Adolescence and Discipline.* New York: Association Press, 1959.

Wyckoff, D. Campbell. *The Gospel and Christian Education.* Philadelphia: Westminster Press, 1959.

———. *Theory and Design of Christian Education Curriculum.* Philadelphia: Westminster Press, 1961.

Zuck, Roy B. *The Holy Spirit in Your Teaching.* Wheaton, Ill.: Scripture Press Publications, Inc., 1963.

There have been many youthful links in the chain of Christian witnesses through the ages. Among them were Timothy, colaborer with the Apostle Paul; John Calvin, called "the most Christian man of his time"; David Brainerd, a young evangelist to the American Indian; Dwight L. Moody, converted as a boy and set on fire by God to bring the gospel to two continents; and today, Billy Graham, world-renowned evangelist who was converted in his teens.

All of these young men were deeply influenced for God before they were twenty. They are symbols and fulfillments of vast numbers of young men and women who to this day derive their principal satisfaction from following and serving Jesus Christ. He inspires young people in all generations to serve Him to the utmost of their capacity for the good of the age in which they live.

MILFORD SHOLUND

4

a historical survey of youth work

LUKE'S ACCOUNT of the fourfold developmental growth of Jesus Christ is a pattern for youth and youth workers. "And as Jesus continued to grow in body and mind, He grew also in the love of God and of those who knew Him." (Luke 2:52, Phillips).

All youth work will be judged ultimately according to Jesus Christ. The center and circumference of all youth activities for the individual and the group must be evaluated in the light of His life and His gospel.

The historical perspective of youth work has meaning and significance in the teaching and work of Jesus Christ. Though the Scriptures and secular history are silent about the life of Christ between the ages of 12 and 30, the account of His childhood and the achievement of His manhood leave no doubt that His adolescent years were years of preparation for the task which God had sent Him to accomplish.

There have been many youthful links in the chain of Christian witnesses through the ages. Among them were Timothy, colaborer with the Apostle

MILFORD SHOLUND, Litt. D., is Director of Biblical and Educational Research, Gospel Light Publications, Inc., Glendale, California.

Paul; John Calvin, called "the most Christian man of his time"; David Brainerd, a young evangelist to the American Indian; Dwight L. Moody, converted as a boy and set on fire by God to bring the gospel to two continents; and today, Billy Graham, world renowned evangelist who was converted in his teens.

All of these young men were deeply influenced for God before they were twenty. They are symbols and fulfillments of vast numbers of young men and women who to this day derive their principal satisfaction from following and serving Jesus Christ. He inspires young people in all generations to serve Him to the utmost of their capacity for the good of the age in which they live.

Numerous early settlers of America were young men and women who had convictions about God and the good life. Some were reared in Puritan homes where the parents insisted on giving attention to godliness. The Puritan young people were heirs of an unbroken practice of catechism in the study of the sacred Scriptures. To catechize meant to instruct by asking questions and receiving answers from students. In religious catechism, the adult prepared not only the question but the answer that was to be given to him by the youth.

Organized youth groups as we know them today were practically unknown in the days of the early colonists, but the young people were nevertheless taught Christian doctrine through the catechetical method. In the Protestant tradition in America, two of the principal works of instruction were the *Westminster Catechism* (1647) and the *Heidelberg Catechism* (1562/63). *The Book of Common Prayer* (1549) also included catechetical sections. Memorizing questions and answers and Scripture portions was inherent in the religious instruction of youth. Catechization profoundly influenced young people in America through the seventeenth and eighteenth centuries.[1] However, another instructional medium was developing—one which was to make even greater impact.

SUNDAY SCHOOL FOR YOUTH

During the nineteenth century the Sunday school was recognized in the United States by various Protestant denominations as the chief instrument for religious education. By 1850, the Bible was regarded as the primary curriculum material replacing the catechism though the latter was still considered important by some denominations.

The founding of the Sunday school is generally attributed to Robert Raikes in Gloucester, England, in 1780. He was motivated by a desire to teach the Bible to children who were neglected, underprivileged and delin-

---

[1]"Catechism," *Encyclopaedia Britannica*, V:25-27 (Chicago: Encyclopaedia Britannica, Inc., 1958).

quent. Before long, Raikes' idea fired the minds of pioneers in America. The first Sunday school in the United States was started in 1785. There was much opposition from clergymen and the established churches. However, within fifteen years Sunday schools scattered along the eastern seaboard were enrolling tens of thousands of children.

The extension of the Sunday school to include youth was begun in Nottingham, England, in 1798. Young working women gathered on Sunday mornings for religious instruction. Through correspondence the idea spread to America, and soon there were young people's classes throughout the eastern section of the country.

THE BEGINNINGS OF YOUTH GROUPS

Along with the growth of the Sunday school there were indications that a youth movement was developing within the churches. Other agencies were soon to attract youth in an effort to guide them in Christian doctrine. The beginnings were obscure, but the results were soon evident. As early as the seventeenth century, there were singing classes for youth. Such a class was held in Boston in 1717. These classes were the forerunners of the Protestant church choir. Through these musical sessions, young people were drawn together for further religious activities.

Social problems accelerated the formation of youth groups in churches. Alcohol ruined many pioneers on the plains and in the growing cities. The idealism of youth was a springboard for temperance societies. By 1829 there were more than a thousand temperance groups for youth in Philadelphia.

From 1787 to 1830 there was a missionary awakening among Protestants. Missionary societies swept over our continent. Among these groups were the following: New York Missionary Society (1796), Boston Female Society for Missionary Purposes (1802), and Witness of Baptist Youth Missionary Society of New York City (1806).[2] The famous Haystack Meeting of 1806 was instigated by a movement of youths who were destined to go to the ends of the earth with the gospel of Christ.

The modern youth movement in Protestant church circles is an outgrowth of the first YMCA founded in 1844. Twelve young men met in London under the guidance of George Williams. The original purpose was religious in nature. By 1851, the work spread to the United States and Canada. Along with the appeal to young men there was one for young women—the YWCA—founded in London in 1855, and in New York City in 1858.

The period from 1830 to 1860 was fertile with ideas for youth groups,

[2]*The Study of Education: Part I, Christian Education Yesterday and Today* (Chicago: International Council of Religious Education, 1947) .

but this stirring was only a suggestion of the rapid birth of youth organizations following the Civil War.

Theodore Cuyler quickened the pace of interest within the churches when he organized a young people's association in his church. Cuyler set a pattern that has been expanded in thousands of churches in America. Three ideas from Cuyler's original plan prevail in churches today: (1) *Coed*: the group should work with both young men and women. (2) *Weekly:* the groups should meet every week. (3) *Participative:* committees composed of the young people should prepare weekly devotional meetings. These three features prevail today in most young people's meetings in Protestant churches across the nation.

The practical young people's meeting soon captured the imagination and interest of pastors. Churches throughout the eastern United States were eager to get young people involved in groups for memorizing Scripture and improving their Christian lives. During this period, the Sunday school movement was developing from an emphasis on Scripture memorization among children, to lectures on all sorts of biblical and related topics.

The evolution of educational theories implemented by Horace Mann in the public schools was soon impinging on the religious education movement. There was considerable unrest with resultant searching for new ways of helping young people. What could not be done by teachers in the Sunday school was supplemented by what was called "juvenile illustrated periodicals."

CHRISTIAN ENDEAVOR SOCIETY ORGANIZED 1881

Doctor Francis E. Clark, pastor of the Williston Congregational Church, Portland, Maine, visited Dr. Theodore Cuyler's church in Brooklyn, New York, and was inspired to organize the *Young People's Society of Christian Endeavor* (1881) as a result of this contact. The object of Christian Endeavor was "to promote an earnest Christian life among its members, to increase their mutual acquaintance, and to make them more useful in the service of God."[3]

The success of Christian Endeavor societies was unprecedented as a religious youth movement. The time was ripe for such an effort.

The nondenominational character of Christian Endeavor groups was a bid for all Protestant churches to participate. However, in less than ten years (1889) the optimism for an interchurch inclusive youth program was eclipsed. The Epworth League was formed from existing Methodist church societies (1889). The Baptist Young People's Union (1891) appealed to the loyalty of Baptist churches while the Lutheran churches rallied their

---

[3]H. Clay Trumbull, *The Sunday School—Its Origin, Mission, Methods and Auxiliaries* (Philadelphia: John D. Wattles, 1888).

efforts around the Luther League (1895). The pattern was clear. Denominational programs were growing. Sunday schools and youth groups were directed from the national headquarters of the various denominations.

At the opening of the twentieth century, organized youth groups in local churches were the rule rather than the exception. The time had come for denominational leaders to use their skills in imagination, inspiration, and ink to guide and stimulate interest and fervor in local youth groups toward eager participation in constructive activities.

FACTORS AFFECTING GROWTH

Several characteristics of the young people's movement in the Protestant churches encouraged their growth: (1) fulfillment of the need for companionship inherent in young people moving to and living in the cities; (2) a sense of belonging, since most of the various groups required some kind of pledge or membership; (3) an involvement in responsibility by participating in the plans and programs (there was hardly a group without a committee-centered approach) ; (4) the enthusiasm and hope which prevailed in the groups, for at that period (1880-1914), the world conditions were conducive to a vigorous outlook for worldwide peace, prosperity and progress; (5) the democratic leadership which meant that young people themselves could participate in and direct their efforts.

1900-1930: EXPANSION AND DEVELOPMENT

Young people demonstrated exceptional ability to mobilize their resources and aptitudes within the framework of the established patterns of their church organizations. They elaborated their purposes, plans, programs and organizations. The period from 1900 to 1930 was a time of expansion and development of the established patterns of young people's societies conceived by Theodore Cuyler in 1860 and developed by youth leaders and pastors after the Civil War. Youth work grew in local churches, in states, and throughout the nation.

The typical local church youth society met once a week, usually on Sunday evening. The program was varied, covering topics on the Bible, the Christian life, devotional readings, temperance, amusements, social problems and world conditions. The appeal to youth was through a varied program. The difference between the typical young people's session in the Sunday school and the young people's society meeting in the evening was the increased activity and expression on the part of the young people in the evening.

In evaluating the various elements of religious education and their positions in the program of the local church, Squires tells us that this typical contrast between the various phases of the youth program continued into the prosperous 1920's: *Informational emphasis:* Sunday school, 90%; Christian Endeavor, 10%; Boy Scouts and Girl Scouts, 25%; weekday church school, 75%. *Worship emphasis:* Sunday school, 6%; Christian Endeavor, 15%; Boy Scouts and Girl Scouts, 2%; weekday church school, 10%. *Expressional emphasis:* Sunday school, 4%; Christian Endeavor, 75%; Boy Scouts and Girl Scouts, 73%; weekday church school, 15%.[4]

GROWING PROBLEMS

The churches were reaching out for a complete program for youth, but the capacity to achieve their aspirations was lacking. The paucity of leadership on a voluntary basis in the local church was staggering. In addition to this problem there were powerful forces working within the Protestant churches as well as outside to weaken the program of religious education among young people in the churches.

Theological tensions were growing in the churches. The accepted orthodox, Bible-oriented setting that had prevailed for three hundred years in America as an acceptable contribution to the contemporary generation of young people was being challenged. The heart of the theological controversy was focused on two basic issues: the nature of Christ and the nature of man.

The traditional biblical views concerning the deity and humanity of Christ were openly disputed. The tide of liberalism swept over Protestantism. The devastation was complete in many quarters. Leaders of youth were being educated in seminaries and colleges that were espousing liberal views of Christianity. Every advancement in learning seemed to be at loggerheads with the existing order of evangelical theology. Critical studies of the Old and New Testaments were in full bloom. Many of the conclusions of destructive Higher Criticism undercut faith in the sufficiency, authority and finality of Jesus Christ and the Scriptures.

Inherent in the interpretation of the deity and humanity of Christ was the study of the nature of man. In the last third of the nineteenth century a ferment of new ideas challenged the traditional concepts of man and his environment. Charles Darwin in his book *The Origin of Species* (1859) opened the gates of inquiry and research concerning the origin and nature of the human race. The enormous breakthrough in scientific studies in psychology confronted the churches with new ideas about the nature and potential of young people that soon affected programming and publications for young people's work throughout the churches.

In the field of religious education all these forces gathered strength in a great convention in Chicago which organized the Religious Education As-

---

[4]Walter Albion Squires, *A Parish Program of Education* (Philadelphia: Westminster Press, 1923), p. 36.

sociation (1903). Internationally known leaders participated in the program. William Rainey Harper, first president of the University of Chicago, advocated more intelligent study in the use of the Bible. George Albert Coe had a genius for coining religious educational terms for the new liberalism. A prominent and provocative speaker at the convention was John Dewey, who certainly had concepts about religion which were radically different from the conservative leaders who wanted a revival of Bible study in the churches.

The problem in the evangelical ranks was the lack of leadership. There was no "Moses" to lead them out of the "wilderness" of critical ideas about the Scriptures. There were many protests from evangelicals. But the die was cast. There was no turning back the forces of cultural change in the American way of life as the revolutionary educational concepts captured the minds of youth leaders.

In liberal churches, evangelism was dissipated in trying to make young people Christian by giving them "refreshing experiences" rather than leading them to spiritual regeneration through the Holy Spirit. The basic teachings of the Bible on the sinfulness of human nature, the atoning work of Jesus Christ on the cross, and the call to worldwide evangelism were lacking in the purposes, plans and programs of young people's organizations.

Of course, as always there was a remnant of true believers. They were scattered throughout the land in churches within the mainstream denominations and in smaller groups.

YOUTH WORK: LIBERAL AND CONSERVATIVE

Protestantism was divided not only into scores of denominations but into two theological camps: liberals and conservatives. The issues were debated and the lines drawn tighter. In 1922 the turning point in organizational relationship culminated in the formation of the International Council of Religious Education. The ICRE, as it was popularly known, was a merger of forty denominational boards and thirty-three state councils of churches. The work of the ICRE was chiefly in local church programs, family life, and community religious education. The significance of the ICRE for youth work was twofold: theological overtones and organizational unification.

For the next twenty-eight years (1922-1950), the ICRE through its youth department exerted an enormous influence on the development of denominational youth programs.[5] The United Christian Youth Movement (1934) provided guidelines for church youth groups to follow as they built their programs. Five themes were considered in the comprehensive view of

[5] In 1950, the ICRE merged with several other national and interdenominational agencies to form the Division of Christian Education of the National Council of the Churches of Christ in the U.S.A.

the program for youth: (1) Christian faith, (2) Christian witness, (3) Christian outreach, (4) Christian citizenship, (5) Christian fellowship.

During this period of ICRE development, fundamental, conservative youth groups were carrying on in their respective denominations and churches, but there was no counterpart to the ICRE for these theologically conservative elements. There was no unifying agency through which they could express or expand their cause.

Youth work in the Sunday school was languishing between 1915 and 1935. The same was true of the Sunday evening youth groups. The spiritual depression throughout the land was equal to the economic depression that gripped America from 1930 to 1937.

The Christian Endeavor movement, so strong in 1910, was rapidly losing its grip in the 30's as an effective channel for the evangelical forces. The United Christian Youth Movement established in 1934 did little to arouse the evangelistic fervor of teen-agers. The idealism of youth needed challenging leadership, but this was lacking.

DEVELOPMENTS SINCE 1935

Youth work during the next thirty years was different from what anyone in 1935 could have safely predicted. Developments were in sharp contrast to the routine of many youth meetings. Parades, campaigns, rallies, small study groups, sensational appeals, coffee houses, recreation, camping, movies, tours—all these and countless other youthful expressions and enterprises constituted the motley assortment of youth work that was soon to appear in an era of economic depression, world war, affluent living, population explosion, race tensions, and moral and spiritual revolt. The clergy and laity were about to be "shocked" and "dismayed" with young people's work in their churches. The denominational machinery was not ready for the rapid changes in youth work. The typical church had "too little too late" to satisfy the younger set swirling with the cultural changes that struck the United States during one generation. Where churches gave attention to their youth, the appeal was usually outside the framework of organized Christian work. Throughout the nation young people were ready and willing to leave their religious moorings and try something new.

EXTRACHURCH YOUTH ORGANIZATIONS

The "something new" was the appeal of the extrachurch activities and organizations. For more than seventy-five years the ministry among young people was closely associated with the local church or an interchurch agency. There were exceptions like the YMCA, YWCA, Boy Scouts and Girl Scouts; but the rise of movements that were diverse, independent, religious, evangelical and evangelistic was reserved for the revolutionary generation from 1937 to 1967.

As an example of this new brand of Christian youth effort, the Young Life Campaign, launched in Texas in 1941, appealed to millions of high school kids on and off high school campuses. The Reverend James Rayburn was burdened for reaching high school students. He was convinced that they could be reached for Christ even though the local churches (in his view) were not making an effective bid for students outside the usual activities of the church.

His approach was different. He went directly to leaders of high school student bodies. Often the appeal was to the school athletes. The approach was personal, informal, and casual. He found that there were many students who wanted to know about Christ and receive and follow Him. They were not beyond the reach of the Christian witness.

The response was encouraging. Before long, Rayburn was confronted with the problem of extending the work to other high schools, then to other cities and states, and finally to the entire nation. More leaders were needed to help the work grow. The leaders would need special training. This would require a staff, equipment, materials and money.

An official organization with a board of directors was incorporated to guide the work and to raise financial support. The scope of the organization became nationwide. Young Life leaders and groups were spread over the entire nation.

Young Life is only one extrachurch movement. There are many other similar movements in the United States appealing to young people in and out of churches. Four other well-known evangelical groups are Youth for Christ International (working with high school youth) and Campus Crusade for Christ, Inter-Varsity Christian Fellowship, and The Navigators (the last three ministering among college youth).[6]

Extrachurch youth movements have common characteristics. They are independently organized and directed by individuals, usually incorporated, and supervised by a board. They are designed to appeal to youth and to help them to come to know Christ, to grow in the Christian life and to serve Christ. These organizations are distinct from interchurch and interdenominational youth organizations because they are not officially guided and supervised by persons elected or authorized by the churches to represent them.

The extrachurch groups are usually vital, energetic and progressive. They show no signs in most instances of abating their efforts to reach youth outside of the typical denominational or local church organizational activities.

---

[6]For a fuller discussion of extrachurch youth movements, see chapter 22.

RENEWED EFFORTS IN CHURCHES

Fortunately for Protestantism, the work of reaching youth in the churches did not diminish. The tangled times offered a challenge to established groups. The Southern Baptists reinforced their Training Unions for education in church membership. They set goals for enrollment and achievement which clearly indicated that the denomination and the local churches were aware of the importance of training youth for Christ and the church.

The Methodist churches in their mergers shifted from Epworth Leagues to Methodist Youth Fellowships. The term "fellowship" became a common label for youth activities in churches. The denominational and regional offices implemented the MYF plans, programs and publications. The spectrum of youth activities included everything from learning the Bible to discussing life-related teen problems and encountering the worldwide dilemma of war and peace.

NATIONAL ORGANIZATIONS

Within the framework of the Federal Council of Churches, a consolidation of youth emerged at the Cleveland Constituting Convention of the National Council of Churches of Christ in America on November 29, 1950. Youth work was placed under the newly formed Commission on General Christian Education, which has defined its purposes as follows: To serve as the medium of the Division for advancing its work in the field of general Christian education; to aid the member boards and agencies in the development of a comprehensive Christian education service for persons of all ages in the home, local church and community.[7] The Commission on Youth Work and the United Christian Youth Movement of the National Council of Churches serve the youth agencies of liberal denominations and local churches.

The National Association of Evangelicals was founded in St. Louis in 1942, amid massive changes in the relationships of churches within the United States. Harold Ockenga, pastor of the historic Park Street Church, Boston, headed the newly formed organization of evangelical denominations, churches and individuals. The NAE emerged as a fellowship of evangelicals and a service agency in many areas related to church needs and problems arising in the World War II period. There was no concerted effort, however, to build, organize, and serve the youth groups of the NAE's constituent denominations.

In 1945, the National Sunday School Association (NSSA) was organized in Chicago. James DeForest Murch, an incisive writer and interpre-

---

[7]Gerald E. Knoff, "Christian Education and the National Council of Churches," *Religious Education: A Comprehensive Survey),* ed. Marvin J. Taylor (New York: Abingdon Press, 1960) , p. 341.

ter of evangelical thought, advocated that means be created for evangelicals to express themselves in Christian education. Under his skillful guidance, the NSSA found a hearty response from thousands of evangelicals who were ready to establish a strong Christian education program for their denominations and churches. The NSSA, somewhat wary of centralized control, projected its main efforts through national and regional Sunday school conventions. Gradually through the years, the NSSA has become for evangelicals the means of drawing together youth leaders—as well as Sunday school leaders. (The title NSSA continues to be used, but today the organization is much broader in its purpose and program than the title indicates.)

The Youth Commission of NSSA was formed in 1957.[8] The purpose of the commission is: (1) to provide a national fellowship for youth executives and leaders throughout evangelical Christendom; (2) to provide a year-round exchange center for the best in methods, materials and procedures; (3) to conduct clinics and workshops at the annual spring convention of NAE, at the annual NSSA convention, and elsewhere; (4) to give attention to the task of collecting, evaluating and communicating to the Christian public the facts and needs concerning the plight of today's youth.[9]

One of the major functions of the NSSA Youth Commission each year is the sponsoring of National Youth Week in January. Promotional and program materials for this special week are produced by the commission and used by many evangelical denominations.

Thousands of youth leaders have attended conferences and workshops sponsored by the NSSA across the nation.

In the seventh decade of the twentieth century, there are four mainstreams of Protestant youth endeavor in the United States: (1) denominational organizations, (2) the Commission on Youth Work and the United Christian Youth Movement of the NCCCA, (3) the Youth Commission of the NSSA, (4) extrachurch movements on regional and national levels.

Denominational offices and independent publishing houses prepare and supply materials for youth in Sunday schools, Sunday evening gatherings, weekday clubs, vacation Bible schools, and camping groups.[10] Professional

[8]For ten years before that, the Youth Commission had been a commission of the National Association of Evangelicals, and was known as the Association of Evangelical Youth International. In 1957 this association (AEYI) discontinued its operation as a separate commission of the NAE and merged with the NSSA to function as its Youth Commission.

[9]Adapted from the constitution of the Youth Commission, National Sunday School Association, Wheaton, Illinois.

[10]For an evaluation of some of these materials, see chapter 25, "Materials for Working with Youth."

leaders are available to inspire, guide and evaluate youth work in local churches.

The interdenominational organizations of the United Christian Youth Movement (NCCCA) and the Youth Commission (NSSA) are chiefly concerned with inspiration, ideas and incentives. Special weeks for youth emphasis are sponsored, and materials are available for various programs. Numerous conferences, conventions, retreats and meetings are conducted for interaction and an exchange of ideas. The difference between the NCCCA and NSSA frameworks is found essentially in theological perspectives rather than in practical viewpoints. The NCCCA functions in the structure of a composite of churches with a liberal ecumenical outlook. The NAE and the NSSA advocate a strong emphasis on a biblical, evangelistic thrust.

The extrachurch youth organizations continue to appeal to churches for their moral, spiritual and financial support. Concurrent with the major thrusts of denominational and interdenominational extrachurch groups has been the development of camping, weekday classes, recreational programs, radio and TV appeals, and books—particularly paperbacks. The opportunity for young people to hear, learn, study and work in the Christian context is unparalleled in the United States in this generation. No period in the history of the Christian church compares with it.

This is not the whole story, however. The forces of evil—hedonism, atheism, materialism, secularism, humanism and war—are making massive appeals to youth. A highly stimulating environment (especially in the cities) of amusement, music, athletics, corrupt literature, and economic affluence tends to make the typical church youth group seem tame, dull, and uninteresting. Determined and dedicated Christian youth, however, can find abundant resources to help them. Alert churches are using more professionally trained youth leaders and ministers of Christian education to plan and direct activities for youth.

SUMMARY

To be effective and significant, youth work must be viewed from the evangelical Christian perspective. This concept includes the authoritative use of the Bible and the vital, transforming power and purpose of Jesus Christ in young lives.

The tendency toward specialization in teaching and training young people in Protestant churches in America began in the eighteenth century in singing and fellowship groups. The development of the Sunday school movement helped focus the attention of churches on the needs of their youth. Young people's societies of the late nineteenth century accelerated the trend to do more for and with young people. The twentieth century brought further evaluation as well as formalization of purposes and programs for youth. The shifting theological scene, the scientific revolution, two world wars, and the inability of the churches to cope with the problems of family life—all of these factors, and many more, created problems which challenged the best that American Christianity could give in leadership.

The potential of Christian youth calls for a deeper understanding of their needs and problems and a biblical, Christ-centered and Spirit-empowered ministry to them.

FOR FURTHER READING

Christian Endeavor Essentials. Columbus, Ohio: International Society of Christian Endeavor, 1956.

CUBBERLY, ELWOOD P. *The History of Education.* New York: Houghton Mifflin Co., 1948.

EAVEY, C. B. *History of Christian Education.* Chicago: Moody Press, 1964.

EBY, FREDERICK, and ARROWOOD, CHARLES. *The History and Philosophy of Education: Ancient and Medieval.* Englewood Cliffs, N. J.: Prentice-Hall, Inc., 1940.

ERB, F. O. *The Development of the Young People's Movement.* Chicago: University of Chicago Press, 1917.

LEBAR, LOIS E. *Education That Is Christian.* New York: Fleming H. Revell Co., 1958.

PRICE, J. M., CHAPMAN, J. H., CARPENTER, L. L., and YARBOROUGH, W. F. *A Survey of Religious Education.* Second Edition. New York: Ronald Press, 1959.

RICE, EDWIN WILBUR. *The Sunday School Movement and the American Sunday School Union.* Philadelphia: American Sunday School Union, 1917.

TRUMBULL, H. CLAY. *The Sunday School—Its Origin, Mission, Methods, and Auxiliaries.* Philadelphia: John D. Wattles, Publisher, 1888.

VIETH, PAUL H. (ed.). *The Church and Christian Education.* St. Louis: Bethany Press, 1947.

ZUCK, ROY B. "Sunday Evening Youth Groups," *An Introduction to Evangelical Christian Education.* J. EDWARD HAKES, editor. Chicago: Moody Press. 1964.

PART II

the contemporary world of adolescence

"*Youth everywhere is exploding into action. Members of the new generation have looked at the world their elders made. They do not like what they see. They are moving hard and fast to change it . . . . But even this headlong pace is not fast enough for youth of the sixties, the war babies who at last have grown up to give voice and vehemence to a generation that has been called 'silent' and 'cautious.'*"
—*George B. Leonard, Jr., Look staff writer.*

GORDON S. JAECK

5

the sociological context of teen-age behavior

> "Teen-agers are the current scapegoats for adult apathy, indifference, lack of responsibility, and lack of imagination."
> —Anthropologist MARGARET MEAD
> "You ought to bury them at twelve and dig them up at eighteen."
> —A MOTHER writing to JUDGE MARY CONWAY KOHLER

THE TENSE GENERATION

IN 1958 HARRISON E. SALISBURY wrote a headline-making book that subsequently won a Pulitzer prize. The book was entitled *The Shook-up Generation,* and dealt with that grouping of our teen-age culture that society has labeled "juvenile delinquents." There would be many, including parents, who might argue the limited application of Mr. Salisbury's title to delinquent teen-agers. In fact Mr. Salisbury himself, in the conclusion to his book, refers to a "shook-up age" and suggests that all our youth are subject to the strong influences of violence, turbulence and amorality which tend to produce shook-upness.[1]

---

[1]Harrison Salisbury, *The Shook-up Generation* (New York: Harper & Bros. Crest Book, 1958).

GORDON S. JAECK, M.A., is Chairman of the Department of Sociology and Anthropology, Wheaton College, Wheaton, Illinois.

But other epithets have been hurled at the mushrooming teen-age segment of our population, much of them suggestive of the distinct culture out of which the segment comes but even more descriptive of the behavior which appears to characterize this period. Consider, for example, the following:

"the spoiled generation"	"the angry ones"
"the cool generation"	"the wild ones"
"the open generation"	"generation in peril"
"the explosive generation"	"the tormented generation"

and the older, disturbing but still-used designation, "generation without a cause."

Recent incidents occurring in widely separated geographic locales have focused attention on our troubled youth—youth whom sociologist David Matza says have been especially "vulnerable to a variety of deviant patterns which manifest a spirit of rebelliousness."[2]

Winnetka, Illinois, twenty miles north of Chicago's loop, is a fashionable, high-income suburb where homes range from comfortably modest to million-dollar estates. On November 19, 1962, a limousine carrying nine New Trier High School teen-agers crashed into a tree in Winnetka. One of the young people, a 17-year-old girl, was killed. Police found evidence that some of her companions had been drinking. All nine of the teen-agers were leaders in their high school, which is rated among the nation's ten best public-supported preparatory schools with 92 percent of its graduates going on to college. All nine came from socially prominent north-shore families. The driver of the car was also a 17-year-old and a candidate for a national merit scholarship at the high school. The incident brought into sharp focus problems familiar to suburban communities all across the nation, and a United Press International reporter wrote of a shocked suburb and stunned parents "taking stock" in an effort to discover where they first failed.

Hastings is an English Channel resort town not unlike American coastal resorts where similar incidents have occurred. In August, 1964, newspaper accounts told of the RAF ferrying in special riot police to quell a three-day rumble of teen-agers in which two youths died. It had been the third major outburst of hooliganism that year. Involved were thousands of Britain's teen-agers, many of them members of two rival groups, the Mods, distinctive for their Beatle-style clothes, and the Rockers, who wore the characteristic leather jacket. Both gangs used motorcycles and were aggressively violent in their attack on the police.

---

[2]David Matza, "Subterranean Traditions of Youth," *The Annals,* 338:102-18 (November, 1961).

In January, 1965, a 16-year-old *Colorado* boy stood trial for the brutal murder of his mother and his physician father in an argument over the son's use of the family car. The jury took only seven minutes to return the guilty verdict and to impose the only punishment possible under Colorado law for this crime—life imprisonment. Newspaper reports stated that the boy "showed no emotion as the verdict was read" and that during the trial he stared "unblinkingly" into the jurors' eyes sometimes with a smile, sometimes with a sneer on his face. The boy and his family were members of an evangelical church in their community.

Darien, Connecticut, is a community much like Winnetka, Illinois. It too attracted national attention when two of its teen-agers were involved in a drinking-driving date that ended up in the death of a pretty and talented 17-year-old girl. The 18-year-old lad was charged with reckless driving and negligent homicide. The accident occurred at 4 A.M. on June 23, 1964. The testimony given by witnesses, including friends of both young people, spoke of debutante parties in private homes preceding the tragedy, of unlimited amounts of liquor served by adults, of date-switching during the evening, and of the young guests (some of whom were barely able to stand up) driving off to nearby beaches. Writing of the trial, presiding judge Rodney S. Eielson, in a courageous and provocative challenge of modern morality, says:

> After listening to witnesses for a day and a half, I realized the case was not routine at all. In fact, it dramatized nothing less than the crucial problem behind our difficulties with today's youth. . . . I have been on the bench for 4 of my 39 years and have long ceased being surprised at any kind of human behavior. Since 1947, I have been a resident of Fairfield County, the most affluent section of New York's "Exurbia," and I am not blind. I know that many of our teen-agers drink and think nothing of it; that the parents of these young people include some of our "nicest" people; and that many of these parents actually neglect their children. The trouble is that these parents would flatly deny this charge. They would refuse to believe it and reject it as preposterous! But as I listened to the testimony in this case, it became increasingly apparent to me that the facts—at least for the first time in my court—established the step-by-step link between this new form of neglect—amid plenty—and its disastrous consequences. Let me be clear: Parental neglect is a universal blight and is not confined to high-income families. But in this case . . . I knew there was nothing uncommon about these practices, and that was the very point of my rising indignation. It was mere luck that the failure of adults to assert their normal responsibility did not result in a senseless roadside killing—like that of Wanda Wyeth [fictitious name]—every weekend of the year. . . . During the next few days, headlines erupted in newspapers across the country: "Judge Puts County Morals on Trial";

"Judge Sees Parents' Guilt in Darien." The unexpected publicity grew to what I thought were astounding proportions. What, after all, was so remarkable about parents' being called to account for their all-too-obvious sins towards their own sons and daughters? . . . Close to one thousand letters and telegrams poured in to me from all parts of the country. And from the unexpected furor, certain facts emerged that commanded my attention not only as a judge but as a parent. First, the overwhelming majority of the editorials I saw and the letters I received supported the Connecticut law and its application in this case. Second, it became apparent that responsible parents did not view the problem as limited to drinking. They felt, as I did, that the moral education and discipline of teen-agers were at stake. How much discipline should be exercised over adolescents? Who has the responsibility for administering it? These are problems which we all face as parents and which I must frequently deal with in my judicial capacity.[3]

In *Chicago, Illinois,* two 16-year-old boys were sentenced for the 1966 holdup-murder of a 66-year-old Railway Express employee who had left his wife and home in the evening to go out and buy a newspaper. These two boys, together with a 17-year-old, blamed pep pills for their savage behavior the night of the killing. And in the widow's presence in open court they said they were "sorry" and hoped that she understood "this wasn't something we picked out to do just to her husband." Added one of the boys: "If I wasn't on the drugs, I might have reasoned out that it was wrong."

Ocean City, New Jersey, was the scene of mass insurrection and immorality in the spring of 1962 as vacationing college students invaded the community and took over one of its summer hotels. When police finally rounded them up, sworn testimony in court indicated that fellows and girls were parading naked on the hotel roof, that beer cans and other objects were hurled at adjoining buildings, and that sexual intercourse was being practiced openly on fire escapes before the astounded and shocked eyes of the inhabitants of a town that does not even permit the sale of liquor. Similar episodes were occurring in other nearby resort towns, on the Florida and Californit coasts, and as far inland as Ohio and Indiana— all bearing stark testimony to the fact that at the Easter season not all young people are gathering in church. Intoxicated 13- and 14-year-olds were found in some of the police lineups on the East Coast. Once again police report parental naïveté and unconcern.

Twenty years ago adults made up more than two-thirds of the national population. Within a few years youngsters and teen-agers will outnumber adults. At the end of 1964, the United States Census Bureau estimated that more than 40 million of the United States' 188 million population

---

[3]Roger S. Eielson, "The Sins of the Parents," *McCall's,* XCII:48-51 (January, 1965).

were under 10 years of age. These millions of children will be in the age of greatest vulnerability even before most of today's teen-agers reach adulthood. In 1965, teen-agers already numbered 12 percent of our population, or 25 million! They increased 30 percent during the past five years while the rest of the population increased only 8 percent. Where will these teen-agers be going?

The incidents mentioned have left in their wake all across America troubled adults seeking answers to troublesome questions:

Is there a distinct teen-age culture that we should know more about?

What are the role and the relevancy of the church with today's teen-agers?

It is appropriate to start with the first of these two questions in an attempt to examine the sociological context in which teen-age behavior occurs, and the implications of these sociological factors for the Christian church.

TEEN CULTURE: FACT OR MYTH?

In the current literature of both sociology and psychology, adolescence is most often described as that unique period in development between childhood and adulthood, distinct from both and characterized by "storm and stress" and by participation in a "youth culture" all its own. Parents and other adults closely associated with adolescents tend to develop serious concerns over both of these characteristics. Revolt is another aspect of behavior most frequently associated with adolescence. A number of factors are commonly identified with the "storm and stress" feature of adolescence, such as sexual frustrations arising out of normal physical maturation, and sanctions and restrictions imposed by society; emancipation-from-parents problems as the adolescent strives to cut apron strings; conflict between generations (i.e., the world of the teen-ager and the world of the adult); and problems of vocational choice.

A counterpart to the individual stress and strain is the significant part played by adolescent friends and associates of the teen-ager. Sociologists refer to this as the "peer group culture," and one of their number, Talcott Parsons, sees this youth culture as easing "the transition from the security of childhood in the family . . . to that of full adulthood in marriage and occupational status."[4] This youth culture includes innumerable general and specific identifying characteristics, such as its romantic concept of life, its bid for independence, its compulsive conformity to teen-group mores, its rejection of adult standards, its distinctive dress and slang, rambling telephone conversations, exclusive social groups (clubs, cliques and gangs),

---

[4]Talcott Parsons, "Age and Sex in the Social Structure of the United States," *American Sociological Review*, VII:604-16 (October, 1942) .

its strong sense of loyalty to each other, its emphasis on fun and popularity, paraphernalia of sports and recreation, the automobile and the hangout.

Sociologists seem to agree that contemporary teen-age culture is essentially a product of affluence and that it is the culture of a leisure class. Jessie Bernard at Penn State University notes that the teen-age culture of younger adolescents is characteristically lower class, that of older teen-agers, upper middle class.[5] As "WASP's" (White Anglo-Saxon Protestants), many of us are more familiar with the older teen-age culture which is essentially a prototype of our own than with the teen-age culture which is identified with the lower class, particularly with the distortions it takes on as it filters through such barriers as poverty and racial discrimination. Examples of this type of teen-age culture will be cited shortly—having been a part of the recent experiences of the writer, on whom these experiences left indelible impressions.

But first let us examine in further detail the teen-age culture of middle and upper middle class society. It possesses both material and nonmaterial traits as sugggested in the foregoing listing of some general and specific characteristics.

Material Teen-age Culture Traits

Today's teen-ager is a relentless consumer of cosmetics, clothes, automobiles, phonograph records, radios and magazines. Industry has long ago discovered the profitable teen-age consumer market and is now gearing much of its advertising and merchandising to this market. In menswear, teen-age clothing accounts for 40 percent of all clothing purchased; and one-third of all sweater sales is to teens. For the past ten years teen-age girls have been setting women's fashions. In 1960 young women under 20 were spending for all items 4½ billion dollars annually—20 million of which allegedly went for lipstick, 25 million for deodorants and 9 million for home permanents. Many car dealers now take it for granted that when a fellow turns 16 he will be in the market for a used car. In 1963 there were 8,200,000 licensed teen-age car drivers who constituted 8.6 percent of the 95,600,000 drivers in the United States. For fellows, particularly, a car becomes an important factor as both a motivating and a socializing force. Much of his time and interest (and money) is given over to his car, which becomes for him and for his friends literally a "clubhouse on wheels." One writer refers to teen-agers as the "Moola Minority" and estimates the present teen-age market at 14 billion annually and expected to reach 20 billion by 1970.

---

[5]Jesse Bernard, "Teen-age Culture: An Overview," *The Annals,* 338:2ff. (November, 1961).

Nonmaterial Teen-age Culture Traits

These include a special language which changes almost as rapidly as it emerges and which has some cultural and geographical variations. Parents and educators have a tough time tuning in, but tune in they must, or run the risk of being permanently written off as "square" and stodgy—members of that doomed and deprived "other world" of adults. At any given time during the past five years you might have been hearing terms like these: cool cat (interesting person), blast (gala party), daisies (shoes), pudding (money), stone ace (best friend), loose goose (eccentric person), the tube (TV).

Contemporary teen-age values also represent nonmaterial culture traits and seem to be the same at all levels of social class. Three stand out—beauty, fun and popularity. These are especially reflected in teen-age magazines and in popular songs. The latter have been subjected to content analysis by many researchers. One sociologist, Donald Horton, has cataloged them into a "drama of courtship" consisting of a prologue and four acts![6] According to Horton's scheme, the Prologue emphasizes wishing and dreaming. Act I deals with courtship; about one-third of all popular songs belong in this category. Scenes in this act deal with the direct approach, sentimental appeal, desperation, questions and promises, impatience, and surrender. Eight percent of all songs are on the honeymoon and constitute Act II. Act III speaks of the downward trend of love and depicts scenes such as temporary parting, threat of leaving, rivalry. This constitutes 14.5 percent of lyrics. And Act IV, "All Alone," accounts for 25 percent!

Another value that research demonstrates conclusively to be far more important than intellectual achievement to teen-agers is athletic prowess. This is based on such criteria as popularity, visibility, composition of leading crowd.

Other significant nonmaterial teen-age culture traits are political apathy, fun-rather-than-work orientation, class distinctions (the "outs," or "clods," still constitute a sizable proportion of the high school population), and double-standard sex codes. All of these have implications for youth leaders, for educators, and for youth-serving agencies and institutions including—especially—the church.

In the matter of work, for example, teen-agers participate in the economy more as consumers than as laborers. In fact, among out-of-school youth, joblessness continues to constitute a major problem today. Close to a million out-of-school youngsters under 20 have literally nothing to do. The rate of teen-age unemployment has gone up 50 percent in the

---

[6]Donald Horton, "The Dialogue of Courtship in Popular Songs," *American Journal of Sociology*, LXII:575 (May, 1957).

past seven years, over 20 percent in the past year. One out of every five of today's unemployed is in the 16- to 19-year-old age group. Former Secretary of Labor W. Willard Wirtz estimates that there are between 5 and 10 million boys and girls in the United States who are today facing futures they are not prepared for and won't be unless something is done about it. Wirtz believes that this "could develop into one of the most explosive social problems in the nation's history." But jobs alone are not the entire answer, concludes Samuel Grafton in *Look* magazine:

> Evidence suggests that many of the youngsters who spend their evenings decorating street corners don't want jobs badly enough to do very much to get them . . . other difficulties are involved, including profound problems of motivation . . . . The American middle class has apparently decided that the only conceivable happy life for its children lies in intellectual activity, preceded by years of academic distinction. . . . Our youngsters have caught this national attitude and often share the feeling that there is something shameful about any work with one's hands (except, maybe, brain surgery). Middle-income-group boys who would like to do manual work are made to feel as declassed as India's untouchables. . . . We have succeeded in creating a class of half-grown rejects of society.[7]

Hollows and Harlem: Two Teen Cultures

Not all teen-age culture is a product of affluence. Disturbing distortions do occur as teen-age culture develops out of the blights of poverty and ignorance and discrimination. Within the past five years massive governmental programs have been set up to deal with these problems of youth and to break through barriers to raise levels of opportunity for the all-too-many disadvantaged children and young people in the United States. One such program has been the President's Committee on Juvenile Delinquency and Youth Crime, created by executive order of the late President Kennedy in 1961. In his message to Congress, President Kennedy expressed his growing concern over steadily increasing rates of juvenile delinquency, and with the related problems of youth unemployment and school dropouts. As a result, during the years that have followed, new and creative programs to deal with these problems have been set up in seventeen communities across America. Most were in large cities (New York, Chicago, Los Angeles, Boston) addressed to the complexities of crowded urban living—the asphalt and blackboard jungles.

But problems like delinquency and poverty are not contained within the boundaries of cities, and two programs were developed in predominantly rural areas. As mentioned earlier in this chapter, the author was identified

----

[7]Samuel Grafton, "The Tense Generation," *Look,* August 27, 1963.

with one of these programs located in that part of the country known as Appalachia. In this remote portion of the United States the writer discovered a whole subculture of teen-agers and adults living in sharp contrast to both the affluence of suburbia and the street corner society of hostile street gangs. Michael Harrington refers to this subculture in his provocative book, *The Other America.* Harrington describes America's invisible poor and in speaking of Appalachia says, "The ordinary tourist never leaves the main highway. . . . He does not go into the valleys where the towns look like movie sets of Wales in the thirties. He does not see the company houses in rows, the rutted roads, and everything black and dirty. . . ."[8]

Those enjoying the loveliness of areas like Appalachia may easily miss the fact that many of the inhabitants of these hills and hollows are under-educated, underfed, underprivileged, lack medical care, and are in the process of being forced from the land into a life in the cities where they are gross misfits.

In Kanawha County, West Virginia, where the writer spent two years helping develop a delinquency prevention program called "Action for Appalachia Youth," he encountered teen-agers living in a rural hillbilly culture that is as unique and removed from the average American's experience as that of an underdeveloped country in the remotest section of the world.

Kanawha County is West Virginia's largest and most prosperous county. Yet within its boundaries exist many of the deplorable conditions found in the rest of the Southern Appalachian region. The county is characterized by sharp contrasts. Among its assets are the facts that it contains the capital city of the state, lovely forested landscapes, a concentration of the world's largest chemical industries, a current industrial worker's average annual income that places Charleston first in the East and fourth in the nation, and a slight gain in population. (The rest of the state showed a 7.2 percent population loss.) A consideration, however, of the prevalence of illiteracy, chronic unemployment among youth and adults, extreme poverty, technological displacement, systematic exploitation of human resources, and wide disparities in basic community services that are at best minimal, leaves little about which to be comfortable or complacent. The population of Kanawha County is 253,000. Eighty-four thousand people (one-third of the population) dwell in isolated mountain hollows scattered over the 914 square miles. These hollows, even though geographically contiguous, are not accessible to one another except by driving out of one hollow on muddy, nonstabilized roads to a main road that leads several miles to the mouth of the next hollow. Many of these

---

[8]Michael Harrington, *The Other America: Poverty in the United States* (New York: Macmillan Co., 1962) , p. 3.

roads leading into mountain hollows are virtually impassable from November through April. Thus the problem of accessibility is complicated in terms of distance and impossible road conditions.

There were 51,221 children and youth ranging in age between 9 and 19 living in Kanawha County in 1960. Over 40 percent of the youth aged 16 to 21 are unemployed. Most of them are school dropouts who, by virtue of limited skills, poverty and inability to communicate effectively, are unable to find gainful employment. The tragic plight of thousands of West Virginia children was dramatized by an editorial which appeared in the *Charleston Daily Mail,* October 21, 1963, carrying the title "Wrong Time, Wrong Place, Wrong Parents; The West Virginia Problem Personalized." The editor was reporting on a recent Department of Public Welfare study which disclosed the following staggering facts:

1. Of the parents in the entire case load (52,000 cases), *only one percent had a high school education* (and this despite the fact that West Virginia has had free public schools and a compulsory school law for many years).
2. *Forty percent* of these parents had *less than a fifth-grade education* and
3. Forty percent of these parents now on the relief rolls account for 94,000 children. . . .

These bleak statistics explain how difficult it is going to be to generate the kind of progress all the rest of West Virginia is talking about and dreaming of. At a bare minimum it has *nearly* 100,000 *boys and girls growing up in an environment so darkened by ignorance and eroded by poverty that the prospect of their maturing into useful, productive, independent parents, citizens and tax-payers is dreadful almost beyond contemplation. . . .* You can dispatch the truant officer. You can cite the compulsory attendance law. But until someone has *figured out a way to interrupt the cycle in which poor, ignorant and demoralized parents produce poor, ignorant and demoralized children,* "you are going to have very little success." . . . It is hard to conceive of any expansion of the economy or any change of the "image" in which there would be a place for *thousands of West Virginians who know nothing, expect little, and inherit from their parents only the worst habits of indolence, indifference and dependency. . . .* The problem is all of these rolled into one and capsulized in the presence of at least *100,000 boys and girls who were born in the wrong time, in the wrong place to the wrong parents.*

From Hollow to Harlem

Hell Gate Station is a one-mile-square area in New York City running from 86th to 110th Street and bordered on the west by Central Park and on the east by the East River. Within this one square mile live 194,000 people—mostly Puerto Ricans, Italians and Negroes. There are 46,816 teen-agers—tough, hostile, dangerous, disturbed, lonely, desperate teen-agers. Theirs is an asphalt jungle of rotting houses and dark stench-filled hallways and alleys. Theirs is the world of drug addicts, drink cadgers (spongers), pimps and prostitutes. And in this world is Youth Development, Incorporated, or YDI as it is called, headed up by big, tough, warmhearted Jim Vaus, who invaded this twenty-third police precinct nearly ten years ago in the interests of reaching out to these teen-agers with the Person of Jesus Christ. Here, too, is a teen-age culture sharply contrasting with the affluent upper middle class society of suburbia. By invitation of YDI, the author and twelve college students moved into this Harlem culture for one summer.

One of the students describes this culture:

> My footsteps crush glass against the concrete ground. Water pushes past me in the gutter. A young boy sits laughing under the open fire hydrant as men and women sit on the stoop . . . talking, watching. Small gray men roll their wagons down the street advertising cherry ices. A rubber basketball bounces heavily on the playground's concrete court. People slouch forward under the burning sun of the long, hot summer . . . summer of crowded park benches and sleeping drunks shifting uncomfortably in the gutters, and kids . . . little kids running and jumping and playing. Never slowing down; never stopping. Babies crying, radios screaming, feet tapping; streets pulsating with the tremor of the beat . . . the steady, wild beat of the big city. And my popsicle drips, making sizzling pink pools of water on the sidewalk as I walk these streets, these stormy streets of Spanish Harlem.
>
> I am a YDI summer staff member. I am in East Harlem for these moments . . . those times when a kid has to stop running and face life and death squarely. I am one, yet I am all. I speak alone, yet speak for all. I look at Harlem through a wrinkled dark glass. The concrete jungle appears blurred and shadowed. And sometimes I wonder why I am here, why I have come . . . and my calculated reasons are distorted, and flutter nebulously before me out of reach. I only know that I belong in East Harlem, that my God has brought me here. And I believe that man's empty, searching soul will never be fully satisfied by anyone but man's own Maker. And because I love my God, I will love all men. . . . And I must tell His people that no matter what they do, or what happens to them, God never ceases to love them. I must remind them of this . . . because so many of them have forgotten. . . . The people of Spanish Harlem call it the jungle. The law of this jungle is the survival of the fittest. The continual noise and activity on the streets often camouflages the misery and hopelessness so deeply entrenched in the lives of the population. Yet, occasionally this attitude of despair unveils itself and crudely exhibits its pitiful form.
>
> Hell's Gate . . . the jungle . . . survival of the fittest . . . desperation. To survive, a man will steal, lie, beg, or fight. If a kid has a

rep to uphold, if a kid has heart . . . he'll fight. And it's not difficult; it's no new thing. He's been fighting since he was born. It's the only way of life he knows.

And so life in the wilds of the jungle goes on at its usual rapid pace, with people hurrying anxiously from here to there, from there to nowhere, and back. Existence is swallowed one day at a time; the concept of any type of really happy future is nebulous. And God? God, in the minds of these men, is too often shoved behind dusty bookshelves and buried beneath moth-eaten scatter rugs and forgotten. Precious are the times when a kid stops running, pausing long enough to search out this God . . . this supposedly loving Being, this good and righteous Power . . . and gives God a chance to show him what He's all about.[9]

East Harlem youth also have a distinctive vocabulary which has developed out of their culture and is as different from Appalachia as the Hollow dialect is from suburban jargon. Some examples are: blade (knife), bop (fight), burn (shoot), busted (arrested), grits (food), hustler (narcotics-seller), vines (sharp clothes).

The Fact or Fallacy of Teen Culture

The preceding accounts would seem to establish clearly the fact of a rather distinct adolescent culture with a set of unique characteristics bearing close resemblance to the larger culture of which it is a part. While sociologists might tend to disagree with the concept of a separate youth culture that is strong and pervasive,[10] all would converge around the concept of some rather distinctive teen-age characteristics. It is with this aspect that the church and other youth-serving institutions need to be thoroughly knowledgeable and intimately related.

Sociologists seem to agree also that teen-age culture is an adaptation or prototype of adult culture, and that contrary to the impression of a new breed of rebellious insurrectionists poised to attack the adult society which gave them birth, America's millions of teen-agers are the bearers of a rather traditional and conservative culture and are consciously or unconsciously complementing us adults by borrowing our values and adapting them to their own needs.

Trends are appearing that suggest that teen-age culture may end with high school graduation. Not only are children entering the teen culture at an earlier age, but current happenings indicate that at the college level, young people are more adult.

---

[9]Beaver Ozols, "Through a Glass Darkly" (unpublished paper). (New York: Youth Development, Inc., 1964), pp. 1-2.

[10]See, for example, "The Myth of Adolescent Culture," by two McGill University sociologists, Frederick Elkin and William A. Westley, in *American Sociological Review,* XX:680-84 (December, 1955).

This chapter might be seen then as a descriptive profile of adult culture as reflected in the teen-age culture which it sponsors.

CONFRONTATION BETWEEN THE CHURCH AND THE TENSE GENERATION

What do today's nearly 25 million teen-agers think of the church—in its corporate, institutional, or personal role? How meaningful and relevant is it to them? Perhaps an even more important question is "How does the church regard the teen-ager?" It cannot ignore them. In 1966 every second person in America was 25 or under. *In less than ten years one half of our population will be teen-agers!*

A number of teen-age surveys have devoted a major section to youth views of the church and/or religion. One of the earliest was the Remmers and Radler *Purdue Opinion Poll* which sampled the attitudes of American teen-agers on a number of important issues over a fifteen-year period beginning in the early 1940's. From a special poll conducted in the early 1950's on American teen-agers' "religious values and feelings." Remmers and Radler concluded:

> The typical American teen-ager today retains a favorable attitude toward the church, attends services about once a week and says prayers once or twice a day. His religious beliefs usually agree with those of his parents. If there is disagreement between the parents, the adolescent is more likely to agree with his mother's religious values than with those of his father. This makes him more of a churchgoer, since the typical mother of a teen-age child attends at least twice a month, while the father does not usually go to church that often.
>
> The average teen-ager thinks of God not as a person but as an omnipotent and omniscient bodiless spirit who exists everywhere. On the average, the teen-ager believes faith serves better than logic in solving life's important problems. He feels that his prayers are sometimes answered. He believes in the hereafter and expects his place there to be determined by his conduct here on earth. He believes that God guided or inspired the writing of the Bible, and that a good human society could not be built without such supernatural help.[11]

The Purdue study also asked boys and girls in grades 9 through 12 to identify the religious problems that troubled them most. It is interesting to note that these high schoolers reported the following (in varying degrees of frequency for each level): confusion in religious beliefs, anxiety over heaven and hell, conflict between the Bible and school subjects, inability to live up to their religion; searching for something to believe in, and confusion over standards of "right" and "wrong."

[11]H. H. Remmers and D. H. Radler, *The American Teen-Ager* (New York: Bobbs-Merrill Co., Inc. and Charter Books, 1957 and 1962), pp. 155-57.

In the area of standards, an earlier YMCA survey of 32,000 Chicago teen-agers showed 42 percent of these youth doubting that religion could be relied on to give them any standard of right or wrong! (In this same survey 43 percent of the boys polled saw nothing wrong with high school students having sex relations; and 33 percent expressed approval of sex relations before marriage.)

One of the most recent and exhaustive studies of today's youth was done for *The Saturday Evening Post,* using the Gallup Poll's scientific facilities.[12] More than 3,000 boys and girls between the ages of 14 and 22 were queried about war, religion, jobs, sex, parents, education and themselves. Of youth views about religion, Gallup and Hill reported: "Seventy percent of our youth believe in God 'very firmly'; 76 percent think of God as an omni-present judge who observes all individual human actions and rewards or punishes them; 78 percent believe in a hereafter; almost two-thirds of the high school and working youth believe the Bible is 'completely true'; . . . and nearly two-thirds of our collegians are 'very firm' believers."

The author recently had occasion to hear the director of a large, well-established evangelical high school academy speak to a group of adults. He began by saying that he had spent the past several years living in a community made up entirely of teen-agers and that on the basis of this he felt very optimistic about the future of this country. He added, however, that one of the characteristics of this teen-age community that stands out is its "revolt against the institutional church" which they feel is "stuffy and irrelevant."

Rev. Carroll Tageson has provided us with an excellent summary of the existing empirical data on the moral and religious development and experiences of adolescents. He presents twelve propositions which comprise one of the best summaries of the growing body of research data about the moral and religious development of the adolescent:[13]

1. The Church is still an important and influential institution in the lives of American youth.
2. There is a trend, however, towards a general decrease in church attendance as adolescence progresses. This is less true for girls than boys, and less true for Catholics, than either Protestants or Jews. Where this phenomenon does occur, however, it seems due less to a disinterest in religion than to the fact that the needs of the adolescent are not being met by existing church programs.
3. Adolescence is not a period of religious or moral upheaval. "Storm and stress" does not seem characteristic of this phase of adolescent

[12]George Gallup and Evan Hill, "Youth: The Cool Generation," *Post,* CCXXXIV:41-42, 44; 63-69 (December 23 and 30, 1961).

[13]Carroll F. Tageson, "Spiritual Direction of the Adolescent" (from a paper presented at the Fourth Workshop of Psychological Counseling of Adolescents at the Catholic University of America, Washington, D.C., June 16-27, 1961; Raymond J. Steimel, editor).

experience. The moral and religious training previously acquired is generally retained, though the *basis* for doing so shifts from loyalty to parents and the prestige enjoyed by authority to peer group influence and more mature rational considerations. Not even college attendance, contrary perhaps to popular opinion, seems to affect religious belief very drastically.

4. Adolescents are no longer satisfied with arbitrary appeals to authority on questions of moral or religious doctrine and practice. They are increasingly interested in the meaning of religion for their lives as adolescence progresses, and they tend to be more tolerant, and less liberal in their interpretation of religious doctrine.

5. Religious affiliation seems to be the most important single variable in the religious development of an adolescent. Eighty-one percent of all adolescents choose the denomination of their parents; and where there is conflict among the parents, a majority of adolescents follow the religious affiliation of the mother.

6. The intellectual maturation characteristic of the adolescent period parallels and seems to determine the maturation of religious concepts.

7. A definite gap exists between knowledge of moral and religious precepts and their practice.

8. Such ideals are formed by reference to concrete models, especially in early adolescence. Parents recede; more remote figures increase in importance in this respect.

9. An exaggerated moral perfectionism is characteristic of many adolescents; *i.e.,* they tend to view moral and religious principles in black and white terms.

10. The peer group is the most important and influential training institution during the adolescent period. Its effects during this period of growth far outweigh those of the home, church, or school. Its standards and values are the ones adopted by the individual adolescent. Usually these are more or less in conformity with adult standards, but the important point here is that conformity to peer group pressures is what determines their adoption.

11. Getting help in the solution of their religious problems is a major continuing problem mentioned by adolescents of all ages.

12. There is no developmental trend away from religion or morality during adolescence.

The Evangelical Church's Outreach to Teens

Certain implications of the sociology of teen behavior must be faced by all of us who have an interest in youth, our own and others, and in the church's outreach to them. The following conclusions and suggestions are intended to be for the help and use of parents, Christian youth leaders, and our Protestant evangelical churches through whose enriching and deeply meaningful heritage many of us emerged from childhood through adolescence to adulthood.

1. *Have a message.* In the instance of teen-agers this message needs to be relevant, attractive, clear and challenging so as to bear evidence of the fact that there is an understanding of the needs and problems with which youth are confronted in today's world. We must make every effort to view the world through the eyes of the adolescent and avoid the deadly clinchés, pious platitudes and careless incoherency which has too often characterized our message.

2. *Know the facts* about contemporary youth culture and be able to relate these meaningfully to your own young people *and* to the youth of your community.

3. *Cultivate a keen sensitivity* to the needs and problems of young people. This means a conscious and continual tuning-in to both their verbal and nonverbal cries for help.

4. *Develop the capacity for communication* with teen-agers. This is no small task but it is vital. This cannot be done obviously or we end up being regarded as even more "square." Communication with teen-agers involves listening mostly (and, we might add *hearing*), talking little (and then never at or to), and sharing.

One minister interviewed by *Look* magazine reporters for their report on the tense generation put it this way: "They feel their isolation. They know they need help. But they can't talk to anybody."

Harvard pediatrician J. Roswell Gallagher and psychiatrist Herbert Harris, in writing of ways to help adolescents, speak of the *art* of listening:

> Listening to an adolescent, though an active rather than a passive process, often calls for silence. When an adolescent really lets his words flow and his feelings go, this is the time to remain silent. Any comment or suggestion should be held in reserve. . . . Later, when the adolescent's stream of thought and feeling begins to dry up, is the time for the listener to prevent the growth of an undesirable degree of emotional tension which a long period of silence might cause. . . . At times it will be worthwhile to change the subject entirely in order to give him a rest from the emotional strain. . . . Everything said . . .should be designed to increase the adolescent's approval and acceptance of the listener, and to establish a warm and friendly relationship.[14]

5. *Identify with youth.* Much has been said about this in all kinds of contexts. Applied to teen-agers it simply involves being yourself, *an adult,* and evidencing a natural empathy. This does *not* include as a technique recalling your boyhood or girlhood days about which teen-agers could care less should they even have a slight interest in going back to those

---

[14]J. Roswell Gallagher and Herbert I. Harris, *Emotional Problems of Adolescents* (rev. ed.; New York: Oxford University Press, 1964) , p. 176.

"dark ages." In fact, consciously applied techniques of identification per se will probably fail.

6. *Involve youth.* This is an amazing oversight and gross deficit in most of our programming for teen-agers in early or late adolescence. We deserve, therefore, to be surprised to discover how well our young people do— given even a little responsibility and the opportunity for being their creative best! As adults we have become enamored of, and addicted to, adult hand-me-downs in the form of everything from Sunday school lessons to recreation programs for teen-agers, on the theory (often erroneous) that "we know what's best."

7. *Be honest with teen-agers.* This sounds like there are times when we might be dishonest. Not knowingly, perhaps. But any degree of phoniness or pretense is dishonesty and will sell you out to teens faster than almost anything. The author learned this very quickly in East Harlem but it's equally true on a college campus. This kind of honesty also implies consistency. Most adolescents are testing adults constantly in a variety of ways. What we end up doing had better add up to what they have been hearing us say or again, "we've had it." Fairy tales are poor substitutes for fact whether the subject is jobs or sex.

8. *Offer support to teen-agers—spiritually and psychologically.* This means more praise and less blame. Psychologically this means helping the adolescent develop a stable, positive self-concept—*i.e.,* good, specific reasons for thinking well of himself. Many teen-age suicides could thus be averted. Spiritual support means consistency in our own lives plus the practical, realistic application of biblical teachings to teen-age living. This calls for an intimate knowledge of our particular teen-ager's personality, an understanding of what wholesale condemnation can do to the teen as a person and, finally, a respect for the chosen friends of our teen-agers.

9. *Trust teen-agers.* Here again we will be surprised, even with troubled or delinquent youth, how they will respond to even a little trust which the adult may invest. The trust must be given without reservation or reluctance but with the expectancy that it will be honored.

10. *Love teen-agers.* All of us as parents know that there will be moments, many or few, when this seems all but impossible—the smashed family car; the third call from the traffic officer; the violent, unreasonable outburst; the relentless and intolerably tantalizing testing!

More and more of our young people are reporting and evidencing the lovelessness within their homes. The capacity for giving and for receiving affection which is so important a part of becoming a marriageable person is learned and received in the home. It flows directly out of the security of two parents who love each other deeply and securely into the lives of their children who, incidentally, must come a natural second to the one parent in the affections of the other.

Within the church it means showing the reality of the love of Jesus Christ to our teen-agers, recalcitrant, rebel, and halo-bearer alike.

Psychiatrist Leo Kanner, in his study of autistic (love-starved) children, stressed the importance of acceptance, affection and approval, all of which are uniquely involved in this concept of love as applied to teen-agers. These three extensions of the love principle are especially applicable to the troubled youth to whom the church all too infrequently reaches out—the delinquent, the emotionally disturbed child, the mentally ill youth, the teen-age unwed mother. These same three "*A*'s" cited by psychiatrists Edward Litin and George Constant are three factors that keep teen-agers from becoming delinquents.[15]

SUMMARY

Society's troubled teens are increasingly requiring the services of the organized church.[16] With these children and youth, assistance in early detection and early referral to appropriate treatment resources is an important role which the church shares with parents and other concerned groups. Too often the church and its personnel attempt to play amateur psychiatrists only to endanger the child's welfare and entangle itself in relationships it is ill equipped to handle.

The church occupies a most strategic place in the lives of young people, and what it has to offer them is singularly unique. The good news of the gospel is that *God gave* in order that a shook-up, tense, "cool," spoiled, angry, lost generation of teen-agers *and* adults might find *the* Way in the person and power and presence of His Son Jesus. Only He can bring us out of the shadows and darkness of sin into the health-giving sunshine and clean fresh air of His forgiveness and presence. And if this were not enough He has also provided us with a Book, the Bible, which, unlike any other book, satisfies the deep hunger and longing and loneliness of our lives. For in what other book could we find these words:

> My son, if you will receive my words and treasure up my command-
> ments with you . . . then you will understand . . . and find the
> knowledge of God. . . . Then you will understand righteousness,
> justice and fair dealing in every area and relation; yes, you will under-
> stand every good path. . . . Lean on, trust, and be confident in the

---

15"Three '*A*'s' for Youth," *Science News Letter,* LXXIX:294 (May 13, 1961).

16Nine specific reommendations made on how religious bodies can assume a larger role in assisting American youth have been offered by various individual and organizational spokesmen to the U.S. Senate Subcommittee to Investigate Juvenile Delinquency. The recommendations are listed in "Widen Youth Ministry to Reduce Delinquency," an editorial in *Christianity Today,* VI:27 (October 26, 1962).

Lord with all your heart and mind, and do not rely on your own insight or understanding. In all your ways know, recognize, and acknowledge Him, and He will direct and make straight and plain your paths (Prov. 2:1, 5-6; 3:5-6, Amplified Bible).

FOR FURTHER READING

BECK, DAVENS, FREEDMAN, HUNT, MARLAND, OETTINGER, et. al. "Children and Youth at the Mid-Decade" (a symposium), Children. Washington, D.C.: Children's Bureau, Department of Health, Education and Welfare, March-April, 1965.

BERNARD, JESSIE, et. al. "Teen-Age Culture," The Annals of the American Academy of Political and Social Science, November, 1961.

BETTELHEIM, BRUNO. "The Problem of Generations," Daedalus, Winter, 1962.

BRODERICK, CARLFRED B. "New Data on Dating," The PTA Magazine, December, 1961.

CHRISTENSEN, HAROLD T. "Adolescence: Mystery, Madness or Milestone?" The PTA Magazine, September, 1961.

COLEMAN, J. S. Social Climates in High Schools. Cooperative Research Monograph No. 4. Washington, D.C.: U.S. Department of Health, Education and Welfare, 1961.

CROW, LESTER D. and ALICE. Adolescent Development and Adjustment. New York: McGraw-Hill Book Co., 1956.

DENNEY, REUEL. "American Youth Today: A Bigger Cast, a Wider Screen." Daedalus, Winter, 1962.

ELKIN, FREDERICK, and WESTLEY, WILLIAM A. "The Myth of Adolescent Culture," American Sociological Review, Vol. 20, December, 1955.

FAEGRE, MARION L. The Adolescent in Your Family. Washington, D.C.: Children's Bureau, U.S. Department of Health, Education and Welfare, 1954.

FRELLICK, FRANCIS I. Helping Youth in Conflict. Englewood Cliffs, N.J.: Prentice-Hall, Inc., 1965.

FRIEDENBERG, EDGAR Z. The Vanishing Adolescent. New York: Dell Publishing Co., Inc., 1959.

FULBRIGHT, FREEMAN. The Young in Crime. Chicago: National Research Bureau, 1960.

GALLAGHER, J. ROSWELL, and HARRIS, HERBERT I. Emotional Problems of Adolescents. New York: Oxford University Press, rev. ed., 1964.

GALLUP, GEORGE, and HILL, EVAN. "Youth: The Cool Generation," The Saturday Evening Post, December 23 and 30, 1961.

GILBERT, EUGENE. "Why Today's Teen-agers Seem So Different," Harper's Magazine, November, 1959.

GLUECK, SHELDON and ELEANOR T. "Why Young People 'Go Bad,'" U.S. News and World Report, LIX: 56-62 (April 26, 1965).

GOTTLIEB, DAVID, and REEVES, JOHN. Adolescent Behavior in Urban Areas, New York: Free Press of Glencoe and Macmillan Co., 1963.

GRAFTON, SAMUEL. "The Tense Generation," Look, August 27, 1963.

———. "When Youth Runs Wild," McCall's, April, 1962.

GRAN, JOHN M. How to Understand and Teach Teen-agers, Minneapolis: T. S. Denison & Co., 1958.

HAMRIN, SHIRLEY A. *Counseling Adolescents.* Chicago: Science Research Associates, 1950.

HECHINGER, GRACE and FRED M. *Teen-age Tyranny.* New York: Wm. Morrow & Co., Inc., 1963.

JOSSELYN, IRENE M. *The Adolescent and His World.* New York: Family Service Association of America, 1960.

KIK, J. MARCELLUS. "Combating Delinquency," *Christianity Today,* III: 13-16 (July 6, 1959).

LANDERS, ANN. *Ann Landers Talks to Teen-agers on Sex.* Greenwich, Conn.: Faucett World Library, 1965.

———. "Why Teen-agers Get Out of Control." *Readers Digest,* June, 1961.

LANDIS, PAUL H. *Coming of Age: Problems of Teen-agers.* New York: Public Affairs Pamphlet No. 234, 1956.

LEE, ROBERT. "7 Myths About Juvenile Delinquency," *Presbyterian Life,* November 15, 1961.

LEONARD, GEORGE B. "The Explosive Generation," *Look,* January 3, 1961.

LITTLE, VIVIAN. "Adolescents Are Human Beings Too," *The Clearing House,* November, 1961.

MALLERY, DAVID. *High School Students Speak Out.* New York: Harper & Row, 1962.

"Man of the Year," *Time,* LXXXIX:18-23 (January 6, 1967).

MEAD, MARGARET. "A New Look at Early Marriages," *U.S. News and World Report,* June 6, 1960.

MILLER, HASKELL M. *Understanding and Preventing Juvenile Delinquency.* New York: Abingdon Press, 1958.

MYRA, HAROLD. "Teen-age Suicides," *Youth For Christ Magazine,* XXII: 9-10 (August, 1965).

NOVAK MICHAEL. "God in the Colleges," *Harper's Magazine,* October, 1961.

PARSONS, TALCOTT, "Youth in the Context of American Society," *Daedalus,* Winter, 1962.

REMMERS, H. H., and RADLER, D. H. *The American Teen-ager,* New York: Bobbs-Merrill Co., Inc., 1957.

ROBERT, GUY L. *How the Church Can Help Where Delinquency Begins.* Richmond, Va.: John Knox Press, 1958.

ROSS, MURRAY G. *Religious Beliefs of Youths.* New York: Association Press, 1950.

SANDERS, AL. "Pornography and Our Youth," *The King's Business,* LIII: 18-19 (May, 1961).

SCHULLER, DAVID. *The Church's Ministry to Youth in Trouble.* St. Louis: Concordia, 1959.

SHEARER, LLOYD. "Our Teen-agers: What Is Society Doing to Them?" *Parade,* March 14, 1965.

SILVA, MICHEL. "Boys and Girls Too Old Too Soon," *Life,* August 10, 1962.

SPOCK, BENJAMIN. "Disturbing Influences in Adolescence," *Ladies' Home Journal,* February, 1962.

STEIMEL, RAYMOND J. *Psychological Counseling of Adolescents.* Washington, D.C.: The Catholic University of America Press, 1962.

STRATON, HILLYER H. "The Church Faces the Problem of Pornography," *Christianity Today,* IX:3-5 (September 24, 1965).

STROMMEN, MERTON P. *Profiles of Church Youth*. St. Louis: Concordia Publishing House, 1963.

Teen-age Drinking. Report to Wisconsin Legislature. Wisconsin: State Department of Public Welfare, Division for Children and Youth, May 15, 1961.

TURNER, RALPH H. *The Social Context of Ambition*. San Francisco: Chandler Publishing Co., 1964.

Understanding Your Teen-ager. New York: Metropolitan Life Insurance Co., 1953. WILKERSON, DAVID, and SHERRILL, JOHN and ELIZABETH. *The Cross and the Switchblade*. New York: B. Geis Associates, 1963.

WITTENBERG, RUDOLPH M. *Adolescence and Discipline* New York: Association Press, 1959.

As all but the most cement-bound of city dwellers know, there is a time each year when life pulsates through all of nature with a surge of sudden growth. The world is covered with a fresh new green, and colorful with early blossoms. There are calm, clear, beautiful, sunny days, and there are the quick drenching rains, gusty winds, late snows, floods, and everywhere growth—along with change and promise.

If April showers bring May flowers, early adolescence is the April of life. Years differ. Spring may come late one year and early another; or it may be mild one year and stormy another. Likewise individual teenagers differ. The constant factor is growth—along with change and promise.

MARGARET JACOBSEN

6

the nature and needs of junior highs

A SUBCULTURE

PERSONS BETWEEN THE AGES of 12 and 14 we call young adolescents, early youth, junior highs, early teens or young teens. The American teen-age group has become a subculture, not just a population segment in transition between childhood and maturity. It is not necessarily an antiadult culture, but it is most certainly nonadult, with ways of behavior all its own.

Someone has suggested that fast-passing fads for early teen costumes such as "granny gowns" are motivated by the desire to find something to wear that mothers won't copy. Reaction against the symbols of childhood leads to the bizarre symbols of early adolescence—the brightest colors and wildest fads in clothes, the heaviest beat in music, the strongest hero worship, the greatest conformity to group pressure. A section of America's economic and entertainment world has exploited and reinforced this age group's natural tendency toward excess in their search for independence

MARGARET JACOBSEN, M.A., is author of *The Child in the Christian Home,* and is former Chairman of the Department of Christian Education, Biola College, La Mirada, California.

and security. The Christian community—home, church and Christian school—is debtor to teen-agers as well as to the children and adults, and must be ready to give them the gospel which is God's power to salvation (Rom. 1:15-16).

Physical Awareness

Many physical changes take place during adolescence. Puberty, the time when secretion of active reproductive cells begins, usually occurs in the early adolescent years. Individual differences are very pronounced. Harbour has commented on the significance of puberty:

> The most phenomenal change during adolescence occurs in the emergence of reproductive power. This is the center of a broad group of other changes, and its significance can hardly be overestimated. Biologically, the young person changes from a derivative to a determinative relationship to the continuation of the human species. Sociologically, the young person is endowed with power to become a cocreator of a basic unit of society, the family. Psychologically, the gift of freedom for individual decision carries heavy burdens of responsibility to other human beings. Philosophically, self-realization expands to concern for social self-satisfaction. In a Christian perspective these movements are very important because they include the relations of a person to society, to nature, to God.[1]

There is a prepubescent period of six months to a year and a continuing postpubescent development of sex glands that extends another year. One out of every ten girls reaches puberty by age 12, eight out of ten, by age 14. In boys puberty occurs on an average of two years later than in girls.

Erratic, rapid growth of the muscular and skeletal system may result in awkward, inadequate coordination. Glandular imbalance may result in skin problems and emotional sensitivity. General health may be unstable and physical endurance lessened, yet restlessness and activity increased.

The sudden and conspicuous emergence of secondary sex characteristics makes young teens very conscious of their physical appearance. Most of them want either to gain or lose weight, would like to have better figures, are seeking to improve their body build. They become critical of their parents' and teachers' appearance too.

Because the desire for approval becomes a preoccupation, teens are a prime target for advertising personnel. Most girls are experimenting with makeup and hairdos by the age of 12. Seventy-five percent of today's youth (boys as well as girls) believe that "correct" clothes are essential to happiness. ("Correct" clothes are chosen for social approval and according to the current fad.) Happily, this attitude will pass. Unless early teen dress

---

[1] Richard L. Harbour, "Adolescence," *The Westminster Dictionary of Christian Education,* Kendig Brubaker Cully, ed. (Philadelphia: Westmister Press, 1963), p. 6.

is immodest, indecent or inordinately expensive, it need not become a constant point of conflict. Guidance, when really needed, is best administered with a light touch.

When, at the age of 12, Ruthie, Charlene, Meri, and Betty Rae were to sing "Fairest Lord Jesus" in a county quartet contest, they exercised initiative, went shopping together, and found exactly the dresses to wear. Solemnly, at the girls' invitation, the mothers assembled in committee at the department store to see four fresh-faced seventh-graders emerge from the dressing room in four black velvet sheaths, high in front, low in back and slinky tight in fit. To the mothers' credit, not one laughed out loud.

After due deliberation, they recommended that the girls buy material they liked and make their dresses, something they would enjoy wearing to school after the contest was over. So the search continued for material and a pattern. The girls had the experience of group choice and the satisfaction of a useful project completed. They can all laugh about it now, but it was serious business then. They could not have taken ridicule.

Intellectual Awakening

The mental powers of early teens are rapidly unfolding with an awakening mental self-awareness and an increased desire for knowledge. They love to read and will learn rapidly from this indirect experience. A visit to the average bookstand with its preponderance of junk will encourage parents and youth leaders to be sure a variety of good reading material for teens is available at home and church. The school and public libraries will be helpful in general material. The church and Christian home must add Christian biography, fiction, and books of information in areas related to Bible study.

Junior highs enjoy investigating and examining evidence, but they find it embarrassing to ask questions about what they are supposed to know. They are alert to the rapid advance of science.

The intelligence of boys and girls is on approximately the same level, though girls as a whole are higher in language and perceptual discrimination while boys excel in performance tests and mathematical manipulations.

Teen-agers like to talk, especially to each other—and particularly over the telephone. By comparison, both children and adults seem almost inarticulate. Teens have not yet developed the important adult ability to initiate and sustain a suitable conversation. Whether they speak in public or private conversation, they need help in expressing themselves in simple truthful ways.

Reasoning power and judgment are growing but are limited by experience. Facts are not always given the proper weight, especially where feeling is involved. Young teens do enjoy lining up the pros and cons of a matter and coming to their own independent conclusion. Parents and leaders can listen and enrich the thinking process by a few simply phrased questions such as "Have you considered this fact?" "How do you feel about the article in yesterday's paper?" It is fun to think in a relaxed atmosphere.

While rote memorization seems to be decreasing because junior highs are actually bored by it, memorizing by association is increasing. They remember what captures attention, what has meaning, what is used. For example, let a class work out a departmental worship service for Christmas using a theme such as "Who is this Child?" See how quickly they can memorize verses that seem to them to answer that question when they know the verses are to be used in a program.

Many early teens, especially ninth-graders, wish they knew how to study better. They say they have difficulty keeping their minds on their studies. To meet this need, some churches have successfully included a supervised study period as a part of their midweek program.

Special interests and abilities continue to develop. This age should have the privilege of experimentation in a variety of interest fields without being required to enjoy or persevere in them all. They lack stick-to-itiveness, even in areas of genuine ability and interest. The more gifted youth have more varied, more intense, and more lasting interests. Some are carried over from childhood, some arise from an expanded environment. Gifted teens can have a remarkable alertness to the world around them, with its challenge of things to know, do, feel and enjoy. At the other end of the spectrum, but suggestive of what many teens feel some of the time, is the boy who wrote, "Dear Sir: It seems like that I never have nothing to do or when I got it to do, it bores me."[2]

Interests are both personal and social. Of prime importance to girls are appearance and friends; boys focus on cars and sports, and attempt to imitate the gestures of male adulthood. Weekday clubs at church provide a variety of wholesome personal and social interests to stimulate experience and achievement, and make practical the reality of the risen Saviour in every phase of life.

Imagination, idealism and a growing appreciation of cultural and aesthetic values spur some junior highs into creative writing, music, art. The increased understanding of symbols opens a world of new meaning to them in cartoons, literature, church architecture, and Bible study.

Social Pressure

Each teen-ager is a product of his own culture pattern. Nevertheless the similarity of attitude and reaction is strikingly evident in cross-culture,

[2]H. H. Remmers, and D. H. Radler, *The American Teen-ager* (New York: Bobbs-Merrill, Inc., 1957), p. 64.

cross-country studies. Popularity is of supreme importance and the social pressure of his own age group is foremost. There is a naïve desire for attention and prestige in the eyes of his peers, and a growing hunger for security.

The most popular young teens are cheerful, friendly, enthusiastic, able and willing to initiate activities.

Social relationships expand as teens go to larger schools farther from home. In the crowd, loneliness assumes terrifying proportions. Most teens want desperately to make new friends. "When you are lonely, and somebody likes you, you'll do almost anything," they say.

Girls are interested in the opposite sex in general, often indiscriminately. The more mature girl is interested in boys older than she and bored with those her own age. Some junior high boys are beginning to have an interest in girls. Perennial questions are "When should I start to date?" "Should I go steady?"

"Going steady" means different things to different people. To some it is a comfortable form of social security, a protection against possible rejection. To others, it is an economic convenience, since first dates with a person you don't know too well should be special and would be expensive. For some, it includes privileges that are neither wise nor good. Interestingly enough, most early teen "steadies" break up with more feelings of relief than of remorse.

Early teen boys fear being turned down for dates, and teen-agers agree that it is the girl who determines what the relationship with a boy will be.

The well-directed church group can meet early teens' needs for social experience if a variety of activities that make for natural companionship are provided. Parents can give some help in providing a family welcome to friends, a sort of "public privacy."

Young teens complain about teachers who aren't fair, aren't interested in things that interest students, use ridicule, are too impersonal or too strict. Teens respond to the teacher who is just, who encourages them to achieve, and who holds a clear standard, yet protects their deepest self-respect. They will be critical of teachers and leaders behind their backs, and at times teens will voice their criticisms to their teachers and leaders directly.

With many teens, their relationship with their parents is a problem. As children, they somehow felt their parents knew everything. Now teens find that their parents can be wrong. Young people tend to overact to this discovery by saying, "My parents are all wrong." Teens hold idealistic views of persons older than they (even youth leaders), and therefore teens are easily critical. As teens' horizons expand, they see and resent the limitations of their parents. A great majority of teens concede that their parents should discipline them when they do wrong, but they feel their parents treat them as being younger than they are—"like children!" "Our parents won't listen to us talk," they complain. "They get there first with the most words and give us looks instead of reasons."

Parents often feel that their well-behaved child has now in his teen years dropped his well-established habits, and that he *won't* talk, at least not reasonably. He seems irritable, inconsistent, impulsive, sensitive, easily embarrassed, and secretive—and at times he is. The emotional climate of the home is no longer monotonous; it becomes suddenly and unexpectedly charged.

Parents are understandably impatient for their child to get through the inconvenient stage, and they often unconsciously communicate that impatience. In addition, they may be concerned about what other people think, or even resent the teen's growing up.

Emotional Sensitivity

So much can be eased in the home by adults who understand the conflict of moods and opposition of impulses of their early teens. These junior highs are real persons with special characteristics. They are living in two worlds, caught between childhood and maturity. They are subject to their necessary striving for independence; but they have to live with themselves whom they do not trust, in a world they do not know. A few years ago, they were learning to walk and talk; now they are learning to live. Moving from the frankness of childhood to the embarrassment of adolescence can be awkward misery. Sometimes they explode in the most secure place they know—home. Sometimes they explode at all that represents the dependence of childhood—home. Either way they feel guilty.

At this point, parents do not need to add resentment or fear to the emotionally tense atmosphere. Love never fails. If a parent is kind and firm in what is right, he need not fear that he will lose his child's love and respect. The parent may need to shun his own subjective, emotional involvement; and for this, he can find help on his knees. *Many parents grow spiritually while their teens are growing emotionally.*

Most of the time early teens are busy, happy and vitally interested in life around them. It is not fair to say they are characterized only by emotional problems. Nor do they profit by a detailed or sentimental explanation of their "problems."

It is said that about one-fourth of the population of the United States is neurotic—not insane, but miserable. The danger signals of a real emotional problem include extreme restlessness; severe inhibition; feelings of being left out, not cared for or loved; a tendency to bully; fears of many things; constant need for reassurance; unusual interest or disinterest in sex; excessive and hurtful teasing; genuinely destructive tendencies; cheating, lying, and stealing. The young person who displays a strong cluster of these traits needs professional help—beyond the ability of a loving parent or an interested youth worker.

The real developmental task of the adolescent is achievement of identity, a sense of self that he can recognize and count on. He is awkwardly trying to speak for himself, to do something himself, to understand for himself, to correct his mistakes himself, to bolster his self-respect. Yet when he so wants to feel adequate and self-sufficient, he is still dependent on others. As a mother in a cartoon said, "Except for making her own bed and ironing her own clothes, Emmy Lou wants to live her own life." A junior high does not yet consistently and realistically acknowledge that he is responsible for the consequences of his own feelings and actions. Yet he is far advanced beyond the emotional immaturity of childhood.

Developing Character

Out of all this physical, intellectual, social and emotional upheaval, there does develop a more self-directed, self-reliant person. The wise parent will stand by and *allow* his child *to learn* by his own experience, to find out what he really is and can do by trial and error. The wise parent will let his teen experiment if it is not dangerous or morally wrong. Where the child is overprotected and overorganized, his experience will be too shallow to stimulate the growth of his own inner resources. He needs to exert himself, to engage in the process of living, to take the responsibility of choice. *It is far better to climb Fool's Hill at 13 than at 23 or even 33.*

The successful Sunday school teacher or church youth leader will work hard to involve individuals in learning and doing for themselves, always standing by with resources, encouragement, appreciation and help in well-timed small doses.

Teens can understand limitations if they are real limitations for real reasons. They can help work out ground rules at home—the work they are to do, the hours they should keep, how they should spend their money, and the privileges they should enjoy.

By explanation and by example, parents and youth leaders can help young people understand that true freedom is guaranteed by living within the limitations of life. Parents are subject to authority too. There is just so much time in the day, just so much money. In a home, the needs of each member must be remembered. A parent bears legal responsibility for his child, and Christian parents are accountable to God for the way they raise their children. Most of the rules of a home can be understood. However, there may be times when on an essential matter a parent will say, "I'm sorry you don't see the wisdom in this, but this is the way it is in our home, so I'm asking you to cooperate cheerfully."

"But everybody else—"

"Well, in our home, we'll do it this way." Some parents have found it helpful to add, "Just tell your friends you have very difficult parents."

"But you don't trust me."

"I think I probably trust you more than I would have trusted myself at your age."

Of course "everybody else" is not doing it, but everybody else *is* giving his parents the same old line. Somebody has to call this perpetual bluff.

To early teens, a few reasonable, definite parental restrictions are a source of both pride and relief. In the conflicting standards of home, church, school, the entertainment world and the peer group, young people have a definite place to stand while they are finding standards for themselves. This does not mean they will always abide by even just and reasonable parental rules, but there is security in having something to rebel against and come back to.

How important that adults hold fast the genuine moral and spiritual principles on which life in Christ is built, and hold loosely the superficial and irritating little things which have no permanent import.

Spiritual Bases

What are the spiritual principles on which junior highs should build their lives?

In the Ten Commandments there is truth that endures for all generations. Junior highs can really hurt themselves by putting secondary things in the place of God in their lives—self, popularity, money, fun (cf. first commandment, Exodus 20:3). They can be hurt by assuming a casual, empty attitude toward God and their responsibility to Him, or by underestimating His plan for a balanced life that includes work and worship (cf. second, third and fourth commandments, Exodus 20:4-11). They can be hurt by failure to honor their parents (cf. fifth commandment, Exodus 20:12), by holding lightly the value of life (cf. sixth commandment, Exodus 20:13), by letting loneliness push them into impurity (cf. seventh commandment, Exodus 20:14), by disregarding the rights of others (cf. eighth commandment, Exodus 20:15), by misuse of truth (cf. ninth commandment, Exodus 20:16), by unlimited and impassioned desire for persons or things (cf. tenth commandment, Exodus 20:17).

Young people can put down roots for fruitful and satisfying living if they come to God through Christ and put Him first in their lives, if they understand the importance of reverence for Him and respect for the authorities constituted by Him. God has a plan for the proper use of time and possessions. He has provided for social relationships through whole-some companionships which are to be maintained in purity. He has placed value on life and truth, and has provided for a release from driving desires into a life of gratitude to a trustworthy Father.

Young teens have sensitive consciences but lack moral judgment. In one survey, over 90 percent of the teens questioned felt they *ought* to do what other people expected them to do. This contributes pressure toward medi-ocrity or even delinquency, as well as pressure toward following socially acceptable acts. A strong sense of personal loyalty can entrap as well as enable. Guilt feelings are real to teens. They distinguish between the "guilt you feel when you get caught" and the guilt when "you feel awful and just hate yourself even when nobody else knows about it." Solutions vary: "Punishment kind of takes it out of your system." "If it's not too bad, it helps to tell." "If it's too bad, it lasts until you do something to redeem yourself. You have to keep on doing something good until the feeling finally leaves you and you forget about it."

The Word of God speaks with certainty and clarity about standards of right and wrong. The Bible transcends feelings, the pressure of friends, and even the opinions of adults. Teens need to know the Word so that their consciences may be educated as well as sensitive. But their greatest need is Christ. He invites them just as they are. He takes away the guilt as well as the guilt feelings. He cleanses the life and gives power. This age is a peak age for conversion to Christ.

Genuine conversion is the work of the Holy Spirit. Christian parents and leaders must look to Him to convict of sin, righteousness and judgment, to take the things of Christ and make them real to teens, and to accomplish the miracle of the new birth. We can pray without ceasing, we can instruct and witness, but when a teen comes to Christ in repentance and faith, he comes as an individual, all alone.

What areas of life demand moral choice for teens?

Profanity increases sharply among junior highs. They consider it a sym-bol of adulthood. The third commandment gives simple, definite instruc-tion regarding swearing. But God's plan goes beyond "no profanity"; it includes active, positive reverence for Him.

Teens feel much guilt in their conflict with their parents. They will profit by considering the fifth commandment and its promise. Youth leaders also need to recognize and strengthen teens' respect for parents.

Jim had been brought by a friend to Bible club, and then to Sunday school. He found Christ as his Saviour and gave evidence of new life. When his Sunday school teacher suggested that he join the church, he said, "I'd like to, but my parents are very much against it." In this case, the Sunday school teacher advised, "Wait a while to join the church. You have Christ, you have Christian fellowship, you are living a Christian life now. You do not need to go against your parents' opposition. Honor them as far as you can without denying Christ." A year later, Jim did join the church with his parents' approval.

On a far less serious but more common level are home rules about what time to be in, the number of nights out a week, how much money can be spent, places to go, and things to do. While the youth leader may feel that some parents are unreasonable, he should recognize that the authority of the parent is in the plan of God. The youth leader should help his young people show love and honor to their parents.

Stealing is a nationwide problem of this age. Most often the purpose of stealing is to have money to buy friends in some way. The Bible says, "Let him that stole steal no more: but rather let him labour, working with his hands the thing which is good, that he may have to give to him that needeth" (Eph. 4:28).

Baby-sitting, paper routes, yard work—these are some of the many ways for enterprising young teens to work so that they can give. The church youth group can provide a healthy amount of responsible work, even by projects such as car washes to make money for camp. But the Scriptures not only say to work rather than steal, but to give rather than take. Junior highs enjoy giving, especially if what they give is in some way their own.

Boy-girl relationships are high on the list of discussion areas for young adolescents. In a Sunday school class of 12-year-old girls, in answer to a written question "What kind of activity interests you most?" six out of ten answered, "Having dates." The astounded teacher questioned several of them individually later on. Oh, no, they never had dates. But it was the activity that they were most interested in.

And no wonder they were interested. In just ten years, most of them would be married. The choices of life partners would determine the rest of their lives.

This is a TV-made generation. Thoughtful secularists are concerned about the emphasis on violence and sex which insistently pushes itself into the American home. More subtle is the absence of a vital moral tone and godly love.

It is a great thing when teens know a happily married young couple and see what Christian love and marriage can be. Teens should have opportunity to talk about God's plan for marriage. They also welcome open but guided discussion on down-to-earth specifics such as age of dating, kissing, going steady, dancing, and how they can keep boys (or girls) interested in them. The leader of such discussions needs to know the Scriptures, young people, and himself. He should be able to listen well, sense the real question underneath the superficial one, and lead teens to understand God's *reasons* for purity as well as the simple "thou shalt not" of the seventh commandment.

Many teens begin to have some form of intellectual doubt about the Christian faith during early adolescence. To be helpful, again an adult needs to be a good listener, one who can hear the real question behind the surface question. Even those who have grown up under strong Christian leadership and instruction at home, church and Christian school are now questioning their own childish notions. This is a necessary step to a more mature understanding of God and His ways.

Some early teens' questions do not suggest deep doubt; they are usually nothing more than the flexing of mental muscle. Use the Bible in answering this type of question, and teens will profit by the exercise of their growing minds. The Word of truth is able to build them up. Take the lead in asking them questions—the kind God asked Job in chapters 38 through 40 of that book. "Where were you when God laid the foundations of the earth?" "How is light divided?" "Can you bring rain?" "Does the hawk fly by your wisdom and stretch her wings toward the south?" There are many awe-inspiring questions in these chapters. Moody Institute of Science films pose this type of question very graphically.

Sometimes there will be a genuine soul-shaking period of doubt in an early teen. The Lord Jesus has said that the truth will make him free, and the teen needs to be assured of Christ's promise that if any man will do His will, he shall know. A willingness to *do* God's will is the pivotal point at which rebellion or obedience determines doubt or faith.

All questions, however, do not stem from personal rebellion against God. God is infinite, we are finite. God is all-knowing, we see through a glass darkly. God sees the end from the beginning, we see only a limited segment of time. God understands *why*, we see only a part of *what*. Our minds are not limited, they are twisted by sin. God's ways and thoughts are higher than the earth. There are some things man cannot understand, but to God there is no mystery. We can trust him. Man is not making scientific law, he is *discovering* it, thinking God's thoughts after Him. God still knows more about the atom and the universe than any man.

SUMMARY

The greatness and the grace of God are great themes for junior high young people. Because of His grace, God loved us and sent His Son to be the propitiation for our sin. By receiving His Son, we too become sons. The Lord Jesus told us when we pray to say "Father." The spirit of the age is to depersonalize God or deny Him altogether. Our teens need the biblical teaching that God is a spirit and seeks persons to worship Him in spirit and in truth. They need to discover that the believer's relationship to the Father, Son and Holy Spirit is *personal.*

The vocational goals of early teens will shift several times as they mature, but the underlying conviction of Christian young people can stay steady. "God has a personal plan for my life. He has chosen me. He has a purpose for me. He will show His way." Jesus Christ will not allow the life yielded to Him to be wasted; He will develop, bless and use it fully.

The Christian life is *eternal* life. Today the junior high can know Christ's salvation, His presence and His guidance into a plan that encompasses all the tomorrows.

FOR FURTHER READING

BARUCH, DOROTHY W. *How to Live with Your Teen-ager.* New York: McGraw-Hill Book Co., 1953.

BLAIR, GLENN MYERS, and JONES, STEWART H. *Psychology of Adolescence for Teachers.* New York: Macmillan Co., 1964.

COLE, LUELLA. *Psychology of Adolescence.* Fifth edition. New York: Rhinehart, 1959.

DOAN, ELEANOR. *Teaching Junior Highs Successfully.* Glendale, Calif.: Gospel Light Publications, Inc., 1962.

GESELL, ARNOLD, ILG, FRANCES L., and AMES, LOUISE BATES. *Youth: The Years from Ten to Sixteen.* New York: Harper & Row, 1956.

GRAN, JOHN M. *How to Understand and Teach Teen-agers.* Minneapolis: T. S. Denison & Co., 1958.

GRIFFITHS, LOUISE. *The Teacher and the Young Teens.* St. Louis: Bethany Press, 1954.

JAARSMA, CORNELIUS RICHARD. *Human Development, Learning and Teaching.* Grand Rapids: Wm. B. Eerdmans Publishing Co., 1959.

LANTZ, EDITH N. *Better Junior High Teaching.* Kansas City, Mo.: Beacon Hill Press, 1962.

LIGON, ERNEST M. *Dimensions of Character.* New York: Macmillan Co., 1956.

MERRY, FRIEDA and RALPH. *The First Two Decades of Life.* New York: Harper & Bros. Publishers, 1950.

NARRAMORE, CLYDE M. *Young Only Once.* Grand Rapids: Zondervan Publishing House, 1957.

PARKHURST, HELEN. *Growing Pains.* New York: Doubleday & Co., Inc., 1962.

REMMERS, H. H., and RADLER, D. H. *The American Teen-ager.* New York: Bobbs-Merrill Co., 1957.

ROGERS, DOROTHY. *The Psychology of Adolescence.* New York: Appleton-Century-Crofts, 1962.

SODERHOLM, MARJORIE E. *Understanding the Pupil, Part III, The Adolescent.* Grand Rapids: Baker Book House, 1957.

TOWNS, ELMER, L. *Teaching Teens.* Grand Rapids: Baker Book House, 1965.

WILKERSON, DAVID, and SHERRILL. JOHN and ELIZABETH. *The Cross and the Switchblade.* New York: B. Geis Associates, 1963.

Young Adolescent in the Church. Philadelphia: Geneva Press, 1962.

Filmstrip: *The Stages of Growth (Later)*. Chicago: Moody Bible Institute. Color, 33⅓ rpm record, and discussion guide.

Filmstrip: *Those Turnabout Teens*. Wheaton, Ill.: Scripture Press Publications, Inc. Color, 33⅓ rpm record, and discussion guide.

High school young people possess a crusading spirit that waits to be challenged. But the challenge must be significant! Dull programs, trite skits, and innocuous recitation will drive young people away. And when they have gone, earnest (but misguided) youth leaders wring their hands and lament the indifference of youth to the things of the Lord.

When the local church involves youth in vital issues, and provides opportunities for them to engage in significant, sacrificial work, the prospects of success are good. High school young people are sensitive to the claims of Christ. They respond to the evangelistic appeal with genuine emotion and idealism. But beyond the teen years relatively few people receive Christ as Saviour.

Lloyd D. Mattson

7

the nature and needs of high school youth

THE FACT that the evangelical church is not content with its ministry to high school youth is evidenced by the frequency with which the topic "Facing the Youth Problem" (or something similar) appears on programs for workers in Christian education.

Youth and *problem* mean about the same thing to some people. Perhaps it is time to begin thinking of the youth *opportunity,* the youth *potential.* Of course, teens' problems should not be ignored. But it is the privilege and responsibility of the church to discover the nature of today's high school teen-ager, to work creatively to meet his needs, and to help him achieve his potential for Jesus Christ.

Ineffective ministries to people often can be traced to the attitude of the leader. Working with teen-agers as the leader *wishes* they were, or as he thinks they ought to be, offers little hope for success. But discovering what life looks like to the teen, and accepting him as he is, promises much good.

The church must minister in distinctive ways to every age-group—from

LLOYD D. MATTSON, Th.B., is Secretary of the Board of Men's Work, Baptist General Conference, Chicago, Illinois.

the infant through the senior citizen. But the middle adolescent years (roughly 15 to 18) represent an especially critical period. To minister effectively to young people in their initial mid-adolescent years, youth leaders should be knowledgeable of the physical, emotional, mental, social and spiritual characteristics of high school youth and the world in which they live.

THE MIDDLE TEENS: WHAT ARE THEY LIKE?

The following paragraphs speak in general terms and may not accurately describe a teen-ager whom you know. But perhaps the total treatment will provide clues to this youth's makeup which will prove helpful. This points up the fundamental principle of *individual attention* in youth work. The needs of each person will differ.

Horrocks emphasizes the importance of knowing individual teens:

> A true understanding of adolescence includes a recognition of the existence of individual differences. Surface similarities may often conceal crucial differences. . . . An understanding of a given adolescent requires a wide and extensive knowledge of his past as well as his present physical and psychological environments. He must be viewed as an adolescent, but he must also be viewed as a human being, and his behavior as an adolescent must be interpreted with the aid of that view.[1]

Brunk and Metzler point out some of the characteristics of this period in a young person's development:

> As youth enters middle adolescence individual differences become more pronounced. The slow student reaches his intellectual level, so that school may be difficult for him. The brilliant young person may be ready for college by the time he is halfway through middle adolescence.
>
> Hereditary characteristics of face and form introduce the appearance of the adult. Emotionally, some may be eleven- or twelve-year-olds, though their physiques are adult. Others, more precocious socially, may marry before the close of the period. Some gain economic independence and become job seekers, while others remain dependent even into the latter part of later adolescence. Many characteristics that are true of early adolescence may still be found in these ages—fifteen through seventeen—and many develop amazingly toward the maturity of later adolescence.[2]

Horrocks suggests that adolescence is a time of physical development and growth, a time of intellectual expansion and development, a time when

[1]John E. Horrocks, *The Psychology of Adolescence* (Boston: Houghton Mifflin Co., 1962) , p. 29.
[2]Ada Brunk and Ethel Metzler, *The Christian Nurture of Youth* (Scottdale, Pa.: Herald Press, 1950) , p. 44.

group relations and status-seeking become of major importance, and a time when values are developed and evaluated.[3] These points suggest the four areas of development to be discussed in this chapter: physical, intellectual, social and spiritual.

Physical Maturation

A young person approaches physical maturity in the middle adolescent years. Many of youth's so-called *problems* grow out of this fact. Girls normally mature physically earlier than boys, frequently gaining full height in early adolescence. Boys catch up in middle adolescence. The erratic energy pattern of junior high years stabilizes. Rapid growth and aggressive interests in active pursuits create voracious appetites among high school teens. Physical maturation brings with it social complications:

> On their fourteenth birthday, 90 percent of the girls are sexually mature. At the same age, only 50 percent of the boys have passed this stage. And not until sixteen have boys gained the percentage of 90. The difference in body growth of adolescents presents a variation in emotional, social, and economic maturity between the sexes of the same age, and explains the air of superiority girls carry toward boys their age.
>
> By later adolescence the average youth has matured physically. The boy has acquired the rich voice of masculinity. His hair is more glossy, and there is a glint in his eye that did not exist before. Shaving has become routine. His shoulders are broad and the boyish lines are gone. His hands and feet no longer cause him embarrassment. He has become big brother to his admiring little brother and sister. The girl, too, is entirely at home with herself physically. She strives to be graceful and self-composed—and beautiful.[4]

Good health and a sense of well-being are reasonably constant, though a degree of moodiness is not uncommon. With physical development comes muscular coordination which equips high school youth for nearly maximum competence in athletic skills.

Physically, then, the young person in mid-teens may be considered an adult. And with physical maturity come the problems of stepping into the complicated adult world.

High school young people are moving toward emotional maturity. Youthful emotions are triggered by such a variety of stimuli that it is precarious to predict a pattern. But for the most part, the sudden tear squalls and pouting piques have passed. Occasional depression, feelings of insecurity, and an undercurrent of being misunderstood persist, but with less violence

[3]Horrocks, *op. cit.* For the reader who desires a thorough study of adolescent development, Horrocks' book is recommended.

[4]Brunk and Metzler, *op. cit.,* pp. 46-47.

and frequency than during early adolescence. Emotions become more subject to reason.

Youth's love for fun and downright giddiness cause adults to despair at times. Young people want to have *fun*. Their emotional makeup demands it.

High school youth tend to be less demonstrative than junior high youth. Displaying affection for parents, siblings, or other relatives seems painful, particularly to boys. Yet high school young people are highly sensitive to injustice. They are idealistic and capable of genuine love—and hatred.

An important part of the work of the church is to enrich a young person's emotional life through worship, music, Christian literature and a sense of personal commitment to meaningful causes. Perhaps this aspect of youth work has often been overlooked.

> In general, the realm of feelings and emotions has not been recognized in the churches' ministry to youth. Most pastors and lay leaders feel less competent to help in this area and as a result give little help. What they emphasize is precisely what they feel most competent to do—give information and exhort. A new awareness is needed of the total person and with it a conscious effort to bring the Word in a way that is meaningful and relevant to youth.[5]

Intellectual Potential

Youth's horizons expand at this period. Earlier the teen was concerned primarily with *self*, his personal wants. Now he begins to discover a world beyond himself, and to learn that satisfaction is found through relating himself to that world.

This growth in concern is accompanied by an increased willingness and capacity to learn. While the last word has yet to be spoken on the nature and accuracy of the IQ, it is obvious that not all teens grasp new concepts or stockpile knowledge for ready use with equal facility. But during mid-teen years the mind rolls up its sleeves for work.

Young people want to work with subject matter that is vital. How will language, or math, or genealogies or doctrines be useful? Philosophy and systematic theology may prove unpalatable, though the adult leader be ever so enraptured by them. Truths that concern youth—his relationship to God and man—these stir the curiosity and imagination.

Given adequate motivation and a proper setting, the teen-ager's craving to express himself will be irrepressible. He holds strong opinions, though perhaps hastily formed. He can muster orderly arguments. He asks not only *what* but *why*. He deplores authoritarian, pat answers. The mind of high school youth may become a hotbed of doubts, to the dismay of deacon and pastor.

[5]Merton P. Strommen, *Profiles of Church Youth* (St. Louis: Concordia Publishing House, 1963) p. 239.

AME _____

DDRESS _____

DEBITS	AMOUNT
Jauth + yours Cheerer	5.95
SALES TAX	
	19
TOTAL	6.14

Guiding youth toward intellectual maturity is the task of the church as well as the school. Brainwork is hard work, and youth shares the common human trait of laziness. Yet the seeds of scholarship can be cultivated, even in the hotbed of doubt. The church should concern itself with the work of introducing youth to the delights of an inquiring intellectual life.

Social Consciousness

The greatest human influence in the life of a young person is another young person. At no other age will he rely so heavily upon his peers. The *clique* becomes a way of life.

During mid-adolescence the peer group includes both sexes. Since there is no cure for this social instinct, workers with youth will do well to utilize it. A youth program can hardly succeed where young people do not enjoy the company of each other.

This is not to imply that the high school youth will not be friendly toward those outside his immediate circle of friends. But almost every youth has a few friends he prefers above others. They may quarrel, even to the extent of temporary severance of relationships, but before long all is forgotten and the group is intact once more.

It is an honor for any adult to become accepted into the collective confidence of such a group. Such acceptance is essential to effective youth leadership. The leader's efforts will be analytically dissected by the group in private discussion, and judgment passed.

Parents and other family members grieve when they discover that their sons and daughters prefer their high school companions to the family circle. But a quiet evening at home with Mother and Dad, brother and sister, rarely excites the teen-ager.

Since young people influence each other, it is important that the church help them form friendships within the fellowship of the church. Aggressive, happy young people provide the church with its most effective tool for influencing nonchurched teens.

The social consciousness of mid-adolescence of course includes boy-girl relationships. Pre-high school dating is most often the product of a regrettable trend among some educators, parents, and a few church leaders to thrust children into dating situations. Often this is not because the young teens have been crusading to date. The practice invariably creates awkwardness for them, and it stimulates a social consciousness which normally should not arise until later years.

The whole area of dating and, ultimately, mating must be included in any thorough ministry to mid-adolescent youth, as Strommen points out:

> Youth's concerns in the area of boy-girl relationships center in questions of a life partner. Their principal life goal is a happy marriage.

Concomitant with this aspiration is a feeling of need to find a Christian concept of sex and marriage. Accentuating this need are the ever-present books, magazines, and movies which tend to negate the sacredness of sex. Even though most youths want help in this area, only a few congregations have felt the freedom or competence to provide it.

Contrary to what adults usually think, half of the sophomores, juniors, and seniors in the study [a four-year study of 3,000 Lutheran high school youth] seldom, if ever, date. Among those are a significant group of late-maturing youth who are troubled because they are *not* interested in dating.[6]

It is the continuing responsibility of the home, church and school to help youth adopt Christian standards and to exercise the personal restraint essential to wholesome boy-girl relationships. Has the church kept pace?

Going steady is an aspect of this growth area. In spite of adult propaganda to the contrary, this relationship is generally accepted by high school youth as normal and desirable. This practice will probably persist. Youth leaders must find ways to provide guidance.

Petting is a common practice among high school teens. Youth need to be taught the hazards and heartaches associated with prolonged intimacies. Unfortunately, the Christian standard of chastity is no longer the community standard. There is an alarming increase among high school youth in illegitimacy, venereal disease, and marriages which end in divorce. Church youth are not exempt from these tragedies, nor can the church ignore its duty to provide teens with a Christian interpretation of sex and marriage.

Spiritual Openness

High school young people possess a crusading spirit that waits to be challenged. But the challenge must be significant! Dull programs, trite skits, and innocuous recitations will drive young people away. And when they have gone, earnest (but misguided) youth leaders wring their hands and lament the indifference of youth to the things of the Lord.

When the local church involves youth in vital issues, and provides opportunities for them to engage in significant, sacrificial work, the prospects of success are good. High school young people are sensitive to the claims of Christ. They respond to the evangelistic appeal with genuine emotion and idealism. But *beyond* the teen years relatively few people receive Christ as Saviour.

The importance of challenging youth to spiritual growth and service is reinforced by this fact: *adult spiritual progress usually follows the trajectory established in mid-teens.* Permitting young people to settle into spiritual complacency almost assures the continuance of the religious mediocrity so

[6]*Ibid.,* p. 238.

much in evidence all about us. Passive, routine youth work will stifle the adventurous spirit of youth and abort the upward thrust of faith.

The mid-teens are the time to challenge youth to dedicate their lives to Christian service. This is best accomplished through actual field service (not tourist jaunts, or pleasant visits to exotic places). Hard work in practical Christian ministries near or far will give youth a taste of the incomparable joy of serving others. It is the task and privilege of the church to guide young people into church-related vocations.

But while the high school teen is amenable to adult leadership, he is repelled by an authoritarianism that provides no place for creativity and initiative by young people. Youth does not insist on autonomy, but he demands a voice. And this voice will not always speak with tact and precision.

As a young person stretches his intellect, a doubt factor is often produced, which causes alarm among adults. A teen-ager who since childhood has confessed a staunch faith may suddenly chill hearts by his questions. "How do you know the Bible is God's Word?" "How can the heathen be lost if they have never heard the gospel?" "Is the Genesis story true?"

Youthful doubting is no cause for hysteria. In fact, honest doubting reflects a maturing faith. Who bothers to question that which has no significance to him? Would he not simply cast it aside and go on?

Youth demands the right to ask, and to *doubt*. Yet he wants help from someone who *believes*. Truth becomes personal when it has passed the test of inner doubting. Truth cannot be harmed by doubts.

Youth is spiritually sensitive to hypocrisy. Nothing is so damaging to faith as spiritual insincerity on the part of professing Christians, particularly those in leadership. Critical, gossiping, compromising adults are a serious stumbling block to spiritual growth among young people.

The basic question, "Who am I?" frequently arises during mid-adolescent years. Youth searches for the integrating factor in life. What is life's purpose? What is fulfillment? Earlier goals of riches, power and fame continue to lure the heart, but for many high school youth there is an awakening to deeper currents of spiritual need.

These currents of spiritual concern are often overlooked in favor of more obvious or immediate problems. Most young people could not articulate this inner cry, yet for many it is very real. Failure to find an answer to this basic question produces the life of frustration and disappointment so common among adults.

Many Christian youth want to know God's will. "Which career should I pursue?" Whom shall I marry?" "Which college should I attend?" And the inquiry reaches beyond religious life: "How does the gospel relate to *all* of life?" "How can I please God in the everyday world?"

The spiritual unity of life and individual self-identity too seldom find their way into the agenda for youth. Certainly it is the task of the church to help young people discover the answers to their deepest questions.

These are some of the characteristics common to high school youth as they mature physically, emotionally, intellectually and spiritually. They are asking questions and craving action.

THE WORLD YOUTH LIVES IN

Youth finds itself in a world of unparalleled opportunity and peril. The second half of the twentieth century must be considered a new threshold for humanity. The affluence, mobility, leisure, knowledge, technology and inventiveness of this day will leave their imprint on youth. The Bomb is a fact, and the psychological effects of a constant awareness of it have yet to be appraised.

But there are lesser bombs. Wars (both hot and cold ones) are apparently a permanent part of our world. Young men must consider military service in their plans. The necessity for higher education conditions the thinking of youth, creating tensions among less capable students.

News media pour torrents of information at youth, educating them in spite of themselves. This education covers the full spectrum of world affairs, including the sordid. Hollywood or Paris sex kittens become national bywords. Learned men, clergy and laity, inform youth that morality is being overhauled, that the "new morality" is acceptable.

A vile flood of obscenity is sweeping America today, with no abatement in sight. Indescribable lewdness in illustration and print is circulated freely among young people.

Many movies, both the theater and television variety, are barely less vile than the printed matter. Much of the popular music flouts chasity or marital fidelity. Sex has become the goddess of America, and with the decay of morality must come the ultimate breakdown of the home.

Youth cannot completely escape the effects of this attack on decency. They must be armed and equipped to stand for Christ. Little help can be expected from society. Even the home seems to be losing an awareness of the peril. The church *must* find ways to undergird youth morally.

But while the contemporary scene has bleak aspects, there is much that is bright. Youth finds itself in a world of opportunity greater than man has ever known. The potential for a rich, satisfying life must not be overlooked. The same affluence, mobility, leisure and technology which threaten morality also can help man to serve Christ.

The church must emerge from a monastic frame of mind and penetrate the world with tens of thousands of alert young people who are committed to Christ. Opportunities are everywhere; the world is asking for leadership. Why not supply *Christian* leaders?

High school young people may bear psychological scars from the contemporary world but they also share bounties of body and mind, the fruit of human progress. They are physically stronger, better educated, and they possess at least the potential for broader vision. The world has shrunk, and it is an exciting world of youth.

MEETING YOUTH'S NEEDS

Programming an effective church ministry to youth is the subject of other chapters in this book. We are here concerned with the principles and approaches which will communicate with high school youth. Ideally the church works together with the home and school, though in practice this may not be entirely possible. In some places the church must compete with the school and, sometimes, the home, if *Christian* education is to be accomplished.

> A youth ministry must recognize the smallness of youth's world and concerns. The problems of adolescence are found within his world of experience, and this world includes four communities of people—his family, school, congregation, and leisure group. Few are troubled by social, political, economic, and international issues. The absence of concern in these areas may simply indicate that this is the size of an adolescent's world while he is in the process of becoming an adult. Rather than label these concerns self-centered, they should be viewed as a developmental stage. Meanwhile each concern, when acknowledged, provides an open door through which an adult can enter youth's world. Once there he can assist youth in his present preoccupation and stimulate him with larger concerns.[7]

Christian education must relate Christian experience to the total life experience.

> Youth need the dynamic which indoctrination alone cannot give. The compelling pressure of mass media, friends, and family background shout the need among youth for an inner power. The evidence [through the study] clearly indicates the limited value of religious knowledge. An increase in cognitive beliefs is quite unrelated to the degree to which youth experience personal assurance, aspirations to service, or are helped to live exemplary lives. What is clearly needed is a ministry that recognizes youth's battlegrounds and helps them find the power inherent in God's forgiveness. Something more potent than a knowledge of right and wrong is needed—and that is a living relationship with Jesus Christ. . . .[8]

Thus we see that Christian education must help youth learn *how* to live for Christ, not merely supply proof texts in support of doctrinal viewpoints. The church must earn the right to youth's loyalty. It is expecting too

[7]*Ibid.,* p. 240.
[8]*Ibid.,* pp. 240-50.

much to assume that young people will respond just because a certain hour has arrived—listed in the church calendar as the "youth meeting."

Public schools continue to enlarge their borders, often including Saturday and Sunday. The school's interest and influence has extended to the student's recreation, social life, health and career interests. School influence also carries over into family life through homework.

Without duplication or a sense of jealous competition, the church must seek to enter more deeply into the life interests of the young person, and in so doing enrich his experiences in the school and home. Rather than the church looking on the public school as competitive, the church can endeavor to reach youth through the school, thinking of the school as a vehicle through which adult youth workers can relate to young people.

Homelife in America has radically changed from earlier generations. Affluence, gadgetry, and television are relatively new features. Many homes have delegated responsibility to the school and church, *responsibilities which will be met in no other way if school and church fail.* Until such time as the home assumes Christian leadership once again, the church must be a spiritual foster parent to youth. While this foster parenthood is less than ideal, it is very real. Great care is required to insure the effective presentation of vital spiritual issues. To believe that traditional, passive youth meetings will maintain interest in this day is naïve. Better tools, better understanding of communication, and imaginative programming and Bible teaching must be used.

Program-building Through Developmental Tasks

Curriculum builders in secular education have sought to relate subject matter to the capacities, needs and cumulative experiences of the learners. They have assigned to the several age divisions certain accomplishments or learning goals which they call "developmental tasks":

> A developmental task is a task which arises at or about a certain period in the life of an individual, successful achievement of which leads to his happiness and to his success with later tasks, while failure leads to unhappiness in the individual, disapproval by the society, and difficulty with later tasks.[9]

Havighurst explains that these "tasks" arise from various sources: physical maturation, cultural pressure, and personal values and aspirations of the individual.[10] He gives two reasons why he thinks this concept is useful: (1) it helps in discovering and stating the purpose of education, and (2) it is useful in the *timing* of educational efforts.

[9]Robert James Havighurst, *Human Development and Education* (New York: Longmans, Green & Co., Inc., 1953), p. 2.

[10]*Ibid,* p. 4.

In regard to this second use, Havighurst discusses what he calls the "teachable moment." "When the body is ripe, and society requires, and the self is ready to achieve a certain task, the teachable moment has come."[11]

This concept has received widespread interest in secular education. Knowing the ten developmental tasks assigned to adolescence[12] (most of which apply to the high school years) can also help *Christian* educators. Knowing these tasks can (1) increase our understanding of adolescent psychology, and (2) suggest subject areas for program building. We herewith list them:

1. Achieving new and more mature relations with age mates of both sexes
2. Achieving a masculine or feminine social role
3. Accepting one's physique and using the body effectively
4. Achieving emotional independence of parents and other adults
5. Achieving assurance of economic independence
6. Selecting and preparing for an occupation
7. Preparing for marriage and family life
8. Developing intellectual skills and concepts necessary for civic competence
9. Desiring and achieving socially responsible behavior
10. Acquiring a set of values and an ethical system as a guide to behavior.[13]

Narramore lists several interests common to teen-agers, a further guide to programming for youth:

1. Teen-agers are interested in fun.
2. Teen-agers are concerned about friendships.
3. Teen-agers continue to be interested in parents.
4. Teen-agers are interested in education.
5. Teen-agers are interested in personality development.
6. Teen-agers are interested in looks.
7. Manners are a serious concern to teen-agers.
8. The art of communication is important to teen-agers.
9. Dating is of special interest to teen-agers.
10. Teen-agers are vitally concerned about military service.
11. Teen-agers are vitally interested in marriage.
12. Teen-agers show a solemn interest in spiritual issues.[14]

[11]*Ibid.*, p. 5.
[12]*Ibid.*, pp. 111-58.
[13]For further discussion of five of these developmental tasks, see chapter 28, "Helping Youth Make Wise Decisions."
[14]Clyde M. Narramore, *The Psychology of Counseling* (Grand Rapids: Zondervan Publishing House, 1960), pp. 142-46.

Helps of various kinds are available from many sources for leaders of youth. Yet *leadership* continues to be the chief obstacle to an effective ministry to young people. While responsibility rests on the entire church, there will always be a need for dedicated, understanding adults who will assume the responsibilities of Christian leadership.

Youth-Adult Relationships

When one considers that teen years either launch a person on his way to a satisfying, enriching spiritual life or persuade him that Christianity and the church are not relevant, it is obvious that the youth worker is a key leader in the church. He may be a Sunday school teacher, a youth fellowship sponsor, a leader of a boys' or girls' weekday club; whatever the role, the church cannot survive without him, for he is the liaison between the church and tomorrow's congregation.

SUMMARY

We have discovered that young people normally prefer the company of their peer group over that of adults. We have learned too that high school teens resent an authoritarianism that makes no provision for self-expression. Yet young people want direction and discipline. Young people are ill at ease when boundaries are not defined.

Wise leaders aid youth in recognizing boundaries, and guide them in self-expression within those boundaries. Youth have no objection to meaningful rules when they are impartially administered.

To discover what a young person is like, and to recognize the world as youth sees it are first steps in serving youth. To achieve that fine blending of authority and liberty which allows youth to mature in Christian experience should be the continuing prayer of all who would lead high school young people into spiritual maturity.

FOR FURTHER READING

BERNARD, HAROLD W. *Adolescent Development in American Culture*. New York: World Book Co., 1957.

BILLETT, ROY, and STARR, IRVING S. *Billett-Starr Youth Problems Inventory: Senior Level*. Yonkers-on-Hudson, N.Y.: World Book Co., 1960.

BOWMAN, LOCKE E. *How to Teach Senior Highs*. Philadelphia: Westminster Press, 1963.

BRUNK, ADA ZIMMERMAN, and METZLER, ETHEL YAKE. *The Christian Nurture of Youth*. Scottdale, Pa.: Herald Press, 1960.

DOAN, ELEANOR. *Teaching Senior Highs Successfully*. Glendale, Calif.: Gospel Light Publications, 1962.

FINEGAN, JACK. *Youth Asks About Religion*. New York: Association Press, 1949.

GALLUP, GEORGE, and HILL, EVAN. "Youth: The Cool Generation," *The Saturday Evening Post* (December 23 and 30, 1961).

GESELL, ARNOLD, ILG, FRANCES L., and AMES, LOUISE BATES. *Youth: The Years from Ten to Sixteen.* New York: Harper & Bros. Publishers, 1956.

HALL, KENNETH F. *So You Work with Senior High Youth.* Anderson, Ind.: Warner Press, 1959.

MADDOX, GEORGE L. "Drinking in High School: An Interpretive Summary," *Bulletin of the AAIAAN,* IV: 3-14 (1958).

NARRAMORE, CLYDE M. *The Psychology of Counseling.* Grand Rapids: Zondervan Publishing House, 1960.

REMMERS, J. J., and RADLER, D. H. *The American Teen-ager.* New York: Bobbs-Merrill Co., 1957.

ROBERTS, DOROTHY M. *Leadership of Teen-age Groups.* New York: Association Press, 1950.

ROSENBERG, MORRIS. *Society and the Adolescent Self Image.* Princeton, N. J.: Princeton University Press, 1965.

SODERHOLM, MARJORIE E. *Understanding the Pupil. Part III, The Adolescence,* Grand Rapids: Baker Book House, 1957.

STRANG, RUTH. *The Adolescent Views Himself: A Psychology of Adolescence,* New York: McGraw-Hill Book Co., Inc., 1957.

STROMMEN, MERTON P. *Profiles of Church Youth.* St. Louis: Concordia Publishing House, 1963.

TANI, HENRY. *Ventures in Youth Work.* Philadelphia: Christian Education Press, 1957.

"U. S. Teen-Agers—The Golden, Confusing Years," *Reader's Digest,* LXXXIX: 50-54 (July, 1966).

Filmstrip: *Doubletake.* Wheaton, Ill.: Scripture Press Publications, Inc. Color, 33⅓ rpm record, and discussion guide.

Transition is the word to describe college and career youth. This transition is often made outside the family context. They are challenging the authority of parents, teachers, church and civil leaders. They are bound by love to very few people, wheeling freely in loose patterns, and often anonymous in the big city or university. They have little sense of community responsibility. They are seeking to make up their minds about what they are like and what they want, so they are taking soundings of themselves and others. They want the freedom to look around; yet they also want the security and delight of friendship. They seem to say, "Don't fence me in—but don't fence me out either."

PAUL FROMER

8

the nature and needs of college-age youth

ONE EVENING at an Inter-Varsity summer camp the writer passed out sheets of blank paper to eighty students and asked them to answer the question "What is the biggest problem you are personally facing?" (See the Appendix to this chapter.) The author took their answers back to his room after the meeting, read them, and was so depressed he hardly slept all night.

The next night, almost in desperation he asked the same students to answer a second question: "What was the biggest thing God did for you last year?" When the writer read those answers he was astonished at the measureless grace of Christ. It was like day after night.

The answers from the two nights seemed to come from two different groups: one almost crushed under great pressure, the other triumphant in Christ. Victorious Christian living for these students evidently didn't mean freedom from problems but a mixture of the hardships similar to those mentioned in I Corinthians 11 and the delights of I Thessalonians 1.

PAUL FROMER, B.S., is Editor of *His* magazine, Inter-Varsity Christian Fellowship, Chicago, Illinois.

In the writer's experience this is an accurate reflection of the inner lives of most college-age young people.

INTRODUCTION

This chapter is concerned with college-age youth (ages 18-22), though later adolescence stretches from 18 to 24. Therefore many of the following observations apply to this more inclusive age-group. People between the ages of 18 and 24 are sometimes referred to as older youth or young adults. (Some educators prefer to think of adulthood beginning with age 21 or 22.) In addition to college students, this age division includes employed single young people and single military servicemen. (In some cases, young married couples under 24 are included in the college-career department, but usually couples, when married, prefer to join the adult department.) Some youth in this age bracket live with their parents, some live on campuses, others have established their own homes, and still others live by themselves.

Robert Frost has written a poem entitled "The Road Not Taken," in which he describes making a major decision as a choice of two roads branching off in a Y. College-age youth are at decision-making cross-roads. They are grappling with issues relating to self-support, life occupation, love, and marriage as well as a view of themselves, their friends, their country, the world and life itself.[1] This is the "twilight zone in which persons are trying on adult life for size."[2]

Transition is the word to describe college and career youth. This transition is often made outside the family context. They are challenging the authority of parents, teachers, church and civil leaders. They are bound by love to very few people, wheeling freely in loose patterns, and often anonymous in the big city or university. They have little sense of community responsibility. They are seeking to make up their minds about what they are like and what they want, so they are taking soundings of themselves and others. They want the freedom to look around; yet they also want the security and delight of friendship. They seem to say, "Don't fence me in—but don't fence me out either."

Keeping company with the opposite sex is a consuming interest, but while many high school students swarm, college students go off in pairs.

Many college-age young people experience a deep sense of guilt. The arrest rate for hard-core crimes is higher in the 18-30 age bracket than

[1]Much of the material in this section is adapted from a 28-page booklet by Allen J. Moore, *Toward Understanding Older Youth—Young Adults* (Nashville: General Board of Education of the Methodist Church, 1962).

[2]*Ibid.,* p. 9.

in any other age group.[3] Rootlessness is common because many youth in this age group are not yet sure what they believe or should believe.

Christian college students face many problems: how to have a meaningful prayer life; how to study the Bible; how to deal with sin and overcome temptation; how to witness; how to find God's will for a life mate and a career; how to correlate Christianity with science.

Between 1960 and 1975 the 18-30 age group will increase 64 percent in America while the rest of the United States population will increase only 17 percent. The church must either come to grips with this group or find its ministry drastically curtailed.

THE WORLD COLLEGE-AGE YOUTH LIVE IN

College-age persons are profoundly (though often unconsciously) affected by the larger world in which we all live.

In the early 1800's the steamboat was invented and the industrial revolution was begun. Science began to affect industry and also philosophy. Today in the United States we live in the advanced stages of the industrial revolution. Cars, computers, color TV's are everywhere, and all share a common characteristic: they are impersonal.

On the tollways we drive up to a booth and drop our thirty-five cents into the hopper, and a green light signals us through. On the light are painted the words "Thank you." Is it the machine who thanks us? Or the guard with his back to us in the change-making booth in the next lane, or the unseen superintendent of highways? Or are they oblivious to our existence? To many people the "Thank you" is meaningless— contrived and impersonal.

We have become so accustomed to machines that can never meaningfully say, "I'm sorry" or "Thank you" that we are conditioned to regard people around us as machines. Worse yet, we can unconsciously regard God in this way too. We tend to feel that He is distant, and that the world He created is likewise mechanical and impersonal. We feel abandoned to a helpless life in a world of complicated, indifferent mechanisms where "research is the key to tomorrow."

The industrial revolution has done more than make life seem impersonal, however. It also has created rootlessness and mobility.[4] A person grows up in Detroit, goes to university there and then gets a job in Los Angeles for five years, Dallas for two, Seattle for three, and Boston for

---

[3]Gertrude Selznick and John Larkins, *What Is Known About Young Adults?* (Berkeley: Survey Research Center, University of California, Monograph 5), p. 1.

[4]Cf. Richard E. and Katherine K. Gordon, and Max Gunther, *The Split-Level Trap* (New York: B. Geis Associates, 1961).

four. By then he has no roots anywhere. The system offers him opportunity, but exacts its pound of flesh in payment.

The impersonal, rootless character of life today is undergirded by a prevailing world view that smacks of the laboratory, and fails to provide a sound base for moral human conduct. In dreary fashion war follows war, and scandal follows scandal.

The impersonal, rootless, multiple-choice, warlike feel to life around the college-age person profoundly affects his answers to all his basic questions. He cannot live indifferently to the formal and subtle influences of his culture.

In light of this, consider some of the psychological characteristics of college-age people.

On the Road

The college-age person is neither adolescent nor adult, but a mixture whose proportions depend less on age than experiences. He is therefore a surprising combination of maturity and immaturity. One minute he is pulling a prank on his girl friend. Fifteen minutes later he is asking your opinion of the cosmological argument for the existence of God.

As Jack Kerouac says in the title of his novel, the young adult is "on the road." He has left "home," but has not yet arrived at his destination. He is an "inbetweener," a tumbleweed loosened from the parent root and rolling free across the expanses.

Where is he going? To maturity. How does he get there? By properly answering three questions: (1) Who am I? (2) How do I relate to others? (3) What should I believe? In other words his questions concern *identity, interrelationships,* and *ideology.*

Identity: Who am I? A person's identity is who he is. To the motor vehicle bureau identity is thought of in terms of name, address, age, sex, weight, color of eyes and hair, license number.

But does this really tell who a person is, or is the answer more profound? The question "Who am I?" actually has to do with such things as personal worth and dignity. This might be rephrased, "What am I good for?" Students fear that the answer is "Nothing much."

Self-esteem is closely related to this. If a person decides that God hasn't created him for some purpose, he may be inclined to spend his life loafing. Our depersonalized culture encourages this by hinting that he is not worth much. It says, "You're an IBM card." It says, "You're the one that caused that accident." It says, "You're a dockhand." So a man begins to wonder if he has a soul or is just a five-fingered hand capable of picking things up and setting them down somewhere.

The college-age person wants to know who he is. If he decides he's worth something, he'll live on the growing edge of his life; otherwise he'll choose the receding edge and be like the person in one of Bergman's works who said that he dreamed he'd returned to his mother's womb, and grown smaller—and smaller—and smaller—till he disappeared.

The author has watched people "disappear." And he has seen others "appear" and grow large, but they've never done it without properly answering the question "Who am I?" or perhaps "Who am I growing to be?" Socrates, when asked formally to define "man," said, "Man is not a vegetable," and would say no more. But it is up to each person to decide whether or not he will be a vegetable, a nobody.

Identity can be approached through the question "For what kind of life does my personality suit me?" *Emotionally* I might be fluttery, phlegmatic, volatile, enthusiastic. I must find out. *Volitionally* I may be strong-willed or easily swayed. *Intellectually* I may be an A student, or B, C, D or F. *Socially* I may be a leader, second in command, follower, introvert, clown, party girl. *Technically* I may be an engineer, professor, musician, linguist. Many students need to discover how busy they can afford to be, too. Rosy optimism here can lead to many unnecessary tensions.

Related to this question of identity is the matter of influence of one's family background. One has to decide how much it should direct him, and how much he should resist it.

The student's search for identity may set him over against his parents and equals. Short liaisons with many groups are common. ("I quit going because I don't know if I want to be like them.") The college youth is free to canvass the possibilities about whom to become now that he's away from home. He'll be lured into many traps. One of them is "I am what I buy." Another is "I am what I pretend." The author recalls being one person to his parents, another to his sister's father-in-law, a third to his teachers, a fourth to his male friends, and a fifth to girls.

Because of Socrates' personal integrity, he is a favorite with many college students. J. Glenn Gray, a professor at Colorado College, says, "Why does Socrates appeal to contemporary students? They respond to his fearless assertion of his right to determine his own conduct despite powerful opposition from the majority of his fellow citizens. The conflict between individual freedom and sociopolitical authority which he dramatizes expresses their own central dilemma."[5]

This reflects the existential feeling of many students. Existentialism asks for authenticity, fiercely calling on a man to be himself. As our conformity-minded age threatens to overwhelm individuality, we are reminded that "to exist" means "to stand out from." "The thing that's wrong with this

[5]"Salvation on Campus," *Harper's Magazine,* 231:55 (May, 1965).

class," exclaimed one of Gray's seniors, "is that none of us is spontaneous."[6]
Of course, too strong an emphasis on individuality can make hopeless any
solution to the problem of interrelationships (to be discussed later in this
chapter).

Ivan Ilych is the precise opposite of Socrates. He is a character in Tols-
toy's famous short story, *The Death of Ivan Ilych.* Ivan was a sort of nineteenth century organization man, an official in the Czarist government who
had a good wife, family, position, income, house. And he was pompous,
artificial and unreal. He thought he had it made until one day, when he
was adjusting a curtain in his home, he fell and bumped his side. As days
passed, the pain increased and began to break up his fictionalized view of
his life. Here was he, who had "done everything right," dying from a bump
on his side. Pretense began to melt away in the face of some sort of religious
experience triggered by his forthcoming death. But until the pain came,
he had never really asked himself, "Who am I?" He had been a fake.

The student who cheats (and many Christians do, sometime in the course
of four years at college) is temporarily abandoning the quest for identity
in favor of pretending to be something he's not. He flees reality for the
dream world where he appears a more intelligent or diligent person than
he is.

The student who is trying to be himself will often set himself against
authority to some extent. It is part of growing up, part of the process of
his trying to be himself instead of what others want him to be. The writer
recalls a night at church in the fall when college had just begun and the
minister was being introduced to the students attending the church for the
first time. The master of ceremonies teased the pastor just a little. But
the laughter, though friendly, was hilarious: it was out of proportion to the
slight humor of the remarks. The students loved to see authority twitted.
Henrietta Mears comments that this "rebellion" is a student's "natural
need for independence that results as he matures."[7]

Percentagewise, not many students have been involved in recent student
civil rights demonstrations. But those who have are reflecting a latent tendency in college-age youth generally. Rebellion is part of the method by
which students find themselves.

Solitude is another part of this method. Though self-understanding requires interaction with people, a student needs time alone to straighten out
his thoughts about himself. Real commitments are almost always made in
solitude.

Another part of the process of discovering one's identity comes from the

---

[6]*Ibid.,* 231:56.

[7]"Teaching College-Age Youth," *An Introduction to Evangelical Christian Education,*
J. Edward Hakes, ed. (Chicago: Moody Press, 1964), p. 193.

presence of "an adult guarantor." He is an adult friend of the student who encourages him to believe that he can make it through the confusions of the transitional stage to adulthood.[8] He assures the student (1) that adulthood is worth the effort, and (2) that the student is worth enough to make the effort. No one buys a thousand-dollar setting for a ten-cent glass "diamond." The adult guarantor must help the student see that he is a million-dollar stone, and worth the expense of a thousand-dollar setting— adulthood. (The way the church can use this concept of the adult guarantor is developed in the last section of this chapter.)

Interrelationships: How do I relate to others? "Each human being who has only himself for aim suffers from a horrible void," André Gide has said. On the positive side, Christ told a scribe that the great commandment is love for God, and that the next is love for others. Essentially the problem of interrelationships ("How do I relate to others?") concerns the college-age person's discovery of his relationship to God. By interrelationship we mean "the relationship in which people know one another, support one another, share . . . interests with another."[9]

The later adolescent is an inbetweener in the matter of interrelationships. He wants to be free of entanglements and responsibility, yet he wants the support and stimulation of fellowship.

The student relates only poorly to his own age group. And since he is in a college society of people who do not know what they are either, he is afflicted by loneliness. Also, study is a lonely occupation, compounding the problem. The student says, "I don't want to go with the crowd; I want to be myself. But I'm afraid that I can't. So I go with the crowd and pretend that it's just what I want." The place of an adult guarantor is strategic in encouraging the young person to be himself and love others.

The student is learning the answer to "How do I relate to others?" as he seeks to establish meaningful relationships with the opposite sex. He does this through casual friendships, dating, going steady. Not being sure who he is, or if he is a person of worth, the student hesitates to let others know him. Further, he hesitates to get to know others because of the responsibility that knowledge would place on him. He also fears that if he establishes a personal relationship with someone, he'll either give or receive hurt. For this reason, Sören Kierkegaard never married Regina, thinking that once he was her husband he might fail her.

Maintaining proper interrelationships demands enough security so that one can give to others. But it is even more difficult to receive something

---

[8] Allen J. Moore, *op. cit.,* pp. 16-17.

[9] Gibson Winter, *Love and Conflict: New Patterns in Family Life* (Garden City, N.Y.: Doubleday & Co., Inc., 1958) , p. 70.

from one's peers (such as thoughtfulness, forgiveness), for this challenges one to give something back, again a test of inner security.

Interrelationship is the opposite of monologue. It means personally knowing the other person. Failure here leads to isolation. Most college students experience immense guilt over sins committed in the area of interrelationships. Paul Tournier's *Guilt and Grace* is an excellent aid here.

Oddly enough, students sometimes provide an indirect commentary on their pastor's failure to solve his own problem of interrelationships. They say, "I can't speak to him because he's all business," or "I can't get a word in edgewise," or "He makes me feel so guilty," or "He doesn't understand me."

This may give a clue on how to serve college-age youth more effectively: We need to learn more about human relations. It is not by accident that Christ said that the great mark of His disciples was love for each other (John 13:35). And in discussing evangelism, He prayed that the disciples "may become perfectly one so that the world may know that Thou hast sent Me" (John 17:23).

Interrelationship, then, is the reverse of the statement "I belong to a party of one, because I live in a world of fear."

Ideology: What should I believe? A third question students ask is "What should I believe?" They are trying to form a world and life view that makes sense out of their kaleidoscopic whirl of daily experiences. They wonder what it all means.

This is closely related to the question of identity and interrelationship. How a person views himself and others depends on his reference points. In fact, the three questions are frequently asked together.

Until a person decides on his ideology, he lacks a "sorter" for his impressions of life. He is like a stranger to his own world and needs to find how to interpret life to save some kind of significance for the person.

Edward D. Eddy, Jr., in a study of students in twenty American colleges and universities—some church-related and some not—found that many of the students were deeply introspective, wanted a frame of reference for their lives, were not anti-religious, yearned for something to which to give their loyalties, and were engaged in an honest search for meaning.[10] This is confirmed by Jacobs' research which revealed that most college students express a "need to believe" and a need for some sort of religiously oriented philosophy of life.[11]

According to the Carnegie Corporation of New York, in a survey of 7,000

---

[10]*The College Influence on Student Character* (Washington, D.C.: American Council on Education, 1959), pp. 115-20.

[11]Philip E. Jacobs, *Changing Values in College* (New York: Harper & Bros. Publishers, 1957), pp. 2, 18.

students at twelve colleges and universities, eight out of ten said they felt a need for religious faith, and only 1 percent described themselves as atheists.[12]

Jencks has called attention to "the failure of college students to gain a sense of the possibilities of life—to go beyond the hackneyed alternatives presented by our everyday culture."[13] If we don't have an adequate world view, we have no vision, and fail to experience that alchemy that transforms the dreary round of life into an adventure of meaning and personal significance. One hundred freshmen in a church-related college were asked by their professor to put in writing their philosophy of life. Many of them admitted they had given the subject very little thought. Others experienced confusion or uncertainty in words like this: "Life to me is one great big mixed-up mess," or this: "At times I am not quite sure what I believe if anything at all."[14]

Marjorie McCorquodot, former candidate for Lieutenant Governor of Texas and now a professor at the University of Houston, asked many students, "Why are you attending the university?"[15] One might think their answers would deal with studies, but the almost unanimous and pathetic reply was "To learn to get along with people." She then asked, "Are you satisfied with your situation? If not, in what way would you like to change it?" "I want to be safe" was the substance of most of the answers. The students didn't want an adventurous, challenging life of highly paid work, but security. As a result they were spectators to life, wanting to be just like everybody else. Based on such a moment-by-moment, useless life, we can guess the answer to a third question, "Is there anything you would be willing to die for? If so, what is it?" The answer: "Nothing. Nothing at all."

Nothing to die for, because nothing to live for.

One striking exception to these answers was given by Shimon Kushmir, a student from Israel studying in Houston.[16] He said:

> I myself faced the death sentence just by being a member of the underground in Israel before the creation of the state, in the time of the British mandate.
> Comparing the situation in Israel and observing the American people, I found out that for a person to be willing to die for something

[12]"The Search," *Time*, LXVI:60 (November 21, 1955).

[13]Christopher Jencks, "The Next Thirty Years in the Colleges," *Harper's Magazine*, 227:128 (October, 1961).

[14]Joseph M. Hopkins, "What Do College Freshmen Think About Life?" *Christian Herald*, LXXXIII:21-22, 61, 77-78 (May, 1960).

[15]Marjorie McCorquodot, "What'll They Die for in Houston?" *Harper's Magazine*, 227:179ff. (October, 1961).

[16]*Ibid.*, 227:182.

he has to: (1) know what he is going to die for, (2) understand the
concept of the thing he is going to die for, (3) know the real value
of the thing, (4) be educated for appreciation of this thing. As a
bachelor I have no family to protect, but my country in a state of
freedom is a thing worth dying for.

Young people will never make commitments, never learn to live responsibly, never reach adulthood, until they find something worth dying for.

Freedom is not enough. We need something to be *for*. Gray has said that
in the 1930's men strove for economic survival; in the 40's, for the defeat
of Germany and Japan; in the 50's there was apathy; now in the 60's a
few are concerned for civil rights. He feels that the real ideological problem
facing students is "to discover some authority, both private and public,
that will make possible authentic individuality."[17] Of course the best ideology, the best world view, is Christianity as explained in God's Word, the
Bible.

THE COLLEGE-AGE PERSON AS A STUDENT

Higher Education in the United States

In 1900 the average American left school to work when he was 12; in
1930 he left at 15; in 1960 at 18; by 1990 it will be 21.[18] The point is that
the nation is investing more and more of its available energy in formal
instruction, and changing the character of the work done to be more and
more professional. In fact, in 1900 only one in 1,100 was professionally
trained. But in 1950 the ratio was one in 60.[19]

This has meant a flight from the humanities to professional specialties
such as education, science, business, law and medicine. The average student therefore spends less classroom time trying formally to understand
himself and the world around him (the objective of humanities courses).
This tends to retard the maturing process.

The demand for education, or at least for training, has produced academic empires. For instance, the University of California has nine campuses, and at only *two* of them (the University of California in Los Angeles
and the University of California at Berkeley) almost 30,000 students are
enrolled! As a result it is now much harder for students to know their
professors and administrators. Colleges are becoming gigantic knowledge
factories. Colleges in the United States will award 10,000 doctor of philosophy degrees this year.[20] Some professors have grotesque ideas about what

[17] *Op. cit.*, p. 54.

[18] Jencks, *op. cit.*, 227:121.

[19] Quoted by J. H. Nederhood from John W. Gardner, "The Great Hunt for Educated
Talent," *Harper's Magazine*, 221:49 (January, 1957).

[20] Jencks, *op. cit.*, 221:124.

students are like simply because they have seldom had a down-to-earth conversation with any of them.

Another characteristic of enlarged universities is increased competition. Just as it is no longer distinctive to become a college student, so it is no longer easy to stay one. The "gentleman's C" is a thing of the past. Partly as a result of this, one half of all who start college drop out.[21] The GPA (grade point average) becomes a hard taskmaster. Students at the University of Florida, for example, are often up until two o'clock in the morning doing homework. And in one year sixty-seven students at an Eastern university attempted suicide.

Why are students working so hard? What is their goal? Most of them (like those at the University of Houston) are not sure. This is reflected in an estimate of the typical freshman class drawn by Christopher Jencks:[22]

1% want serious scholarly or scientific training.

2% want a more general intellectual education.

5% want an introduction to an upper-middlebrow culture and upper-middle class conviviality followed by technically distinguished graduate training.

20% want technical or semiprofessional training, painlessly.

20% merely want certification as ambitious and respectable professional employees.

50% don't know what they want, and will never get a degree, though they might "find themselves" during their stint in college.

The Main Distinctive of the Student

We may be tempted to think that there are two kinds of college students when we look at the above statistics: those who respect thinking and those who do not. But this would be a serious mistake. According to Nederhood:

> The distinguishing feature of an educated individual is not simply his having attended college; he is distinguished by the result of this attendence. . . . A college education should develop a thoughtful approach to life. Thoughtfulness, whether a present or a potential quality of each educated individual, is the quality which makes it necessary for the church to subject him to special scrutiny.[23]

Not every student is presently thoughtful. But almost all gain a potential for thoughtfulness that distinguishes them from most of those who do not go to college. As a result, students respect thought, and want to be treated

---

[21]*Ibid.*, 221:121.

[22]*Ibid.*, 221:128.

[23]The writer is especially indebted for much of the material in this section to J. H. Nederhood, *The Church's Mission to the Educated American* (Grand Rapids: Wm. B. Eerdmans Publishing Co., 1960), p. 55.

as thoughtful persons. In fact, they reserve their attention for that group
of adults who will treat them as thoughtful people. In some cases students
are no more thoughtful than nonstudents, but they think they are; and this
prejudice must be recognized if we want to communicate to them.

College Influences

We have seen that educated America is a distinct group, resting on a
base of college education. To understand the student, therefore, is to understand a person who is more than a youth in transition. He is a student
too.

"The church must seek to know the thought patterns, the prejudices,
and the peculiar anxieties of the various types of American citizens. Moreover the witnessing church must seek to know what its message actually
means to nonbelievers when they hear it."[24] If we come to understand the
way our message strikes the collegiate non-Christian, we'll be better able
to understand the problems of the Christian student, since both breathe
the same campus air.

Four areas are worth considering: (1) the impact of science on students,
(2) prejudices of the academic community, (3) misinterpretations of
Christianity, and (4) the conflict between Christian students and secularism.

1. Science has caused students to accept the following: (a) a wonder at
the magnitude of the universe; (b) the hypothesis of evolution (with religion being a high point in man's intellectual development, not a result of
God's existence); (c) a psychological evaluation of people and things (Luther's position would be examined in terms of, say, his childhood rather
than his reasoning); (d) a comparative approach to religion; (e) indis-
criminate reading of popularized studies of religious data (such as the spate
of material on the Dead Sea Scrolls).[25]

2. The academic community unconsciously holds three basic prejudices
against Christianity:[26] First, an instinctive negative reaction to anything
which non-Christians feel demonstrates a *dogmatic* attitude. The tendency
of religion to speak in absolute terms often infuriates them, because they
fear that religionists have elevated opinion to fact. The non-Christians' dis-
trust of *theology* comes partly from this too. Tentativity is so much a
characteristic of the scientific method that "Thus saith the Lord" sounds
out of place. The church's emphasis on *faith* also rankles the academic
community. For them, faith operates only in the area beyond recognized
fact. "It is practically impossible for the educated person to escape the im-

---

[24]*Ibid.*, p. 53.

[25]*Ibid.*, p. 94.

[26]*Ibid.*, p. 97.

pression that theology is but a massive systemization of personal opinion and fantasy."[27]

3. The academic community's meaning of the terms "God," "Bible," and "sin" differs from that of Christians,[28] so the Christian student has to sort out the divergences. Many think of God as no greater than His universe; others look at Him as vague and distant. They feel that the church has made more out of Christ than He did Himself, thinking that He was only an effective moral teacher. The Bible is usually looked on as a literary masterpiece, though for some it is merely an illustration of a primitive view of the universe.

"Sin" is of great interest because everyone sees its effects, but "original sin" means only that sin is inevitable ("Of course I sin; I was born that way") and it doesn't produce the biblical effect of stopping every mouth before God (Rom. 3:19). Many people see sin as a wrinkle in our natures, possibly to be ironed out in the future. To many present-day authors, sin does not convict men, but equalizes them.

4. Other elements in the present academic situation produce tensions for the Christian student. At college, people *ask,* thus asserting their freedom and detachment from the object of their inquiry. However, the average Christian student hasn't asked, but only followed an authority (parent, pastor, youth leader).

College life also often invites skepticism, so students are inclined to doubt. Doubting can be a valuable, hardheaded way of replacing second-hand conviction with firsthand ones, but some Christians tend to look at doubt as something to be ashamed of rather than as a trigger for firsthand study into a problem. Christians must see that God has given us minds so that we can evaluate alternatives, think them through, commit ourselves and act.

In college, the Christian student's authority (the Bible) is ridiculed or ignored. He then feels that if an unsaved friend won't accept the infallibility of Scripture, he can't use it with him. The notion of distinguishing historical reliability from infallibility for the purpose of witnessing has never occurred to him.

These, then, are some of the influences brought to bear on the college student not because he is a young person in transition but because he is a student. It should be pointed out, however, that the secular college can be an immense stimulus to the Christian to become realistic about his faith, mature in his theological judgments, and sympathetic toward non-Christians.

[27]*Ibid.*
[28]*Ibid.,* pp. 102 ff.

THE CHURCH AND THE STUDENT

To minister effectively to older youth, church workers must know the Lord and His Word, must understand students, and must seek to help them see the relevance of Christianity.

Pastors and youth workers must be intimately acquainted with the Scriptures and with the God of the Scriptures. To depart from the Bible is to ignore reality. One man who understands students well, has little to say to them because he is confused about God. He gets there "firstest with the leastest." Students respond to Christian leaders and activities if they sense and can see that Christianity, the church, and the Bible possess the qualities of *vitality and relevancy.*[29]

Why do college students often say that the church is irrelevant to them? Surely not because God is irrelevant. And not because students are especially resistant to truth. Perhaps it is because many "adult" Christians are playing at religion, not facing life squarely in light of the demands of Christ's lordship. If so, a student who is in search of the authentic sees us as adult phonies. We say that the gospel leads to fellowship with God; but do we spend significant times with God privately each day? And do we love one another, bear one another's burdens, witness eagerly, hunger and thirst for righteousness, confess our sins?

Or possibly the student thinks our message is irrelevant because we don't see the special way his problems come at *him.* If we don't see them from his viewpoint, we fail to phrase our answers in the striking life-terms that show him that what he needs is what God offers.

Churches can help college students in three areas: instruction, love and risk.

Instruction

By this I mean that the church should *teach.* This can be done through expository preaching, substantial Sunday school discussion classes, Sunday evening or weekly discussion groups. We should start with the facts of Scripture, move on through systematic theology and apply all this to the specific needs of students. The needs itemized earlier in this chapter might be considered in regard to each passage studied. Teachers should help students work out an ideology that interprets the facts of daily experience in the light of biblical revelation.

Here is an example of a student problem and how Bible teaching from the pulpit and in classes and discussion groups can help solve it:

Many Christian students unconsciously have adopted the idea that the universe is impersonal and that God is vague and distant. They think

---

[29]This is confirmed by Eddy's survey of students in 20 colleges and universities. See Eddy, *op. cit.,* p. 122.

that the Bible records what God once did, that it is now some sort of magical book, incapable of directing present-day people to God. God has retired from the field, leaving His world to be directed by others. To counteract this, youth leaders should emphasize the doctrines of creation and providence, that is, that God created the world, created each of us, gave us certain abilities, and is concerned that we learn to use them to His glory. They should also stress the doctrine of the person and work of the Holy Spirit—emphasizing His indwelling, empowering and sanctifying ministries. Also the death of Christ should be taught, considering the wrath of God, His love, our sin, and Christ's sacrifice from the viewpoints of redemption, reconciliation, substitution and justification. Pastors, Sunday school teachers, and other youth workers should read information on current problems faced by students. They should read quality books describing older adolescents (including those from secular sources) and some of the novels and texts students are reading. They should also talk periodically with the deans at a nearby college about student problems as they see them.

Love

The maturing student needs instruction in God's Word, but he also needs the genuine interest and love of the one who instructs.

Specifically, Christian students need an "adult guarantor"—one who can guarantee the worth of adulthood as a goal, and convince the student that he is worthy to seek it. Spiritual adulthood, of course, is equal to maturity in Christ. "Him [Christ] we proclaim, warning every man and teaching every man in all wisdom, that we may present every man mature in Christ" (Col. 1:28).

A church should provide a climate where such a relationship between a college-age person and a Christian adult can develop. What kind of person might this adult guarantor be? God gave the writer several such adult helpers in his student days: first, his father and mother; then an uncle, for whom the writer worked during his summers between school at college and who helped him start thinking and acting responsibly.

During the author's junior and senior years at Syracuse University, he came to know a sane, intelligent pastor who respected him and tried to help him solve some immense intellectual problems he was facing with regard to the infallibility of Scripture. At seminary two professors were of special help. One gave him confidence in Christian theology, and the other gave him commonsense counsel on how to live in light of Scripture.

In addition, an Inter-Varsity staff member, by his example and advice, taught the writer the way to act responsibly. The following incident illustrates how this staff member worked: At the end of a summer conference, the counselors were evaluating the week. Each time the leader threw out a question about the conference, he directed it at the same hapless person—the writer—until it became very noticeable. Afterward he explained privately, "I did it because I've noticed that you usually wait to see which way the wind is blowing and then you jump in on the winning side. You need to learn to make up your own mind."

This sort of person is an adult guarantor, a sort of father in Christ especially needed by students in light of their problems relating to identity, interrelationships and ideology.

A friend of the writer who, together with his wife, teaches a Sunday school class for college-career students, displays certain characteristics that help show the kind of person these older youths need and appreciate. He is not a rich man, nor necessarily an intellectual, nor the life of the party, but God is using him greatly. He has not read Tillich, but does read pretty broadly and, if necessary, will seek out a specialist to find answers to advance problems that turn up. He has these qualities:

1. *Sympathy* for young people. He understands them.

2. *A permissive spirit* both in class and in private conversation. Anything anyone says is received without the suggestion that it is unfitting or unimportant. He tries to find what is good in every comment and never implies that a person has pulled a boner. Several in the class have said, "Our class is the only place where this is true." He encourages them to come and talk to him. The fellows talk with him; the girls with his wife.

3. *Humility.* He recognizes his personal shortcomings. If a man is satisfied with himself, young people will consider him a phony.

4. *Wisdom* about life. He has lived a lot, and learned from God in the school of hard knocks, which gives realism to what he says and does.

5. *Time.* Preparing discussion questions for his Bible class, conversing privately with his students, inviting them to meals at his home (he lives within walking distance of campus)—these all take time. But the rewards in terms of pleasing Christ and helping young Christians are immense.

6. *Enthusiasm.* While he's not young chronologically, he is young-hearted. He has a sense of humor, is adventurous and not too rigid.

7. *Impartiality.* He is absolutely impartial with the members of his class. He may see more of some than others, but that is because they initiate it. Some drop by his home three or four times a month. Some never come. All know they can come.

8. *Love.* He and his wife let them know that they are concerned for them. He sends out a dittoed letter to them once a month: a chatty, informal bunch of paragraphs on things he's been thinking about. Even during the summer he drops them notes.

9. *Firmness.* He places demands on the students to resolve their problems

and keep moving ahead in the maturing process, yet he does it in a spirit of kind understanding.

In addition to seeing the students on Sunday mornings, he may have one or two over every week or so for dinner. "We're having steak. Want to come over?" Once they had a hay ride and his wife gave the wagon owner two dollars extra "to make sure they had plenty of hay." Afterward the students had a hymn sing in the leader's home, and the next day he found little pieces of hay all over the house but said it was worth it.

Class attendance averages about 90 percent of those on the roll. (He limits enrollment to about twenty.)

Risk

Even if the student is given (1) information about God and life by way of preaching, Bible study and conversation, and (2) love through association with an adult guarantor, another element is still needed—risk. Abraham believed God and left Ur. Moses believed and left Egypt. Noah believed and built an ark. Christian maturity develops as we get out of our depth in response to God's direction. "Playing it safe" is unchristian. The students at the University of Houston, cited by Marjorie McCorquodot, were driven by fear of apathy and wanted only safety. God, on the other hand, expects students to learn to act in faith.

One of the most common risks He asks Christians to take concerns witnessing. Here the student has to show love to someone he disagrees with, state his case clearly, pick himself up when he is defeated in argument, pray in secret for power and boldness, free himself from hypocrisy, seek an authentic private and public life, and trust the Lord for spiritual direction and power. Perhaps in no greater way does the Lord bring maturity to the Christian student on the secular campus than through the stimulus of witnessing. Identity, interrelationships, ideology and "studentness" are all bound together in the act of befriending non-Christians, winning the right to be heard, and speaking about Christ, judgment and salvation.

The church must encourage students to witness. It should continuously be training them, praying for them and helping them to speak for Christ.[30]

Students should be encouraged to join a campus group of witnessing Christians. They need to be with a group who are charged by God with the responsibility of evangelizing the campus, not with a professional off-campus leader. This forces them to face God in remarkable ways.

God will call some college-age Christians to Bible institutes or Christian colleges though proportionally this group may decrease in the next

[30]For more on the church's responsibility to college students, see chapter 20, "Reaching Youth in College."

twenty years as costs of private education skyrocket, facilities become crowded, and the secular colleges develop extensive, low-cost programs. Also the church will be seeing more vividly the great vigor God can give to a student who on the one hand participates in a witnessing fellowship on a secular campus and on the other hand receives vital help from his local church.

However, many will go to Christian institutions, and these must seek opportunities to witness off the campus. They should engage themselves in situations where they are outnumbered by non-Christians, or their Christian vitality will decrease. Risk (or to say it another way, faith) must be demonstrated in the hard situations if the young college student is to grow spiritually.

SUMMARY

This chapter has sought to show that college-career students are in transition from adolescence to adulthood, a process generally going on between the ages of 18 and 24. They are asking three questions: "Who am I?" "How should I relate to others?" and "What should I believe?"— the three I's of identity, interrelationship and ideology.

Students in college experience special pressures and opportunities not common to nonstudents of the same age.

Churches should help older youth become mature in Christ. Churches can (1) help college-age persons answer their three great questions from a biblical standpoint, (2) surround older youth with a loving fellowship of Christians, and (3) stimulate them to "risk" themselves in faith, especially in the area of witnessing.

APPENDIX

"What is the biggest problem you are personally facing?" Below are some of the answers given by eighty student leaders at an Inter-Varsity summer conference in 1965.

I. Quiet time (also discipline, busyness)

Getting enough time on such basics as Old Testament study, prayer and Scripture memorization.

I need help in my daily devotions. I find it hard to sit down and study the Word. I would like help and a few pointers in this area.

My biggest problem is personal Bible study and prayer which are essential to following in the light God wants me to follow. How can I follow what I am ignorant of?

Personal discipline, especially in regard to apportioning time so that I will be able to spend more time with the Lord.

I'm having a problem in a consistent quiet time. When I neglect this, my entire day is not smooth. Naturally all areas of my life are affected. A good place to have it, a quiet, isolated spot is hard to find.

More time with the Lord would help, but presently an unchristian family at home keeps me concerned about ineffectual home witness, future plans, etc.

Quiet time and fitting it into a regular place that won't get lost in my ridiculously busy schedule. Also a problem facing me at the moment is the proper selection of a mate. How will I know "he" is the right one for me?

Lack of fellowship with Christ.

My unwillingness to *make* time during a busy academic schedule for quiet time with God, or for individual witnessing for Christ.

Keeping a regular quiet time.

I don't have the discipline in prayer and study which is needed for spiritual growth and strength.

My individual relationship with Christ in maintaining a personal quiet time, Bible study, and a daily walk and commitment.

II. Witness

Trying to really live for Christ and witness on campus as I should.

My biggest problem is developing a real concern for my fellow students. I find it too easy to sit back and do nothing.

I believe it is personal evangelism. I can "live" a Christian life but find it difficult to "speak" one.

How personal witness (word and action) can be more effective and fruitful.

Personal witnessing on campus to non-Christians.

I don't know my responsibility as an evangelistic Christian—on or off campus.

How can I make my personality and actions a constant witness?

Really committing myself fully to the Lord's work. If I could through God's help be continually committing myself, my witness would come much easier and the Lord's name be blessed.

III. Sin, temptation, self, surrender, forgiveness

Obedience to God's Word especially in the area of daily discipline.

I think my biggest problem is self-discipline. I am unable to use my time and to discipline my desires and responsibilities; both my spiritual and physical likes are a disappointment and a constant battle.

Pride and lack of self-discipline.

My biggest problem is self—which is caused by being too busy in the wrong things.

Handling sexual desires.

To accept God's forgiveness for sin and to forget and move on. They [sins] come back and haunt me.

The need for totally surrendering my will to God's, and for the life which such surrender would bring.

My unwillingness to die for Christ. If I were put in a situation where I must choose life or Christ and death, I am not sure which I would choose. I think the basic reason behind this is that I am not totally in *every* way committed to Him.

The Bible says a man can never serve two masters. For me there is a basic conflict between a career and work for God. I don't know when I'll come to a decisive point.

I face the problem of allowing God to take complete hold of my future. I have surrendered myself to Christ, and I am now attempting through prayer to allow the past not to block my future.

My biggest problem is staying close to the Lord. When I draw away a little, I don't do my best for Him.

Failing to rejoice in Christ. Allowing "feeling" to reign.

Pride—the almost unconscious tendency to rely on myself and what I think are my abilities instead of looking to God for guidance and strength.

At times I find myself not being completely open to God. As a result I allow many opportunities to serve Him to slip by.

Lack of boldness, also the lack of time to adequately do my schoolwork and the great work that needs to be done on our campus for the Lord.

IV. Dating, homelife.

I find it very difficult to submit my desires and will to those of God, particularly about my future life with one person. I am filled with too much pride.

Trying to understand myself and my feelings toward a certain other person.

I am concerned with my breaking up with my fiancé, at least temporarily.

My biggest problem is to carry on cheerfully my home duties because illness is with my family and it seems that things will not improve. I need spiritual strength to carry my burden and to keep a cheerful outlook on life.

I feel God has told me to leave home and desert my father even though I know he needs me. I am having a rough time deciding how, when, and if to go.

V. Life profession

A life profession. I am not positive whether God wants me to teach or preach, or what He wants me to do when I graduate from college.

VI. Problems as an IVCF chapter officer

As a new executive member, my job requires much work and can really make the Inter-Varsity group grow if done in the right way. Also [I wonder] if I can find enough members who are willing to help.

Knowing when and when not to disagree with other members. In other words, understanding their views and acting accordingly.

How can I as a leader in the campus Inter-Varsity group communicate to others the personality of Jesus Christ?

VII. Intellectual problems

(Interestingly enough, only one student listed anything here, though it became evident as the conference proceeded that the problems existed. Some students think they do not have such problems, but a little probing always reveals them.)

The devil, fallen angels, evolution, and other teachings I used to consider fundamental. How conservative does the Christian have to be? Essentially, what is a Christian? How liberal can I be and still be a real Christian?

FOR FURTHER READING

Apolegetics and Doctrine

ANDERSON, J. N. D. *Evidence for the Resurrection*. Chicago: Inter-Varsity Press, n.d.

GERSTNER, JOHN H. *Reasons for Faith*. Grand Rapids: Baker Book House. 1960.

HOLMES, ARTHUR. *Christianity and Philosophy*. Chicago: Inter-Varsity Press, 1960.

LITTLE, PAUL E. *Know Why You Believe*. Wheaton, Ill.: Scripture Press Publications, Inc., 1967.

MANLEY, G. T. and OLDHAM, H. W., editors. *Search the Scriptures*. Chicago: Inter-Varsity Press, 1955.

STOTT, J. R. W. *Basic Christianity*. Grand Rapids: Wm. B. Erdmans Publishing Co., 1959.

WALSH, CHAD. *Campus Gods On Trial*. New York: Macmillan Co., 1962.

Understanding and Teaching Older Youth

EDDY, EDWARD D., JR. assisted by PARKHURST, MARY LOUISE, AND YAKOVAKIS, JAMES S. *The College Influence on Student Character*. Washington, D.C.: American Council on Education, 1959.

FORDHAM, FORREST B., and ALESSI, VINCE. *Teaching Older Youth*. Philadelphia: Judson Press, 1959.

HALLECK, SEYMOUR L. "The Roots of Student Despair," *Think*, XXXIII:21-24 (March-April, 1967).

International Journal of Religious Freedom, February, 1958. Special issue on church & college.

JACOB, PHILIP E. *Changing Values in College*. New York: Harper & Bros. Publishers, 1958.

"Man of the Year," *Time*, LXXXIX:18-23 (January 6, 1967).

MEAD, MARGARET, "Problems of the Late Adolescent and Young Adult," *Survey Papers* (1960 White House Conference on Children and Youth).

MEARS, HENRIETTA, "Teaching College-Age Youth," *An Introduction to Evangelical Christian Education.* J. Edward Hakes, editor. Chicago: Moody Press, 1964.

MILLER, ALEXANDER. *Faith and Learning.* New York: Association Press, 1960.

NEDERHOOD, J. H. *The Church's Mission to the Educated American.* Grand Rapids: Wm. B. Eerdmans Publishing Co., 1960.

RIESMAN, DAVID, GLAZER, NATHAN, and DENNY, REUEL. *The Lonely Crowd* (abr. ed.). New Haven, Conn.: Yale University Press, 1953.

SELZNICK, GERTRUDE, and LARKINS, JOHN. *What Is Known About Young Adults?* Berkeley: Survey Research Center, University of California, Monograph 5.

SNYDER, ROSS (ed.) *The Young Adult.* A special issue of the Chicago Theological Seminary *Register,* XLIX (November, 1959) .

SYMONDS, PERCIVAL M., and JENSEN, ARTHUR R. *From Adolescent to Adult.* New York: Columbia University Press, 1961.

TOURNIER, PAUL. *Guilt and Grace.* New York: Harper & Row, Publishers, 1962.

PART III

youth and the
local church

*Providing a comprehensive youth program
calls for coordinating the various functions.
But a church must be careful not to diagram
an organizational and programming scheme
which looks good on paper, but is not workable. Coordination should be viewed against
the demands of the teens' home and school
life and not against the background of theoretical programming. If a plan cannot easily
be implemented in practice, it would be best
to reconsider its value to the total youth
endeavor.*

DONALD S. AULTMAN

9

organizing for youth

THE INABILITY OF THE CHURCH to communicate with and minister effectively to adolescents is a constant problem which seems to have intensified in this decade.

> We are bothered that we feel our failure in the areas of study, creative expression, action, fellowship, stewardship, and worship, that we feel we have not really communicated in the church or neighborhood or beyond our circle; and that we sense a lack of relevance to the modern world, and the modern soul.[1]

In view of these facts youth leaders should be sure that local church youth activities—including Sunday school classes and departments, youth groups, weekday clubs, vacation Bible school, socials, service projects, rallies, retreats, camps—are so organized that they achieve their aims in the best possible way. This may call for constant evaluation. Organization

---

[1] D. Campbell Wyckoff, *Theory and Design of Christian Education Curriculum* (Philadelphia: Westminster Press, 1961), p. 138.

DONALD S. AULTMAN, B. A., is National Sunday School and Youth Director for the Church of God, Cleveland, Tennessee.

once adequate, and programs once appealing, may become outmoded unless they are constantly evaluated and, if necessary, reshaped and updated. While certain guiding principles of Christian education do not change, the implementing of those principles should not become static. To maintain vitality, youth activities must be Christ-centered and life-related. But they should *also* be based on the best principles of organization.

ORGANIZATIONAL PRINCIPLES

To be meaningful to young people an organization must be structured for *quality* and *growth*. It should therefore follow principles which assure a program that is well ordered and full-orbed, and which draws youth into activities that provide for participation, fellowship, discipline, spiritual insight and nurture.

The organization should be purposeful. Any youth organization in the local church should have a distinct purpose, a definite *raison d'être*. Organization should exist for the sake of people, not people for the sake of organization.

> Organization exists for the sake of program. . . . Participation in organization and administration results in educational experience for the participants. The ways in which persons are organized and administered are factors in their experience of the Christian fellowship.[2]

A primary test of organization should be, Is it essential? The rapid proliferation of programs and multiple youth agencies demands that youth leaders ask, Are these activities really necessary to meet the needs and interests of young people? If an organization or activity cannot be justified as to purpose, then continuation of it may well be questioned. "Any organization which exists for its own sake and does not contribute to better program is superfluous."[3] To be functional, a youth organization must be flexible. For efficiency, organizational framework should be held to a minimum. Each youth agency must be able to function freely without infringing on related agencies.

Historically, youth work has been related to people ranging in age from 12 to 24. It has been suggested, however, that the increasing tempo of maturation in young people, new forms of youth education and entertainment, and the prosperity of "teens" earning billions of dollars annually have made youth more sophisticated and are consequently gradually lowering the age of participating youth in the church. But we will consider the traditional years of 12 to 24 as the age bracket for the church's youth division.

---

[2]Paul H. Vieth, "The Local Church Organized for Christian Education," *Religious Education,* Marvin Taylor, ed. (Nashville: Abingdon Press, 1960), p. 247.
[3]*Ibid.,* p. 249.

Since the size of a church determines the number of specific age group-ings, it is necessary to build on a flexible base that can be adapted to large and small groups. The following age divisions can be adjusted as the size of the congregation increases. Age groups here are treated as departments in any agency of the church.

A new department may be formed when there are 15 or 20 young people of a particular age group.

DEPARTMENTAL DIVISIONS

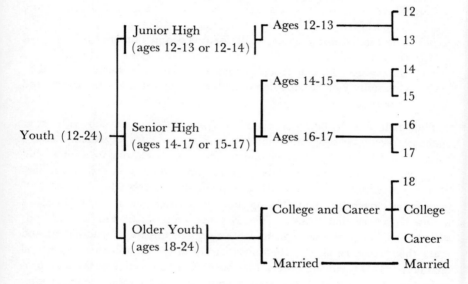

Smaller churches may be limited to a single youth department, whereas larger churches might have as many as three to five departments. Of course in large churches some agencies (e.g., Sunday school) may need more di-visions than other agencies. The point here is to be sure that the youth or-ganizations are flexible so that they can divide as they grow in number.

While the small church has unique organizational problems, it also has some definite advantages. The term "small church" is used as a reference to churches with less than one hundred members and less than five meeting rooms. The most obvious problems are lack of facilities, groups too small for advanced organization, lack of creative leadership that really under-stands youth work, a "small-church complex" with consequent failure in attempts to duplicate large church programs and compete with community youth programs.[4]

[4]Rachel Swann Adams, *The Small Church and Christian Education* (Philadelphia: Westminster Press), pp. 16-19.

It can readily be observed that most of these problems can be turned to positive advantages. A small church need not try to compete with community programs or duplicate large church efforts. In a small group, members can easily get acquainted, thus forming lasting friendships ideally suited for Christian fellowship. Adam suggests that a small church has these advantages:

1. The home becomes a natural setting for many church groups.
2. The small church can use the out-of-doors for teaching.
3. The small church can use its total environment for teaching.
4. There is concern across age lines (also wider acquaintences and friendships).
5. The family unit is more easily identified and nurtured in the small church.
6. The values of small group participation are more easily achieved.
7. Creativity can be stimulated in the use of facilities, personnel and resources.[5]

The small church should specialize in doing an adequate job with fewer agencies, providing programs that will involve its youth in worship, study, training and fellowship. It is erroneous for a small church to assume that effective youth work can be done only in large groups and colorful rallies.

In the beginning of new youth groups in the church where no set patterns have developed, the following suggestions might be helpful: (1) Have a stated purpose that is acceptable to youth and adults. This should constitute a challenge to their spiritual life that will fire their imagination and make them resourceful. (2) Relate the group to the church through official channels. (3) Provide resources that will yield productive ideas and programming aids. (4) Let the youth work out the rules for membership, with adult guidance guarding against the formation of cliques. (5) As soon as possible organize separate groups for junior highs, senior highs, and college-age youth. When they are all in one group, the older ones tend to drop out or the younger teens feel dominated. (6) Carefully inform the youth what is expected of them. Give them the guidelines, keeping rules simple, expecting cooperation and allowing freedom within this framework.

The scope should be comprehensive. The organization should provide activities for youth of all ages, taking into account their varied interests as well as their spiritual, social and intellectual needs.

> With respect to each person organization is properly comprehensive when at the program planning level he may be seen as a whole person, and provision made for his total Christian education. Individual persons will usually be related to more than one agency. For example, a junior

---

[5]*Ibid.*, pp. 14-16. Also see Virgil E. Foster, *How a Small Church Can Have Good Christian Education* (New York: Harper & Bros. Publishers, 1956), chapters 6-7.

high school boy may be in the Sunday church school, the vacation church school, Boy Scouts, junior high fellowship, church membership class, and attend the church service of worship. Good organization should make possible planning for the total interests and needs of this boy and should help each agency contribute its share without conflict or overlapping with others.[6]

Providing a comprehensive youth program calls for coordinating the various functions. But a church must be careful not to diagram an organizational and programming scheme which looks good on paper, but is not workable. Coordination should be viewed against the demands of the teens' home and school life and not against the background of theoretical programming. If a plan cannot easily be implemented in practice, it would be best to reconsider its value to the total youth endeavor.

Of course the primary concern is for quality, for spiritual results in the youth activities. This is that which puts fiber on the skeletal framework of an organizational plan. Many churches provide for the following educational functions through these agencies: (1) study of the Bible and Christian doctrine—Sunday school and pastor's instruction classes; (2) training in Christian living and leadership—weekly youth groups and weekday clubs; (3) spiritual, social and physical development—weekday activities;[7] (4) evangelism and Bible study—vacation Bible school.

The program should be church-related. Youth work in the church exists to help the church in its mission of evangelism and nurture. Each group should be seen as a part of an overall educational program, administered by the board of Christian education, which in turn is answerable to the congregation or official church board. The following chart illustrates this fact and summarizes the organizing principles discussed.

Some churches have a youth committee. This committee consists of an adult representative from each youth agency. This would include the junior high, senior high, and college-age departmental superintendents in the Sunday school, the head sponsor of each of the three youth groups, the head leader of each of the youth weekday clubs, and the director of Christian education (and/or youth director) and the pastor. All the committee members may be on the board of Christian education, or only the committee chairman may be on the board.

The function of the youth committee is to coordinate and evaluate the activities of all the youth agencies. It may also plan functions that would include all three age groups (junior high, senior high, and college-age) where all three may be involved. Examples of such functions would be a youth rally or retreat, a career clinic, a work project.

---

[6]Vieth, *op. cit.*, p. 249.

[7]"Weekday activities" include socials, recreation, service projects.

ORGANIZATIONAL DIAGRAM

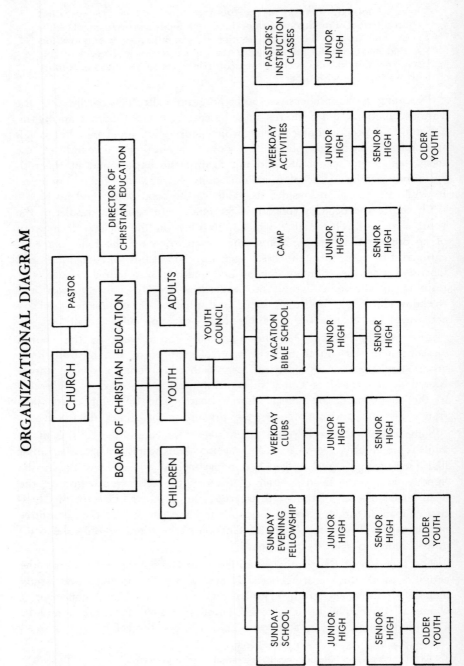

In churches not large enough to require a youth committee, these co-ordinating functions may be done by one person. He may be known as the youth chairman or youth coordinator.

Some large churches have a junior high coordinator, a senior high co-ordinator, and a college-age youth (or older youth) coordinator. Each of these three leaders is responsible for overseeing and correlating the total educational program for his particular age group.

A youth council is optional. It consists of adult representatives from the youth agencies (one from the Sunday school, one from the youth groups, and one from the weekday clubs) *and* teen representatives (a junior high, a senior high, an older youth). The purposes of the youth council are identical with those of the youth committee, but the council differs from the committee in two ways: (1) the council has less of an official voice in the planning, coordinating, and evaluating, and (2) the council is not a part of the board of Christian education, whereas the youth committee members or its chairman are.

ADMINISTRATIVE FUNCTIONS

Seven administrative functions are necessary if a group is to succeed. Ineffectiveness in church group programming can usually be traced to poor work on one or more of these functions. They are planning, organizing, executing, supervising, coordinating, publicizing and evaluating.[8]

Planning should be done by capable persons who are aware of the ob-jectives of the group. *Organizing* should be in keeping with the basic prin-ciples already discussed. *Executing* is putting into practice the objectives of the group. *Supervising*, the oversight and directing of a project, should be done by someone who knows the aims of the planners and who has the authority and insight to suggest changes where needed. *Coordinating* the program insures harmony and helps avoid unnecessary overlapping and competition. *Publicizing* makes the church community aware of the what, when and where of every activity. *Evaluating* the program can be a means of measuring quality, progress and attainment of goals.

The following questions may be asked when seeking to evaluate a youth agency or activity: Is it Christ-honoring? Is it leading young people to Christ for salvation? Is it helping them grow spiritually? Does it have a purpose distinct from the other youth activities and is this known and un-derstood by the youth and their adult leaders? Does it provide opportu-nities for personal social adjustment? Does it employ the best in educa-tional techniques? Does it provide opportunities for seeking Christian

[8]Lee J. Gable, *Christian Nurture Through the Church* (New York: National Council of Churches, 1955), pp. 36-38.

answers to basic life problems? Are the needs and interests of young people being met?

LEADERSHIP GUIDELINES

It has become increasingly apparent that young people do not leave church because they have no interest in religion but because our approach has failed to interest them. The greatest single need in youth work is for youth leaders who will give themselves to the exhausting task of seeking to understand, love and guide the impressionable lives of young people.

Youth leaders let youth belong. Young people learn best when they "belong" to a group which seems significant to them. When youth are asked about the kind of groups they prefer, they usually indicate that they like a group with a feeling of oneness, a sense of belonging, and an atmosphere of warm friendliness.

Youth leaders let youth share. Teens gain a sense of belonging to an organization as they have opportunity to share in it and contribute to it. This means that adult leaders must avoid the two extremes of a dictatorial, do-it-all kind of control and a laissez-faire, onlooking, do-nothing attitude.

The adult must be a sponsor, a guide. But this role is often misunderstood.

> He is not a dictator who decides exactly what the group ought to do.
> He is not a clown, who woos and wins with his great personality. The
> sponsor is an advisor. He is a manager or, better still, a coach. . . . The
> sponsor is very busy behind the scenes. Though he is not always in
> front of the group, he is always there.[9]

This principle applies primarily to Sunday evening groups,[10] but it also relates to Sunday school teaching. A Sunday school teacher of teens should not "do all the talking" nor should he let the class ramble aimlessly in endless discussions. Instead he should be a guide, helping the young people discover the truths of God's Word for themselves. As the teacher guides, the teens *share* in the discovery of God's truths.

Though the leadership is to be shared with the youth, some planning must be done by adults alone.

> Would that not rob youth of participation? No! Clear thinking will
> suggest that this over-all survey by adult workers in no wise overlaps
> youth's own areas for planning. There are some things youth cannot
> do! Likewise there are some things—those within the experience range
> and abilities of the age level of youth involved—adults should not rob

---

[9]Donald S. Aultman, *Guiding Youth* (Cleveland, Tenn.: Pathway Press, 1965) , p. 75.
[10]For more on the sponsor's role, see chapter 13, "Sunday Evening Youth Programs."
Also see Roy B. Zuck and Fern Robertson, *How to Be a Youth Sponsor* (Wheaton, Ill.: Scripture Press Foundation, Inc., 1960) , chapters 2-3.

them of their chance to do. But short-sighted "letting youth do it all" may mean failure on the part of adult workers to attain a level of youth work worthy of a Christian church.[11]

The following "advice to advisors" from a survey of 609 Presbyterian young people offers candid insight into the role adults should take in youth work:[12]

"Don't act as if you own the group."

"Get to know everyone. Don't try to control the meetings. Let us do as much as we can."

"Don't be dictatorial, but do be firm. Above all, don't be childish."

"Be friendly. Ask 'the gang' over after the meeting."

"Be religious but not stuffy."

"Lead a life worth copying."

"If you are not a true Christian with an exceptionally good personality and the ability to recognize the flippant cruelty of youth, you'd better not take the job."

"Just act like folks and be a cooperative soul."

"Have genuine love, understanding, and respect for young people."

"Be more than just an advisor; be a friend, and help the young people when they need you."

Youth leaders let youth participate. Youth agencies and activities should be organized to allow for maximum participation by the young people.

Many young people have qualities of leadership far beyond their opportunity to exercise them. To capitalize on the dynamics of the peer group relationship and teens' yearning for adult acceptance, the adult sponsor should let young people take part. But he must know them individually, so he can know in what ways they can best participate.

> Not only is it true that belonging or not belonging to a Fellowship makes a difference; it is also true that the role one plays, the position one occupies within the structure of the Fellowship, makes a difference. Longing to be recognized, to feel that he has made a worthwhile contribution, the senior high may never have an office, never have a responsibility. Then, he may reluctantly agree to take a part on a program and fail miserably. Gradually he comes to feel inferior. No one helps him find the thing he can do, so that he can have a sense of worth. . . . Or take the person who always occupies the limelight, who always has the key office. Too much success may prove even more dangerous than not enough. Is someone going to keep in mind the individuals in the group and their individual needs?[13]

---

[11]Clarice M. Bowman, *Ways Youth Learn* (New York: Harper and Bros. Publishers, 1952), p. 38.

[12]Sara Little, "Adult Leaders of Youth," *Handbook for Senior High Fellowship* (Richmond, Va.: John Knox Press, 1952), p. 9.

[13]*Ibid.*, p. 27.

The wise youth leader or teacher will (1) let each member of the group or class know that he is accepted, (2) create an atmosphere of responsible freedom in which there is opportunity to discuss freely, (3) identify with the youth, (4) reach young people at their point of need, and (5) come to know the young people and their families.

In Sunday school and youth groups young people appreciate opportunities to be officers—presidents, secretaries, treasurers. They enjoy taking part in Sunday school opening assemblies, and in ministering musically in youth groups and church services.

In youth groups, leadership can be shared as teens serve on committees and planning groups. There are better reasons for committees than "we have always had them and couldn't get along without them." These reasons include the following: (1) to get the work done, (2) to develop young people's leadership potential, (3) to train young people in teamwork, in working with others.[14] Some of the possible committees in youth groups include missionary, social, publicity, membership. The planning of programs should be in the hands of planning groups, with each young person in a group.[15] Of course at camp, banquets, socials, rallies, teens may be given responsibilities on various short-term committees.

VITAL RELATIONSHIPS

The *pastor* is related to the youth work as an ex-officio member of the youth committee (and/or youth council) and the board of Christian education. He should be a personal friend to youth and available for counseling. As the spiritual leader and chief administrator of the church he should be apprised of all program plans in regular reports from the adult leaders. He should respond by demonstrating a positive interest in all the youth activities.

The *director of Christian education* is the chief resource person to the youth work. As the administrator of the total educational program he should be aware of all youth projects and activities. Relating the plans of the board of Christian education to the various youth leaders, his advice and evaluation should help steer the entire youth program. He attends youth meetings and social functions as time permits. In some larger churches these functions are carried on by a full-time or part-time youth director in addition to or in place of the director of Christian education.[16]

Informed *parents* can lend significant assistance to the youth program. The adult leaders should keep teens' parents informed about youth

[14]Arthur Flake, *Baptist Young People's Administration* (Nashville: Convention Press, 1952), pp. 27-28.

[15]For a detailed discussion of how this planning group works, see chapter 13, "Sunday Evening Youth Programs."

[16]For duties of the full-time youth director, see chapter 18, "Adult Leaders for Youth."

activities and policies, enlist the prayer support of Christian parents, get to know the parents, urge them to cooperate with the youth program, and occassionally ask them to assist in various youth activities.

Since the Sunday school is the agency most likely to reach the largest number of youth, the youth *departmental superintendents* have an important relationship to the total youth program. They should become personally acquainted with the young people and should encourage their participation in all aspects of the church's youth program.

The *Sunday school teachers* should be close friends and advisors to youth. As key people in the educational program, they have a major responsibility in the ministry to youth. To many teen-agers, Sunday school is one of the most boring hours of their entire week. If teaching methods are noncreative, if young people are treated like children, and if Bible study is irrelevant, dull and less challenging than public school studies, teens find it difficult to get excited about Sunday school. Therefore it is the responsibility of Sunday school teachers to teach creatively, to treat young people as adults, to make the study of God's Word challenging and teen-slanted.

Finally, the total youth program should be related to the church through the *board of Christian education*. All adult workers with youth should be approved and/or appointed by the board of Christian education.

SUMMARY

All youth activities should be worthy of the gospel and should be representative of the purposes and standards of the church. Youth should be led to recognize that they are under the umbrella of the church and, as such, should participate in the work of the Lord on a churchwide basis. That such a relationship to the church can be deeply appreciated by young people is borne out by a 16-year-old who said, "I feel I am becoming more and more a part of my church." This is the purpose of organizing for youth—to help them grow in the Lord as they take part in (and thus sense that they are a part of) God's program of evangelism, worship, instruction and service.

FOR FURTHER READING

ADAMS, RACHEL SWANN. *The Small Church and Christian Education.* Philadelphia: Westminster Press, 1961.

AULTMAN, DONALD S. *Guiding Youth.* Cleveland, Tenn.: Pathway Press, 1965.

———. *Learning Christian Leadership.* Cleveland, Tenn.: Pathway Press, 1960.

BOWMAN, LOCKE E., JR. *How to Teach Senior Highs.* Philadelphia: Westminster Press, 1963.

BYRNE, H. W. *Christian Education for the Local Church.* Grand Rapids: Zondervan Publishing House, 1963.

CARROLL, JOHN L. "One of These Days We've Got to Get Organized," *Baptist Leader*, XXVIII:4-6 (January, 1967).

FORDHAM, FORREST B. *Our Church Plans for Youth*. Philadelphia: Judson Press, 1953.

LITTLE, SARA. "Adult Leaders of Youth," *Handbook for Senior High Fellowship*. Richmond, Va.: John Knox Press, 1952.

LOTZ, PHILIP HENRY, editor. *Orientation in Religious Education*. Nashville: Abingdon Press, 1950.

NEWBY, DONALD O. "The Church's Ministry to Youth," *Religious Education*. Marvin Taylor (ed.). Nashville: Abingdon Press, 1960.

PERSON, PETER P. *An Introduction to Christian Education*. Grand Rapids: Baker Book House, 1959.

ROBERTS, DOROTHY M. *Leadership of Teen-age Groups*. New York: Association Press, 1950.

VIETH, PAUL H. "The Local Church Organized for Christian Education," *Religious Education*. Marvin Taylor, editor. Nashville: Abingdon Press, 1960.

ZUCK, ROY B. "Sunday Evening Youth Groups," *An Introduction to Evangelical Christian Education*. J. Edward Hakes, editor. Chicago: Moody Press, 1964.

ZUCK, ROY B., and ROBERTSON, FERN. *How to Be a Youth Sponsor*. Wheaton, Ill.: Scripture Press Foundation, 1960.

Nikolai Lenin and J. Hudson Taylor had one thing in common. Both of them made momentous though vastly different decisions concerning God during adolescence. In so doing, these two young men were quite normal because adolescence is a time when life-changing decisions are made. This is what makes the evangelism of youth so imperative. During these stormy years, teens are making significant decisions about a future vocation, a life partner, values, goals, God! How important, then, that priority be given to presenting to teen-agers the claims of Christ!

EDWARD D. and FRANCES F. SIMPSON

10

evangelism of youth

DEFINITION

IN A GENERAL SENSE, an evangelist is a person so convinced of the truth-fulness of that which he believes that he attempts by various means to convince others also. Christian evangelism is the persuasive presentation of the gospel for the purpose of bringing men to Jesus Christ for salvation from sin. The gospel, or evangel, is the good news of God's saving grace through Jesus Christ. Thus the person presenting this gospel to the lost is called an evangelist. He himself saves no one. Only God can do that.

The evangelist merely proclaims the gospel which is "the power of God unto salvation to everyone that believeth" (Rom. 1:16). Such presentation may take various forms, such as proclaiming passionately from a pulpit, talking exicitedly in a dorm, chatting quietly in a den,

EDWARD D. SIMPSON, Th.D., is Dean and Chairman of the Division of Christian Ministries, Fort Wayne (Ind.) Bible College.

FRANCES F. SIMPSON, D.R.E., is Chairman of the Department of Christian Education at the same school.

living transparently on a campus, or writing lovingly in personal correspondence. Whatever the situation, Christian evangelism means witnessing effectively with our whole being to the gospel of God's grace (II Cor. 5:18-20). It is the solemn obligation and blessed privilege of every Christian (Mark 16:15; Acts 1:8).

Obviously, evangelism of youth is the presentation of the gospel to young people. It is the purpose of this chapter to outline effective ways of reaching young people of the twentieth century with the ageless message of salvation through Jesus Christ.

MOTIVATION

Challenge of the Word

Youth evangelism shares basic motivation with other forms of Christian evangelism, namely, obedience to the commands of Christ (Mark 16:15; Acts 1:8), and compulsion of the love of Christ (II Cor. 5:14, 20). In addition, rewards are promised to those who faithfully carry the message (Isa. 52:7; II Tim. 4:5-8), infinite blessing accrues to the person evangelized (James 5:20), and salvation causes rejoicing in heaven (Luke 15:7).

More specifically, however, there are particular reasons for making special efforts to reach *young* people for Christ. The Bible has a special message to young people: "Remember now thy Creator in the days of thy youth" (Eccles. 12:1); in the book of Proverbs Solomon directs much of his wisdom to youth; Paul advises, "Let no man depise thy youth; but be thou an example" (I Tim. 4:12); and John says, "I write unto you young men, because ye have overcome the evil one" (I John 2:13).

There are many examples of youth who served God. At the age of 12, Christ was busy about His Father's business (Luke 2:42, 49); young Miriam served as custodian of Baby Moses; young David smote the enemy-giant Goliath; young Timothy assisted Paul; and young Mark accompanied Paul and other apostles.

Needs of Youth

Another powerful urge is found in the desperate spiritual needs of youth as reflected in their surging doubts and confusion during these years. Such studies as the Mooney Problem Check List, Science Research Associates Youth Inventory, Billett-Starr Youth Problem Inventory, and Lutheran Youth Research Inventory attest to universal concern of American youth over matters of faith and their relationship to God.

Response of Youth

A third factor which should drive Christians to reach adolescents for Christ is the fact that people are more responsive to religious influence during this period than later in their lives.[1] Various studies have indicated that many people come to Christ in their teen years. For example, in a San Diego evangelistic crusade, 75 percent of those in attendance on Youth Night were in their teens and twenties, and 33 percent of those making decisions for Jesus Christ were between 15 and 18 years of age.

> It was youth who trooped to the stadium [Balboa] night after night, sometimes in rain, cold, and wind. . . . It was youth who listened and puzzled and pondered the challenging words of the speaker. And when the appeal was made to receive Christ as Savior, it was youth who responded with buoyancy and eagerness.[2]

Crisis of Youth

However, it is also during teen years that the great "war of independence" is declared; and consequently many Sunday school pupils leave the church. Beyond this, it is estimated that of the more than four million college students in America today, no more than one out of ten attends worship services anywhere.[3] It seems that many young people today are being swept along on the swift "Niagara" current of chaos, confusion and conflict until they are beyond the reach of those who stand on "Redemption Point." What further motivation is needed than the sight of those who have been carried over the brink of the falls into lives of waste, sin and crime? "Judges testify that 97 percent of the youths convicted of crime had no religious training of any sort."[4]

Effect of Reaching Youth

Reaching youth in time provides them with firm anchorage and steady rudder.[5] Not only is a soul saved for eternity and a life rescued from sin and waste, but also a life of blessing and service is made possible. The end and aim of youth evangelism is not only to bring young people into conscious and intimate relationship to Jesus Christ as Saviour, but also to the Holy Spirit as Guide and power for a life of happy and fruitful service. Thus youth must not be taken for what they are alone, but for what they can become by the grace of God. This investment of life in service is illustrated by a group of leaders in Youth For Christ who were converted at the (average) age of 15. These men now spend themselves in seeking to reach teen-agers for Jesus Christ.[6]

---

[1]See chapter 1, "The Challenge of Today's Youth."

[2]"News Report," *Moody Monthly*, LXV:19 (September, 1964).

[3]Stanley Smith, "Your Place in the Campus Ministry," *Key*, III:63 (January-March, 1965).

[4]James DeForest Murch, *Christian Education in the Local Church* (Cincinnati: Standard Publishing Co., 1943), p. 360.

[5]Ted W. Engstrom, "All Out for Youth," *Moody Monthly*, LVII:25 (July, 1957).

[6]Mel Larson, *Youth for Christ* (Grand Rapids: Zondervan Publishing House, 1947), p. 99.

PROBLEMS

To be certain, there will be roadblocks to encounter in taking the path of a youth evangelist. Attention is drawn to two: attitudes of youth toward the local church; and the influences of a secular environment on young people.

Attitudes of Youth Toward the Local Church

Young people are frankly critical of the church program. The following comments, reported in a nationwide survey on teen dropouts made by the Research and Youth Commissions of the National Sunday School Association in 1962, are expressive of the complaints young people have regarding the youth program of the church:[7]

"Not enough church activities or opportunity for teen participation"
"Inconsistency of adults in church"
"Boring, unchallenging lessons and youth programs"
"Sermons on subjects which do not interest young people"
"Youth meetings unplanned and disorderly, subjects uninteresting"
"Socials offer no fun, are not planned, are too juvenile"
"Young people of the church are not friendly"

This study revealed further that of those who dropped out of church, 26 percent were between 11 and 14 years of age, 24 percent were 18 and over, and 50 percent were in the 15-17 bracket.[8] Since 56 percent of the dropouts profess to be Christians, several questions arise: Do they assume they are Christians when actually they are not? Why were not more of them reached before they dropped out? Why is the church losing professing Christians?[9] The picture becomes even darker when it is cited that "85 percent of church membership comes from the Sunday school, but less than 20 percent of the Sunday school finds its way into the church program."[10]

In looking for causes of this teen exodus, undoubtedly it will be discovered that there are weaknesses in the program and personnel of the church which triggered this negative attitude on the part of youth.

Influences of Secular Environment

A second roadblock encountered in the struggle over the souls of teen-agers is composed of intriguing secular influences which lure them from good intentions. These influences include the counteracting effects

---

[7]Roy B. Zuck, "Why Do Teens Quit Church?" *Link*, XI:6 (March, 1963).
[8]Roy B. Zuck, "Why Do Teens Quit Church?" *Link*, XI:5 (February, 1963).
[9]*Loc. cit.*
[10]Herbert W. Byrne, *Christian Education for the Local Church* (Grand Rapids: Zondervan Publishing House, 1963), p. 162.

of secular education, the deadly impact of pernicious literature and entertainment, the discouraging pall of parental neglect, and the withering breath of evil companions and environment.

To the problem-conscious youth worker here is cause for immediate resignation. But to the power-conscious Christian this situation becomes the opportunity for God to show what He can do. For God is not looking for great men, but for men who will let God show the world through them how great He is!

STRATEGY

An attitude of dependence on the omnipotent God to perform the supernatural work of regeneration in such unlikely candidates is the first qualification necessary for becoming a usable tool in the hands of God. Ultimately only God can bring about spiritual birth—and the evangelist must work from this premise.[11] But he must be aware also that God has chosen to use men—prepared men—as tools by which He performs such supernatural works. Thus he must seek that preparation which makes him a sharpened instrument in the skilled hands of the Holy Spirit.

PREPARATION

As a general trains his soldiers before sending them into battle, so the church must prepare its "soldiers" (youth leaders) for spiritual warfare. To prepare for "boot-camp inspection" the leader might check himself against the following list of spiritual and personal qualifications:

Spiritual qualifications	Personal qualifications
Vital relationship to Christ	Pleasing personality
Appreciation for God's grace	Sincere friendliness
Faith in the power of God	Genuine interest in youth
Dependence on the Holy Spirit	Understanding and patience
Utter confidence in prayer	Tactfulness and grace
Radiant, current testimony	Willingness to take time
Love for the souls of men	Ability to communicate with teens
Urgent desire to reach youth	Sensitivity to reaction
Consistent everyday life	Creative imagination
Working knowledge of the Word	Sense of humor

To prepare for his finals at "officers' training school," the leader may wish to evaluate his understanding of and interest in those he is seeking to win. Much help in this may be found in chapters 5-8 of this book. Obviously, the "evangelist" (the one seeking to win another to the Lord) needs a genuine interest in the young person he is seeking to win. The

---

[11]Roy B. Zuck, *The Holy Spirit in Your Teaching* (Wheaton, Ill.: Scripture Press Publications, Inc., 1963), pp. 162ff.

Christian needs to be actively and genuinely interested in and involved with the unsaved teen. And the truth of God must be incarnate in the life of the soul-winner.

Introducing a person to Christ includes having a point of common interest for initial contact, asking specific questions to lead into spiritual conversation, giving a simple explanation of the plan of salvation and providing opportunity for a decision. Several books on personal evangelism, listed under "For Further Reading" at the end of this chapter, outline excellent plans to follow. A favorite set of verses used by many personal workers includes Romans 3:23; 6:23; John 1:12; 3:16. The Holy Spirit may lead along a different path in the actual situation, but it is wise to plan each step beforehand, and let the Spirit lead in any digressions. Since Christianity is essentially a person—Jesus Christ—evangelism is basically an effective introduction to that person.

On the "front line" the youth leader will find it necessary to remind himself often that youth may not need to be entertained, but they need to be interested; the gospel may not have to be highly intellectual, but it must be relevant; a young person may not respond to a program, but he will warm up to a person. The youth leader may discover that a teen-ager wants a God he can trust more than a creed he can recite; a faith to live by, not a feeling to remember; a cause in which to invest his life rather than a safe into which he may deposit it; a powerful Person who conquers his will rather than a complex code which enslaves his soul; a God who can save and deliver him from his sin and rescue him from himself.

Explanation

But to say that the gospel need not be intellectual is not to say that it need not be intelligible. In fact it is the obligation of the evangelist to make clear exactly what the Bible declares to be God's requirement and provision for man's salvation. The gospel must be understood by the mind, desired by the heart, and accepted by the will. This may be seen clearly in the act of conversion which is the voluntary change in the mind of the sinner in which he turns *from* sin *to* God (I Thess. 1:10).

Turning from sin is repentance, and involves:
Intellectual: recognition of sin as personal guilt and defilement
Emotional: heart-sorrow for sin as committed against God
Volitional: renunciation of sin

Turning to God is faith, and involves:
Intellectual: belief in the existence of God and teaching of Scripture
Emotional: personal trust in Christ as the only Savior from sin

Volitional: surrender to Christ and present confidence in Him as Savior and Lord.[12]

Jack Wyrtzen frequently uses the following explanation:

Sin is a disease of the soul, worse than any disease known to medical science. Only the Great Physician can provide the sure cure for sin, but the remedy must be received and applied. After each point has been seen in Scripture, prayer is urged so that the person making the decision may confess his sin, ask for forgiveness and cleansing, and receive Jesus Christ as his Savior.[13]

Decision

Perhaps the most common error committed at this point is to become so involved in an explanation of problems and answers to questions that a consistent movement toward decision is sidetracked. A young person may understand the way of salvation, and desire to be saved, but unless the will is involved in a favorable decision the process is incomplete. As a drowning swimmer must "let" a life-guard save him, so the sinner must turn completely to the Saviour and trust Him for salvation. Once this act of the will is performed in a prayer for salvation from sin, the Scriptures should again be used to provide assurance and confidence.

Follow-up

After spiritual birth has taken place, spiritual growth should be encouraged. One may help a new convert by suggesting a plan for Bible study, by securing a spiritually mature friend who will counsel and take a personal interest, and by encouraging him to join an evangelical church with a vital program for youth. He should be urged to tell others about his experience with the Lord, to consistently read good Christian literature, and to practice obedience to the Word.

One can easily understand the joy and satisfaction which comes to an evangelist when he sees his spiritual children "walking in truth" (II John 4). But such privileges are not limited to a pastor, missionary or Bible teacher.

ROLE OF THE HOME

"Homemade" evangelistic opportunities provide a natural setting for initial spiritual experiences as well as for continuous and practical spiritual growth.

---

[12]George P. Pardington, *Outline Studies in Christian Doctrine* (Harrisburg, Pa.: Christian Publications, 1926), p. 314.

[13]Jack Wyrtzen, "Teen-agers Can Be Reached," *Christian Life*, XIX:16 (October, 1957).

Parental Responsibility

God has given parents the responsibility for the spiritual welfare of their children (Deut. 6:7; Eph. 6:4) and the privilege of influencing the home for Christ (I Tim. 1:5). The family rather than the church is the primary agency for spreading Christianity. There is nothing a person can do for Christ which will count for more than the maintenance of a truly Christian home.[14]

> When young people are brought up in a happy, wholesome, properly disciplined Christian home where the Word of God is read daily, prayer is offered and hymns are sung, and where parents set an example of honor, integrity, love and purity, parents will have little or no difficulty with their children. The idea of giving children free rein so that they won't develop any frustrations is like trying to train a wild colt by turning it loose. Delinquency starts when family life stops.[15]

Today's teens are pleading for spiritual reality in the lives of their parents. They wish parents would maintain regular family worship at home. Perhaps young people have shown keener insight into the weakness of the modern American home than many parents would care to admit. Youth rebel at a kind of scotch tape brand of piety—hastily stuck on when life starts to come apart at the seams.[16]

Church Supplement

The vital role of the home in youth evangelism cannot be played by the church. But the church can supplement the efforts of the home by offering additional opportunities for instruction and decision, for public witness to spiritual growth, and by offering training for parents so that they might more adequately fulfill parental responsibilities. From the church, the home receives inspiration and guidance. From the home, the church receives cooperation and support. From church and home, youth receive a strong foundation.

ROLE OF THE CHURCH

While the church does not provide "professional parents" who can be hired to fulfill spiritual obligations otherwise neglected, nevertheless in each of its agencies there are evangelistic opportunities which supplement those of the Christian home.

Sunday School

This teaching arm of the church has the dual responsibility of providing

---

[14]Albert H. Gage, *Evangelism of Youth* (Philadelphia: Judson Press, 1922), p. 112.
[15]Jack Wyrtzen, *ibid.,* p. 15.
[16]Robert A. Cook, "What Does Your Teen-ager Expect of You?" *Christian Life,* XIX:11 (December, 1957).

instruction for the unsaved so that they learn of the saving grace of God, and instruction for the saved so that they may grow to spiritual maturity. To accomplish this, curriculum materials must be selected which provide opportunities for such teaching, and teachers must be trained to capitalize on such opportunities. Further evangelistic opportunities occur when visits are made into homes by Sunday school workers, and other contacts with members of the family arise in parent-teacher meetings, recreational and social events, and canvassing campaigns.

Vacation Bible School

In addition to opportunities described above, vacation Bible school often reaches many unchurched neighborhood youth who might otherwise be unreached. It also provides more time for teachers to counsel personally with students. Moreover, if an evangelistic message is included as a part of the closing demonstration program, visiting parents and relatives may be reached.

Youth Programs

The training hour (or youth fellowship) provides additional opportunities for youth to invite friends to "their own" meetings. But perhaps the greatest assistance in evangelism is the instruction and practical experience it affords in training Christians *for* personal evangelism. Gospel teams may be formed, instructed, trained, and then sent out to reach other youth for Christ.

Worship and Evangelistic Services

The regular church services offer opportunities for decision and/or public witness, formally or informally, and give teen-agers a chance to bring unsaved friends in contact with a skilled presentation of the gospel. Some churches schedule rallies, retreats, or conferences designed particularly to reach young people. Special decision days afford a time for teens and others to make a decision or give public witness to a previous decision for Christ.

Weekday Activities

Numerous activities are conducted by churches on weekdays, such as clubs, study groups, recreational activities and special interest groups. These can be geared to provide opportunity for personal contact and counsel which Sunday activities may lack. Effort should be made to reach "fringe followers" and unsaved youth and to lead them into a meaningful relationship to Jesus Christ.

Camping

The advantages of weekday activities over Sunday contacts are magnified even more in camping situations because of round-the-clock contact, close living, natural setting, on-your-own feeling, and comparative isolation—all of which provide multiplied opportunities for counseling and winning the unsaved.

Other Agencies

The church library can have an evangelistic influence by providing books on Christian biography, doctrine, apologetics, Bible study, and Christian fiction. Choirs and ensembles have been the means of evangelism both among those participating and those who listen. Then there are a host of extrachurch arms of evangelism at work in the neighborhood and on campus.

Adult workers with youth should be alert to opportunities the Lord provides for them to witness and win non-Christian youth to Himself. For example, one youth leader saw three or four boys playing basketball in the afternoon on a school ground. He asked them if he could play with them. They agreed. After getting acquainted with them while playing ball, he bought them cokes at a nearby drugstore. Then he invited them to attend the Sunday school he teaches. Result: the boys were in his class the next Sunday! All that the church does should be geared for evangelism and edification—to win others to Christ and then build them up in Christ.

ROLE OF YOUTH

While God has placed responsibility for the spiritual life of children on parents, and while it is the business of the church to evangelize the world (including youth), it is also true that most young people are influenced more by their peer group than by their parents or the church. One of the best ways to win youth to the Lord is through the witness of Christian teens.

Importance

The average adolescent is very sensitive to group conformity.[17] Young people often attest to the fact that it was the encouragement of friends their own age which influenced them most in religious affairs.[18]

Young tells why many unsaved youth can best be reached by certain *teens:*

---

[17]Karl C. Garrison, *The Psychology of Adolescence* (New York: Prentice-Hall, Inc., 1946), p. 102.

[18]Roy B. Zuck, "Why Do Teens Quit Church?" *Link,* XI:6 (February, 1963).

... students who are owned and indwelt by Christ are the best possible missionaries for reaching other students. They speak the same "language," have common interests, spend their time together. And of prime importance, the Christian student can in no way be considered a "professional" missionary paid by outsiders to do a job.[19]

Of course this is not to suggest that adults shirk their responsibility of witnessing to youth. Nor does it suggest that in every case young people can reach other young people more effectively than adults can reach teens. But it *is* to suggest that more Christian youth should be witnessing to their peers because of the advantages Young says they possess.

Activities

Creative imagination is the only limitation on the types of purposeful contact a Christian young person can have with an unsaved teen, when evangelism becomes a major chord in his life. He could be challenged to inculcate an evangelistic thrust in various activities, such as these:

Canvassing	Year of voluntary service
Visitation	Fishermen clubs
Open-air meetings	Parent-teacher teas
Mission services	Billboard posters
Vacation Bible school	After-game socials
Christian peace corps	Game nights
Traveling choirs	Hobby or craft clubs
Breakfast clubs	Campus forums
Singspirations	Prayer cells
Gospel films	Camp counseling
Youth centers	Literature distribution
Weekend conferences	Summer mission safaris
Retreats	Campus teas or coffees
Family conferences	Study groups
Gospel teams	Sports leagues
Vacation evangelism	Radio, TV programs
Weekday club activities	Sorority and fraternity meetings[20]

Precautions

Though youth may be very effective in reaching other youth, there are problems to be avoided or solved. Potential soul-winners should be taught and trained before being sent out alone in evangelistic endeavor. When coupled with veteran workers, youth may be called on for personal testimony, Scripture reading or prayer—with great profit to themselves as well as to others. In addition, such limitations as the "same-age" problem,

---

[19]Robert Young, "A Philosophy of Student Work," *His*, XVII:19 (June, 1957).
[20]For information on witnessing on college campuses, see chapter 20, "Reaching Youth in College."

"equal-sinner" problem, "zeal-without-knowledge" problem, can be solved if youth are teamed with more mature and experienced counselors. When properly planned and prepared, evangelistic endeavors of youth can have great results both on the unsaved and in the lives of Christian young people.

Training for Evangelism

An Illinois church held a series of six Friday night training sessions for its young people. The teens learned how to gain spiritual boldness for witnessing, how to know to whom one should witness, how to turn a conversation to spiritual matters, how to present the plan of salvation, how to lead a person to a decision, how to follow up a convert.

Only a few weeks later the entire church rejoiced when several of the young people in the course led some of their friends to Christ.

SUMMARY

On behalf of the millions of young people across America and through-out the world, let the home and church resolve to go about their major business. Whether it is the counsel of a parent, the preaching or teaching of a Christian worker, or the casual conversation of a teen-ager, the most important factor in reaching youth for Christ is the proclamation of the Word of God in the power of the Holy Spirit! It has been commanded. We have been commissioned. Youth are waiting for it to be communicated.

FOR FURTHER READING

EDWARDS, GENE. *Here's How to Win Souls.* Tyler, Tex.: Soul-Winning Publications, 1960.

ELLIS, HOWARD W. *Evangelism for Teen-agers.* Nashville: Abingdon Press, 1958.

ELLIS, JOE. *The Personal Evangelist.* Cincinnati: Standard Publishing, 1964.

GAGE, ALBERT H. *Evangelism of Youth.* Philadelphia: Judson Press, 1922.

HARRISON, EUGENE MEYERS. *How to Win Souls.* Wheaton, Ill.: Scripture Press Foundation, 1952.

LARSON, MEL. *Youth for Christ.* Grand Rapids: Zondervan Publishing House, 1947.

LOVETT, C. S. *Soul-Winning Classes Made Easy.* Baldwin Park, Calif.: Personal Christianity, 1962.

————. *Soul-Winning Made Easy.* Baldwin Park, Calif.: Personal Christianity, 1959.

WOOD, FREDERICK P. *Challenging Youth.* Grand Rapids: Zondervan Publishing House, 1946.

The Bible is extremely practical, intensely relevant, and strikingly contemporary. It has answers to current problems faced by today's young people. Most youth are not interested in the Bible if it is presented as a book of impractical theories and irrelevant concepts. Effective Bible teaching, then, helps young people see what the lessons imply, by way of illustrations and principle, for their lives.

Lloyd M. Perry

11

youth in bible study

MANY SURVEYS of teens' Bible knowledge have revealed an appalling biblical illiteracy among our generation of young people.[1] Many Christian leaders are concerned about this problem and rightly so. For *though Bible knowledge does not guarantee spiritual growth it is an essential step toward it.*

The Bible itself makes it clear that spiritual maturity cannot come apart from the study of God's written Word, applied by the Holy Spirit. "Desire the sincere milk of the Word that ye may *grow* thereby" (I Peter 2:2). "All Scripture is given by inspiration of God and is profitable for doctrine, for reproof, for correction, for instruction in righteousness" (II Tim. 3:16).

God's Word brings salvation (II Tim. 3:15; I Peter 1:23; James 1:18), gives guidance (Ps. 119:105), helps Christians overcome temptation (Ps.

---

[1]See, for example, Joseph M. Hopkins, "Is Your Sunday School Teaching the Bible?" *Christian Herald,* LXXVIII:20-21, 45-47, 67 (April, 1955) , and Robert H. Mounce, "What in the World Are We Teaching Our Children?" *The Standard,* LIV:11, 23 (June 22, 1964) .

LLOYD M. PERRY, Th.D., Ph.D., is Chairman of the Division of Practical Theology, Trinity Evangelical Divinity School, Deerfield, Illinois.

119:11), gives cleansing (Ps. 119:9; John 17:17), and nourishes the soul (Heb. 5:12-14; I Peter 2:2).

It is striking that Hopkins in a survey of one hundred college freshmen discovered "that there *is* a high correlation between knowledge of the Bible and maturity of religious thought and experience. Conversely, ignorance of the Bible and confusion of religious direction and motivation go hand in hand."[2]

Hopkins further observed that "students who are well grounded in the Scriptures tend to be considerably more inclined toward Christian commitment than students who have not had the advantage of effective Bible training."[3]

Thus it behooves Sunday school teachers of junior highs, senior highs, and college-career youth to do their best in enabling teens to understand and apply the teachings of the Scriptures.

However, it is no hidden fact that many young people in evangelical churches do not enjoy studying the Bible. Unfortunately many teens feel that Sunday school classes are irrelevant, uninteresting and therefore boring.[4]

CHARACTERISTICS OF AN EFFECTIVE BIBLE TEACHER

What constitutes a challenging and effective Bible teacher? Several factors may be suggested.

The effective Bible teacher guides young people to discover Bible truths for themselves. Young people are not content merely to sit listening to their teacher report what *he* learned from *his* study of the Bible lesson. They prefer the teacher who realizes that the purpose of the class is to help *them* learn the Bible.

The class that interests teens is the one in which they are learning firsthand through guided discovery what the Bible teaches and what it means to them. This implies that the teacher think of himself as a *guide,* leading his students on a venturesome tour of truth. As such, they become "searchers," looking, sharing, discussing right in class what *they* see in the Bible passage or topic. With this approach in mind, Wald calls such Bible study "the joy of discovery."[5] Our Lord exhorted believers to "search the Scriptures" (John 5:39).

One writer explains this approach to teen Bible study in this way:

2Hopkins, "What Do College Freshmen Think of Life?" *Christian Herald,* LXXXIII:22 (May, 1960).

3*Ibid.,* p. 61.

4Roy B. Zuck, "The Problem of Spiritual Dropouts," *Christianity Today,* X:14, 16-17 (February 18, 1966).

5Oletta Wald, *The Joy of Discovery* (Minneapolis: Bible Banner Press, 1956).

Youth planning a program for their annual Fall retreat were asked
by the adult leader, "Do you want someone to come in and present the
subject, or would you rather dig out the facts for yourselves?" The
response came quickly, "We would rather find out for ourselves." This
involved more time and effort on the part of the adult leader, but it
revealed that youth want to discover for themselves. They are interested
and eager to study the Bible if properly directed. They will come to
church school, carrying their own Bibles, if the hour is spent in a
meaningful study of its contents. They are interested in sharing their
ideas. The leader becomes a guide for their use of the Bible. The class
period must be more than a lecture and a few verses of Scripture read
by the students.[6]

Because the teacher's role is to facilitate learning, he is to be more
than a transmitter of subject matter. He is also to be a resource person
directing learners in the process of inquiry. This leads to a second feature
of good Bible teaching of teens.

*The effective Bible teacher encourages young people to become active
participants in the study of God's Word.* Interest is often directly proportionate to the extent of involvement. If young people are mere spectators
in a class, they soon lose interest.

*The effective Bible teacher enables young people to see the practical
nature of the Bible.* A teacher who stops short of applying the truth does
not fulfill his mission. Understanding the Bible—comprehending it and
accurately interpreting its content—is not to be an end in itself. Instead
it is to be a step toward applying the truth to one's life.

The Bible is extremely practical, intensely relevant, and strikingly contemporary. It has answers to current problems faced by today's young
people. Most youth are not interested in the Bible if it is presented as a
book of impractical theories and irrelevant concepts. Effective Bible
teaching, then, helps young people see what the lessons imply, by way of
illustration and principle, for their lives.

The effective Bible teacher challenges young people to think. Young
people do not appreciate having Bible information spoon-fed to them.
Instead they want to think it through for themselves. Thought-provoking
questions, brain-stimulating discussions, idea-challenging debates—these and
other methods that genuinely stimulate thought are appreciated by teens.

*The effective Bible teacher utilizes a variety of teen-related teaching
methods.*[7] The fact that students remember 10 percent of what they hear,
50 percent of what they see, 70 percent of what they say, and 90 percent

---

[6]F. William Godtfring, "Printed Passage or Your Own Bible?" *Baptist Leader,* XXVIII:
11 (September, 1966). Also see chapter 5, "The Use of the Bible in Teaching," in Lois E.
LeBar, *Education That Is Christian* (Westwood, N.J.: Fleming H. Revell, 1958).

[7]For a more complete discussion of teaching methods, see chapter 24, "Using Creative
Methods."

of what they do, highlights the importance of students seeing, discussing and interacting with Bible truths as well as hearing them.

Discussion, properly led, will stimulate interest and a spirit of inquiry, and also encourage personal expression on the part of the class members. A good class discussion demands preparation on the part of the teacher. The teacher must have the ability to keep the discussion within the confines of the general interests of the class rather than allowing it to be monopolized by an item of interest to a minority.

Various forms of discussion include brainstorming, buzz groups and case studies.

One of the aims of teaching is to help students become individual thinkers and independent investigators. *Research* as a teaching method is especially helpful in developing the thought processes of the students. The teacher assigns to one or more teens a part of the lesson to investigate for themselves. During the class each student has an opportunity to present his findings. Direct investigation of the Scriptures—sometimes called *Scripture search*—is another means of encouraging independent investigation of the Word.

Though the *lecture* method permits a smooth and systematic development of the lesson, the advantages are often overshadowed by its serious limitations. Mere lecturing does not necessarily challenge young people to think, does not give them opportunity to express themselves, and may lead to boredom. When lecturing is used, it is usually more effective if accompanied with one or more other methods such as visuals or discussion.

There are several aids for teaching which, effectively employed, can make class sessions more enjoyable and meaningful.

Maps and pictures help visualize Bible locations and customs. Words, sentences and diagrams on a *chalkboard* can capture the attention of the class. *Slides and filmstrips* serve as useful devices in visualizing Bible truth. *Objects* can attract attention and visually clarify Bible facts.

The *teacher's lesson manual* is designed as a helper for the teacher. It is his guide and counselor—not a substitute for the Bible. The manual should be used to gain information on how best to present Bible information to the pupils in the class. It is best to use the teacher's manual in preparing for the class, but not to use the manual *within* the class session. The effective teacher never allows himself to become a "manual wired for sound."

The *student's manual* should serve as a workbook. It is ideal that the workbook material be completed at home so that (1) the class may make use of its information in the regular period and (2) the students may come to class with a degree of readiness for the lesson. The primary concern of the teacher should not be that the students present orderly and neat manuals, but rather that the students learn to investigate Bible truth on their own. These student manuals should have areas to be completed in writing, suggestions for items to be checked and Bible references to be located, provocative thought questions, and pertinent observations on how the truths apply to life.

A problem common to many teachers is how to get their students to complete the manuals.[8] One senior high departmental superintendent conducts a brief "dedication service" at the beginning of each quarter, dedicating the manuals and the teens' study of them to the Lord. This dramatizes to the students the importance of the manuals. A teacher of junior highs encourages her class members to sign a pledge which states they will endeavor to complete them week by week. In a junior high department, adult workers grade the manuals outside the department room each Sunday during the opening assembly.

The teacher who makes it a habit to refer to questions and comments in the student's manual shows he feels that completing the manual is important. Eventually the students will get the same impression too!

The effective Bible teacher reflects a personal interest in each class member. Teens can quickly sense whether a teacher is genuinely interested in them as individuals. The effective teacher respects each teen, seeks to know his problems and needs, and is interested in helping him in whatever way possible. This means an interest which goes beyond the limitations of the Sunday school class.

Jacobs lists several traits which college students appreciate in their instructors. These same traits should be evident in those who teach the Bible to youth:

(1) Ability to arouse interest and enthusiasm. Depending upon the students, this may imply either skillful showmanship or intellectual excitement and provocativeness.

(2) Interest in students, cooperativeness and sociability, or more positively put, "empathy" for students. . . .

(3) Tolerance and respect for students and their ideas, and giving those that want it an opportunity to get into the act in the teaching process; sympathetic consideration of their objections and complaints.

(4) Clarity in the presentation of the subject matter, an ability to explain and to "structure" the material so that students can easily follow, understand and remember.

Conversely, students dislike teachers who do not plan their courses well, do not explain clearly what is expected on examinations, over-simplify or overcomplicate or are just plain dull. But the blackest trait

---

[8]See Elizabeth W. Crisci, "Lesson-Book-Itis," *Sunday School Success,* XVIII:22-23 (Summer, 1966) .

a teacher can have is disrespect for the students. He incurs acute disapproval if he talks down to them or otherwise belittles them.[9]

FEATURES OF AN INTERESTING CLASS FOR YOUTH

Jacobsen lists several features that college-age young people welcome in a Sunday school class. Many of these suggestions would also apply to junior high and senior high classes:

Honesty. "We don't want to be limited to the answers that are expected of evangelical Christians—we want to be free to say what we really think, and to ask what we really want to know."

Permissiveness. "We want the right to disagree with you without being made to feel that we are morons, backsliders or incompetents. We want to be accepted as individuals regardless of what we believe and think."

Intellectual integrity. "We want help in coming to right conclusions, but we want to make up our own minds after we think through the evidence. If we believe simply because someone tells us to, we'll never be able to defend our convictions or communicate them effectively."

Participation. "We get enough lectures in our classes, and we listen to a lecture [sermon] every Sunday. Give us a chance to ask questions, make comments, and discuss the subject we are studying."

Sharing. "When we have had an experience with God or with His Word, and it is relevant to the topic at hand, we want an opportunity to share it with the group as a means of mutual encouragement."

Problem-solving. "We think our discussions ought to center on problems that are relevant to our life on campus. We aren't too much interested in what is purely abstract and theoretical."

Understandability. "We want truth expressed in a way that is readily understandable rather than beclouded by metaphysical or philosophical terms."

Originality. "We know very well that truth does not change, but we'd surely appreciate its being expressed in language more meaningful than some of the time-worn stereotypes that no longer make people think because they have been used so often and so long."

Validation. "We'd like to examine whatever we are asked to believe, so that we will know why we can believe it. We believe that God is reasonable—didn't He invite Israel, 'Come, let us reason together'? We believe that God's truth will stand the searchlight of honest investigation."

Depth study. "When we are specially challenged by some truth in a lesson, we'd like to sidetrack the curriculum long enough to explore that particular area 'in depth.' "

---

[9]Philip E. Jacobs, *Changing Values in College* (New York: Harper & Bros. Publishers, 1957), p. 80.

Preparation for witnessing. "We'd like to feel that as a result of being in this class we are better prepared to deal with the unsaved, with skeptics, and with other Christians who are spiritually needy."

Fellowship and friendship. "We'd like to feel part of a group linked together by strong ties of genuine Christian love."[10]

WAYS TO ENCOURAGE YOUTH TO STUDY THE BIBLE FOR THEMSELVES

Teachers of young people face the task of how to get teens interested in Bible study. Teens do not appreciate being threatened or driven to study the Word.

Sometimes young people can be encouraged to *read* the Bible by holding contests, requiring regular reading reports, and having projects such as reading the Bible through each year. One soon learns, however, that such techniques do not necessarily guarantee that the teens have actually *learned* Bible content or found information which will be of assistance in daily living. The best way to come to know the Bible is by *studying* it.

Bible study includes searching, meditating, understanding and applying.

"*Search* the Scriptures . . . for they . . . testify of me" (John 5:39). This verb "search" means to investigate and to explore. The Bereans in Acts 17:11 searched the Scriptures daily.

Meditating on the Scriptures means seriously contemplating the meaning and implications of the Word. "But his delight is in the law of the LORD; and in his law doth he *meditate* day and night" (Ps. 1:2).

Wise students of Scripture seek to *understand* what they read. "Which things also we speak not in words which man's wisdom teacheth but which the Holy Ghost teacheth; comparing spiritual things with spiritual" (I Cor. 2:13).

The next step in Bible study is the willingness to *apply* the Word to life. Being a hearer and not a doer of the Word brings self-deception (James 1:22).

But how can a teacher get teens to follow these steps, to actually enjoy studying the Bible for themselves? These are a few answers to that question which may apply to group Bible study as well as individual study:

Encourage teens to read Bible versions in modern-day English and to use special study Bibles. Suggest that students compare Bible lessons in the King James Version with one or more of the following reliable translations:

Norlie, Olaf. *Norlie's Simplified New Testament,* 1961

Phillips, J. B. *The Four Prophets,* 1963

[10]Henry Jacobsen (ed.), *Adult Teacher* (Wheaton, Ill.: Scripture Press Publications, Inc.), XIV:3 (July, 1966).

Phillips, J. B. *The New Testament in Modern English,* 1958

Taylor, Kenneth. *Living Psalms and Proverbs,* 1967

Taylor, Kenneth. *Living Gospels,* 1966

Taylor, Kenneth. *Living Letters,* 1962

Taylor, Kenneth. *Living Prophecies,* 1965

The Amplified Bible, 1965

Verkuyl, Gerrit, editor. *The Berkeley Version in Modern English,* 1945, 1958

Way, Arthur S. *The Letters of St. Paul,* 1921

Young, Robert. *Literal Translation of the Holy Bible,* 1877; reprinted 1953

The works of Phillips and Taylor are especially appealing to teen-agers because of their contemporary expressions. One parent commented that her teen-age boy, a Christian, had little interest in Bible reading *until* he began reading Kenneth Taylor's *Living Letters.*

A number of study Bibles can be examined in Christian bookstores. These Bibles—with explanatory notes, cross references, concordances, dictionaries, topical indexes—can aid teens in their understanding of the Bible.

Have teens search the Scriptures right in class. If a teacher simply tells his students what the Bible says without giving them opportunity to search the Word in class to discover what it says and means and implies for their lives, he can hardly expect them to search the Word during the week on their own. How the Bible is taught in class determines, to a large extent, the degree of interest the students will have in the Bible during the week.

Suggest that teens look for answers to questions as they study Bible portions. The following questions may be asked when a Bible book is being studied:

What can you discover about the author of this book?

Where was the book written?

When was the book written?

To whom was the book first sent?

What problems in the lives of the immediate recipients of the book made the book necessary?

What are the peculiar and repeated words and phrases?

What does the book teach about God?

What is the main theme of the book?

What are some of the key verses of the book?

What are some of the places within the book where major divisions of thought seem to occur?

How would you outline the book?

What are some of the outstanding chapters and paragraphs in the book?

In studying a Bible chapter, paragraph in a chapter, or a single verse, the following questions may be asked:

What is the theme?

How may the contents be outlined?

What words and phrases need definition?

What differences in wording do you note in other translations?

What characters are referred to?

What places are referred to?

What was the purpose behind the inclusion of this portion?

What conclusions can be gained from this portion regarding what we should believe and how we should live?

What do you consider to be the best verse?

Are there any commands we should obey?

Are there any promises we should claim?

Are there any lessons we should remember?

What errors of living should we seek to avoid?

Which words and phrases did you like best?

Interest youth in studying Bible personalities. Young people will discover some answers to life's problems as they see that Bible characters were confronted with similar problems. They will discover that the Bible does not set forth pat answers for all personal problems, but gives timeless principles for living. Many of the answers to teen-age problems will be found as the teacher guides the students in the study of Bible personalities. When studying a Bible character, encourage teens to look for answers to some of the following questions:

What is the meaning of the individual's name?

What is the ancestral background of this individual?

What significant religious and secular crises occurred in his life?

What advantages for personal development were enjoyed by this individual?

What traits of character were manifest?

What important friends did this individual have?

What important influences did this individual exert?

What failures and faults occurred in his life?

What one main lesson in his life is of special value to you?

What influence did the culture of the day and the location where he lived exert on this person?

What important contributions were made by this individual?

If this individual were in our present society, what might be his occupational status?

Engage youth in studying various topics in the Bible. For example, young people can come to understand more about prayer by studying the prayers recorded in the Bible.

Printed Sunday school curriculum materials for youth which include units of study on Bible books, personalities, and topics provide a balanced scriptural diet.

Guide youth in following the basic steps of inductive Bible study. Whether the Bible is studied by books, paragraphs, verses, personalities, or topics, these steps should be followed, usually in this order:

Observation—What does the Bible say?

Interpretation—What does the Bible mean?

Application—What does the Bible mean to me?

Each Sunday school lesson should help young people discover (not just hear, but discover for themselves) what the Bible is saying, how what is said is to be interpreted or understood, and how it relates to their lives.

Provide weekly opportunities for Bible study beyond the Sunday school. The study of the Scriptures should be the primary purpose and function of the Sunday school. Of course a number of churches provide other Bible study opportunities for youth to supplement the Sunday school ministry. Many churches have *released-time classes* once a week during school months for children and early teens. Several denominations have produced study materials for released-time classes (e.g., the Lutheran Church—Missouri Synod, and the Southern Baptist Convention).

Pastors' instruction classes (called confirmation classes in Lutheran churches, and communicants' or catechism classes in some other churches) usually consist of a series of studies for junior highs (sometimes juniors and senior highs too) on Saturday mornings or schoolday afternoons. The courses may include a survey of Bible doctrines, a survey of biblical history and/or denominational church history.

Midweek services can also give teens additional opportunity to study God's Word.

In an Illinois church, senior highs look forward to Wednesday night prayer meetings because they have their own separate study and prayer time, geared to their interests. Junior highs in that same church welcome the practical helps they receive in their midweek studies on how to study the Bible.

An occasional in-depth study in *Sunday evening youth programs* challenges teens to "get into the Book." For example, one group spent the entire hour studying the book of Philemon. Some of the teens wrote a brief modern-day skit based on the book; others discussed the issue of slavery, and still others researched what the book teaches about Christ, sin and salvation. Then the groups shared their findings. They did these things right in the youth program while seated around tables. Another group did an exploratory study of Ecclesiastes.

Introduce youth to out-of-the-ordinary opportunities for Bible study. A church in Dallas, Texas, found that their senior high young people welcomed the opportunity to study Bible doctrines in a special class on Tuesday nights in the home of the youth director. This was a kind of "home Bible class" for teens.

Many young people have been refreshed spiritually as they have taken part in a Christian fellowship group at school. In these groups the teens eat lunch together and then briefly share their observations about a Bible passage they study together.

Christian students in secular colleges often welcome informal Bible studies such as those afforded in fellowship groups by Campus Crusade, Inter-Varsity, The Navigators, or denominational "student centers" on or near the college campus.

Various opportunities for group Bible study such as these help encourage youth to study the Scriptures on their own.

SUMMARY

The way in which some people read and study the Bible resembles the process of sand sifting through an hour glass. The information runs into the mind and out again, leaving nothing behind. There are others who study the Bible after the manner of the action of the sponge. The sponge soaks in and then deposits what it has taken in without any change in the sponge itself. Some study the Bible after the manner in which jelly used to be made with the use of a jelly bag. The berries were put into a bag suspended over a stove until the juice from the berries had soaked through the bag and dropped into the pan below. Only the seeds and skins were left behind. That which was of real value had gone. As some people study the Bible, they allow the real goodness to escape, holding from their study only a few meaningless trick questions or witty impractical quips.

But the real student of God's Word works as carefully as one panning gold. He carefully searches for and sifts that which is of value to him. Such diligence in study will show teens that the Bible is a priceless possession, more valuable than money or food (Ps. 19:7-10; 119:72).

FOR FURTHER READING

BOWMAN, LOCKE E. *How to Teach Senior Highs.* Philadelphia: Westminster Press, 1963.

DOAN, ELEANOR. *Teaching Junior Highs Successfully.* Glendale, Calif.: Gospel Light Publications, Inc., 1962.

ERDMAN, CHARLES R. *Your Bible and You.* Philadelphia: John C. Winston Co., 1950.

GETTYS, JOSEPH M. *How to Enjoy Studying the Bible*. Richmond, Va.: John Knox Press, 1950.

HALL, KENNETH F. *So You Work with Senior High Youth*. Anderson, Ind.: Warner Press, 1959.

HOWSE, WILLIAM L. *Teaching Young People in the Sunday School*. Nashville: Sunday School Board of the Southern Baptist Convention, 1939.

JENSEN, IRVING L. *Independent Bible Study*. Chicago: Moody Press, 1963.

JOHNSON, CARL E. "Attention and Interest," *The Sunday School Journal*, L:8-11 (June, 1965).

MOODY, D. L. *Pleasure and Profit in Bible Study*. Chicago: Moody Press, n.d.

MCGEE, J. VERNON. *Briefing the Bible*. Grand Rapids: Zondervan Publishing House, 1956.

PERSON, PETER P. *The Church and Modern Youth*. Grand Rapids: Zondervan Publishing House, 1953, Chapter 7.

PERRY, LLOYD M., and HOWARD, WALDEN. *How to Study Your Bible*. Westwood, N.J.: Fleming H. Revell Co., 1958.

PERRY, LLOYD M., STRICKLAND, BRUCE, and HOWARD, WALDEN. *Introducing the Bible*. Peabody, Mass.: Powell Publishing Co., 1957.

RIDOUT, SAMUEL. *How to Study the Bible*. New York: Loizeaux Bros., 1947.

SMITH, WILBUR M. *Profitable Bible Study*. Boston: W. A. Wilde Co., 1939.

STIBBS, ALAN M. *Understanding God's Word*. London: Inter-Varsity Fellowship, 1950.

TENNEY, MERRILL C. *Galatians: The Charter of Christian Liberty*. Grand Rapids: Wm. B. Eerdmans Publishing Co., 1950.

THOMAS, W. H. GRIFFITH. *Methods of Bible Study*. New York: Harper & Bros., 1926.

TOWNS, ELMER. *Teaching Teens*. Grand Rapids: Baker Book House, 1963.

TRAINA, ROBERT A. *Methodical Bible Study*. New York: Ganis and Harris, 1952.

VOS, HOWARD F. *Effective Bible Study*. Grand Rapids: Zondervan Publishing House, 1956.

WALD, OLETTA. *The Joy of Discovery*. Minneapolis: Bible Banner Press, 1956.

Worship is more than an outward form, a performance, an opening exercise, an artistic act, a ceremony, a custom. It is an inward experience of those redeemed by Christ Jesus, indwelt by His Holy Spirit, who with Paul can say they "worship God in the spirit, and rejoice in Christ Jesus" (Phil. 3:3).

HAROLD E. GARNER

12

youth in worship

THE NEED AND DESIRE to worship are inherent in youth's nature. Youth will worship someone or something. Each has his god. Someone has suggested that one's god is that person or thing around which his life revolves; that which one prefers above all else; that which demands one's loyalty. To some this is the living God; to others, success, fame, wealth, possessions, personal relationships.

WHAT IS WORSHIP?

The primitive Anglo-Saxon word *weorthscipe* became *worthship* and then *worship,* meaning, according to Webster, "courtesy or reverence paid to worth; hence, honor, respect."

To the Christian, worship is "the honor and adoration which are rendered to God, by reason of what He is in Himself, and what He is for those who render it."[1]

---

[1] J. N. Darby, *The Collected Writings,* Vol. 2 (London: G. Morrish, n.d.) , p. 134.

HAROLD E. GARNER, D.D., is Chairman of the Department of Christian Education, Moody Bible Institute, Chicago, Illinois.

"When given to God, worship involves an acknowledgement of Divine perfections. It may express itself in the form of direct address, as in adoration or thanksgiving, or in service to God; and may be private or public."[2]

Jesus said, "God is a Spirit; and they that worship him must worship him in spirit and in truth" (John 4:24).

> Worship must be of a spiritual nature—must spring from the heart, through the influence of the Holy Ghost: and it must be in TRUTH, not only in sincerity but performed according to that Divine revelation which He has given men of Himself. A [Christian] man worships God in spirit when, under the influence of the Holy Ghost, he brings all his affections, appetites, and desires to the throne of God; and he worships Him in truth when every purpose and passion of his heart, and when every act of his religious worship, is guided and regulated by the Word of God.[3]

Worship is more than an outward form, a performance, an opening exercise, an artistic act, a ceremony, a custom. It is an inward experience of those redeemed by Christ Jesus, indwelt by His Holy Spirit, who with Paul can say they "worship God in the spirit, and rejoice in Christ Jesus" (Phil. 3:3).

The Bible frequently calls believers to worship. "O come, let us worship and bow down; let us kneel before the LORD our maker" (Ps. 95:6). "Worship the LORD in the beauty of holiness" (Ps. 29:2). "The Father seeketh such to worship him" (John 3:23).

The Bible demonstrates worship clearly even though it does not give a systematic outline of all that is involved in Christian worship. It states that God is worthy of adoration and honor, and that believers should express their adoration, respect and love for God in what they say and do. "If any man be a worshipper of God, and doeth his will, him he heareth" (John 9:31).

Both God and Man Involved

Worship involves both God and man. The result of objective worship of God should be the subjective response of the worshiper. It is actually both inward and outward. It must be inward before it is outward. It is first the vertical relationship of a son to his father, then a horizontal relationship of man to man. It is first a Christian young person "practicing the presence of God," then practicing interpersonal relationships in which the presence of God is demonstrated in love and concern for others.

The outgrowth of worship with the lips is the total dedication of self. "With eyes wide open to the mercies of God, I beg you, my brothers, as an act of intelligent worship, to give him your bodies, as a living sacrifice,

---

[2]*Pictorial Bible Dictionary* (Grand Rapids: Zondervan Publishing House, 1963), p. 899.
[3]*Clarke's Commentary* (six vols.; New York: T. Mason and G. Lane, 1837), V:541.

consecrated to him and acceptable by him" (Rom. 12:1, Phillips). Worship is not only an act of adoration and love but an active life of dedication and practical living, as God is loved with all of one's heart, soul, strength and mind, and one's neighbor as oneself (Luke 10:27).

Both Private and Corporate

Group worship is more significant in the lives of youth when it is coupled with regular times of private worship. Adolescents naturally appreciate periods of solitude. When each young person in a youth group dedicates a special time each day to meet with God in a quiet time of Bible reading, meditation and prayer, there is not only the resulting joy of personal fellowship with the Lord but also spiritual food to share with others. Youth leaders should seek to encourage youth to form the important habit of a daily devotional time with the Lord.

The young people of our churches could well be encouraged to pray the prayer of St. Richard:

> Day by day, dear Lord, for these
> three things I pray:
> To see Thee more clearly,
> To love Thee more dearly,
> Follow Thee more nearly,
> Day by day.

Thus group worship services do not take the place of private prayer and Bible reading; they supplement them.

Both Formal and Informal

Informal worship experiences may emerge as a part of one's private devotions or as a result of a group activity such as learning a new hymn, discovering the depth of a biblical passage, planning a service activity, meditating outdoors by a lake shore, on a hike, or at other times of fellowship.

Formal worship in church services, Sunday school, youth groups, clubs, or camps may be based on special themes which meet young people's needs, the departmental unit of Bible study or a special seasonal emphasis of the church year. These services open or close the session, or are within the framework of it. No one time is "best" for group worship. It should be timed when it will be most meaningful.

Other planned worship experiences for teens may include midweek prayer meetings, before-school prayer groups, Thanksgiving Day breakfasts, New Year's Eve watchnight services, weekend retreats (outdoors in summer or indoors in winter), hymn sings, group devotions, campfire fagot services, family worship times.

A youth director of a Midwest church found that the young people who met at the church for prayer every Tuesday morning at seven o'clock were far more spiritually alert and concerned than before.

THE NEGLECT OF WORSHIP

Unfortunately not all evangelical churches are noted for worship. Many "worship services" fail to lead youth to adore the Lord. Often more attention is drawn to the leaders of the service, announcements, special music, than to the Lord Himself.

Many Sunday school "opening worship" sessions in youth departments offer little more than a lively (or not so lively!) song fest, with little time or opportunity for real worship.

> Some church programs with youth—imitating those of schools, clubs, and other agencies—become so crammed full of activities that worship is all but crowded out. A young president announced to his fellow officers at council meeting, "We have so many items to discuss at this meeting that we will just dispense with the opening worship."[4]

Unfortunately a number of Christian youth are apathetic toward church worship services and prayer meetings. Could it be that we have not trained our youth how to worship? Has the idea of worship been relegated to a peripheral issue of the church rather than being made the very *heart* and life of the church? Have we been guilty of encouraging youth to develop the habit of daily Bible reading merely for habit's sake without guiding teens in how to enjoy personal communion with God?

GUIDING YOUTH IN WORSHIP

The superintendent or youth sponsor is the key person in guiding the group to full participation as he helps plan and conduct worship opportunities. The adult must have a vital personal relationship with Christ if he is to be successful in leading others in a meaningful worship experience.

The youth worker must know the reality of personal worship. Young people are quick to spot a phony. And a person can teach effectively only what he knows through experience. Corporate worship must be an outgrowth of a regular daily pattern of private worship. Young people do not usually worship when the leader is spiritually inept.

He must recognize his own inadequacy to produce worship. "Without me ye can do nothing" (John 15:5). He must recognize the adequacy of the Holy Spirit. "No man can say that Jesus is the Lord, but by the Holy Ghost" (I Cor. 12:3).

He must have a spirit of spiritual expectancy. The worker with youth

4Clarice M. Bowman, *Ways Youth Learn* (New York: Harper & Bros. Publishers, 1952), p. 24.

must expect something to happen at the worship service; he must expect to meet God. "Draw nigh to God, and he will draw nigh to you" (James 4:8). The leader must know and feel that the service is important, otherwise it will not be important.

He must know the characteristics of youth in general and his own young people in particular. Young people do not worship as children nor do they express themselves as adults. They are young people, and must worship out of their own youthful experience. The content and conduct of group worship services will be modified by the present interests and abilities of the group. Elements of a worship service (hymns, Scripture, prayer, etc.) should be chosen to fit a theme and to meet the needs of young people. In the average youth group the participants have had varying experiences of worship. Each is an individual with his own present capacity for spiritual response. All may be repeating the same passage of Scripture or singing the same hymn; but each responds in his heart in his own way.

He must be sincere, humble, warmhearted, friendly, reverent, dedicated, Spirit-controlled. The leader can help young people understand the purpose of the worship service and their part in it. He must teach them that an occasional default in carrying out the order of service is unavoidable, even with the most carefully laid plans. If changes occur, the sponsor should instruct the young people to carry on with the service without apology. Knowledge of the sponsor's understanding will help the young person keep his poise.

LEARNING TO WORSHIP

Young people learn by example, instruction and participation.

Adult example is potent—but not enough. Worship must be taught as well as "caught." When the disciples asked, "Lord, teach us to pray," Christ did not refer to His own example, as He might have done; rather He immediately taught them (Luke 11:1-13).

Young people must understand the biblical basis for private and corporate worship. They must also understand the principles involved in preparing and leading worship services. They must have guided experiences in leading those services. Such training may be given during the Sunday school hour in the youth department. By mutual agreement with the teachers, the departmental superintendent (working with the pastor or director of Christian Education) could plan to use the first twenty-five minutes each Sunday morning for a few weeks to teach and train youth in worship. Or a similar series could be conducted during the evening youth fellowship hour. Such projects of study may also be developed for vacation Bible school, camp and special formal training classes. It is advisable to plan such training for the time when the largest number of young people can be involved.

As a result of a thorough discussion of the need in a Midwest high school youth group, their leaders carefully thought through and outlined a course of special studies on worship. These covered several months of instructional and expressional activities.

ELEMENTS OF A WORSHIP SERVICE

Scripture, prayer and music constitute the three basic elements of a worship service.

Scripture

"Seek ye out of the book of the LORD, and read" (Isa. 34:16). "Hear the word of the LORD" (Jer. 7:2).

Inasmuch as "man shall not live by bread alone" (Duet. 8:3), the high points of any worship service are the times when God speaks from His written Word.

The above-mentioned group spent several sessions studying how Scripture can be used in group worship as calls to worship, responsive readings, readings in unison, verse-speaking choirs, silent readings. They selected portions of Scripture appropriate for these uses. Of course they found the book of Psalms to be resourceful in this way.

Prayer

"Pray with the spirit, and . . . pray with the understanding also" (I Cor. 14:15).

To some young people prayer is but a thoughtless repetition of a few memorized sentences or a monologue resulting in subjective blessing. The young people in the Midwest group learned, however, that prayer is to be the quiet listening to and speaking with God out of the inmost depths of the heart. They discussed the importance, meaning and proper form of prayer. They learned that prayer is:

ADORATION (Ps. 111:1)
CONFESSION (Ps. 51)
THANKSGIVING (I Thess. 5:17-18)
SUPPLICATION (I Tim. 2:1-2; I John 5:15)

They also learned that prayer is an affirmation of faith and an expression of one's personal willingness to obey as he renews his vows of dedication to God.

Music

"Praise him with stringed instruments and organs" (Ps. 150:4). "Teaching and admonishing one another in psalms and hymns and spiritual songs, singing with grace in your hearts to the Lord" (Col. 3:16).

Ordinarily nearly one half of a church worship service consists of music.

Music draws young people nearer to the Lord in worship, and to one another in Christian fellowship. It is a unifying medium.

The group learned:

Why and how to listen to the prelude, special numbers and offertory

How to concentrate and think about the words of a hymn in order to sing thoughtfully from the heart

The differences between a hymn (basically centered in God and objective) and a song (basically centered in the first person and subjective)

That light songs and shallow choruses are out of place in a worship service

Offering

In addition to the study of the basic elements of worship the group learned that the offering is also an act of worship for it symbolizes the dedication of self and talents. It is not merely a collection—just a necessary part of a youth assembly—but a part of the stewardship of life.

Visuals

The group learned that simple visuals—such as pictures, bulletin board displays, an open Bible on a table at the front of the room, a globe with a cross—can enhance worship.

Stories, Poetry, Devotional Thoughts, Testimonies

The use of these formed the closing sessions of study. The youth learned that these means are to be used to help young people worship, not to show off talent or to "fill in" time. These parts of the program should be short and relevant.

WORSHIP SERVICES IN THE CHURCH

The next phase of the special learning project was a four-week observation of the morning worship services of the local church. With the cooperation of the pastor, the young people developed a set of questions which guided them in evaluating the services. The questions pertained to the unity of the service, the various elements of worship, the environment, distractions, and participation of the congregation. The pastor met with the young people each week and led in the discussion of their observations. This helped them understand the practical outworking of the principles they had studied.

PLANNING AND CONDUCTING WORSHIP SERVICES

After weeks of study, observation and evaluation, the young people were ready to build their own fifteen-minute worship services. The teens were divided into four groups. Each chose a leader and developed a pertinent theme with music, hymns, Scripture and prayer, all carefully analyzed and woven into a progressive worship service. After all participants were briefed, and an interest center was prepared and the room carefully arranged, the young people presented the service to the entire youth group. The leader then called for an analysis and evaluation. Much helpful discussion followed.

The four groups were asked to present their services for various organizations in the church. For example, one group led in an outdoor worship service at the young married people's Sunday school class outing.

YOUTH DEVELOPING WORSHIP SERVICES

In the youth department of a Sunday school in the ast, the following questions and comments were frequently voiced: "How do you get young people to come for the opening of Sunday school?" "How do you get them to participate in the opening when they do come?" "We never seem to be able to start on time." "Teachers and young people come straggling in after we do start." "There are so many interruptions." "What can we do to make this opening worship time meaningful and worthwhile?" The workers agreed that something had to be done about these problems.

First, the teachers decided on the amount of time for teaching the lesson: thirty-five minutes. The "opening exercises" had represented the most wasted time in the Sunday school hour. A committee of leaders and young people discussed ways to change this. They settled on a timing that would help make each detail of the twenty-five minute assembly a worthwhile venture:

> Special feature—3 minutes
> Instruction—10 minutes
> Fellowship—3 minutes
> Worship—9 minutes

To solve the perennial tardiness problem, it was decided to begin on time with a three-minute "special" (not the traditional singing of the same songs each Sunday). These well-planned specials used the young people's musical talents, a series of filmstrip frames on missions, a short Bible quiz contest. The young people soon learned that the opening minutes of Sunday school were planned with them in mind, and they responded heartily.

A ten-minute period of instruction followed in which two new hymns and a short passage of Scripture were taught. These had been carefully chosen for the departmental worship service. It usually took four weekly instruction periods for the teens to become thoroughly familiar with the new hymns and Scripture. By learning these one month and using them in the worship service the following month, the young people actually memorized them.

Since at the beginning of the class period much valuable time had been wasted in announcements and marking class rolls, it was agreed to care for these items in a three-minute fellowship time in the assembly. Each class could then begin with prayer and the study of the lesson.

At the close of the fellowship time, ushers received the offering. The offering dedicatory prayer and offertory response opened the nine-minute worship service. This was conducted each week by a worship committee of high schoolers who had accepted the assignment the previous month.

Long-Range Planning

Long-range planning is a "must," whether the worship services correlate with the Sunday school lesson or youth program or are based on chosen relevant themes.

In working out the above plan, the leaders met for three two-hour sessions in May to plan for the new Sunday school year which began in October. They outlined a year's program of twelve monthly themes based on suggestions in their teaching manuals, around which the young people later built the complete worship services month by month. For example, for November:

Theme—"We Praise God for Himself"

Scripture—Psalm 138:1-5

Hymns—"Praise Ye the Triune God"

"Praise Him, Praise Him, Jesus Our Blessed Redeemer"

PRINCIPLES TO OBSERVE

The Theme

One central theme should be used throughout the worship service. This theme should determine the choice of hymns and Scripture. Each segment of the service should be selected to bring the young people into communion and fellowship with God—not merely to give overall unity to the theme. The aim is not to choose a great amount of material on a theme, but to encourage genuine fellowship with God through the use of meaningful correlated material.

"A theme is more than a title. A title is descriptive; a theme presents a principle and intimates a purpose. For a Christmas program of worship, for instance, 'The Birth of Christ' would be a title; but 'God's Greatest Gift' is a theme."[5]

The theme provides the path of thought down which one moves to the climax of worship—dedication. For example, in the young person's life

[5]Gerrit Verkuyl and Harold E. Garner, *Enriching Teen-Age Worship* (Chicago: Moody Press, 1950), p. 71.

there is a need to express awe and wonder in the presence of God. A theme of adoration—"How Great Thou Art"—might be chosen as the path down which the young person would move in expressing worship and personal dedication to the God of "wondrous works." Other themes may grow out of other needs: to express dependence on God; to confess sin (based on a keen realization of sin and failure); to give praise and thanksgiving for God's gift of Christ, for Christ's sacrifice on Calvary, for the Holy Spirit's ministry, to acknowledge the guiding ministry of Christ the Shepherd; to intercede for the missionary work of the church or for the success of the young people's outreach; to pray for guidance in the making of decisions, for courage to live for Christ, for strength of character, for victory over temptation.

Scripture

This should correlate closely with the theme. It will preferably be familiar, perhaps a passage that has been previously discussed. It may be used as a call to worship, a prayer, a testimony, thematically interspersed with hymns, offering dedication or response, meditation, or benediction. It may be read by an individual or by the group in unison, or responsively, as a litany, or as choral speaking. It may be read aloud, or at a given time all may read silently.

The Scripture should be assigned early. This will help the reader to familiarize himself with the text and to read it interpretively. Time for preparation will also save the reader the embarrassment of stumbling over unfamiliar words. The reader should practice reading the Bible text aloud. He should be instructed to read clearly and distinctly. This will help to arouse interest and to create a climate in which God's Word may reach the heart. The Scripture should be read from an open Bible rather than from a printed bulletin.

Although many prefer the majestic cadence and familiar wording of the King James Version, other versions may be used in a worship service with genuine profit. Sometimes when reading a short portion of Scripture, several versions may be compared. For example, three young people might read—one using the King James Version and the other two reading identical verses from other versions for a clearer understanding of the passage.

Prayer

Young people should be taught to pray with simplicity, reverence and a sense of God's nearness. They should be instructed to pray in a voice sufficiently loud and distinct to be heard by all present. The subjects for group prayer should represent the interests and concerns of the group. Those not leading in prayer should be encouraged to follow along inaudibly but consciously. Sentence prayers, prayer in unison, silent prayer, praying a Scripture passage, singing a prayer hymn, are all ways to provide variety in the exercise of the spiritual act of prayer.

Instrumental Music

This may be used in a variety of ways in worship: prelude, interlude, special number, prayer background, prayer response, offertory, benediction response, postlude. The music may be played on a piano or organ. Recorded music can also be used effectively when it is well planned.

Since it is natural for young people to come to a meeting in a social mood and engage in friendly conversation, the prelude should (1) be an invitation to attention, (2) serve as a transition from the street to the sanctuary, (3) create a reflective mood of anticipation and meditation, and (4) be a preparation for worship.

In Sunday school the spirit of worship should not be lost by a disorderly dismissal to classes. A well-chosen postlude is helpful.

Hymns

These can be used effectively as (1) a call to worship, (2) with a Scripture reading, (3) with poems, (4) with hymn stories, (5) with the offering, (6) as the conclusion to a season of prayer, or (7) as a benediction response.

The great enduring hymns of the ages need to be learned, appreciated and used by young people as a medium of expression. Hymns selected should be relevant to the theme, meaningful and expressive of young people's feelings. The hymns should be used progressively—they must not only fit the theme but develop it step by step toward the climax.

The text of a hymn must be scripturally and theologically correct. The hymn should have literary value and a message worthy of God, making it worthy of memorization. The music to which the hymn is set must be of a high quality. It should not be flippant or racy, but compatible with the words, appealing and easy to sing.

How a hymn is taught makes a big difference in the way it will be used. Young people need to be guided in the interpretation of what they are saying to God as they sing. The hymn should be analyzed and unfamiliar portions of it taught. Facts about the hymn writer and the background of the hymn will give a greater appreciation of it. Bowman exhorts us pointedly, "Revive hymn singing!"[6]

---

[6]Bowman, *op. cit.*, p. 26.

YOUTH LEADING WORSHIP SERVICES

Since young people are creative they will if sufficiently challenged, throw themselves wholeheartedly into a project. They want to get involved, to participate, to be more than onlookers. They want to discover for themselves. Adult Sunday school leaders in youth departments should appoint their young people to serve on youth worship committees that rotate on a monthly basis, and whose responsibilities are to:

1. Meet a month before the opening worship service is to be conducted.
2. Recognize the importance of Spirit-led preparation.
3. Pray for the Lord's wisdom and guidance.
4. Thoroughly discuss the Scripture and hymns chosen by the departmental workers as a basis for the worship service. Add other familiar theme-related hymns, Scripture and further highlights. Develop an outline. For example, prelude, call to worship, hymns, Scriptur reading, offering response, meditation, special music, benediction, postlude. (Vary the order of these elements from month to month.)
5. Choose participants carefully, remembering that each young person is at a different stage of readiness for worship, and at a different stage of skill development. All must be sincere, warmhearted and friendly, prompt and reliable, humble, recognizing that there must be no self-display. They can by their very attitude create an atmosphere conducive to worship.
6. Enlist participants. Encourage but do not force participation. Some young people may hesitate because they fear failure before their peers. Assure them of the committee's readiness to help.
7. Assign responsibilities early so that there may be sufficient time for preparation. Be specific; be sure that each fully understands his part.
8. Guide and brief the participants. Be sure that all have copies of the service outline and that they are familiar with it. Be sure that all speak distinctly with conviction. Confidence and poise can be developed if the presentation is practiced (except the prayers). In some youth departments this is done in presession time. Be sure that practicing does not become artificial or an end in itself. To avoid this, begin and close each practice session with meditation and prayer.
9. Prepare the worship setting. What young people observe as they enter the room will many times affect their mood. The room should be clean, orderly, well-lighted, well-ventilated, chairs neatly arranged in the order desired and so arranged that the entrance is at the back of the room (eliminating the disturbance of late-comers). The group should not face glaring sunlight streaming through the windows or

bright low-hanging electric fixtures. Meaningless drab pictures and banners should not line the wall.

To draw attention to the theme a simple worship interest center may be placed at the front of the room. It should have teaching value as it silently and sometimes subtly suggests the theme. It may be symbolic—using symbols to which deep meaning is attached. For example, the open Bible may symbolize the centrality of the Word; a globe may speak of the outreach of missions.

SUMMARY

The fundamentals of worship can be taught. The spirit of worship can be caught. The service of worship can be carefully planned. The service itself can be meticulously conducted. Yet all of this will never guarantee true worship. More basic than all the planning is the grateful outflow of the heart to God.

A young person who has had a deep personal experience of redeeming grace—one who understands what is involved in his redemption and who so loves the Redeemer that his heart *must* overflow in adoration and love and his will *must* respond in total commitment to his Lord—experiences true worship.

"The Father seeketh such to worship him" (John 4:23).

FOR FURTHER READING

Abba, Raymond. *Principles of Christian Worship*. New York: Oxford University Press, 1957.

Allen, J. P. *Reality in Worship*. Nashville: Convention Press, 1965.

Armes, Woodson and Sybil. *What Is Worship?* Nashville: Convention Press, 1965.

Barber, Estelle. *Guiding Intermediates in Worship*. New York: Abingdon Press, 1946.

Blackwood, Andrew. *The Fine Art of Public Worship*. Nashville: Cokesbury Press, 1939.

Bowman, Clarice M. *Guiding Intermediates*. New York: Abingdon-Cokesbury, 1943.

———. *Resources for Worship*. New York: Association Press, 1961.

———. *Restoring Worship*. New York: Abingdon-Cokesbury, 1951.

———. *Ways Youth Learn*. New York: Harper & Bros. Publishers, 1952.

Bryant, Al. *Time Out*. Grand Rapids: Zondervan Publishing House, 1961.

Cranford, Clarence W. *The Devotional Life of Young People*. Valley Forge, Pa.: Judson Press, 1940.

Cummings, Oliver deWolf. *The Youth Fellowship*. Philadelphia: Judson Press, 1956.

Dobbins, Gaines. *The Church at Worship*. Nashville: Broadman Press, 1962.

Gudnason, Kay. *Complete Worship Programs for College Age*. Grand Rapids: Zondervan Publishing House, 1956.

MacInnes, Gordon. *A Guide to Worship in Camp and Conference*. Philadelphia: Westminster, 1962.

Massey, James Earl. *The Worshiping Church*. Anderson: Warner Press, 1961.

McDormand, T. B. *The Art of Building Worship Services*. Nashville: Convention Press, 1958.

Miller, Randolph Crump. *Education for Christian Living*. Englewood Cliffs, N.J.: Prentice-Hall, Inc., 1956. Chapter 16, "Methods of Worship."

Pearce, J. Winston. *Come, Let Us Worship*. Nashville: Broadman Press, 1965.

Person, Peter P. *The Church and Modern Youth*. Grand Rapids: Zondervan Publishing House, 1963. Chapter 8.

Raycroft, Coy Herman. *How to Conduct a Worship Service*. Valley Forge, Pa.: Judson Press, 1951. Copyright by F. B. Fordham.

Rinker, Rosalind. *Prayer, Conversing with God*. Grand Rapids: Zondervan Publishing House, 1959.

Schalm, Bernard. *The Church at Worship*. Grand Rapids: Baker Book House, 1962.

Sellers, E. O. *Worship, Why and How*. Grand Rapids: Zondervan Publishing House, 1941.

Stanfield, V. L. *The Christian Worshiping*. Nashville: Convention Press, 1965.

Tozer, A. W. *The Pursuit of God*. Harrisburg, Pa.: Christian Publications, Inc., 1948.

Urang, Gunnar. *Church Music for the Glory of God*. Moline, Ill.: Christian Service Foundation, 1956.

Verkuyl, Gerrit, and Garner, Harold E. *Enriching Teen-Age Worship*. Chicago: Moody Press, 1950.

Wygal, Winnifred. *How to Plan Informal Worship*. New York: Association Press, 1955.

The strength of future evangelical churches depends on the type of leadership training today's teens are receiving.

Ten years from now, who will be teaching the Sunday school classes in our evangelical churches? Who will be the future elders and deacons in our churches? Will these future leaders be dedicated men and women, ready and willing to stand for Christ, and to serve in places of responsibility? Training in youth groups today should help build this kind of leadership.

FERN ROBERTSON

13

sunday evening youth programs

LIMITATIONS OF SUNDAY SCHOOL HOUR

INSTRUCTION IN GOD'S WORD is basic to Christian education, and traditionally the Sunday school hour has been reserved for study of the Scriptures. But many educators admit that the Sunday school does not provide sufficient time for activity and expression required for developing skills in Christian leadership and for exploring life-related topics of concern to youth.

For example, in Sunday school, teens may study Christ's commission, "Go ye into all the world, and preach the gospel to every creature" (Mark 16:15). The students may be motivated to follow Christ in obedience to this command. But they need further time and opportunity to explore questions such as these: "How do I present the gospel to someone who is a follower of another religion?" "What mission fields need workers today?" "How can I discover where God wants me in His service?" "How should I apply to a mission board?" "How can I prepare to become a missionary?" "What missionaries from our church are doing the kind of work I'd like to do?"

FERN ROBERTSON, B.A., is Editor of Youth Programs, Scripture Press Publications, Inc., Wheaton, Illinois.

ADVANTAGES OF SUNDAY EVENING YOUTH-GROUP MEETING

The above questions can best be answered in a time supplementary to the Sunday morning Bible study hour—the Sunday evening (or weekday) youth-group meeting.

Excellent Training Means

The youth group should exist for the purpose of training young people in Christian living and leadership. Of course other church agencies contribute to spiritual training too, such as weekday clubs and camp,[1] but more churches should utilize the youth group as a means of such training.

As subjects related to Christian living and leadership are included in the youth-group curriculum, training is provided. But an unplanned hit-and-miss type of programming can at best meet only a few of the teens' needs.

Properly organized, the group can provide training in leadership skills. This calls for a youth-centered program which gives the teens opportunity for expression as well as for experience in leading.

Expression to Bible truths they have learned in Sunday school can be given through testimonies, debates, discussions, role plays, brainstorming, skits, reports. Service projects planned by youth-group committees also give opportunity for expression and for developing leadership skills. For example, giving a gospel service at a convalscent home helps teens develop skills in program planning and in the use of their musical talents for the Lord.

The purpose and function of the youth group determines the type of leadership to provide, the kind of organization to have, and the curriculum to follow.

Splendid Loyalty Stimulus

The youth group is an excellent means of involving young people in the work of the local church and challenging them to be loyal to Christ and the church. The youth group should be an integral part of the total church program. Thus the missionary projects of the youth group should fit into and be a part of the missionary activity of the local church. No youth organization outside the local church should hold precedence over the youth group of the church.

Definite Maturing Aid

Influences of the screen, the school and the social world tend to draw

---

[1]See chapter 14, "Weekday Clubs," and chapter 23, "Camping and Conference Work."

teens away from Christ rather than toward Him. Teens must swim against the tide if they are to be successful Christians in today's secularized society. Therefore they need instruction and training in stewardship, dating, college preparation, standards of right and wrong, witnessing, personality development, vocational choices. They need opportunity to examine their own Christian faith and test it against the teachings of today's society as well as against the beliefs of other religions and cults. To grow, youth need to discuss these subjects with their peers under the guidance of mature, understanding Christian adults.

Christian young people also need experience in developing Christian leadership skills: to speak boldly for Christ at school, to be willing to serve others by taking an active part in school and community service projects, to serve Christ by being a Christian witness as a school leader. A strong youth training program in the local church can help prepare Christian teens for these leadership roles.

Future Leadership Resource

The strength of future evangelical churches depends largely on the type of leadership training today's teens are receiving.

Ten years from now, who will be teaching the Sunday school classes in our evangelical churches? Who will be the future elders and deacons in our churches? Will these future leaders be dedicated men and women, ready and willing to stand for Christ, and to serve in places of responsibility? Training in youth groups today should help build this kind of leadership.

Will the homes in our communities ten years from now be Christian homes? They will be if our teens are being trained now for Christian dating, marriage and home responsibilities.

Young people must also be learning to be dependable, cooperative and adjustable. One youth leader suggests that teens should develop these leadership qualities: responsibility instead of dependence; cooperativeness instead of competitiveness; a giving rather than a receiving attitude; gentleness, kindness and goodwill instead of hostile feelings; adaptability instead of stubbornness.[2]

Weekly youth meetings, properly planned and conducted, can be a strategic means of providing youth with this kind of training.

VALUE OF ADULT LEADERSHIP FOR YOUTH GROUPS

The pastor and/or director of Christian education are responsible for the training of the youth of the church, but obviously they cannot be

---

[2]Verna Joiner, *What Teens Say* (Anderson, Ind.: Warner Press, 1962), p. 20.

responsible for every youth group and every meeting. This responsibility should be delegated to capable lay leaders who are designated as youth workers and usually referred to as youth sponsors or advisors. Each youth group should have enough sponsors— adults from the local congregation— so that one sponsor is responsible for no more than eight to ten young people.

Supervision

For each age group one adult should be appointed as the head sponsor or overseer of the entire group. He calls sponsors' meetings, delegates responsibility, attends quarterly planning meetings for setting up forthcoming programs, works with the youth-group officers in planning ahead for the year's activities, meets with the officers in regular business meetings, helps in the training of the officers, and reports to the board of Christian education or the Christian education director.

All the youth sponsors should be trained for their important task. They should know the purpose of the youth group, the goals that are set for the group, how the group is organized, how to work with teens in program planning, how to counsel teens in their personal problems.

The pastor and/or director of Christian education and the board of Christian education should be responsible for choosing and training youth sponsors, and selecting youth curriculum materials.

It is usually best to have married couples serve as sponsors so that an effective ministry to both fellows and girls can be carried on. But often a dedicated single person of either sex can do an outstanding work with youth. More than one couple or a combination of couples and single adults should be enlisted if the group includes more than sixteen young people.

Example

Spiritual maturity and a growing Christian life are the prime qualifications for effective youth sponsors. They should be students of the Word, and should be experiencing the joy of the Lord in their daily lives. They must be examples to the young people, and be able to say with the Apostle Paul, "Those things, which ye have both learned, and received, and heard, and seen in me, do" (Phil. 2:8).

Counsel

Youth sponsors should be emotionally mature. Teen-agers are faced with many emotional upheavals. They are tossed by the storms of growing up. Sometimes when teen-agers are going through emotional crises they need an adult to whom they can go for comfort, counsel and security.

At a time when a teen-ager thinks he hasn't a friend in the world, a mature counselor can point him to Christ, the truest Friend.

A love for young people and a concern for their spiritual growth are indispensable assets of effective sponsors. They should be willing to give of themselves. Their time, love, concern, prayers and home must be given unselfishly as they show Christ's love and guidance to the teens in their group.

RESPONSIBILITIES OF ADULT LEADERSHIP

Youth sponsors should organize, plan ahead, and keep the youth group moving toward stated goals. Many of the sponsors' duties are determined by and related to the type of organization the group has.

> The ideal youth sponsor is a coach . . . ; the coach sponsor is one who helps or assists the young people in doing their own programming. Like the athletic coach on the football field, he helps the young people carry the ball themselves. As the coach seeks to inspire and motivate his team to do their best, so the sponsor seeks to encourage and motivate his young people to do their best in the programs they plan. As the coach is on the sidelines more than he is on the field, so the sponsor is behind the scenes more than he is before the group. As the coach, the sponsor seeks to help his young people build confidence in themselves. He coordinates their activities. He counsels with them individually and in a group and seeks to help them improve. He is interested in each person individually. He receives no honor to himself; all the honor goes to the young people who are learning and growing as he helps them do so.[3]

Three General Areas of Responsibility

Organizing and project planning. The sponsors should attend all officers' meetings and plan with the officers for the year's activities. Very often the sponsor is the one who must make suggestions for worthwhile activities such as missionary and service projects, retreats, trips. The sponsor should make the suggestions not as commands but as challenges for the teen-agers to consider. But the teen-agers themselves should be the ones to work out the details and follow through on the plans once they are made. Here again the sponsors serve as coaches.

Program planning. Because many young people do not always know what they need, the youth sponsor should oversee the choosing of good program material. A sponsor should work with each planning group, meeting with them as they plan their programs, and making suggestions when necessary. The sponsor does not necessarily participate in all the youth meetings, but he should always be present. Often the sponsor will find

---

[3]Roy B. Zuck and Fern Robertson, *How to Be a Youth Sponsor* (Wheaton, Ill.: Scripture Press Publications, Inc., 1960) , pp. 13-14.

it necessary to guide a discussion, point the group to God's Word, or give a summary or closing challenge.

Personal counseling. As programs and personal contacts reveal to the sponsors the spiritual needs of individual teens, the sponsors should be available for personal counseling. For example, casual conversation with a young person may reveal that he has a problem in his life. Or program discussions may bring problems to light. The sponsor should invite the teen to meet with him at some specific time when they can be alone. If the sponsor feels incapable of meeting the need, he may suggest the teen make an appointment with the pastor.[4]

It is important that the youth sponsor keep clearly in mind the goal of the youth group—training youth for Christian living and leadership. He should then work toward this goal step by step under the power and guidance of the Holy Spirit.

ORGANIZING YOUTH GROUPS

If the youth group is to build Christian leadership, the young people must learn to lead by leading. The organization of the youth group should be simple and functional.[5] The best organizational plan is that which enables the teens to develop leadership potential, thus making for efficient planning.

One organizational plan is the *committee plan,* with a program committee, membership committee, missionary committee, social committee. The major difficulty in this kind of organization is in program planning. Since the one program committee is responsible for every week's youth program, the bulk of the work of the group falls on this committee. Also program participation is often confined to a few talented individuals, and many who are less talented and less aggressive may be overlooked. Those who do not have an opportunity to participate may lose interest in the group.

Another organizational plan is built around program *planning groups.* The teens are divided into four groups (or more in exceptionally large groups). Each group is responsible for planning one program a month. In addition to planning groups, other committees may be established if necessary. Usually it is best to have each planning group also serve as a committee: the first planning group may also be the missionary committee, the second planning group the social committee.

However, with junior highs it is important to remember that committees should be "short-term" for the duration of the job to be done. For example, instead of having a junior high social committee serve for six months or

---

[4]See chapters 26-28 on counseling.
[5]Also see chapter 9, "Organizing for Youth."

so, choose a committee to work with the adults in planning one social, and then appoint another committee later for the next social.

It is best to assign *one sponsor to each planning group*. Often two couples work nicely in this kind of arrangement. (One of these adults should be appointed head sponsor.)

Many youth groups have experienced these advantages of planning groups:

1. The responsibility of program planning is divided among four groups and does not fall on one committee or one or two young people.

2. The training of all the teens in the group is made possible because *every* young person in the group has an opportunity to help plan and present the programs.

3. Because everyone is involved, more interest is created and attendance growth is stimulated.

4. The sponsors' work load is shared. Each sponsor has more time and opportunity to get to know the teens in his planning group. He can devote his time to personal counseling and to supervising program planning.

5. Healthy competition between planning groups may be generated as each group vies to have the "best" program of the month. The quality of programs is thus upgraded.

The planning-group organizational plan for a group of sixteen or more members may be set up as indicated in the following chart.

Additional members may be added to the planning groups as the youth group grows. From four to ten teens may be on a planning group. If the youth group is larger than forty, then add one or two more planning groups. Or consider having the committees separate from rather than identical with the planning groups.

Membership in planning groups should be rotated every six months in junior high groups and every twelve months in senior high groups.

The officer, planning-group leaders, and sponsors constitute the officers' planning council. In larger groups, where the average attendance is more than forty, the officers' planning council may be enlarged to include chairmen of the missionary, social, membership and service committees. Larger groups may also want to appoint other leaders such as a prayer chairman, a librarian, and a music chairman. Every committee chairman should be given specific responsibilities (in writing) and should be required to report regularly to the officers or sponsors.

The officers' planning council, meeting once a month, plans the schedule for group activities such as missions projects, socials, service projects. The planning council chooses the program subjects and assigns them to the planning groups four weeks to three months in advance. That way

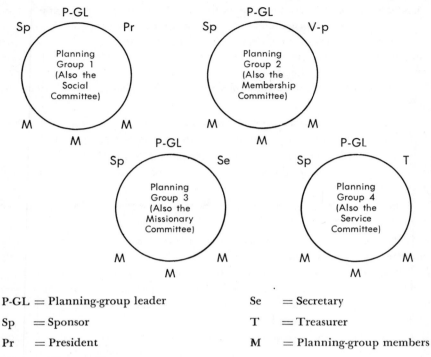

P-GL = Planning-group leader   Se   = Secretary

Sp   = Sponsor   T   = Treasurer

Pr   = President   M   = Planning-group members

V-p   = Vice-president

each planning-group leader knows what program topics his group is responsible for.

Each planning group should meet once or twice, two or three weeks before the date of the assigned program. Some programs require more advance planning than others. Many groups find that the hour before the regular youth meeting is a convenient time for scheduling planning meetings. Others prefer to meet at their sponsor's home on a weeknight. If this is done, the sponsor should be sure the meeting does not interfere with homework, and that the meeting is dismissed at an early hour. Some sponsors have found that a dinner meal in connection with the planning meeting enables them to get to know their teens better.

The planning-group leader should work closely with the sponsor. The planning-group leader's position provides him with a perfect opportunity for learning leadership skills. As he leads the group, he should encourage them to express their ideas. When someone fails to come to a planning meeting, he should first of all exercise patience. When others do not take seriously the things he is trying to get them to do, he should evaluate his own attitude toward those who attempt to lead *him*.

The efficient planning-group leader studies the program ahead of time so that as the group assembles he can lead them in discussing the program, pointing out the aim, overall program plan, and methods suggested for presentation. Then as he works with the group he can lead them in adapting the program to fit the needs of the teens in the youth group. He should encourage the teens to suggest and use their own creative ideas as much as possible. He should try to involve every planning-group member in planning and presenting the program.

The sponsors should pay particular attention to these questions: Are the teen-agers learning first of all that God has a plan for their lives and that their responsibility is to follow His plan? Are they learning to be prompt, faithful and good stewards of the time they use in the planning meetings and officers' meetings? Are they being trained to have good attitudes toward the work of the church, their responsibilities to the Lord, the sponsors, other teens—both Christian and non-Christian? Are they learning to work together in the power and wisdom of the Holy Spirit?

CREATIVE METHODS IN YOUTH MEETINGS

The youth meetings themselves give opportunity for expression and activity. Maximum participation by the teens is one of the keys that unlocks the door to interest and enthusiasm. A steady diet of programs where teens are only spectators will not maintain interest or build leadership within the group. As programs are planned, each teen on the planning group should be given a part in the program. Creative methods, chosen to fit the topic of the meeting, should be used. Some methods that encourage participation are discussions, buzz groups, debates, role plays, brainstormings, panels, symposiums, interviews, skits, monologues, pantomimes, Scripture searches, case studies, circle conversations, reports, quizzes, testimonies, checklists.[6]

Youth Program Curriculum

Zuck discusses various possibilities in curriculum plans for youth groups:

> A curriculum for youth may be established in many ways: (1) Follow a prescribed course of published materials. (2) Determine the interests of the group through an "interest finder," and use only those printed materials which match these determined interests. (3) Undertake projects which relate to Sunday morning Bible study. (4) Use the first Sunday of each month for a "chain" of related programs, the second Sunday for another "chain," etc. (5) Allow the programs to go as they will, according to the whims and wishes of the youth. It is generally considered best to follow, to some reasonable extent, regularly released printed materials, so that there will be some order, or sequence, and so

---

[6]See chapter 24, "Using Creative Methods."

that both overlapping and overlooking of teen-agers' needs may be avoided.

No program material should be used slavishly. Adaptation to local needs is always necesary. Curriculum materials must be altered to suit the present needs of the youth group. Local situations or problems may need to be introduced, some ideas extracted, and other new ideas incorporated.[7]

Some of the needs of young people which should be met through the program topics are how to witness, how Christian teens should conduct themselves on dates, how to find the right life partner, how to find God's will for a life vocation, how to have an effective devotional life, how to study the Bible for oneself, how to be a faithful steward of one's time and talents and money, how to get along with family members, how to have a Christ-centered personality.

A good youth curriculum will include programs on the following subject areas:

1. Witnessing

In a sermon or class, teens may be *motivated* to witness. But beyond this they need to know the principles and techniques of effective witnessing. Many Christian teens face questions such as these: "How can I begin to talk to someone about Christ?" "How can I turn a conversation to spiritual things?" "How can I help a person grow in the Lord after he has received Christ as Saviour?" "How can I meet the differing spiritual needs of my friends?"

Each of these questions needs to be answered for young people—not by just telling them the answers, but by leading them in discussion and study so that they discover the answers. One group of teen-agers, in connection with a youth program, interviewed friends at school on their religious views. The interviewing opened many opportunities for witnessing and gave the teens practice in talking to their friends about Christ.

2. Missions

More than the traditional missionary challenge through speakers and films is needed to train teens for missionary service. Program topics in this area may include various kinds of missionary service (radio, aviation, medicine, literature, education), a history of missions, problems missionaries face, how to prepare for the mission field, theological issues in missions such as the spiritual condition of the heathen.

A vital area, related to witnessing and missions, is world religions and cults. As Christian teens study what people in other religious groups believe, they are better equipped to witness to them. The beliefs of various world religions (Catholicism, Judaism, Islam, Hinduism, Buddhism, Animism)

---

[7]Roy B. Zuck, "Sunday Evening Youth Groups," *An Introduction to Evangelical Christian Education,* J. Edward Hakes, ed. (Chicago: Moody Press, 1964), p. 328.

and of the cults (Jehovah's Witnesses, Mormonism, Christian Science, Seventh-Day Adventism) should be explored so that the young people know why and how the teachings of these groups differ from the Bible.

Many youth groups have found that practical missionary training through missionary projects has helped interest and train their youth for future missionary service.[8]

3. Church leadership

The church leaders of the next decade should be in training today. Subjects that will help train for church leadership are church history, Bible doctrine, church membership, the work of the local church. Through the youth group, teens can learn of the history of their local church and denomination, the doctrines of the church, and the work involved in carrying on the ministry of the local church. Through holding offices and learning to serve in youth programs, young people can learn to become better church leaders. As teens take a vital part in the church, their loyalty to Christ and His work is strengthened.

4. Stewardship

How can the youth group help train young people in biblical stewardship? As teens are encouraged to contribute toward the group's budget, they are trained in the stewardship of money. As the teens work and serve in service projects, they learn to give of their time and talents. Training in the stewardship of time and money is gained as teens in youth programs evaluate their daily schedules and their spending, and discuss with sponsors and other teens how they can best use their time and money to the glory of Christ.

5. Dating and family living

How can leaders train teens for the future responsibility of establishing Christ-honoring homes, and for living for Christ now in their present families? Teens must be taught that dating conduct should be guided by biblical standards. Teens should see that God's Word gives guiding principles for teens regarding questions such as these: "Should I date a non-Christian?" "Should I go steady?" "Should I date someone of another faith?" "Is necking wrong?" "Where can Christian teens go on dates?" "What is a Christian marriage?"

A good youth curriculum includes programs on various aspects of dating, courtship and marriage—programs in which biblical standards are set forth. Only when such training is pursued on a large scale by churches across the land will Christian young people escape the avalanche of moral decay and divorce that threatens young people in today's "new morality."

---

[8]See chapter 16, "Missionary Education of Youth."

6. Vocational guidance

"For what vocation am I best suited?" "How can I know what God wants me to do?" "What kind of training will I need for the vocation I would like to follow?" "What kinds of vocations are open for Christian young people today?" "Should I attend a Christian or a secular college?"

Where can Christian teens find the answers to these questions? Many high schools have good vocational guidance counselors. But few of these counselors direct young people to seek God's will in their vocational choices. Few counselors encourage young people to enter church-related vocations. Few recognize or appreciate what it means for a Christian young person to have a definite call by God for a specific Christian vocation.

Programs on vocational guidance can include how to find God's will for one's lifework, how to determine one's vocational aptitudes, how to establish good work habits, how to prepare for various vocations, and how to serve the Lord in whatever vocation He may lead.

7. Worship

Opportunity for worship should occasionally be included in the youth-group curriculum. A worship service, planned by the teens themselves, may involve the entire group for the youth hour. Worship may culminate a meeting. A worship program may be held outdoors at a specially planned spot. In youth programs teens should be learning what genuine Christian worship is, what are the elements of a worship service, how to plan for worship, and what their response to worship should be. Worship then becomes a reality, a meaningful spiritual experience.[9]

8. Bible study

Unfortunately many young people do not know how to study the Bible for themselves. Youth programs can help teens see how to use Bible study tools, how to use various Bible study methods, how to maintain a personal devotional life, how to know and follow biblical standards for Christian living.

9. Personality development

In Christ's great intercessory prayer, He asked God the Father, "I pray not that thou shouldest take them out of the world, but that thou shouldest keep them from the evil [one]" (John 17:15).

Today among Christians of all ages, including teen-agers, there are many cases of emotional disturbance. This tendency may increase as the time for Christ's return draws nearer and as the pressures of Satan and the world grow greater. Consequently, it becomes more and more important for churches to enter into the task of training Christian young people to cope with anxieties, fears, tensions and pressures that cause emotional disturbances. An emotionally upset Christian cannot be an effective witness for Christ. The youth-group curriculum should provide for finding answers

---

[9]For more on this subject see chapter 12, "Youth in Worship."

to questions such as these: "How can I control my thoughts?" "What is the cause of anxiety?" "What does the Bible say about one's personality?" "Can I be popular and still be a Christian?" "How can my personality be more Christlike?"

10. Stalwart Christian living

Our secular materialistic culture makes it extremely difficult for Christian teens to live for Christ. Teens face a tough world—a world in which morality is considered relative, Christianity is belittled, the Bible is mocked, and faith in Christ is considered unintellectual and nonscientific.

Well-planned youth programs can make a contribution to teens in this area, in helping them to be spiritually stalwart. Obviously insipid youth meetings consisting of little more than choruses and testimonies hardly prepare today's young people for the rigors they will encounter in the secular university, in military service, in a sex-obsessed society.

One church conducts annual special "Senior Seminar Studies" for its twelfth graders. This series, which lasts for several weeks, is designed to prepare these future high school graduates for college living. Subjects discussed include the new morality, the inspiration of the Bible, neoorthodox theology, psychology and Christianity, problems in science and the Bible, witnessing to college students.

The mere reading of parts in a program week after week is woefully inadequate as a means of helping youth know the essentials of Christian life and enabling them to have more than a secondhand faith. But discussions that realistically face the problems of Christianity, situational ethics, racial and other social issues; studies that avoid an obscurantist head-in-the-sand attitude, and that help teens come to grips with significant issues for the Christian in today's world—only these kinds of programs can adequately train teens for stalwart Christian living.

SUMMARY

How can you know whether you are accomplishing anything in your youth group? What are the signs of growth which you should look for in your youth? How can you be sure you are training your young people?

Look for these indications of growth in spirituality:

A growing interest in God's Word
A greater concern about winning the lost to Christ
An increased love and concern for one another
A concern that their conduct pleases Christ

Look for these indications of growth in expression:

Interest in and ability to speak about spiritual things and share
spiritual experiences with one another
Freedom in witnessing to the unsaved

Interest in discussing with the sponsors problems that relate to
  Christian living

Greater poise and confidence in witnessing

Look for these indications of growth in leadership ability:

Willingness to serve in the church program

Faithfulness in fulfilling an accepted task

Ability to cooperate with others, not always insisting on having
  their own way

Initiative and creativity in thinking of work that needs to
  to be done

Perhaps one of the most rewarding events in the life of a youth sponsor
is to see someone whom he knew as an insecure, stammering, self-conscious
junior higher stand before a group of children as an older teen-ager and
teach God's Word, or to see him as a college student clearly presenting
the claims of Christ to a fellow student, or to see him as a young adult
establishing a Christ-honoring home.

"Therefore, my beloved brethren, be ye stedfast, unmoveable, always
abounding in the work of the Lord, forasmuch as ye know that your
labour is not in vain in the Lord" (I Cor. 15:58).

FOR FURTHER READING

AULTMAN, DONALD S. *Guiding Youth*. Cleveland, Tenn.: Pathway Press, 1965.

BRUNK, ADA ZIMMERMAN, and METZLER, ETHEL YAKE. *The Christian Nurture of
  Youth*. Scottdale, Pa.: Herald Press, 1960.

COLBURN, RALPH J. *Secrets of Success in Youth Work*. Redondo Beach, Calif.:
  Christian Workers' Service Bureau, 1956.

CUMMINGS, OLIVER DEWOLF. *Guiding Youth in Christian Growth*. Philadelphia:
  Judson Press, 1954.

GUDNASON, KAY. *Complete Worship Services for the College Age*. Grand Rapids:
  Zondervan Publishing House, 1956.

HOGLUND, GUNNAR. *Better CYF Youth Groups*. Chicago: Harvest Publications,
  1960.

———. "Fact and Fiction for Your Youth Group," *Moody Monthly*, LXII:37-39
  (November, 1961).

———. "Sponsoring a College-Age Group," *Tips*, XIII:4 (April, 1965).

SANTA, GEORGE F. *Youth Leader's Handbook No. 1*. Redondo Beach, Calif.:
  Christian Workers' Service Bureau, 1955.

TANI, HENRY N. *Ventures in Youth Work*. Philadelphia: Christian Education
  Press, 1957.

ZUCK, ROY B. (ed.). *Success Tips for Youth Leaders*. Wheaton, Ill.: Scripture
  Press Publications, Inc.

———. "Sunday Evening Youth Groups," *An Introduction to Evangelical Christian Education*. J. EDWARD HAKES, editor. Chicago: Moody Press, 1964.

ZUCK, ROY B., and ROBERTSON, FERN. *How to Be a Youth Sponsor*. Wheaton,
  Ill.: Scripture Press Foundation, 1960.

Filmstrip: *From Boston to Brownville*, Wheaton, Ill. Scripture Press Publications, Inc. Color, 33⅓ rpm record and leader's guide.

The church that will survive the challenges of this era must develop and adapt to meet the needs of a changing world. For many centuries there was no Sunday school, but, as its value was recognized, it became a universal part of evangelical Protestantism. Now the church needs to take a careful look at its traditional youth program of Sunday school, worship services, training hour and socials to see if conditions require a new dimension in Christian education to meet the needs of contemporary youth. If it neglects to do so, it may develop a high-quality program, yet fail to accomplish its task of reaching, winning, teaching and training youth.

Joseph B. Bubar

14

weekday clubs

ARE EVANGELICAL CHURCHES reaching and holding their young people? Are church leaders providing activities in which teens take an active interest? Is the evangelical church in America meeting the social, physical, emotional, mental and spiritual needs of contemporary youth with its traditional one-day-a-week program? How much value is there in filling youth with biblical thoughts on Sunday and turning them loose for idleness or purely secular activity the other six days of the week?

There is reason to ask these questions in light of a survey taken among teen-agers who dropped out of church. This study, conducted by the National Sunday School Association,[1] indicated that 80 percent of the evangelical churches surveyed had dropouts—with an average of 8.5 dropouts every two years! "If the problem were simply that evangelical churches are not reaching teen-agers, the answer would be relatively easy—go reach

[1]Roy B. Zuck, "Why Do Teens Quit Church?" *Link,* January, February, March, April, 1963.

JOSEPH B. BUBAR, B.D., is General Director of Christian Service Brigade, Wheaton, Illinois.

them! But the problem is more acute than that—one out of six of the teens we are reaching is not being retained."[2]

Some of the reasons given by these dropouts for quitting church were: "Church is boring," "My friends aren't there," "Church adults aren't interested in teens," "My parents didn't encourage me." But the chief reason was: "Not enough church activities for youth!" Interestingly, pastors who also were quizzed rated this reason twelfth in a list of more than twenty causes for teen dropouts.[3]

INADEQUACY OF TRADITIONAL CHURCH YOUTH PROGRAM

Obviously, teen-agers and pastors are not agreed as to the value and need for more youth activities in the church program. Perhaps this explains why weekday youth programs have not been fully accepted as a basic element in American evangelical churches.

The church that will survive the challenges of this era must develop and adapt to meet the needs of a changing world. For many centuries there was no Sunday school, but, as its value was recognized, it became a universal part of evangelical Protestantism. Now the church needs to take a careful look at its traditional youth program of Sunday school, worship services, training hour and socials to see if conditions require a new dimension in Christian education to meet the needs of contemporary youth. If it neglects to do so, it may develop a high-quality program, yet fail to accomplish its task of reaching, winning, teaching and training youth.

What are some of the conditions in mid-twentieth century America that demand reevaluation?

Waning Influence of the Home and Parent Image

The varied pressures of modern society have diminished the strength of the father-son, mother-daughter relationship. Attendance at church, social, civic and business meetings along with increased job responsibilities has reduced the amount of time which parents can spend with their children. Coupled with the rising divorce rate, this often creates a situation where young people have no adult who provides a proper model of conduct, no one to whom they can go for counsel. Too often the formal situations of the traditional church program do not lend themselves to building close adult-teen relationships. But weekday activity programs provide a climate in which close friendships can develop and flourish.

---

[2]*Ibid.*, February, 1963, p. 4.
[3]*Ibid.*, March, 1963, p. 7.

Mounting Influence of Secular Activities

School functions, community affairs and entertainment, usually devoid of positive Christian thought, have combined to produce a secular mentality which does not include God in its framework. Subtly children and teens are adopting an approach to life which leaves God out. But weekday programs teach the essential unity of the Christian life: all of life is spiritually significant, not merely those experiences which occur in church. This is demonstrated, rather than lectured about, through the normal range of teen-age interests and activities which are built into the weekly club meeting and achievement program.

Limitations of Sunday-centered Christian Education

In the interest of reverence for the Lord's Day, most Sunday youth activities do not include the action and adventure that appeal to modern teens. Also, no Sunday program can divorce youth from the thought that Sunday is a special day. The natural thing is for Christian youth to "act Christian" on Sunday. A weekday program helps youth relate what they learn on Sunday to the life they live during the week.[4] To use an illustration from athletics, it becomes the practice field for the "plays" learned on Sunday.

Insufficient Leadership Development

In recent years sound training programs have been designed to appeal to a broad spectrum of youth interests and to give teens training in formal group leadership. However, teen-agers also need to experience leadership responsibility in a direct spiritual ministry to other teens. Some have distinguished the difference between these two as training for *churchmanship* and training for *leadership in real life*. Obviously there is need for both kinds of training. Sometimes leadership involves a formal meeting, but often the setting is an unstructured situation. An effective weekday program builds on the concept of one teen-ager having a direct responsibility for other teens in the program through a system of junior leadership. Thus it meets a vital need in the modern church's training program.

The weekday program built on solid principles can become an integral and valuable part of the evangelical Christian education program. In fact, many have concluded that it has become an essential part of the program already and that the lack of it is the "Achilles' heel" of the church.

THE WEEKDAY ACTIVITY/TRAINING PROGRAM

At this point it is important to clarify what is meant by "weekday activity program." Many kinds of weekday activity have been and are being

[4]*Guidebook for Counselors* (Grand Rapids: Calvinist Cadet Corps, 1962), p. 4.

used by churches to interest youth, but not all of these can rightly be called "weekday activity/training programs." Midweek Bible studies, hobby or craft clubs, catechism classes, released-time classes, game nights, sports leagues or parties may occur during the week, but are not accurately described as "weekday activity programs." Essentially, this Christian educational agency is the local church at work reaching boys and girls and training them for Christian service and mature Christian adulthood within an informal activity- and achievement-centered context.

A weekday activity program that meets the needs of youth will reveal certain principles that are necessary to an effective long-range ministry (see illustration).[5] Five principles make up the hub of the wheel and are central to an adequate approach:

The Lord. The total program must be consecrated to God. It is essential that it be openly identified as Christian, and expressly dedicated to God. Such dedication must be real, effectual and continually affirmed.

The Word. The Bible must permeate the literature, the achievement program, the leadership education system, the actual meeting program and the individual's experience. The written Word must be recognized by leaders and youth as divinely inspired (God-breathed) and authoritative in both life and doctrine.

The effectiveness of this emphasis is measured by the degree to which the individual youth as well as the individual leader learns to discover and understand the truths of the Word of God for himself, to realize their relevancy to his own daily life and to put them into practice. This requires more than parroting a select number of memory verses.

An effective weekday program will encourage a young person to follow a schedule of Bible reading and memorization which is graded according to age and spiritual growth, while at the same time he is exploring nature and reaching out in physical development. This is not to say that the program is "activities plus the Bible." Everything centers in Christ and finds its meaning in relation to the Scriptures.[6]

The church. A weekday program for youth will succeed, bear fruit and endure only if it is a vital part of the local church's program of evangelism and education. Its main purpose is not "to keep the kids off the street," but to reach and disciple them for Christ through purposeful action. Thus, it is an arm of the church rather than a civic effort with humanitarian goals. As such, it contributes to the church's strength and manpower, for many future church leaders will be those who have grown up in the church.[7]

---

[5] *A Key to Effective Christian Boys' Work Worldwide* (Wheaton, Ill.: Christian Service Brigade, n.d.), p. 4.
[6] "The Word of God in the Brigade Program," *Brigade in Action*, Summer, 1964.
[7] *Boys for Christ* (Wheaton, Ill.: Christian Service Brigade, 1962), p. 16.

The leader. Spiritual, mature adult leadership is essential to guide young people in the Christian life. The full effect of such leadership will be realized only as God works in the lives of young people through personal contact with leaders of their own sex who love the Lord and serve Him heartily. Reaching boys for Christ is a man's job; and similarly girls need to see at close range the dedication of devoted women. Such leaders must know their youth in the context of their home and community life to understand them adequately.

The youth. The adolescent should be the focal point of the weekday program.[8] By helping teens through this critical and difficult period of their lives, the church can effectively meet the dropout trend, capitalize on the potentialities of youth for present and future leadership,[9] and meet some of the many social and spiritual needs of teens. Spiritually, the adolescent is seeking a personal faith to be the basis of his life. An adequate weekday program aims to make the Word of God become part of the fiber of life during formative years, forming a foundation for "an authority within" which can be used by the Holy Spirit in building mature adult Christian behavior.

Youth's needs are satisfied and their lives are given direction only as

---

[8] A correlated program for preadolescents may greatly increase the effectiveness of the teen program, as certain foundations are laid and built on in the preadolescent years.
[9] *Boys for Christ,* pp. 25-26.

they meet Christ personally, as they discover spiritual truth through individual Bible study, and as they build a satisfying relationship to the church. Dedicated men and women, themselves active in the local church program, may be used of God to stimulate and guide boys and girls in Christian growth and discipleship.

GOALS OF THE WEEKDAY PROGRAM

Even casual study will show that the aims of the church and the Christian weekday activity program coincide. Because of the variety of programs and organizations, however, each church must compare and evaluate each organization's effectiveness in carrying out the following aims:

Reach the unchurched youth of the community and win them for Christ. This gives the church a positive missionary outreach into its own neighborhood.

Make disciples of young men and women. Some evangelical churches have drifted toward a principle of entertainment in their frantic endeavor to attract and hold youth through the adolescent years.

Many secular and Christian youth organizations are "wringing their hands" in search of some new gimmick that will attract youth. In contrast, Communism appeals to the principles of discipline and responsibility in calling young people to the task of establishing a new world order. Gang leaders waste little time on entertainment when enlisting youth for their causes. They have successfully applied some of the principles of biblical discipleship, while the church has often settled for cheap substitutes. The weekday program that is focused on meeting of the needs of youth will stress discipleship rather than mere entertainment. Of course there is a difference between an entertaining kind of program in which teens are spectators, and activities which, because of their interest and attractiveness, involve youth.

Build a strong relationship between the young person and the church during the critical years of adolescence. At a time when other church activities may be losing their appeal, the teen-ager frequently finds new interest in the church through the weekday program. This is his church and there is a place for him in it. As the teen participates in junior leadership, he recognizes that this is a kind of service that only a teen-ager can do. Now in a new way he feels a part of the church.[10]

Help teen-agers build a value system based on the Scripture. Jesus said, "If ye continue in my word, then are ye my disciples indeed; and ye shall know the truth and the truth shall make you free" (John 8:31-32). As teen-agers meet achievement requirements based on a personal study

---

[10]*Ibid.,* p. 20.

of the Bible and learn to apply the Word to their lives, they experience this truth. Not only does the Word of God make believers free; it builds within them an arsenal of truth to meet the self-centered, pleasure-seeking solicitations and philosophies of the world. In the final analysis, such a system of thought is built as the individual meditates on the Word of God. He cannot buy such convictions from others.

Assist young people in developing skills that will enrich their lives and increase their usefulness to Christ. The task of skill training cannot be left entirely to the public school when the church has a great resource in trained Christian leadership. The weekday activity program provides a unique setting which combines the physical, mental, social and spiritual aspects of life. This helps to produce an integrated view of the Christian life and to help teens develop well-rounded Christian lives.[11]

Train future leaders through built-in leadership and service opportunities. The weekday program is designed to help youth serve Christ while they are teen-agers. As leaders focus attention on the needs and opportunities on God's battlefield, young people will respond to the call to Christian service both at home and "to the ends of the earth."[12]

ORGANIZATION OF THE WEEKDAY PROGRAM

Normally a one- to two-hour weekly session is used to accomplish basic objectives. There are usually three elements involved: (1) a time for physical action, (2) a time for growth in skills and insights, and (3) a time for spiritual challenge and growth. Each of these elements involves "purposeful action," designed to appeal to both the needs and interests of youth, and to be a definite training thrust. An effective weekday program seeks to break down the distinction between *spiritual* and *secular* and helps the young person relate his Christian faith to every area of life. Each part of the meeting should spur the youth to walk with Christ every day of his life.

Leadership of the weekday activity program should come from the local church. The pastor, Christian education director, board of Christian education and a steering committee all play a vital part in guiding the youth work. Dedicated men and women from the congregation form the corps of workers who actually lead the youth. Regardless of the curriculum or content, the effectiveness of the weekday program is largely determined by the quality of its leadership. For this reason it is important to evaluate both the standards for local leaders and the training opportunities available to them, when selecting a particular fellows' or girls' work program.

A number of service organizations have arisen to assist local churches

---

[11]*The Pioneer Girl Guide* (Wheaton, Ill.: Pioneer Girls, 1963), p. 7.
[12]Herbert Cook, "Training Guerilla Fighters," *Brigade Leader,* Summer, 1965, p. 122.

in their weekday ministry. Some of these function as departments in particular denominations; others are independent ministries serving churches of many denominations. The basic goals of these organizations are (1) to provide training for local leaders and churches and (2) to supply them with the necessary publications and program materials. Each organization provides (in varying degrees of quality and efficiency) program literature, training materials, periodicals, leadership conferences and seminars, staff consultation service, and a central office for communications and records.

THE HIDDEN POTENTIAL OF A WEEKDAY YOUTH PROGRAM

It is wise to appeal to the basic interests of those to be reached in a given ministry—adults or teens. It is equally important to insure that the program meets the needs of those for whom it is planned.

A program which is developed solely to meet teen interests (without meeting needs) runs the risk of being both shallow and useless. On the other hand, a program characterized by "We're going to give you this because you need it, whether you like it or not" is likely to meet resistance from teen-agers. A third alternative uses a "false front" program, hiding the Christian content behind a screen of attractions and entertainment. This may bring an impression of success, but teen-agers often see through the disguise and become disillusioned. A better choice is to make the program both useful and interesting, edifying and attractive. This is the goal of a healthy weekday church youth program.

The value of such a program is that it attracts teen-agers to the local church, involves them in interesting activities which may lead to their conversion and provides a setting for the training of those who decide to follow Christ. This is accomplished by building on a program foundation including five basic elements, all of which are both attractive and needful. An examination of these (see illustration on page 229) will reveal how this is accomplished.

Purposeful Action

Action characterizes this approach to youth and often distinguishes it from other aspects of the church's program. An abundance of creative activity is necessary to expand and develop a teen-ager's physical, mental and spiritual capacities. But attractive as it may be, it should never be employed as mere bait. Action *with purpose* is part of a teen's spiritual training and should be included in weekday programs for its own inherent value. One weekday youth organization states the following activity aims: "(1) personal fitness on a high level; (2) self-discipline and sportsmanship; (3) spiritual development of the individual boy in his Christian life and in his relation to others."[13]

The activity element in weekday programs also appeals to the interests of boys and girls. Both sexes want action, although a different kind. Teen-age "boys are interested in active, vigorous games—games involving muscular dexterity and skill, and games involving competition—whereas girls are more interested in . . . sedentary activity and activities involving a restricted range of action."[14] This is why the separation of fellows and girls in most weekday programs is an advantage, not a disadvantage as frequently supposed. By having separate programs, each individual can engage in activity that will challenge his or her skills and keep his or her interest.

Achievement Progress

Adolescents want something to do; they crave new experiences and need the satisfaction of having succeeded at some task.[15] An achievement (or advancement) program is appealing to teens because it satisfies these desires. It also provides a standard to live up to and helps them progress on the road to maturity by means of intermediate goals. A sound achievement program offers the following benefits:

1. Develops skills a teen-ager needs for Christian service now and in the future.

2. Assists a teen-ager in choosing his future vocation by broad exposure to many areas of knowledge.

3. Helps the teen-ager build a view of life that integrates the secular and the spiritual into one viewpoint.[16]

4. Involves the teen-ager in a program of inductive Bible study as a normal part of his everyday life.

5. Teaches a teen-ager to make good use of his leisure time.

These and other important goals work together, meeting the needs *and* interests of teens in a program that is an integral part of the church's ministry to youth.

Group Dynamic

A weekday activity program makes a strong appeal to a teen's yen for companionship. Authorities conclude that an adolescent "needs the sup-

---

[13]*Physical Education in Christian Service Brigade* (Wheaton, Ill.: Christian Service Brigade, n.d.) , p. 3.

[14]Harvey C. Lehman and Paul A. Witty, *The Psychology of Play Activities* (New York: A. S. Barnes & Co., 1927) , p. 106.

[15]Paul H. Landis, *Adolescence and Youth* (New York: McGraw-Hill Book Co., Inc., 1952) , p. 80.

[16]*Boys for Christ, op. cit.,* pp. 44-45.

port, approval and proximity of age mates in order to satisfy the need for companionship."[17] An adolescent needs "someone to go around with, someone to confide in, someone to give him support in his ventures.[18] The basic social needs of teen-agers—special friendships, social adjustments and acceptance by a gang—are met through weekday groups.

A weekday youth program also establishes a peer group of teen-agers with positive Christian standards. The average teen-ager's desire for acceptance by peers creates fear of "deviating from the generally accepted [code and] hesitancy in expressing opinions contrary to common beliefs."[19] Because the weekday program encourages and facilitates the formation of a closely knit Christian social group, Christian teens are strengthened in their walk with Christ because "the dynamic of the group helps each member live for the things he really believes and not be swayed by the predominant peer culture."[20]

One reason the weekday youth program can build on the group dynamic and use it so successfully is that most programs are *not* coeducational. This is true because "the opposite sex is still pretty much of an enigma to the adolescent and each side, uncertain of itself and the other, hesitates to let down its guard."[21] One weekday organization for girls puts it this way: "An all-girl club is in fact a relief from the pressures and tensions of a boy-filled world. . . . [It] is a place where they can cease to seek attention and can be themselves, safely experimenting with new materials and new ways."[22] When a teen-ager is with those of the same sex in the informal setting of a weekday club, he or she can easily build deep friendships and the confidence needed for normal personal development and effective Christian living.

Service Concept

Growing young people reach their greatest potential when they are dedicated to a purpose outside themselves. Adolescents are not as much challenged by a program provided *for* them to entertain them as by one that is *by* them for which they feel responsible. This dedication to service

---

[17]Harold W. Bernard, *Adolescent Development in American Culture* (New York: World Book Co., 1957), p. 452.

[18]M. Malm and O. G. Jamison, *Adolescence* (New York: McGraw-Hill Co., Inc., 1952), p. 121.

[19]Robert Havighurst and Hilda Taba, *Adolescent Character and Personality* (New York: John Wiley and Sons, Inc., 1949), p. 87.

[20]Daniel C. Jessen, *Distinctive Contributions of the Weekday Activity Program to the Teen-age Boy and to the Church* (unpublished Master's thesis, Department of Christian Education, Wheaton College, Wheaton, Ill., 1963), p. 85.

[21]Joseph L. Stone and Joseph Church, *Childhood and Adolescence* (New York: Random House, 1957), p. 288.

[22]*The Pioneer Girl Guide, op. cit.,* p. 16.

is only complete when the object of their service is the Lord Jesus Christ and the spirit of their service is one of serving heartily. As the Apostle Paul puts it, "And whatsoever ye do, do it heartily, as to the Lord, and not unto men" (Col. 3:23).

Leadership Example and Opportunity

Studies have shown that adolescents are "influenced greatly by attractive and visible young adults. The data indicate that . . . the objects of imitation tend to be attractive young adults and successful middle-aged citizens."[23] Though some adolescents will reject the advice and guidance of their parents, they will often accept such help from other adults. Teenagers want to discuss their personal problems with someone whom they respect and trust.

The weekday youth program brings exemplary men and women into direct contact with teen-age boys and girls, helping to meet their needs during these highly formative years. The example that men and women set will help teens form their own standards of behavior.

The weekday youth program also provides a laboratory where young teens can develop their leadership ability. Most of the programs provide a rank rating which encourages improvement of latent leadership qualities and ample opportunity to exercise their abilities.

In the call and training of the disciples, the Lord Jesus demonstrated the basic training element in weekday activity programs. As young men and women have opportunity to accept responsibility for themselves and for others in the service of Christ, they are preparing for the load of leaderships which will come to them in their maturing years.

CONSIDERATIONS FOR SELECTING A WEEKDAY YOUTH PROGRAM

As stated earlier, there are a variety of such programs in existence. This variety makes a wise choice imperative for the church which is vitally concerned in reaching and holding its teens. The following questions should be answered by the committee involved in choosing a program:

1. Is its philosophy scripturally and educationally sound?

2. Is its tie-in with the local church solid and inherent in its structure?

3. Although preadolescents may be included, is priority placed on the adolescent fellow or girl?

4. Is its program adequately developed with a balanced emphasis on all areas of life, with Christ as the integrating core?

---

[23]Havighurst and Taba, *op. cit.,* p. 80.

5. Is the program effective? What success have other churches had in reaching and training teens?

6. Are adequate leadership training opportunities and program materials available?[24]

SUMMARY

If the church dares to face the needs of its youth squarely and courageously, "it will admit that a gap exists between vital Christianity and the average young person's daily life. Will it supply the missing link by an effective bridge, one which takes into account teen-age interests and needs? It cannot isolate itself by pretending the problem does not exist. It must present Christ preeminent in every phase of life—between Sundays as well as on the Lord's day,"[25] and help teen-agers make this come true in their lives.

FOR FURTHER READING

BARNES, JOHNNIE. *The Royal Rangers Leader's Manual.* Springfield, Mo.: Gospel Publishing House, 1962.

Boys for Christ. Wheaton, Ill.: Christian Service Brigade, 1962.

Brigade in Focus. Wheaton, Ill.: Christian Service Brigade, n.d.

COOK, HERBERT. "Training Guerilla Fighters," *Brigade Leader,* Summer, 1965.

Counselor Guidebook. Grand Rapids: Calvinist Cadet Corps, 1962.

HURT, EDWARD, JR., BLACK, FRANK, and GODFREY, NORMAN. *The Ambassador Counselor's Guide.* Memphis, Tenn.: Brotherhood Commission, Inc., Southern Baptist Convention, 1962.

HURT, EDWARD, JR., and BLACK, FRANK. *The Pioneer Counselor's Guide.* Memphis, Tenn.: Brotherhood Commissions, Inc., Southern Baptist Convention, 1961.

JESSEN, DANIEL C. *Distinctive Contributions of the Weekday Activity Program to the Teen-age Boy and to the Church.* Unpublished Master's thesis, Department of Christian Education, Wheaton Colege, Wheaton, Ill., 1963.

Key to Effective Christian Boys' Work Worldwide. Wheaton, Ill.: Christian Service Brigade, n.d.

LANDIS, PAUL H. *Adolescence and Youth.* New York: McGraw-Hill Book Co., Inc., 1952.

Leaders' Handbook. Chicago: Awana Youth Association, 1953.

Physical Education in Christian Service Brigade. Wheaton, Ill.: Christian Service Brigade, n.d.

Pioneer Girls Guide. Wheaton, Ill.: Pioneer Girls, 1963.

RUSSELL, EUNICE. *The Development of Pioneer Girls' Philosophy.* Unpublished Master's thesis, Department of Christian Education, Wheaton College, Wheaton, Ill., 1959.

---

[24]Eunice Russell, "Weekday Youth Clubs," *An Introduction to Evangelical Christian Education,* J. Edward Hakes, ed. (Chicago: Moody Press, 1964), pp. 290-291.

[25]*Ibid.*

STEEVES, DIMMOCK. *Reaching Boys with a Christian Program*. Chicago: Moody Press, 1954.

STONE, L. JOSEPH, and CHURCH, JOSEPH. *Childhood and Adolescence*. New York: Random House, 1957.

"Word of God in the Brigade Program." *Brigade in Action*, Summer, 1964.

ZUCK, ROY B. "Why Do Teens Quit Church?" *Link*, January, February, March, April, 1963.

Leisure, essentially a block of time when feelings of compulsion are minimized, has now become the property of practically every American. Reduction of the necessity to work long hours, proliferation of time-saving devices designed to accelerate living, and the availability of a vast range of recreative opportunities are now within the grasp of most Americans. The "affluent society" is upon us.

The teen-ager, reared in the midst of all this, is not exempt from the beneficial—and detrimental—effects of an abundance of free time. It is the opinion of this writer that leisure itself poses no threat to youth. If leisure is a threat to society, and especially to its youth, it is not because there is so much leisure time (with more to come) but because we lack the creativity to use it constructively.

EDWARD L. HAYES

15

recreational activities

PROBLEM OF INCREASED LEISURE

INCREASE IN LEISURE TIME has been heralded as a blessing to mankind. "Leisure for everybody," writes Neumeyer, "may prove to be the most revolutionary thing that has ever happened."[1] The suddenness with which our society has come upon free time may have taken all of us by surprise. Never before in the history of civilization has leisure been so widespread as it is now. This is especially true in the United States.

It should be remembered that leisure has always been used in one of three ways: (1) idleness, (2) activity lacking constructive qualities, often leading to the deterioration of character, or (3) opportunity for the enrichment and enhancement of life.[2] Thus, it may be assumed that the

---

[1]Martin H. and Esther S. Neumeyer, *Leisure and Recreation* (New York: Ronald Press Co., 1958, 3rd edition), p. 3.

[2]Charles K. Brightbill and Harold D. Meyer, *Recreation* (New York: Prentice-Hall, Inc., 1953), p. 37.

EDWARD L. HAYES, Th.M., Ph.D., is Chairman of the Department of Christian Education, Conservative Baptist Theological Seminary, Denver, Colorado.

239

extent to which leisure is used constuctively depends on how well individuals are prepared for it.

The relationship of leisure and recreation is readily seen. While leisure implies free time, recreation includes any way people spend their leisure. In a broad sense, forms of recreation are free activities, and many leisure pursuits have some recreational value.

The place of recreation in modern society cannot be fully understood unless the significance and development of leisure are also considered. The dawn of leisure is hidden in antiquity. The desire to play seems almost universal. However, two important factors led to the rise of leisure and recreation: the division of labor and the emergence of a leisure class. Stratification of class society led to the emergence of an aristocratic, elite group whose main objective was play. Indulged in by the feudal lords of Europe, leisure time in the Middle Ages took on wider significance. Knights gave tourneys, and gentlemen practiced fencing and hunting, while people in general indulged in a plethora of activity.

The reaction of the churches of the Reformation was a natural consequence. Alarmed by the brutality, debauchery, and unconstructive recreational activities, churches took a firm stand against certain forms of sports, dances, theatricals and betting. This reaction culminated in a general taboo of pleasure-seeking.

The modern era, with technological change and urbanization, has produced more free time than ever before. Leisure of children and youth has increased considerably. The reduction of child labor, the extension of the school period, the deferment of marriage, and the introduction of modern living conditions reducing numerous time-consuming chores have played a part in giving our youth new leisure. Youth find themselves with time on their hands. Relaxed parental control; conflict with traditional standards, prohibitions and taboos; spontaneity and freedom; all combine to aggravate the problem of a young person's use of free time.

THE RELATION OF RECREATION AND THE CHURCH

Leisure and recreation have always been tied closely to religion. The Olympic Games of ancient Greece had their origin in the religious tributes to Zeus. The dilemma between religion and play, as epitomized by the Greek use of play activity *toward* God and the Roman activity *away from* God in brutal and corrupt entertainment, is of long standing. While the Reformation freed churches from unswerving dogmas and intolerances, work was honored and play was frowned on. Idle hands were considered the devil's workshop. And repeatedly churches have spoken out against varied forms of recreation.

But today most churches encourage wholesome recreation. Churches have always been concerned with the way their young people use their leisure hours. The church supper and Sunday school picnic have given way to a variety of acceptable recreational activities. Many churches also provide special recreational facilities, and a growing number of churches have come to consider recreation a major concern of church programming and administration.

A Christian View of Recreation and Leisure

Recreation and Christianity have sometimes been thought to be incompatible. Asceticism has died a slow death. What we need today, in the face of radically upset patterns of life and the proliferation of recreational opportunities for our new-found leisure, is a Christian interpretation of recreation and leisure.

The early efforts of E. O. Harbin to set forth a philosophy of recreation were commendable.[3] Any present or future discussion of the subject must of necessity build on his well-laid foundations.

A Christian interpretation of recreation and leisure can be built upon three premises: (1) the wholeness and sanctity of life, (2) the santification of time, and (3) the necessity of character-building. These premises have little meaning apart from a working definition of recreation.

The Athletic Institute published the outcomes of the Second National Workshop on Recreation and included this definition of recreation, which has now become a classic: "activity voluntarily engaged in during leisure and motivated by the personal satisfactions which result from it."[4] Recreation may be antisocial or social, degenerative or rehabilitative, private or community-sponsored, organized or unorganized, planned or spontaneous, commercial or noncommercial. The by-products that may result from recreation, though not its objectives, are similar to the goals of education and Christian education.[5] Such a comprehensive scope defined by Brightbill may be useful to church leaders.

A Christian emphasis, however, is needed, and the three previously mentioned premises help bring the subject into focus:

The wholeness and sanctity of life. Man is not a splinter. A Christian view of man sees him as created in God's own image, a sinner by nature and choice, potentially Godlike in character through redemption and useful to both God and man. The wholeness of man suggests that what he does to his body, soul and spirit is either harmful or helpful. To the Christian the treatment of the body is always subject to the scriptural

---

[3]E. O. Harbin, *The Recreation Leader* (New York: Abingdon-Cokesbury Press, 1952). See chapter 2, "A Philosophy of Recreation," pp. 19-24.

[4]*The Recreation Program* (Chicago: The Athletic Institute, 1954).

[5]Brightbill and Meyer, *op. cit.*, p. 51.

truth that the body is the temple of the Holy Spirit. Whatever a Christian engages in mentally is to be brought always into captivity to Christ (II Cor. 10:5). Salvation by Christ refers to the total man—not just his soul. Therefore the Christian attaches a sacredness to all of life.

The sanctification of time. Unlike the spaceman to whom all hours are alike, the Christian values time and eternity. Every hour is unique and endlessly precious. The ancient Hebrews attached holiness to time, and Christ taught His disciples to care for eternity. Clear dichotomies do not always exist between good and bad uses of time. Often the distinction should be made between the better and the best use of time. The proper use of time can be spiritually beneficial, therapeutic and thus rehabilitative. Churches can and ought to help people use time properly. Pope John XXIII, in September, 1959, issued a letter in which he stated what can be considered a Christian interpretation of time: "According to the Christian vision of life, all time—working and leisure time—is a value entrusted by God to the freedom of man, who must utilize it to the glory of God."

Quite understandably the Catholic position regarding life and practice centers in church and divine authority. But the Christian, accepting the Scriptures as the only rule of faith and practice, finds no contradiction between a wholesome use of recreation and his faith in Christ. While the Bible denounces idleness and indolence, it is full of expressions of joy, fullness of life, and temperate use of the body and time. The incompatibility of recreation and Christianity is to be found only in the abuse and disuse of leisure time and the human body.

The necessity of character-building. A biblical view of education and recreation places the building of character in an important place in church programming. The older school of thought that character education was the starting point of the regenerate Christian experience is rejected by evangelicals. A Christian view of character growth begins with nurture leading to conversion. Growth in character, character researchers discovered, is not automatic, and the mere knowledge of "rightness" does not produce right behavior. Only the inner dynamic life of the Holy Spirit operating in the believer will produce the fruit of the Spirit, the character traits of a Christian.

The importance of recreation to character-building may be seen in relieving social and personal tensions, demonstrating desirable moral habits, developing a sense of loyalty, and contributing to a sense of values useful to society.[6]

The place of recreation in deterring delinquency cannot be minimized. At

[6]Harbin, *op. cit.*, pp. 25-35.

the same time, it cannot be overemphasized. Brightbill has stated the following:

> To be sure, a youngster cannot be using his leisure constructively (as in wholesome recreation) and get into trouble at the same time. This is not to say, however, that delinquency can be erased, or even substantially reduced, by merely multiplying the number of recreation centers or clubs for youth. It is not as simple as ping-pong versus sin![7]

The Christian use of recreation is not eliminating delinquency so much as it is helping to hold the line against character disintegration by providing for character development, achievement and recognition. The delinquent must first be changed inwardly. This does not preclude the role of recreation in bringing the delinquent to a place where the gospel can be communicated and received.

In summary it may be stated that recreation can provide youth with a wonderful opportunity for an enriched, abundant and satisfying life. Through properly guided recreation, character may be both fostered and displayed. Genuine character change, however, must come from within. Environment, while it may be beneficial and may serve to create a climate for spiritual change, cannot regenerate. "Christian recreation," writes Harbin, "should develop individuals who behave like Christians because of inner controls that 'constrain' them to be good rather than because of outer pressures that compel them."[8]

Recreation and the Church Program

How can recreation be utilized by a local church? Should a church provide facilities on its property for recreation? These two questions are important ones and are rather pivotal to any discussion of recreation and youth.

The old query "How can recreation be utilized in the church?" is misleading. Recreation, properly understood, is not a tool, device, gimmick or bait for the unsuspecting. It is not mere amusement, entertainment, participation in games or sports. To hold such views is to be victimized by outdated interpretations. The church which seeks to use recreation in such ways is guilty of relegating recreation to lower levels. A high view of recreation sees recreation as a natural outflow of recreative activity motivated by enjoyment, personal satisfaction, enrichment of life, character and personality growth, and growth in Christlikeness.

A church would do well to give serious thought and planning to the following considerations: (1) The church has a responsibility to help its young people see that recreation is a necessary element in Christian

[7]Charles K. Brightbill, *Man and Leisure: A Philosophy of Recreation* (Englewood Cliffs, N. J.: Prentice-Hall, Inc., 1961) , p. 272.
[8]Harbin, *op. cit.,* p. 26.

experience. (2) The church has a responsibility to help its young people discern between right and wrong choices of recreational activity. (3) The church has a responsibility to help its young people properly use their leisure time wherever they may find themselves.

If the truth were known, we would discover that often young people's parties, club programs, and attractive facilities are included in the church's program only as bait to lure people to the church. This use of recreation is not Christian. Used as a "hidden persuader," recreation is cheapened and the gospel is viewed as related to and dependent on gimmicks. Evangelism ought to make use of what is supernatural—the winsomeness of the gospel lived out dynamically in a changed life. Let it be perfectly clear, the Christian's whole life should be given to bringing glory to God. This life purpose finds its expression in worship, work and play. The non-Christian will be converted by the power of God. He will be convinced when he sees God's principles embodied in real Christian lives. Wholesome recreational activities, while they may afford a context in which youth may observe the reality of the Christian experience, ought to be an expression of that Christian reality and not a device to be used. The question then is one of motivation—and any use of free time that is forced is not recreation, at least not by this definition.

Should a church provide recreational facilities? This question is discussed more fully later in this chapter but a few guiding principles may be useful here. Those who answer "Yes" to this question argue that since society is corrupt, the church must make every provision for the recreational time of its youth. Consistent with this view is the conviction that the church has every right to provide for the total life of the individual including his recreation. But this viewpoint tends to make the church a "Christian ghetto," with undue demands on a person's time. An extreme position in this regard would hold that the church has the right to bring the member into physical proximity for protection from the evils of society. Such a view, of course, is monastic.

On the other hand, others maintain that it is not the church's business to engage in recreational programming of its members, or to invest in expensive gymnasiums and other recreational facilities. The church must first be itself, it is argued. If it expends effort on tangents it ceases to be a church. But, on the other hand, the provision of such facilities enables the church to become all things to all youth.

Obviously there are weaknesses in both viewpoints. Would it not appear practicable to build a working philosophy of youth recreation on elements from both viewpoints? Certainly a church is to be a church. In so doing it is to help young people be Christians twenty-four hours a day. It is to equip them to do their work as believers in the world. It is to provide for the expressions of fellowship, and in so doing may provide certain facilities to foster this within the life of the church. Wherever possible the church may serve the community needs of youth by providing the finest of facilities within the framework of church policy, purposes and financial ability.

Recreation can become a dynamic part of the church when church members become aware of the need and place of recreation in Christian living. Its role may be fulfilled in enriching human life, developing and deepening fellowship, maintaining good morale, attracting new members, and complementing the whole program.

Programming for Christian Recreation

It has already been stated that recreation does not consist merely of games, sports and social activities. The church recreational leader will make his first mistake by assuming such to be true. Such an activity-centered concept may serve to fill the calendar with fun nights, swimming, bowling and the like, but the recreational needs of youth may not best be served.

Programming for youth recreation must first take into account the basic age groups and sex differences of youth. The young teen (ages 12-14) may lack physical coordination and skill to enter into highly competitive sports. Individual interests and supportive group activities, which do not tend to emphasize sex differences in recreation, are to be fostered. Senior highs and young adults enjoy feats of skill, group activity with both sexes, and vicarious experiences of watching others perform. There is almost no limit to the recreational possibilities of Christian youth regardless of age.

Programming for youth recreation, furthermore, must take into consideration the various categories of recreation. The following classification is often used by recreational leaders:

> Arts and crafts
> Drama
> Games, sports and athletics
> Hobbies
> Music
> Outdoor recreation
> Reading, writing and speaking
> Social recreation
> Special events
> Volunteer service[9]

Another and perhaps more useful classification may be as follows:

> Creative-cultural activities
> Social activities

---

[9]*The Recreation Program, op. cit.* p. 5.

Camping and outing activities[10]
Physical activities
Competitive sports

No single classification is complete. Any arbitrarily devised list of program possibilities in recreation will leave much to be desired, but the reader may benefit from the following partial listing of recreational possibilities:

Creative-Cultural Activities

Arts and Crafts
  Basketmaking
  Bead craft
  Block printing
  Cabinetmaking
  Carving
  Ceramics
  Costume design
  Drawing
  Dyeing and coloring
  Embroidery
  Etching
  Knitting
  Leatherwork
  Metalcraft
  Model airplanes
  Painting
  Photography
  Pottery
  Rug making
  Sand painting
  Sculpture
  Sketching
  Tincraft
  Toy making
  Weaving

  Wood carving
Collecting
  Antiques
  Books
  Buttons
  Coins
  Furniture
  Glassware
  Guns
  Indian craft
  Paintings
  Ships
  Stamps
Drama
  Charades
  Festivals
  Impersonations
  Informal dramatics
  Making scenery
  Marionettes
  Mask making
  Masquerades
  One-act plays
  Pageants
  Pantomimes
  Parades

Play reading
Puppetry
Stage craft
Story plays
Storytelling
Three-act plays
Mental
  Book clubs
  Debates
  Discussion groups
  Forums
  Guessing games
  Lectures
  Mental games
  Public speaking
  Puzzles
  Reading
  Study groups
  Tricks
  Television watching
Musical
  Bands
  Barber shop quartets
  Glee clubs
  Orchestras
  Solo instruments

Social Activities

Banquets
Basket suppers
Beach parties
Carnivals
Conversation
Dinners
Family reunions
Parties
  Birthday
  Block

Costume
Seasonal
Pencil and paper games
Potluck suppers
Scavenger hunts
Table games
  Anagrams
  Caroms
  Checkers

Chess
Crokinole
Dominoes
Monopoly
Parcheesi
Pick up sticks
Picnicking
Ping-pong
Treasure hunts

---

[10]See chapter 23, "Camping and Conference Work."

Camping and Outing Activities

Bait and fly casting
Barbecues
Boating
Camping
Canoeing
Corn roasts
Clambakes
Crafts from native materials
Fish fries
Hiking
Horseback riding
Hosteling
Mountain climbing

Nature study
  Astronomy
  Bee culture
  Birdhouse building
  Caring for pets
  Collecting
    Animals
    Birds
    Bugs
    Flowers
    Minerals
    Mosses
    Rocks
    Snakes

Gardening
Making nature trails
Rifle shooting
Skeet shooting
Skiing
Snowshoeing
Snow tracking
Tobogganing
Trap shooting
Trapping
Walking
Wiener roasts
Visiting zoos

Physical Activities

Archery
Badminton
Baseball
Bicycling
Bowling
Box hockey
Boxing
Croquet
Darts
Deck tennis
Driving
Fencing
Field hockey
Football

Golf
Handball
Horseshoes
Ice skating
Jacks
Kite flying
Lacrosse
Mass games
Ping-pong
Roller skating
Rope skipping
Rope spinning
Shinny
Shuffleboard

Soccer
Softball
Speedball
Squash
Stunts
Tennis
Track and field
Tumbling
Volleyball
Wading
Water polo
Weight lifting
Wrestling

Competitive Sports

Archery
Archery golf
Badminton
Baseball
Basketball
  Foul shooting
  Spot shooting
  Twenty-one
Bowling
Curling
Distance running
  Half-mile, mile, two-mile
  Relay races, baton passing, shuttle hurdles

Fencing
Fly and bait casting
Football
Golf
Gymnastics
Handball
Hockey
  Ice
  Field
Horseshoes
Hurdles
  High, low
Jump events
  Running high jump
  Pole vault
  Running broad jump

Running hop, step, jump
Lacrosse
Paddle tennis
Ping-pong
Riflery
Rowing
Shuffleboard
Skiing
Soccer
Speedball
Squash
Swimming and diving
Tennis
Touch football

Track and field events	Trap and skeet shooting	Shot-put
Sprints	Volleyball	Discus throw
100-, 200-, 440-yard	Water polo	Javelin throw
dashes	Weight events	Wrestling

Organizing for Church Recreation

Most churches have the basis for a recreation program if they have a Sunday school, training hour youth groups, or weekday club programs. Providing for Christian recreation is part of the program of these groups. Some committee or group is desirable, however, to correlate, coordinate and, if need be, increase recreational activities.

The recreation committee. Appointed or elected by the church, this committee would work closely with the board of Christian education and leaders of the various groups working with young people to provide an adequate youth recreation program. The scope of this committee's responsibility would extend beyond youth recreation to churchwide concerns as well.

A chairman should be chosen who has demonstrated his interest in church recreation and who has proven himself faithful in church activities. Membership may be small, consisting of three to six people representing various age groups in the church. Young people of high school or college age may well serve on this committee since much of the church recreational program benefits them directly.

The committee is responsible to the board of Christian education for planning and carrying out the church's recreational program. Some of the duties of the committee might include the following:

1. Making a survey of recreational interests
2. Creating interest in Christian recreation
3. Surveying church facilities to see what areas or rooms can be adapted to recreational activities
4. Planning a church calendar for the year, which provides for balanced fellowship and recreational activities for the year in consultation with group leaders.
5. Promoting an occasional all-church recreational activity.
6. Helping secure proper equipment and provide for the administering of the program utilizing facilities and equipment.

Most churches may not have developed their recreational program to the point that a committee will be needed, so the burden of providing for a balanced recreational diet may rest on the board of Christian education. In the case of the small church, group leaders, adult sponsors and other interested persons may demonstrate their concern for Christian youth recreation by pooling their talents and efforts to see that adequate recreational opportunities are provided under the auspices of the church.

The organization may be minimal or expansive, depending on the size of the congregation, the needs of the youth, community factors, and the will of the congregation.

This discussion has been included because it is felt that any organized youth recreation program ought to be a part of the total church endeavor.

Providing adequate leadership for youth recreation. The need for specialized training of recreational leaders in churches has been recognized only recently. Communities usually make provision for certified recreational leadership to supervise playgrounds and other recreational centers. Any church which views recreation as more than simple social gatherings may do well to consult with community leaders on all facets of recreation.

Leadership training materials for recreational leadership are abundant at the community level. Only recently, however, have churches attempted to provide specialized help to church recreational leaders. Efforts of the Church Recreation Service of the Southern Baptist Convention have been outstanding, and materials prepared under the leadership of Agnes D. Pylant may be helpful to any church which desires to improve its recreational program.

A few larger churches which have well-developed recreational programs hire trained personnel for supervising recreation. But most churches rely on volunteer leadership to work with youth. Every youth worker, teacher, or sponsor ought to appreciate the place of recreation in the lives of youth. Lay workers can receive help in being better recreational leaders. Concerning desirable personality traits, a recreational leader (1) is fair and impartial, (2) plays no favorites, (3) has a good sense of humor, (4) plays and mingles with the group, (5) is interested in each person, (6) possesses a cheerful disposition, (7) is patient, (8) does not "fly off the handle," (9) praises good work, (10) encourages the slower ones, (11) dresses appropriately, (12) is always willing to help, (13) is punctual, (14) is courteous, (15) has varied interests.[11]

But the Christian recreational leader must possess more than these traits. He must know how to help the group grow *spiritually* through the experiences of play and fellowship.

The effect of supervision can do much toward improving the program. Rapport between leader and group calls for a two-way road of respect. The pastor, youth director, Christian education director or other leader in charge of church recreation will help leaders become better leaders with young people if the leader's work is evaluated and adequate assist-

---

[11]H. Dan Corbin, *Recreation Leadership* (Englewood Cliffs, N.J.: Prentice-Hall, Inc., 1959, 2d edition), p. 23.

ance is given. Teachers planning class parties, sponsors and youth officers planning banquets, young people planning meaningful use of free time— all these personnel need resources. Church leaders will seek to be as well informed as possible on the various facets of church recreation.

Building for Church Recreation

Recreational facilities are no panacea for a weak educational ministry with young people. Planning for building space should come only after careful study of the existing educational and recreational programs. "Recreational facilities will not assure an adequate church recreational ministry. Rather, the strength of a program will determine the need for additional facilities."[12]

Principles for providing recreational facilities. The following principles reflect wise use of recreation in the church and may be helpful to church leaders who are planning for new educational and recreational facilities.

1. Every church can and should provide for recreation.
2. Provisions for church recreation should be an integral part of the total educational program.
3. Recreational facilities should be provided only after the needs of the basic educational organizations have been met.
4. Recreational facilities should complement those activities of a wholesome nature provided by the community.
5. Need for facilities should be considered before cost.
6. Cost of leadership must be considered in initial planning. Good leadership is far more important than buildings.
7. The cost of maintenance should be considered in the early planning stages of any recreational building.
8. Whenever possible, plans should allow for later expansion and modification of the facilities.
9. Planners and architects alike should make extensive use of recreational specialists.
10. Planning of any recreational area should take into consideration its use by all the age groups of the church family.[13]

Churches with limited facilities. Some churches with vision have determined to keep expenses at a minimum and utilize community facilities wherever possible. Bowling, skating, swimming and golf facilities are often available to church groups. There are the wide open spaces of public camps

---

[12]Bob Boyd, *Building for Church Recreation* (Nashville: Church Recreation Service and Church Architecture Department, Baptist Sunday School Board, n.d.) , p. 3.
[13]*Ibid.,* p. 6.

and forest preserves, parks and recreation areas which every church can put to greater use.

Churches can utilize parking lots, grassy areas, vacant buildings, basements and church members' homes. A church may not need a gymnasium. There may be facilities available to a church that will be more satisfactory. The following are some possibilities:

1. Larger rooms which may be cleared for parties and table games
2. Wide halls suitable for shuffleboard, portable bowling or ping-pong
3. Small rooms where craft activities may be conducted
4. Below-grade area which might be cleaned up, painted and equipped as a recreational area
5. The sanctuary or an assembly room where religious drama may be presented
6. Residential property by the church
7. The hut built by the church for Scouts or other youth groups
8. Former recreational space which has been misused or abandoned
9. Unused buildings in the area (vacant schools, churches, offices)
10. Outdoor areas:
(a) Grassy areas for volleyball, croquet, horseshoes, archery and badminton
(b) Parking area suitable for skating, badminton, basketball, tennis, shuffleboard, tetherball
(c) Undeveloped church property
(d) Vacant lots for softball, baseball and touch football
(e) Nearby city parks which can be reserved
(f) Nearby school grounds and facilities
(g) Large flat roof areas with sufficient structural support to allow conversion to recreational space

11. Community and commercial facilities which may be used by the church.[14]

Building new facilities. Planning must precede expansion. No extensive recreational building ought to be built until the following questions are carefully considered: (1) Does the church really need a special building, or can other buildings, rooms, or outdoor space be utilized? (2) Is the church merely duplicating what is already available in the community? (3) How will the church staff and supervise the building and its use? The last question is often overlooked. In some ways it is best not to engage in a full-scale recreational program in a gymnasium if it is poorly planned and inadequately supervised. Professional assistance should be sought before any large-scale building of recreation facilities is undertaken.

---

[14]*Ibid,* pp. 4-5.

SUMMARY

The new importance of recreation is dawning. The fact that youth are becoming more and more aware of their tomorrow with its "free time" ought to cause churches to look seriously on recreation not as a cure-all for church ills, or as a necessary evil to "keep young people in the church," but as a force to be utilized for the growth of persons and the glory of Christ.

FOR FURTHER READING

Books

BRIGHTBILL, CHARLES K. *Man and Leisure: A Philosophy of Recreation.* Englewood Cliffs, N.J.: Prentice-Hall, Inc., 1961.

BRIGHTBILL, CHARLES K. and MEYER, HAROLD D. *Recreation.* New York: Prentice-Hall, Inc., 1953.

CORBIN, H. DAN. *Recreation Leadership.* 2d edition. Englewood Cliffs, N.J.: Prentice-Hall, Inc., 1959.

EDGREN, HARRY D. *1000 Games and Stunts.* New York: Abingdon Press, 1960.

EISENBERG, LARRY and HELEN. *Omnibus of Fun.* New York: Association Press, 1956.

HARBIN, E. O. *The Recreation Leader.* New York: Abingdon-Cokesbury Press, 1956.

———. *The Fun Encyclopedia.* New York: Abingdon, 1940.

JACOBSEN, MARION. *Good Times for God's People.* Wheaton, Ill.: Scripture Press Foundation, 1952.

KAPLAN, MAX. *Leisure in America: A Social Inquiry.* New York: John Wiley & Sons, Inc., 1960.

NEUMEYER, MARTIN H. and ESTHER S. *Leisure and Recreation.* 3d edition. New York: Ronald Press Co., 1958.

PYLANT, AGNES D. *Church Recreation Program.* Chicago: Athletic Institute, 1954.

Recreation and the Church. New York: National Recreation Association, 1946.

Significant journals

Church Recreation. Published by Department of Church Recreation, Southern Baptist Convention, 127 Ninth Avenue, North, Nashville, Tenn. 37203.

Recreation. Published by National Recreation Association, 8 West Eighth Street, New York, N.Y. 10011.

Journal of Health, Physical Education and Recreation. Published by American Association for Health, Physical Education and Recreation, National Education Association, 120 16th Street N.W., Washington, D.C. 20006.

Sources of information

Athletic Institute, 209 South State Street, Chicago, Ill. 60604.

Church Recreation Service, Baptist Sunday School Board, 127 Ninth Avenue, North, Nashville, Tenn. 37203.

National Recreation Association, 8 West Eighth Street, New York, N.Y. 10011.

An awareness of the needs of given mission fields, an understanding of the work of specific missionaries from the church or mission board, and a recognition of the ever-present need of additional workers do not necessarily constitute missionary education, particularly with young people. An occasional presentation of missionary facts is one small facet of what churches should be doing to teach missions to their young people.

William V. Bynum

16

missionary education of youth

To assert that any church is slighting its missionary obligation in relation to the educating of its people would make some congregations irate. Is the church not giving missions its proper place with the observance of a missionary Sunday every month? And doesn't the women's missionary society meet regularly? This is an all too prevalent attitude toward missionary education in the local church.

The Place of Missionary Education with Young People

The great missionary task of the church is evangelistic—bringing others into a personal relationship with the Lord Jesus Christ. As an examination of the Word of God reveals, all believers (adults and youth) are to be witnesses for Christ. The local church exists for the twofold purpose of winning people to Christ and helping believers become grounded in the Word, built up in the faith, and skilled in witnessing and service.

William Bynum, D.R.E., is Chairman of the Division of Bible Studies, Biola College, and Professor of Christian Education, Talbot Theological Seminary, La Mirada, California.

The program of the church must therefore include missionary education in order to encourage and challenge young people to witness by life and by verbal testimony.

Christian youth should be encouraged to share their experience in Christ in a number of ways: by a life filled with the compassion of Christ; by a practical, workable knowledge of the Word of God which fortifies this experience and gives depth to that witness; and by a desire to see this experience duplicated in other lives as they give forth the good news.

This missionary spirit is noted in three major aspects of a Christian young person's life: (1) conversion, resulting from someone else witnessing to him; (2) awareness of the will of God—a plan and purpose for his life; and (3) obedience to the will of God, expressed in service. Being in the will of God means being, in a sense, a missionary regardless of one's geographical location.

The Challenge of Missionary Education for Young People

But why should we be concerned with providing missionary education for young people?

1. Because of the nature of adolescence. Many of the physical, mental, emotional, social and spiritual characteristics of young people can be channeled into missionary interests, and many of the needs of teens can be met by an active missionary educational program. For example, junior highs are altruistic—concerned for the needs of others. This means that junior highs can readily become interested in and burdened about the spiritual needs of people abroad and of those apart from Christ in their local schools.

Furthermore it is a fact that a large proportion of missionaries respond to the call to missionary service while in their teen years.[1]

2. A close examination of world conditions leaves little doubt as to the necessity of such an educational program for young people. Newby states that the world situation in which youth find themselves is characterized by change, confusion and consternation.[2] Churches should help young people see that answers to these world problems and to their own problems are found in Christ. As teens' lives are changed by Christ, the missionary program of the church should instill within youth the desire to make Christ the Answer known to others around the world.

3. The indigenous principle suggests that missionary education is needed by today's teens. The missionary endeavor abroad has been operating successfully under the "indigenous church" concept for a number of years

---

[1]See chapter 1, p. 18.
[2]Donald O. Newby, "The Churches' Ministry to Youth," *Religious Education: A Comprehensive Survey*, Marvin J. Taylor, ed. (Nashville: Abingdon Press, 1960), pp. 124-25.

now. If this philosophy has strengthened national churches by developing believers and spreading the gospel, surely the same philosophy will work here "at home." If we encourage young people in their various church-related activities to be self-supporting, self-propagating and self-governing, the missionary concept will not be so foreign to them.

Applying the indigenous principle to our work with youth involves making missions an integral part of the church's program, and not an appendage to it. When we encourage young people to plan and execute means whereby the missionary spirit can be manifest, we are following the indigenous principle of self-propagation. As we do this, missions may become the permeating spirit of the church and not just an afterthought.

4. Missionary activity for young people is important because they learn best through involvement. Bowman points up a number of experiences by which youth learn:

> Experience and common sense suggest that when the learner is merely listening to words someone says, he may be virtually inactive; he may respond but tentatively. . . . On a higher level of efficacy as a method of learning (because it involves the learner more fully himself) is *observation* on his part—seeing, either through pictures or going to see for himself. Yet even here the learner may remain merely a spectator. On a much higher level of effectiveness, because the learner is involved more deeply, is learning through *vicarious experience*. The learner moves over from the role of spectator to feeling with a person or situation. On the highest level, because potentially involving the learner more fully, is firsthand *direct experiencing*.[3]

Learning involves (1) knowledge, (2) appreciation, inspiration and challenge, and (3) active, outward conduct-response to knowledge gained and inspiration received. A vital program of missionary education should provide for each of these. All three are necessary if Christianity is to be "learned" in the fullest sense. Likewise the learning of missions requires all three. This does not suggest that any one of these is more vital than the other but that each has its essential place in effective teaching and learning.

Objectives and Principles of Missionary Education with Youth

The following goals are basic to a successful missionary program with youth:

1. Developing in youth an awareness of the purpose and plan of God for their lives. A knowledge of this plan can help lead teens to follow God's will in obedient service.
2. Helping teens know and practice the great objective of the church by witnessing for Christ by lip and life.
3. Leading young people into a concern for the spiritual needs of others.

---

[3]Clarice M. Bowman, *Ways Youth Learn* (New York: Harper & Bros. Publishers, 1953), p. 91.

around the world and into sacrificial support of missions, by expending abilities, efforts, money and time.

4. Providing frequent opportunity for young people to give their lives to the Lord for specific missionary service.

These four goals may be stated in terms of one overall objective: To bring young people to the place of spiritual maturity wherein there is total commitment of life to the purpose and program of God—personal discipleship and the extension of the church.

These aims are met through (1) *apprehension* or knowledge of the Scriptures, of the concept of discipleship, the conditions of mankind throughout the world, the history and program of missions, and the program of the local church and denomination; (2) *appreciation* and understanding of others and their spiritual needs, of the duty and privilege of discipleship and service, the relevance of the gospel, what constitutes a missionary call, and the needs, requirements and programs of various mission boards; (3) *activities* which allow for self-expression in a positively scriptural and purposeful way, which provide Christian fellowship so vital to young people, and which enhance character development and leadership training, and which promote the missionary spirit.

The planning and carrying out of a missionary educational program among youth will be successful to the extent that these principles are followed:

1. Encourage adult workers with youth to be missionary-minded and vitally interested in the missionary program of the church.
2. Provide missionary education through the existing organizations for youth such as Sunday school,[4] camp, weekday clubs, vacation Bible school, youth groups. Leaders in these groups should be encouraged to coordinate their efforts.
3. Make missions an integral part of the church's total program. Stress that missionary service involves commitment to the will of God and discipleship in service at home and abroad.
4. Teach missions throughout the year, not just seasonally or occasionally.
5. Involve youth in missionary activities "at home" in your church, neighborhood, and town. This makes missionary service more "tangible." In some churches, a missionary committee (consisting of several youth and an adult) in the youth group plans such activities.
6. Encourage youth not to look down on others in an attitude of condescending pity, but to have, instead, a God-given compassion and intelligent concern for their spiritual needs.
7. Relate missionary education to the age groups being taught, and provide for knowledge, inspiration and conduct-responses.

---

[4]See the leaflet *How to Emphasize Missions in the Sunday School,* published by World Vision, Inc.

8. Help young people see that dedication to the will of God is the ultimate purpose of true missionary education—not merely the giving of money, time or talents. Conversion is in answer to Christ's call, "Come unto Me"; discipleship answers His command, "Follow Me"; and both should be climaxed with obedience to the exhortation, "Serve the Lord with gladness."

Program Elements in Missionary Education for Youth

As mentioned earlier, missionary education provides opportunities for many kinds of learning experiences. A well-rounded missionary educational program incites young people to think, feel, will and do—to see and hear, to desire, to decide and to act. This includes (1) vicarious learning experiences, (2) observation of missions, and (3) direct experiences in missionary activity.

Vicarious learning experiences are those opportunities to learn through the experiences and methods of others. *Stories* are always of great benefit, and there are multitudes of books with missionary stories, biographies, adventures, which challenge the minds and hearts of even the least inquisitive. In your church library be sure to include books on these subjects. In Sunday school opening assemblies, occasionally have reports by teens on missionary books they have read.

Visual helps such as pictures, posters and objects are valuable tools for the missionary educator. Using these with a lecture or demonstration increases the extent of learning. Visuals help missionary speakers explain their work, the geographical location, the customs of foreign peoples. Many denominational mission boards have a number of visual aids along this line.

Tape recordings are very useful in vicarious learning. Playing a recording from a missionary creates interest and intrigue. Teens also enjoy "writing" to nationals or enjoy missionaries by tape. Some junior highs enjoy having a pen pal in a foreign land.

Drama, when used to promote missions, has great appeal and strengthens learning. A skit, dialogue, tableau or play might be given on the life of a contemporary or historical missionary, or on how a missionary ascertained the purpose of God for his life. Drama also allows for additional learning experiences as the young people participate in its production. This is more of a direct experience with its own specific values to the learner.

Related to dramatics is the use of *readings*. The oral interpretation of missionary material or a dramatic interpretation in monologue can be very impressive.

Recreation offers a different kind of educational experience for youth. It may not be immediately recognized as a means of missionary education. But at teen socials the playing of games representative of various countries can unconsciously give young people a greater worldwide perspective.[5] Or an entire social or a banquet may be planned around a missionary theme, including food, games and costumes typical of foreign lands, a missionary speaker or film.[6]

The possibilities of *observation of missions* are unlimited. These teaching-learning experiences take a little more time and effort and are therefore often slighted. *Flats* (missionary pictures mounted for use) and *graphics* (charts and graphs) can be a source of information and challenge to action—if well prepared and wisely used. A kit of several interesting charts on world religions is available from the Church Literature Department, Baptist Sunday School Board, 127 Ninth Avenue, North, Nashville, Tennessee 37203. (Order the "World Religions Kit.") The *National Geographic Magazine* is an excellent source of pictures on missions. (Attractively display these on posters and bulletin boards.)

Films and filmstrips with a missionary emphasis are "legion." *The Audio-Visual Resource Guide* lists several hundred films and filmstrips directly related to missions. Many evangelical mission boards—both denominational and independent—as well as several evangelical film producers have produced numerous films and filmstrips on various aspects of missionary endeavor and on various mission fields.[7]

Exhibits include displaying maps, flags, collections of curios, stamps, coins, Christian literature in other languages, diagrams, dioramas, missions scrapbooks.

Field trips are an invaluable teaching tool. Occasional excursions to the headquarters of missionary agencies give young people information and understanding of the missionary task beyond the mere listening techniques. For example, they could visit the headquarters of a mission board, tour a rescue mission, see other missionary organizations.

During summers and vacation periods more and more youth leaders are taking carefully selected Christian young people from their churches to observe missions firsthand. Some have gone to Mexico, some to Alaska, others to Arizona Indians, and still others to rural work in Kentucky. Thus young people have firsthand opportunity to see how missionaries work, to learn of conditions in these locales, and to contribute to the work of missions by helping in work projects, conducting services, visiting

---

[5]See E. O. Harbin, *Games of Many Nations* (New York: Abingdon Press, 1954), and the "Fun and Festival Series" of booklets (New York: Friendship Press).

[6]For a catalog of numerous, inexpensive accessories for use at parties and banquets to create a missionary atmosphere, write to The Wright Studio, 5264 Brookville Road, Indianapolis, Indiana 46219.

[7]See chapter 25, "Materials for Working with Youth," for a listing of independent evangelical film producers.

homes. Certainly an excellent way to create enthusiasm for missions is an actual visit to a mission field.

The opportunity of hearing missionary speakers and talking with them is an excellent means of fostering teens' interest in missions. In fact, it is significant that in a survey of 709 missionaries 58 percent of them said they received their call through a missionary.[8]

Two programs being used to involve young people in *direct experience in missionary activity* during the summers are worthy of mention. One is the Rural Outreach Program under the auspices of the American Sunday School Union. This program gives young people training and experience in vacation Bible school work and in camp counseling. The Practical Missionary Training program offers the same type of expression but takes place in an actual missionary situation. Information may be obtained by writing to the American Sunday School Union, 1816 Chestnut Street, Philadelphia, Pennsylvania 19103, and to Practical Missionary Training, Inc., Box 628, Fullerton, California 92632.

The enthusiasm and strength of learning through such firsthand experiences cannot be underestimated. Every youth counselor should give some thought to what he might do along this line with his young people.

Worship, a vital aspect of the church's activity, offers a number of educational opportunities directly related to the missionary spirit. This includes numerous hymns and gospel songs related to dedication and to the missionary purpose and vision. The fact that the reading of the Scriptures should have a place in this instructional task hardly needs emphasis. Prayer can also be missionary in spirit as intercession for missionaries and for worldwide needs is brought to the Lord. Each youth group or Sunday school class should have a young person record the group's missionary prayer requests and answers. This will help make young people aware that God does work through prayer and that their lives and the lives of those in specific areas of service are affected by it.

Stewardship is ultimately a missionary concept. Some Sunday school classes of youth have taken on partial support of a missionary, a national orphan, or a missionary child. Others have given toward a specific project such as the purchasing of a mimeograph machine for Japan or a set of books for India. Rural teens have raised calves, sold them, and given the money to missions. But the sacrificial giving of money to support missionary programs is only one aspect of stewardship. According to the Bible, stewardship includes the giving of one's self for the purposes of God. Consequently the use of one's time and talents—life itself—is a part of Christian stewardship and of missions.

---

[8] J. O. Percy, "Where Are the Recruits?" *Missions Annual, 1959* (Ridgefield Park, N.J.: Interdenominational Foreign Mission Association, 1959) , p. 34.

Youth can be involved in missionary *activities* right at home—in the church or community. The most readily available activity is the church visitation program. Leaders can encourage teens to express their concern for the lost by participating in church visitation. Training the youth in how to visit will result in their increased empathy and interest.

Or youth may be involved in vacation Bible school work in tenement areas or in a Spanish (or other immigrant people) settlement. Some of the teens could be encouraged to instigate and operate a children's Bible club on Saturday mornings or on a weekday afternoon. Or the leaders might interest them in supplying gospel tracts in tract racks at bus and train depots.

In the summer young people should be encouraged to volunteer their services for improving the appearance of a room in the church. Teens make good painters and hangers of drapes! Or the offices of missionary organizations may need assistance in stuffing and addressing envelopes. Other activities may be suggested by the church missionary committee.

It is important to involve youth in *special missionary programming*. For example, during a missionary conference, a teen banquet should be planned in which missionaries would be seated with the young people to converse with them about missions. Some churches have young people enter a poster-making contest just before a missionary conference. Then the posters are displayed and judged during the conference. Other churches involve teens in booth-making contests. And still others have used teens in manning the booths.

A few churches have sponsored an annual School of Missions—a week of courses on missions, with a graded program for the various departments and a combined meeting each night for the entire congregation.

Special days can be used for missionary instruction, including Christmas, Thanksgiving, a missions day in Sunday school once a quarter. Teens should be encouraged to give a special "missionary Christmas offering" for some mission project. Some groups suggest that Christmas cards to church members be eliminated and that the money saved in this way on cards and postage be given to some missions project. Other activities such as sharing foodstuffs with families in need are also practiced by many churches. Other seasonal events can be used to great advantage by creative, missionary-minded leaders.

Also *youth programs* may deal with various questions regarding missions: What is a missionary call? Are the heathen lost? Who are some of the great missionaries of the past and present? What are the various avenues of missionary service? (Aviation, education, evangelism, literature, medicine, radio.) Why do so few young people volunteer for missionary service? What opportunities for missionary service exist in our own country?

How can young people best prepare for missionary service? Are foreign countries closing to missions?

SUMMARY

Missionary education is central in the Scriptures and essential in Christian education. It is vital to the spiritual growth of young people. The foregoing suggestions are presented to stimulate youth leaders to investigate the many areas in which missions can be taught and ways by which each young person might be challenged to present himself "a living sacrifice . . . unto God" (Rom. 12:1).

FOR FURTHER READING

ADENEY, DAVID H. *The Unchanging Commission.* Chicago: Inter-Varsity Press, 1956.

ALLEN, ROLAND H. *Missionary Methods: St. Paul's or Ours?* Grand Rapids: Wm. B. Eerdmans Publishing Co., 1962.

BOWMAN, CLARICE M. *Ways Youth Learn.* New York: Harper & Bros. Publishers, 1952.

CARVER, WILLIAM OWEN. *Missions in the Plan of the Ages.* Nashville: Broadman Press, 1955.

———. *The Course of Christian Missions.* Westwood, N.J.: Fleming H. Revell Co., 1956.

COOK, HAROLD R. *Introduction to the Study of Christian Missions.* Chicago: Moody Press, 1954.

———. "The Missing Link in Missionary Recruitment," *Moody Monthly,* LXVI:20-21, 45 (December, 1964).

CULLEY, PAUL G. *The Missionary Enterprise.* Wheaton, Ill.: Evangelical Teacher Training Association, 1954.

GATES, HERBERT WRIGHT. *Missionary Education in the Church.* Boston: Pilgrim Press, 1928.

GLOVER, ROBERT HALL. *The Bible Basis of Missions.* Chicago: Moody Press, 1964.

GRIFFITHS, LOUISE B., *Wide as the World: Junior Highs and Missions.* New York: Friendship Press, 1958.

HARNER, NEVIN C., and BAKER, DAVID D. *Missionary Education in Your Church.* New York: Friendship Press, 1950.

———. *Youth Work in the Church.* Nashville: Abingdon Press, 1942.

HOUGHTON, A. T. *In Training.* Chicago: Inter-Varsity Press, 1946.

HOWSE, W. L. *The Sunday School and Missions.* Nashville: Convention Press, 1957.

PEARSON, DICK. *Missionary Education Helps for the Local Church.* Palo Alto, Calif.: Overseas Crusades, 1966.

PIERCE, ROBERT. *Emphasizing Missions in the Local Church.* Grand Rapids: Zondervan Publishing House, 1964.

SOLTAU, T. STANLEY. *Missions at the Crossroads.* Grand Rapids: Baker Book House, 1954.

"Try These Foreign Games," *Tips* (Baptist General Conference), November, 1964.

TROUTMAN, CHARLES H. "What Really Keeps Students from Volunteering for Missions?" *Evangelical Missions Quarterly,* II:193-208 (Summer, 1966) .

WYCKOFF, D. CAMPBELL. *In One Spirit: Senior Highs and Missions.* New York: Friendship Press, 1958.

It is important that the church serve as
a channel for youth's Christian service. A
youth group too often functions as an auxiliary rather than as an integral part of the
church. There is the danger that service
projects will become peripheral rather than
pertinent to the life of the church. While
young people will often be organized and
grouped for practical purposes, their service
activities should always be seen as an important part of the church's ministry.

ROBERT A. CRANDALL

17

youth serving the church

THE CHURCH can be a great school of Christian living and service for her youth.[1] She can provide answers to their questions, a faith for their quest, and an avenue for their abilities. Often, however, the opportunity for service is lacking. "It is lacking, not for want of vision on the part of the young people nor because the older persons have failed to dream dreams."[2] Every youth leader has the responsibility of helping the church see the worth of her youth, and in turn helping youth dedicate themselves to the work of the church.[3]

Byrne has pointed out that service activities are beneficial both to the church and to the young people in it:

---

[1] H. W. Byrne, *Christian Education for the Local Church* (Grand Rapids: Zondervan Publishing House, 1963), p. 27.

[2] Kathryn L. Higley, "Go Forward and Serve," *Workers with Youth*, XVIII:38 (October, 1964).

[3] Ada Zimmerman Brunk and Ethel Yake Metzler, *The Christian Nurture of Youth* (Scottdale, Pa.: Herald Press, 1960), p. 114.

ROBERT A. CRANDALL, B.D., is General Director of Free Methodist Youth, Winona Lake, Indiana, and editor of *Youth in Action* magazine.

Participation in service activities has many advantages, among which are contributions to the social happiness of others, character-forming elements, and practical training for the membership in actual practice of gospel truths and obligations.[4]

THE NEED OF YOUTH FOR SERVICE

Significant service in the church can provide for many of the basic needs of youth.

Youth need a sense of purpose. They not only need a creed to believe but a cause which demands their fullest effort. "One great need in youth work is to help youth gain a sense of mission and purpose."[5] "Where youth have seen themselves as the church in action, they have moved out in power, often to the surprise of their elders."[6] Through challenging Christian service teens see what can be accomplished by God through dedicated lives and talents.

Youth need a sense of participation. One reason young people drop out of church is that they find it boring, uninteresting, and lacking sufficient activities.[7] In many churches youth are only spectators, forced to observe without opportunity to contribute. Wise youth leaders recognize that involvement is one of the keys to working effectively with adolescents. As Bradford points out, "A simple sense of participation often adds the essential meaning and purpose to life that breaks lackadaisical indifference."[8] There can be a place of service for every young person in the church, regardless of talent or ability.

Youth need practice. Learning is often accompanied by trial and error. But proficiency is gained as one performs the service or task. Service training, therefore, provides teens with necessary practice.

Youth need to produce. They need the opportunity to achieve and accomplish. Much of the church's ministry is intangible and thus largely immeasurable. But through service projects a young person can see what his contribution means in the life and outreach of the church.

Youth need praise. Recognition of achievement is important. Through well-performed service a young person can win some honor, public acknowledgment, or a word of personal commendation from the teacher or leader.

---

[4]Byrne, *op. cit.,* p. 30.

[5]Merton P. Stommen, *Profiles of Church Youth* (St. Louis: Concordia Publishing House, 1963) , p. 234.

[6]Robert L. Browning, "The Church's Youth Ministry," *An Introduction to Christian Education,* Marvin Taylor, ed. (Nashville: Abingdon Press, 1966) , p. 187.

[7]Roy B. Zuck, "Why Do Teens Quit Church?" *Link,* XI:6 (March, 1963) .

[8]Jack Bradford, "The Care and Keeping of Young People in the Church," *Christian Life,* XXIV:59 (May, 1962) .

Unless the church meets these needs of her young people she runs the risk of losing them. For this reason, service projects of various kinds should be explored and encouraged. Finding a place of service for every adolescent may well require some imagination and initiative. But the maxim, "Use me or lose me" is as appropriate today as ever.

Years ago, in his book *Church Work with Young People,* Harry Thomas Stock listed six opportunities the church has in helping youth meet their needs. The last one he mentions is "to promote opportunities in sharing significant service."[9] In providing such opportunities, the church can meet the needs of her youth and hold them. Talents will be utilized and abundant energies channeled. In this way the need of youth for the church and the need of the church for her youth will both be met.

Promoting service opportunities may not be easy, but it is important. As Frederick W. Stewart has written:

> It is a large challenge! How best to serve youth and to let youth serve in turn, while at the same time keeping the church, as it must ever be, a chronological cross-section of society, with every age represented. . . . The fact is that emotional life, aesthetic life, mysticism, idealism, and opportunity for service—these are normal adolescent needs, which will die out, if not satisfied, and the church can best meet these needs.[10]

Furthermore, many Christian young people *welcome* rather than reject opportunities to serve the Lord in tangible ways. As Browning points out, "Ministering to others, the life and work of service, is much more highly valued by youth than we have supposed."[11]

SERVICE AS A LEARNING EXPERIENCE

A well-balanced program for youth consists of instruction, worship, fellowship and service.[12] Together these help accomplish the comprehensive aims of Christian education which include "making one's contribution to the church, reaching lost men, and assuming responsibility as a Christian citizen in the community and the world."[13] These aims can hardly be fulfilled without service, for learning in Christian nurture occurs through life's experiences as one shares ideas and deeds.[14] Service therefore becomes

---

[9]Harry Thomas Stock, *Church Work with Young People* (Boston: Pilgrim Press, 1929), p. 10.

[10]Frederick W. Stewart, *A Study of Adolescent Development* (Philadelphia: Judson Press, 1954), pp. 164-65.

[11]Browning, *loc. cit.*

[12]Lois E. LeBar, "Curriculum," *An Introduction to Evangelical Christian Education,* J. Edward Hakes, ed. (Chicago: Moody Press, 1964), p. 93.

[13]*Ibid.*

[14]Robert R. Boehlke, *Theories of Learning in Christian Education* (Philadelphia: Westminster Press, 1962), p. 22.

a method of learning, an expression through activities which give to the didactic presentation symbolic or practical meaning.[15] Youth-group meetings can thus "carry out the implications of the Sunday school class in the form of practical problems and service projects."[16]

Youth want to be doing something. After a period of training they should be given opportunities for putting that training to work. Peter Person reminds us that "the most important permanent learning does not come by way of textbooks and lectures, but through actual doing."[17]

In Christian education a balanced curriculum should include instruction in Christian service and leadership.[13] Leaders of youth today are aware that today's adolescents desire a religion which is relevant and practical. For this reason, unselfish service, as a Christian learning experience, can be a stabilizing factor when teens face periods of questioning and doubt.

PHILOSOPHIES OF SERVICE FOR YOUTH

The effectiveness of service opportunities depends on the philosophy of service held by the adult leaders, and how well that philosophy is transmitted to the young people with whom they are working. Christian service should certainly not be mere activity for activity's sake. Nor is it merely performing some task to earn a merit badge, a new rank or other achievement in a youth organization. Even the idea of "learning to do by doing," while valid, is too limited a concept for Christian service.

An adequate philosophy of service by which to guide youth should have three characteristics. I must be *Christ-centered, others-directed* and *church-channeled.*

Christian service begins with the awareness that Christ was a servant. In all His earthly ministry Jesus gave Himself for others. Christian young people should be impressed with the idea that as followers of Christ they must be known in the world for their life of service.[19] One youth manual has challenged young people in these words: "The church's ministry is that of its Lord. As the people of the church we are called to a life of service."[20]

Iris Cully suggests that youth leaders convey the idea that deeds of loving

---

[15]Victor Hoag, *The Ladder of Learning* (Greenwich, Conn.: Seabury Press, 1960), p. 140.

[16]LeBar, *op. cit.,* p. 94.

[17]Peter Person, *The Church and Modern Youth* (Grand Rapids: Zondervan Publishing House, 1963), p. 66.

[18]See chapter 13, "Sunday Evening Youth Programs."

[19]W. L. Jenkins, *A Message Concerning the Church's Ministry with Senior Highs* (Philadelphia: Board of Christian Education, United Presbyterian Church), p. 34.

[20]*Ibid.,* p. 24.

service are not to be performed because God loves us and expects us to return His love in this manner. Rather, love for God is shown because the persons cannot do otherwise. Love for God is a gift to be shared.[21] The sharing of this gift, love in action, is Christian service. The danger of reducing the intangible love of God to a set of suggestions in a program activity guide is a real one. It is easy to get sidetracked into the performance of service for some lesser motive. "Religious training must be oriented to the experience of joy in service to God."[22]

Love to Christ will find expression in service to others. Young people should see little of self-aggrandizement in a particular service activity. For this reason those who offer rewards for service should be very careful to outline the greater reward of serving others. The idea that we are persons who have received particular gifts from God to be employed in service to *others* must be transmitted to our youth.

It is important that the church serve as a channel for youth's Christian service. A youth group too often functions as an auxiliary rather than as an integral part of the church. There is the danger that service projects will become peripheral rather than pertinent to the life of the church. While young people will often be organized and grouped for practical purposes, their service activities should always be seen as an important part of the church's ministry.[23]

MOTIVATING YOUTH FOR SERVICE

A proper philosophy of service serves as a broad base for motivation. However several methods may have to be used to get young people engaged in serving the Lord. While most young people are "eager to do something," they may not manifest an interest in serving. Or they may wish to adopt an unsuitable project.

The general approach to the three adolescent age groups will also vary. These approaches might be stated in this way: for junior highs, "Service is what you *should do*"; for senior highs, "Service is something you *could* do"; for young adults, *"Would* you do service?" Perhaps these different approaches, together with specific suggestions for motivation, can best be considered by considering each group separately.

Junior Highs

The young adolescent has a strong sense of group loyalty, is a hero

---

[21]Iris Cully, *The Dynamics of Christian Education* (Philadelphia: Westminster Press, 1958), p. 154.

[22]Jan Waternik, *Basic Concepts in Christian Pedagogy* (Grand Rapids: Wm. B. Eerdmans Publishing Co., 1954), p. 134.

[23]Jenkins, *op. cit.,* p. 45.

worshiper, and has intense joy in personal accomplishment.[24] "He has a vision for service. He wants to do something for the Lord. He is ready to act, but he does not know what to do."[25]

Action in this group, therefore, can be secured through the personal appeal of the teacher or leader whom the adolescent idolizes, through an urging to support the project adopted by the group, and through the offer of some award for achievement. Since youth in this age group need considerable guidance, and are generally responsive to it, an appeal on the basis of "oughtness" is effective. But there is danger in overdoing it. "Preachiness" is resented, while practical suggestions are rewarded.

Senior Highs

Middle adolescents have the capacity for an increasing desire to help others, especially those less fortunate than they. Since they often view service as something far away, they need to see in the common task the possibilities for service.[26] Teen-agers are also creative, idealistic, open to suggestions by their peers, and eager to belong to a well-organized social group.[27]

For these reasons teens in this group should be encouraged and allowed to use their initiative in selecting a project. But an adult, by dropping suggestions to key young people, can give real though indirect guidance. Whatever the project selected, responsibility for organization, publicity and follow-through should be carefully assigned. The key to response from this group is to channel energies by showing what can be done, thus getting them personally involved.

Young Adults

Young adults, properly challenged, relish opportunities to serve and manifest a crusading zeal.[28] Yet if a young adult thinks he does not have a particular talent, he may feel there is no place for him in the Lord's work.[29] He may also question the significance of certain service.

To activate young adults, request their assistance, provide service opportunities, and make them feel the importance of the tasks.

---

[24]Marjorie E. Soderholm, *Understanding the Pupil, Part III, The Adolescent* (Grand Rapids: Baker Book House, 1962) , pp. 22-23.

[25]*Ibid.,* p. 32.

[26]Soderholm, *op. cit.,* p. 51.

[27]*Ibid.,* pp. 45-46, 49.

[28]F. L. Reynolds, "You and the Class of '62," *Christian Herald,* LXXXV:60 (May, 1962) .

[29]Soderholm, *op. cit.,* p. 86.

PRINCIPLES FOR SELECTING SERVICE PROJECTS

Service projects assigned to individuals or selected for or by a group are more likely to enlist their interest and participation if the projects are *real, relevant, realistic* and *rewarding.*

Teens in a youth group had been discussing Christian stewardship. They asked their leader, "What can we do to help out in the church? We'd like something real to do!"[30]

Something *real* to do! Yes, the assignments and projects must be real ones. Young people will quickly see through a sham schedule of concocted chores given them as "busy work." They want opportunity for service filling genuinely significant needs of others.

A project is relevant to the extent that it helps youth put into practice what they are learning in instructional and worship times. This calls for close coordination between the Sunday school and the youth group. It is also well to explain how such service relates to the life and ministry of the church. Within the youth group some coordination between programs and service projects will make both more meaningful.

A service project that is *realistic* will be related to youth's abilities and will be achievable. Young people may fail to realize their capabilities or capacities. Or they may wish to select a project which is too ambitious or complicated for them to carry out. There is as much danger in undertaking a project that demands too little effort as in one that demands too much. Ordinarily a project involving the entire group should be relatively short in duration so that interest can be maintained.

Anticipating some reward for service can help a group see a project to its completion. Reward in the form of personal satisfaction is often as meaningful as public recognition.

One handbook gives several practical dos and don'ts in selecting a youth project.[31]

> Some Dos:
> 1. Keep your eyes open for a need to be met. If you can't find one, check with your pastor.
> 2. Investigate thoroughly whatever problem has presented itself. Seek the help of adults who know. Appoint committees to collect all the information you need.
> 3. Decide exactly what you are to do. Outline a course of action. Assign responsibilities definitely.
> 4. Arrange for the participation of as many people as possible.

---

[30]Clarence C. Stoughton, *Whatever You Do* (Philadelphia: Muhlenberg Press, 1949), p. 57.

[31]Adapted from *Senior High Fellowship Handbook* (Richmond, Va.: John Knox Press, 1962), pp. 250-52.

5. Watch for opportune moments that suggest action, such as when the completion of one project may suggest another to follow.
6. Carry through your plans, revising them as necessary, and doing further study as needed. Expect big things of yourselves!
7. Let one project lead to another. Develop within your group an attitude of sensitivity to needs and unchristian conditions around you.
8. Evaluate the work you have done, as to its effect on others and on your group.
9. Do everything in a spirit of prayer.

Some Don'ts:
1. Don't begin your project from a selfish motive. If you do, it may be of little help to you or anyone else.
2. Don't plunge into something without knowing what it is all about and without careful and prayerful planning.
3. Don't attempt to "sell" the group on something you "cooked up" for them; instead, carefully motivate interest by planning *with* the teens. Concentrate on the need to be met, the *privilege* of serving and the potential for participation by everyone.
4. Don't give up. You may have to change plans, but you owe it to the group to see that the project is successfully completed. It is important to select projects within the ability of the group so they can be carried through.
5. Don't carry out the project for the young people. Do it *with* them. Don't concern yourself only with what you are doing.
6. Don't have all your projects of one type. Giving Thanksgiving baskets and Christmas toys year after year, and doing nothing else, may kill the interest of your group in becoming involved in other kinds of equally meaningful projects.

The kinds of projects planned will vary according to the age groups. Projects for junior highs should be uncomplicated but not childish. For senior highs a project should be timely, demanding initiative and effort, but not so involved that interest quickly wanes. Young adults require projects through which they can feel that a vital contribution is being made to a person or to the church.

SELECTING SPECIFIC PROJECTS

Possibilities for service projects are everywhere. Some needs may be obvious. (For instance, the church carpeting may be worn or the hymnals ragged.) But the most urgently needed service is not always apparent. Research, by asking the pastor or community leaders, or by making a survey, may be required.

The handbooks of nearly all denominational youth organizations, such as Christian Service Brigade[32] and Christian Endeavor,[33] also list a variety

---

[32]*Brigade Trails* (Wheaton, Ill.: Christian Service Brigade, 1958), pp. 184-86.
[33]*Guide for Action*, a pamphlet published by International Society of Christian Endeavor (Columbus, Ohio), which suggests service activities for each month of the year.

of ideas. Bowman lists 83 service project ideas.[34] Other resources for general and specific service projects are listed with the bibliography at the end of this chapter.

Below are some possible projects youth may perform for the church, in the community, or as special summer services. Some of these may be carried out for the pastor or other church leaders. Some are related to worship, and others to an outreach ministry of the church.

These suggestions are by no means exhaustive. Any youth leader or group, by using imagination, may be able to select something which fits their group better than any of these. Originality in selection is halfway to success, since the group is thus already involved.

The age group to which the project seems most likely suited is designated by the following code: J = Junior High; S = Senior High; O = Older Youth. You will note that some projects may be carried out by more than one group while some others seem limited to one. And some projects are suited more to an individual, while others may involve the entire group.

Service to the Church:

1. Assist with church janitorial work.   (J S O)
2. Assist the pastor and/or the pastor's wife with personal and/or household chores to give them more time for church work.   (J S)
3. Help direct traffic at the church parking area.   (J S)
4. Operate projection equipment at special services, and be responsible for its care and maintenance.   (S O)
5. Provide transportation to church for invalids or children.   (S O)
6. Purchase visual education equipment; hymnals or chorus books; carpeting; other necessary items for the church and Sunday school. (S O)
7. Assist children's workers or teachers in storytelling, preparing teaching equipment, gathering materials.   (S O)
8. Provide flowers for the church, and distribute them to shut-ins following the service.   (J S O)
9. Care for hymnals, Bibles and other worship equipment.   (J S)
10. Assist with the secretarial work of the church (for the pastor, church secretary, Sunday school superintendent, minister of music). (S O)
11. Publish a church newspaper.   (J S O)
12. Establish and sponsor a scholarship fund for a deserving student at college or seminary.   (O)
13. Sponsor an overseas orphan.   (O)
14. Keep in touch with men and women of the church who are members of the armed forces.   (S O)
15. Establish, sponsor or assist in a church nursery.   (J S O)
16. Visit newcomers in the church.   (S O)

---

[34]Clarice M. Bowman, *Ways Youth Learn* (New York: Harper & Bros. Publishers, 1952), pp. 154-60.

17. Provide ushers for church services.   (S O)
18. Operate a baby-sitting service for parents so they can attend adult functions of the church.   (J S)
19. Form a youth choir or help sponsor a children's choir.   (S O)
20. Begin or help maintain a church library, including a visual aids section.   (S O)
21. Sponsor a youth-conducted evangelistic series.   (S O)
22. Sponsor a missionary project, such as raising funds for a specific need or collecting and mailing needed items.   (J S O)
23. Paint and distribute signs and posters for the church.   (J S O)
24. Supply music for Sunday school and/or church services (including vocal and instrumental solo or ensemble) .   (J S O)
25. Compile a church directory showing names, addresses and telephone numbers of officers of various organizations and departments, and a listing of regularly scheduled services.   (J S O)

Service to the Community:

1. Visit all newcomers in the community.   (S O)
2. Organize group activities for older members of the church.   (O)
3. Make recordings of special church services and take them to shut-ins. (J S O)
4. Make tray favors for hospitals and rest homes for special days, or for any ordinary day, as a special surprise.   (J S)
5. Conduct services in jails, hospitals, rest homes, sanitariums or other institutions.   (S O)
6. Launch a branch Sunday school, with guidance from the pastor or Sunday school superintendent.   (S O)
7. Conduct a community census to secure prospects for your Sunday school or church.   (S O)
8. Distribute invitations to special meetings.   (J S)
9. Provide for services in abandoned churches or unchurched areas, with cooperation and approval of your pastor.   (S O)
10. In rural areas try a "Lord's Acre" project (growing a crop on a portion of land, turning proceeds over to church) .   (J S O)
11. Prepare a float for a community parade.   (J S O)
12. Assist in preparing and manning a church-related booth at a county fair or community exposition.   (J S O)
13. Launch and participate in a high school Bible club.   (S)
14. Conduct a "news service" to report church activities to local papers. (S O)
15. Collect food, used clothing, used repairable toys, for benevolent institutions; then sort, mend, repair, paint, ship.   (J S O)
16. Distribute gospel portions or devotional materials in hospitals, rest homes, county homes.   (J S)
17. Minister to migrant workers, if you live in a community served by them.   (S O)
18. Collect items to send to Goodwill Industries, Salvation Army. (J S O)
19. Give assistance to community welfare and service agencies.   (S O)
20. Join in a community clean-up campaign.   (J S O)

Summer Service:

1. Serve as counselors or workers in church-sponsored summer camps. (S O)
2. Provide scholarships for a week at camp for some youngster (s) who would otherwise not be privileged to attend. (O)
3. Assist in vacation Bible school. (S O)
4. Help with construction or maintenance on camp or conference grounds. (J S O)
5. Form a crusade team to tour a conference or a state, conducting Bible schools in unchurched areas or helping to revitalize other work. (S O)
6. Assist with cleaning, painting, repairing, varnishing of a local church, including yardwork and the maintenance of the parking lot. (J S O)
7. Help pay the way of a person participating in voluntary missionary service (short-term) or in a summer work camp. (S O)
8. Form a work group to go to a nearby mission or smaller church that needs help in painting, redecorating, cleaning. (S O)
9. Have a gardening project and give proceeds to church. (Boys could raise a vegetable garden; girls could grow flowers.) (J S O)
10. Help with leadership of summer playground activities in the community. (S O)
11. Visit a foreign mission field to assist missionaries in needed projects. (S O)
12. Sell Christian books in downtown high-rise apartments. (S O)

REWARDS FOR YOUTH SERVICE

There are rewards in service both to the participating individual and to the church. To the young person there is the reward of personal satisfaction and the opportunity of preparing for service in the future. The enjoyment of Christian fellowship, the learning of social graces, and the acquiring of leadership experience are possible by-products of service activities. While there may be some honor or public recognition, the greater commendation is our Lord's "Well done, thou good and faithful servant" for young people who have performed a task to the glory of God.

Perhaps in some respects the local church is more a beneficiary of service activities than the youth themselves. With each song rendered, each youth office held, each visit to a shut-in, each box of clothing packed, youth are maturing in preparation for adult leadership. As Stoughton has said, "God's best lieutenants of tomorrow will be those youth who serve Him in the ranks of today."[35]

Hopefully through such activity many young people will be called into *vocational* Christian service. Many people who later became ministers or missionaries participated meaningfully in the life of the church when they were teens.

---

[35]Stoughton, *op. cit.*, p. 62.

The assimilation of youth into the work of the congregation tends to infuse it and them with enthusiasm. Youthful zeal proves a tonic to lethargic adults.

SUMMARY

The church's greatest resource of reproduction is through the winning and holding of her own youth. These youth may lack motivation but the potential is there. Happy is the church—and happy are the youth in it—that provides its young people with the opportunity to serve Jesus Christ.

FOR FURTHER READING

BOWER, WILLIAM CLAYTON, and HAYWARD, PERCY RAY. *Protestantism Faces Its Educational Task*. New York: C. C. Nelson Publishers, 1949.

BOWMAN, CLARICE M. *Ways Youth Learn*. New York: Harper & Bros. Publishers, 1952.

BRADFORD, JACK. "The Care and Keeping of Young People in the Church," *Christian Life*, XXIV:58-59 (May, 1962).

BUTLER, J. DONALD. *Religious Education*. New York: Harper & Row, 1958.

Design for Diligent Witness, Official Guidebook for Free Methodist Youth. Winona Lake, Ind.: Free Methodist Publishing House.

HAMMOND, PHILLIS ETTER. *How to Plan a Youth Retreat*. Philadelphia: Baptist Youth Fellowship, 1953. (Copyright by Forrest B. Fordham.)

HOGLUND, GUNNAR. *Better CYF Youth Groups*. Chicago: Harvest Publications, 1960, Chapter 8.

HOGLUND, GUNNAR, and GRAYBILL, VIRGINIA. *Youth Leaders' Handbook*. Wheaton, Ill.: Miracle Press, 1958.

Junior High Crusader's Guide. Winona Lake, Ind.: Free Methodist Publishing House, 1961.

MEEKER, HUBERT M. *How to Publish a Church Paper*. Philadelphia: Baptist Youth Fellowship, 1953. (Copyright by Forrest B. Fordham.)

MURRAY, HERBERT J., JR. "Youth Are the Church Now!" *Baptist Leader*, XXVIII:24-25 (January, 1967).

SMITH, JEANNE K. "Should Senior Highs Teach?" *The Christian Educator*, VI: 3-4, 20 (April-June, 1963).

TANI, HENRY N. *Ventures in Youth Work*. Philadelphia: Christian Education Press, 1957.

"He's great! I feel I can ask him for spiritual help and get it, without being blasted by a ten-point sermon."

"I like him, all right—but I don't think he really knows the score on being a youth sponsor."

"He's just not with it. I don't even think he really likes teaching us."

These are comments teens might make about successful and not so successful adult workers with youth. These remarks indicate that not every adult who works with young people in the church clicks with teens. Many factors contribute to genuine success in this difficult role. These factors include personal qualifications, training, and awareness of the duties of one's task.

WILLIAM R. GOETZ

18

adult leaders for youth

IMPORTANCE OF GOOD ADULT LEADERSHIP

A LACK OF ADEQUATE LEADERSHIP in youth work showed up very pointedly in the nationwide survey of teen dropouts from church conducted in 1962 by the Research Commission and the Youth Commission of the National Sunday School Association.

More than half the dropouts' complaints against Sunday school pertained to the teachers.[1] One problem with youth meetings, said 15.5% of the dropouts, was poor adult leadership. Dropouts also expressed dissatisfaction with leaders who do not seem to be really interested in young people, or seem to be unable to understand them.

On the other hand, scores of Christians (among them many of the leaders of evangelical churches in America) have pointed to the help given them, as youth, by capable adult leaders. They have described this help as being life-changing in its influence.

---

[1]Roy B. Zuck, "Why Do Teens Quit Church?" *Link,* XI: 11ff. (March, 1963) .

WILLIAM R. GOETZ is Associate Pastor and Christian Education Director, Tenth Avenue Alliance Church, Vancouver, British Columbia.

Strong, spiritually healthy youth groups, classes and organizations can be attributed, in large measure, to strong, understanding, spiritual adult leaders. Experience has shown that the adult leader is the key to the success of the youth organization which he guides.

"Four indispensables are to be found in every successful youth group," Gunnar Hoglund writes. "[They are] program, organization, morale and leadership—but the greatest of these is leadership."[2] And of the two types of leadership in youth groups—adult leadership and youth leadership— the adult is of greater importance, since proper adult guidance will develop and strengthen youth leadership.

Young people need adult friends in whom they can confide and whose example they can follow. Church youth workers who "measure up" can meet this need in a unique sense.

This is borne out in the response of dropouts to the final question in the previously mentioned NSSA survey. To the query, "What do you think churches need to do to improve their ministry to young people?" many dropouts replied in effect, "Enlist better adult leaders!"[3]

The fundamental importance of reliable, spiritual leadership is also illustrated profusely in the Bible. Moses, Joshua, Gideon, David and other godly men and women are examples of good leadership in Israel. The apostles gave the early church sound spiritual leadership.

In similar ways God calls today for consecrated adults who will recognize the importance of ministering to youth—adults who will accept it as a commission from God and who will accomplish the task in the strength God imparts.

Function of Adult Workers

The basic function of the adult worker with youth is to guide toward spiritual maturity those youth entrusted to his care. Spiritual maturity begins with the new birth, and subsequent spiritual growth in Christ continues until "we all come in the unity of the faith, and of the knowledge of the Son of God, unto a perfect man, unto the stature of the fulness of Christ . . . growing up into him in all things, which is the head, even Christ" (Eph. 4:13, 15*b*).

Spiritual maturity involves not only knowing Christ conceptually but also growing daily in Him through His Word and prayer, and being equipped to render effective service in the will of God.

How young people progress toward this goal will vary from teen to

---

[2]Gunnar Hoglund, *Better CYF Youth Groups* (Chicago: Harvest Publications, 1960), p. 28.

[3]Roy B. Zuck, "Why Do Teens Quit Church?" *Link,* XI: 5 (April, 1963).

teen. Some may not even be alive spiritually; others may be making little progress in the Christian life; while still others may be growing rapidly.

The adult leader of youth is one of the channels—a very important one—through which the Holy Spirit desires to work in the lives of young people to accomplish His will.

Thus the adult worker with teens is a guide, a counselor, a leader fulfilling his role as an instrument of the Holy Spirit—to help lead youth toward greater spiritual maturity.

Qualifications of Adult Leaders

What sort of person is qualified to be a leader of youth? Who will serve acceptably as a Sunday school teacher of teens, a club leader or guide, a youth fellowship sponsor or a camp counselor?

Qualifications will differ slightly, depending on the educational agency served. And yet there are a number of basic, essential qualifications desirable for *all* adult workers with young people:

Salvation and a radiant Christian life. It is obvious that a youth worker must know and love Christ if he is to lead others to know Him. Only the new birth can place within an individual the God-given love essential for effective youth leadership: love for God, for His Word, and for those who have been committed to the leader's care.

Consistent, exemplary Christian living must go hand in hand with salvation. Youth are quick to detect—and despise—hypocrisy. The inconsistency of adults was the second-ranking complaint made by the dropouts surveyed by the National Sunday School Association.[4]

A youth worker must be a Christian whose whole life shows the job of a daily, growing experience with God!

Real love for and sympathetic understanding of youth. Genuine love will often accomplish with youth what nothing else will. Love will overlook the thoughtlessness, moodiness and ingratitude of which youth are capable. Genuine concern for teens will find ways to lead them on spiritually. The worker who shows love will be honored with the privilege of confidence entrusted by youth: counsel sought and advice accepted.

Understanding that teens are in a period of change—physically, mentally, socially and often spiritually—is an important key in dealing with youth. A youth worker improves his leadership if he makes a sincere effort to understand the problems, viewpoints, conflicts, dreams, needs and fears of young people.

This suggests the quality of "contemporaneity"—the ability to get along with today's teens, to sense something of the peculiar problems of young

---

[4]Zuck, *op. cit.,* XI: 7.

people in *this* generation, to be on the "wave length" of present-day youth. This is not to suggest that a leader must necessarily be young in years. In fact some older adults work better with youth than do some younger adults. Being young at heart is not always synonymous with being young in years.

When the dropouts responding to NSSA's survey discussed what they would prefer in adult leaders, they requested adults who *understand* youth.[5] Such understanding involves the ability to discern personal needs and tactfully offer help without being inquisitive and nosy.

A firm foundation in the Word of God. The answers to young people's needs and problems are given in God's Word. Consequently, an important qualification of a leader of youth is a good grounding in the Bible. This does not necessarily mean a Bible college education—but it does mean familiarity with the truths, doctrines and precepts of the Bible.

Time and capacity for hard work. Youth work takes time and hard work—if it is to be done properly. The adult leader of youth should possess an abundant capacity for work and personal sacrifice in the interests of his youth. Adequate lesson preparation takes time and effort; club work, properly done, is most demanding on one's energies and time; a Sunday night youth group requires hours of tactful coaching; and a youth camp can occupy one's entire vacation period.

These facts need to be realized by would-be adult workers with youth. The cost should be counted, and the requirement of a large expenditure of time and effort realistically faced.

Faithfulness and dependability. It is "required in a steward that a man be found faithful" (I Cor. 4:2). How important that a youth worker be found faithful when the spiritual welfare of young people is in his hands! Without dependability, the most impressive qualifications lose their luster—for if the adult worker is not faithful to his responsibilities and dependable in discharging them, he cannot hope to lead youth aright. Faithfulness in other areas of church life should be a prerequisite to the privilege of youth leadership.

Maturity—spiritual and emotional. A sensible and emotionally balanced person possesses qualities to which youth respond with respect. These include drive, ambition, enthusiasm, good judgment and a sense of humor. A pleasing personality and organizational ability are also important. The ability to see the potential in young people, to appreciate and patiently develop it, is a part of these important qualifications.

Willingness to learn. Adults who work with youth can learn with them by being open for help and instruction which will enable them to know and serve their young people better. This may include reading helpful

5Zuck, *op. cit.,* XI: 5.

books, attending conferences and training sessions, and talking with other youth workers.

Ability to counsel youth. A youth worker needs more than a burden for and an interest in young people; he also needs to be able to help them with their problems.

Acquaintance with and adherence to cardinal rules of counseling promote confidence and trust in adult leaders. These include the following: Never betray a confidence; do not express shock at what a teen tells you; do not ask too many questions; never preach; do not expect a pleasant time with every counselee; and do not be disappointed if obvious results are not always produced.

Counseling includes listening well, questioning tactfully and wisely (so that the youth can see his problem for himself), and guiding the counselee in finding answers to his needs in God's Word.[6]

Awareness of the total church program and his share in it. The alert leader should realize that his service with his teens is a part of a larger, total ministry of the church. The well-rounded total church ministry provides for instruction, worship, training and fellowship for each individual. Each agency ministering to young people should fulfill its part of the whole; no agency should feel it is *the* whole or even the most important segment of that whole.

Specific ministries like camping, club work, teaching or directing church youth musical groups naturally demands special qualifications suited to these requirements. The specific service will suggest these special necessary qualities.

Each youth worker may feel that he does not match perfectly the foregoing characteristics and qualifications. Nevertheless these are ideals toward which he may aspire. Growth in them will contribute toward his own spiritual maturity and improvement in his service to youth.

Recruitment of Youth Workers

Recruiting people to work with youth is not easy. Not all adults readily respond to the challenge of working with young people. And not all adults should!

Recruitment should be the task of the Christian education board or committee—so that the total needs of the church may be kept in view, and so that the best possible personnel for each job can be secured. If individual church agencies are left to "compete" for the available potential leaders, the probability of an orderly fitting of persons to proper responsibilities is decreased, as are the chances for successful recruitment.

---

[6]For more on this subject see chapter 26, "Principles of Counseling Youth."

The board which is faced with personnel needs in its youth departments should follow a carefully planned sequence of activity in all recruitment efforts.

First, the board members should, in earnest prayer, seek God's direction and blessing in the important task of recruiting youth workers.

Next, a list should be made of all persons who might qualify—taking into consideration the necessary qualifications.

Then the list of possible candidates should be rated and aligned on the basis of that rating.

The representative of the board appointed to the task should then make an appointment with the person (or persons, in the case of couples) first on the list. Recruitment for a job of the magnitude of youth worker should be done through a planned personal contact.

From a list of desirable qualities and the services performed by a youth leader a church may define the role of a youth leader in a printed statement. Such a statement could explain the opportunities one has for personal growth and Christian service in working with youth as well as acquaint him with some of the problems youth leaders often face.

The candidate should be urged to consider prayerfully the proposition and reply within a reasonable length of time.

If he says no, the recruiter may go on to the next person on the list. The recruiter must be careful about pressuring people into a task as demanding as that of youth worker.

Several things can be done to create a favorable climate for the recruitment of youth leaders in a church.

One is to impress on the congregation the importance of this ministry— and the necessity for able leadership. An occasional sermon on the heritage of and responsibility to youth in the church will be helpful.

Using the church bulletin, bulletin boards and pulpit announcements to keep the youth ministries before a congregation is one effective way of increasing awareness of and concern for youth.

The use of young people's groups in church services on special occasions— such as Youth Week, Pioneer Girls or Brigade Sunday—will also help build an awareness of the work.

Making the youth ministries and their adult leaders the subject of prayer in the midweek services will also lead to a climate in which recruitment will be made easier.

Training of Youth Workers

The recruitment of adults for work with youth is only the beginning of a church's responsibility to them. Local church Christian educators who truly believe that youth leaders have a significant task to perform will see that they are given as many training opportunities as possible. Some of these can be:

Ensuring that the job to be done is clearly understood by the leader. The supply of a written job description, and the necessary materials, records and reviews will show leaders good leadership in action.

Encouraging leaders to attend conferences, workshops, seminars, clinics and leadership institutes. The alert Christian education leader will see to it that as many as possible of his youth leaders attend such gatherings. Churches near large centers where national or regional Sunday school conventions are held can take advantage of these opportunities.

Conducting local church leadership training classes. Many churches conduct one or more such training classes annually. Some offer these as a training hour or Sunday school class for as many as three quarters in a year. Prospective leaders are enrolled and present leaders brought in on a rotation basis.

A number of excellent books, records and filmstrips are available to use as aids in such classes. See "For Further Reading" at the end of this chapter for the books by Hoglund, Narramore, Robertson, Soderholm, Washburn and Zuck.

The Moody Bible Institute (Chicago) has produced two series of filmstrips, "Successful Teaching" and "Know Your Child." The filmstrips in these areas which deal with teens and youth are excellent.

Scripture Press Publications, Inc. (Wheaton, Ill.) has an outstanding series of sound-color training filmstrips called the "Royal Commission" series. The ones on juniors ("Welcome to the Club"), young teens ("Those Turnabout Years") and senior highs ("Doubletake") provide splendid training for youth workers. Gospel Light Publications, Inc. (Glendale, Calif.) has produced a set of training records.

Denominational Christian education headquarters have their own leadership training programs—for which recognition is usually granted to all who meet the requirements of the course.

Where a church is not large enough to conduct a *class* for the few youth leaders within it, other arrangements can be made. One of these is to consider the possibility of combining forces with several other area churches for a class or series of classes. Another is to schedule weekend retreats of youth workers from several churches for the purpose of training in departmental or agency workshops. Another alternative is the following suggestion:

Enrolling leaders in correspondence courses, or personal study courses.

The leadership training provided and required by the Christian Service Brigade and Pioneer Girls organizations is an example of the value of this type of training.

This sort of help can be a real boon to youth workers. Many of the excellent correspondence courses available through The Moody Bible Institute (Chicago) or Biola College (La Mirada, Calif.) will be beneficial to adult workers with youth.

Christian Workers' Service Bureau (Redondo Beach, Calif.) and Awana Clubs (Chicago) also offer assistance by mail in training leaders.

Directing youth leaders to read helpful youth periodicals. Even a small church can subscribe or encourage youth leaders to subscribe to and read some of the many excellent youth magazines available. Often much youth know-how can be absorbed by keen adults through such reading.

Training *can* be accomplished if the leaders of the church attach sufficient importance to it—and truly seek ways to provide it for their adult youth workers.

RELATIONSHIPS OF ADULT WORKERS AND YOUNG PEOPLE

The relationship between adult leaders and their youth should be a warm friendly one—marked by proper respect for each other.

The adult should not stand on his dignity as an adult—nor should he adopt a hail-fellow-well-met, backslapping pseudoteen attitude. He should be himself. Teens appreciate adults who are good sports—who can act their age and yet permit teens to act theirs.

Winning the respect of teens is basic to a lasting friendly relationship. Love, understanding, concern and encouragement can be given by visiting with the youth, following up on absentees, being open to listen to and counsel them, keeping them busy and involved, and making room for them in his home and in the church.

Another aid to a good relationship is tactful discipline—as it may be needed. Youth respect the leader who will kindly but firmly insist on what is right and who at the same time helps them work out their own standards for conducting their services.

Building such a relationship will take time and effort, but the influencing of one life by another cannot be done by remote control. It will require personalized attention of the leader to each youth.

If a youth leader says, "Who is sufficient for these things?" let him be reminded that this kind of relationship is to be his desired goal, and he may move toward it as the Lord enables him.

DUTIES OF YOUTH WORKERS IN SPECIFIC CHURCH AGENCIES

While the function of all adult workers is basically the same—to guide youth to spiritual maturity—the duties of the workers vary within the different agencies of the church.

Duties of Sunday School Teachers

1. Attend Sunday school each week—on time!
2. Prepare lessons thoroughly and prayerfully, avoiding use of the teacher's manual in class. Teach interestingly, with a variety of methods.
3. Seek to know each class member well—both as a member of an age group with general characteristics and as an individual.
4. Share in planning class functions. Attend social events.
5. Visit pupils and arrange for personal, extraclass contacts. Be ready to counsel youth.
6. Set a good example by attendance at church services, and by cooperation in Sunday school activities and conferences.
7. Seek to develop greater facility in teaching and youth work by attending conferences and other training sessions.
8. Pray—for themselves, their teaching and their young people.

Duties of Youth Group Sponsors

Duties of sponsors vary depending on the age level served. With juniors and younger children, adults have to assume more responsibility, but must be willing to allow the youth to assist as far as is feasible. Strong adult leadership is necessary in young teen groups, but here the teens can be involved more fully in leadership responsibilities.

High school youth need leaders who are able to coach them and encourage them to lead and learn.

Older youth can fully assume responsibility, with adult help available as needed. Adult duties, in light of this fact, include the following:[7]

1. Attend Sunday night youth meetings. Be regular and on time.
2. Attend executive and planning-group meetings. Be prepared to offer advice as necessary. Do so positively with suggestions.
3. Attend social functions of the group. Use these as opportunities to get to know each person.
4. Set a good example by church attendance and cooperation.
5. Take every opportunity to improve ability to effectively sponsor the group. Attend training sessions and conferences.
6. Pray earnestly for themselves, for their group and for each youth.

[7]See also chapter 13, "Sunday Evening Youth Programs."

Duties of Weekday Club Leaders

The duties of adult leaders of weekday clubs can vary a great deal—because of the wide age spread in club groups, and their variety of approach. However, certain basic duties are similar:[8]

1. Be present and early for all club meetings. Join in informal pre-meeting activities.
2. Be sure that all is in readiness for the activities, crafts, achievement tests and message.
3. Be available to lead and direct outdoor club activities.
4. Counsel and guide youth in their achievement program. (This program in clubs is designed to set up counseling situations.)
5. Learn to know youth well in total-life situations (e.g., camping, sporting).
6. Pray!

Duties of Full-time Directors of Youth Work

Person suggests the following:

The specific duties will vary with the different churches even within the same denomination. It would be unwise to attempt to formulate a fixed pattern, but some general suggestions may prove helpful.

1. He shares with the local youth in the planning of their program of activities. There is always the temptation for the trained director to want to plan *for* rather than *with* the youth. It is after all *their* program, not *his*.

2. He is present and shares in the social functions. This does not necessarily mean that he leads them. His presence is not that of a police officer to guard against unchristian conduct but to inspire to fine fellowship and pleasant participation for all present.

3. He is particularly concerned about the spiritual nurture of the individual members. In a sense he is their pastor, that is, their shepherd. He is not a substitute for the regular pastor of the church, but an assistant who is able to work more intimately with the adolescents than is the regular minister of the church.

4. He interprets the interests and needs of the youth to the pastor, the board of Christian education, and to the congregation as a whole. He represents the youth in the planning and programming of the church.[9]

Duties of Other Lay Leaders

Church camp directors, counselors and workers; directors of youth

---

[8]See also chapter 14, "Weekday Clubs."

[9]Peter P. Person, *The Church and Modern Youth* (Grand Rapids: Zondervan Publishing House, 1963), p. 54. In this book (pp. 49-59, 117-18) Person also discusses qualifications for youth directors, problems in professional directing of youth work, and how a church should call a youth director. Also see Philip B. Harris, *The Local Director of Youth Work* (Nashville: Convention Press, 1956).

choirs or musical groups; recreational directors and others, naturally have specific duties related to their tasks.[10]

A CHURCH'S APPRECIATION OF ITS YOUTH WORKERS

Those who work with youth will find their satisfaction and reward in a youth's confidence, in the privilege of seeing a teen's problem solved, or in the joy of watching youth grow spiritually.

A Christian education board would be wise in planning some form of public recognition and thanks to youth workers. An ideal time for this is National Youth Week, when the church's ministry to youth is spotlighted. Some churches prepare citations of appreciation, and present them to all who have served faithfully.

Or appreciation can be voiced during services of dedication, when adult workers are publicly committed to their responsibilities and when the prayers of the congregation are solicited for them.

Personal words or notes of appreciation from pastors, Christian education directors, or other church leaders are also in order. Regardless of how it is expressed, thanks should not be overlooked—for youth work *is* difficult. Adult workers are as human as anyone else, and just as subject to discouragement. Often a sincere commendation will lift a discouraged worker.

SUMMARY

Youth workers should remember the importance of being faithful—faithful to the Lord and to those whom He has called them to serve. For all who are faithful, in the strength which God provides, there awaits the prospect of His commendation in that day when the results of faithful labor will be revealed: "Well done, thou good and faithful servant!"

FOR FURTHER READING

Boys for Christ. Wheaton, Ill.: Christian Service Brigade, 1962.

HALL, KENNETH F. *So You Work with Senior High Youth*. Anderson, Ind.: Warner Press, 1959.

HARRIS, PHILIP B. *The Local Director of Youth Work*. Nashville: Convention Press, 1956.

HILTON, ROBERT M. "Mature Adult Workers," *Baptist Leader*, XXVIII:20-21 (January, 1967).

HOGLUND, GUNNAR. *Better CYF Youth Groups*. Chicago: Harvest Publications, 1960.

LACKEY, J. V. *Young People and the Sunday School Challenge*. Nashville: Convention Press, 1960.

[10]For books which give detailed lists of duties in these areas, see "For Further Reading" at the end of this chapter.

MATTSON, LLOYD D. *Camping Guideposts*. Chicago: Moody Press, 1962.

NARRAMORE, CLYDE M. *The Psychology of Counseling*. Grand Rapids: Zondervan Publishing House, 1960.

———. *Understanding and Guiding Teenagers*. Grand Rapids: Zondervan Publishing House, 1961.

OVERTON, GRACE S. *Living with Teeners*. Nashville: Broadman Press, 1950.

PERSON, PETER P. *The Church and Modern Youth*. Grand Rapids: Zondervan Publishing House, 1963. Chapter 6.

Pioneer Girls Guide. Wheaton, Ill.: Pioneer Girls, 1963.

SANTA, GEORGE F. *Youth Leader's Handbook No. 1*. Redondo Beach, Calif.: Christian Workers' Service Bureau, 1955.

SODERHOLM, MARJORIE E. *Understanding the Pupil, Part III, The Adolescent*. Grand Rapids: Baker Book House, 1961.

Tested Ideas for Teachers of Teen-agers. Elgin, Ill.: David C. Cook Publishing Co., 1963.

TODD, FLOYD and PAULINE. *Camping for Christian Youth*. New York: Harper & Row, 1963.

TOWNS, ELMER. *Teaching Teens*. Grand Rapids: Baker Book House, 1963.

WASHBURN, A. V. *Young People in the Sunday School*. Nashville: Convention Press, 1955.

ZUCK, ROY B., and ROBERTSON, FERN. *How to Be a Youth Sponsor*. Wheaton, Ill.: Scripture Press Foundation, 1960.

PART IV

youth beyond the local church

The church youth organization, like any organization in the Christian church, is not an entity in itself. It is part of a larger picture —the total program of the denomination and the worldwide cause of Christ. How well it fits into this wider domain will determine in large measure its degree of success or failure.

GUNNAR HOGLUND

19

denominational and interchurch activities

A COMPARATIVELY SHORT TIME AGO, participation by young people in interchurch activities was limited by problems of travel. Even a ten-mile trip by horse and carriage was an all-day endurance feat. But with the advent of the automobile and the telephone, with the development of modern highways and sleek new methods of transportation, no section of the country is exempt from comradeship for young people.

On both the denominational and the interdenominational scenes, many youth organizations are isolationist in spirit. They refuse to blend their efforts with others of like faith and practice. This go-it-alone spirit, it must be said, brings injury to the young people they are trying to assist and in numbers of cases imposes great loss on the total cause of Christ. Church youth groups need not succumb to this disease. They should cooperate, joining hands and hearts with those who pursue the same goals.

THE DENOMINATIONAL YOUTH PROGRAM

Some people and causes on the denominational level with whom church youth groups should cooperate are:

GUNNAR HOGLUND, B.D., is Director of Youth Work for the Baptist General Conference, Chicago, Illinois.

The denominational Sunday school program. Denominations usually run interchurch attendance and loyalty campaigns, and the more their young people get involved in these activities the better.

The camp leaders. Denominations sponsor extensive camp and summer assembly programs where young people can spend a day or two (or an entire week) in study, worship and fellowship. Camp, in fact, has become a foremost arm of evangelism and an effective means of leading Christian teens to dedicate their lives to Christ.

The boys' and girls' club program. If the denomination runs a club program, the youth groups should find out about it and get into step. This may involve rallies, retreats, training conferences and conventions; it may also involve the use of an endorsed program involving procedures, materials and standards.

The denominational youth organization. Usually this is linked most closely with the weekly youth group program. What is its organizational set-up? How does an individual group gain membership? What are its obligations, financial and otherwise? Where are the rallies and conventions held?

Most denominational youth organizations have a "youth council" of some kind in which regional or district youth leaders give direction on a denominational level. Some denominations, in addition, hold super youth conventions every three or four years—gatherings which supplement district and state get-togethers.

A great number of youth organizations also run contests and drives on a denominational level. Many denominations publish various materials for their youth programs. Youth workers can find out about the aids their denomination provides, and then obtain them and put them to work. The denomination may belong to a worldwide organization (such as the Baptist World Alliance for all Baptists), thus providing another outlet for witness on a worldwide level.

Numerous denominations sponsor Youth Week observances which enable each church, once a year, to focus attention on youth and youth work. The dates for Youth Week are usually the last full week of January, and materials for these events are often provided through denominational Christian education or youth offices.

Youth activities on a denominational level, whether a weekend rally, a retreat or a conference, have purposes which should be kept in mind. These purposes are to help train young people for leadership, for effective personal witness, and for responsible living at all levels of life. Many youth accept Christ as Saviour at such gatherings. Such activities should also provide young people with Christian fellowship—comradeship and companionship with other young people who share their faith in Christ. And expressional opportunities should be given too, where teens can pour out a little of themselves in song-leading, playing or singing, program planning, message preparation, activities that bring to the surface the best of their skills and leadership potential.

Denominational officials seek to present a wide-ranging program of activities for young people—activities that are available to all their young people, in urban and rural areas alike. Specifically, denominational youth leaders should:

1. Give adult guidance and direction to the total program.
2. See that youth activities are integrated into the total denominational program of missions and evangelism.
3. See that spiritual objectives of the program are kept to the fore.

INTERCHURCH YOUTH PROGRAM

What about the local church unaffiliated with a denomination? In such cases fellowship can be obtained by seeking out like-minded churches in the neighborhood or community or state, and arranging for joint activities.

Whether or not a church belongs to a denomination, its youth can participate in the following forms of interchurch youth activities:

Weekend Conference

In planning such a conference (or convention, as it is often called) the nature of the event must first be determined. The get-together could be for churches in an entire district or state, or for a number of churches in one area. As many as five hundred churches can take part, or as few as two or three. The convention could be a regular event, held every spring, for example. Or it could be a just-this-once sort of thing.

About six months before the convention the cabinet or planning committee should consider three matters: date, location, committees. The date should be a time most convenient to the largest number of young people, and least likely to conflict with already-scheduled events. A weekend, Friday evening through Sunday afternoon, is the best time for the convention. Friday evening through Saturday, though, and Sunday only are also acceptable times. Or the convention may be planned for a Saturday and Sunday, or for a Saturday only. Three-day events allow more time, of course, for achieving the objectives in mind.

Next the location must be selected. The place (usually a church, though a conference or camp ground can also be used) must provide adequate housing, food, meeting and recreational accommodations. The conference should not be held in the same spot year after year.

The number and size of the committees to be chosen will depend on the size of the undertaking. But here are a few suggested committees.

Advertising committee. Its task is to send out preliminary materials—such as mimeographed posters—to pastors and youth-group leaders about three months before the date of the event. This initial mailing should be followed by a stream of notices—letters and reminders—each one giving additional details. This committee's job, in addition, is to publicize the event in church bulletins. A mimeographed notice inserted in the church bulletin is a sure attention-getter.

The Chamber of Commerce or a resort agency will be glad to supply literature and flyers describing the city where the event is to take place. These can be slipped into mailings. Local newspapers where the convention will be held should be given news releases, including photos. The advertising committee's final assignment is to prepare signs on a placard stock—welcome signs, theme signs, a banner for the book table, and arrow signs telling where workshops, meetings and other events will be held.

Registration and housing committee. This committee's job is to send registration materials to churches six weeks before the event. This mailing naturally should correlate with the advertising committee's mailings. Also, this committee should assemble packets—including an attractive name badge for each delegate to wear—to be given out at the registration table. This packet should include a complete array of literature depicting the who-what-why-when of your gathering. The committee should also set up an easy-to-find table for registration, and man it adequately with responsible people. As to housing, this committee should arrange for homes, motels and hotels, and should prepare housing assignment cards.

In addition, this committee should arrange for a courtesy car, parking facilities, and an information booth where questions can be answered and where lost and found items can be processed. They should also arrange for a convention photographer who can take shots for use in publicizing future events. If the photographer wishes, he can also take single pictures of convention-goers, then sell them to the young people. This committee should also prepare a list of recommended restaurants for delegates to patronize.

What public transportation will be needed? What time should delegates arrive? What about housing for speakers and other leadership personnel? These are only a few of the other matters that will occupy this committee's time. Who will arrange for chairs, visual aids, hymnals, and provide ushers and handle the offering? All these details are the responsibility of this committee.

Banquet committee. These people are to arrange for banquet decorations, menu, location, program, serving and cleanup. Because the banquet is such a colorful part of the total weekend, it deserves a special committee of its own.

When planning the convention, the committee must not be afraid to try novel ways of doing things. There was the fellow, for example, who sent a three-inch string to all the churches with a note saying, "This is the string you'll use to tie your winning attendance banner to the wall—if you win it!"

Arranging the conference around some special activity is sometimes wise—like a basketball, softball or volleyball tournament (one team from each church or area, for example), or some other special event. In one district the young people gathered the same week as a world championship ski tournament. The group may want to meet during the Christmas vacation, or on New Year's Day, over Thanksgiving weekend—or on Memorial Day. Sports, when tied into the convention, should not be overemphasized, crowding aside the basic spiritual purposes of the weekend.

Now and then youth conventions weave music and talent contests into the schedule. These can include competition in music (vocal and instrumental) as well as in speech, song-leading, Bible quizzes and other forms of talent display. However, the rules must be clearly stipulated, and age levels separated so competition is fair. Also, the judging must be of mature and competent caliber. The awards should be attractive.

The delegates should be asked to register beforehand in order for the committee to have an idea how to plan the housing and meals. The committee should plan a registration procedure that is quick and simple. Many a conference-attender balks at the last minute when confronted by a confusing registration card. It is a good idea to plan a "conference captain" in every church to insure that the event gets sufficient promotion.

The main speaker—or speakers if there are several—has heavy responsibility thrust on his shoulders. He can make or break all the dreams and prayers for the convention's success. He must be God's man to deliver God's message. Therefore he must be selected with meticulous care.

Here are qualifications to look for in a convention speaker:

1. Genuine spiritual-mindedness. It may sound trite but it is true that young people can spot a leader whose Christian convictions are only skin-deep.

2. Skill in communicating with young people. Not all Christian leaders have this knack.

3. Ability to inspire and challenge. A primary quality of successful convention messages is that they rouse young people to receive Christ as Saviour, to witness, to dedicate their lives for Christian service and to consider the great issues of the Christian gospel. In short, the messages should fire young people up. They should stir their minds, their wills, their emotions. The type of message that is primarily instructional in nature has its place, but not at a youth convention.

4. Reputation for messages that deal with matters of vital concern, that come to grips with pertinent issues in the everyday lives of young people. The speaker who majors in the trite, the obvious, and the cliché should be avoided.

After the committee obtains the speaker, it must provide him with careful and adequate instructions (in writing) as to what it has in mind. All arrangements must be absolutely clear. The committee should not be afraid to approach top-name speakers. But it should remember that just because a man is well known does not necessarily mean that he is the best speaker for the situation.

When the speaker arrives at the convention, the group will treat him with Christian courtesy, of course. And when the gathering is over, they will send him a thank you letter and will complete the financial arrangements.

What about workshop and panel discussion leaders? Here the purposes are primarily instructional—selected. It is essential to choose as leaders those who can draw out discussion, stimulate thought, and give young people fresh, enlightening information. Never tolerate sermons at workshops!

Once the convention opens, what then? Friday evening should major in getting acquainted. After delegates register and pin on their name tags, some "mixers" will help put them at ease. A devotional will end the evening profitably. They should be cautioned on some dos and don'ts of being a guest in a home overnight. Or if they are assigned to a dorm, a counselor should keep them in line.

Saturday morning should accent discussions, classes and panels. Saturday morning—if this is the number one gathering of the year—should also feature the annual business meeting of the organization.

Afternoon is excellent for recreation, outdoors and indoors. The banquet, complete with awards, stunts and a pointed Bible message, is ideal for Saturday evening. Sunday should find the delegates in Sunday school (maybe a special session for the conference attendants) and worship services. In the afternoon there can be a climaxing rally or, if time is a factor, a short testimony time when all sum up the blessings of the weekend. Everyone should be reminded to send thank you notes to their hosts, and cautioned to drive carefully going home.

Friendliness, good publicity, a wide range of youth-styled activities, strong leadership and plenty of prayer preparation—these are the essential ingredients. Mixed well, they can help a convention become a success and contribute greatly to the spiritual enrichment of young people.

Weekend Retreat

Youth retreats are different from youth conferences and conventions in two ways. First, they are usually held in an outdoor setting rather than a church. And second, they are conducted in most instances for a specialized clientele rather than for the entire range of young people. By inserting one or two retreats a year in the youth program, a church can extend a great favor to the younger set.

A retreat can be held any time, though early fall or late summer usually is best. Memorial Day and Labor Day weekends are especially popular. A winter retreat is a great experience, too, since most young people's camp experience doesn't include snow. If the retreat is primarily for planning, it should be held immediately after new officers are elected—or just before the fall season.

To be successful, a retreat must be carefully planned. Here are matters that deserve attention:

Purpose. What does the group have in mind? Is it to rally the young people at the end of the summer and charge them up for the season ahead? Or to inspire and alert them personally? Is it for officers to chart a year's activities? Is it for leadership training? Does it have a deeper-life emphasis. The group must choose the type of retreat theme that best fits its needs.

Place. A state or district campsite may be available for the end of August or early fall. Or a cabin or country home of some interested family may be secured. It is important that there be space for outdoor recreation and provision for active indoor play in case the weather gets bad. For a snowy weekend, the place must be winterized.

Costs. Individual cost depends on several factors: number of youth attending, amount of food that will be donated, number of meals served, distance to camp, means of transportation, cost of renting the site, total of honoraria and expense-money for speakers, amount of insurance and amount the treasury can donate to keep expenses down. After adding the costs, a fair fee can be established.

Adult leaders. The retreat will benefit greatly by an athlete to direct games or teach skiing, a speaker to bring down-to-earth devotions, an educator to advise on the year's plans, a discussion leader to draw out ideas, a successful youth leader to offer new ideas. A good cook or two, a nurse, a lifeguard (if the weather is right), and counselors should be on the list too. Some of these jobs, of course, can be handled by the more mature young people. Upon deciding on the number and kind of leaders required, the committee then should search them out several weeks beforehand and brief them on their assignments.

Transportation. Safety regulations require that all cars be insured and drivers licensed. Mimeographed directions or maps should be provided if the itinerary is tricky.

Food. Detailed menus should be written out ahead of time, also a list of waitresses, dishwashers and busboys. Planning should allow for easily prepared meals and paper plates where possible. The committee must be sure to provide plenty of food!

There is no ready-made schedule to fit all retreats. The determining factors to bear in mind are: (1) Friday evening's activities should essentially constitute a "get acquainted" time. (2) Eight to nine hours of sleep are usually needed. (3) Saturday morning should be given over to the principal business in mind, the afternoon to recreation, and the evening to a combination of fun and the serious (a banquet often works well). (4) Sunday morning should be worshipful, followed by a closing testimony and sum-up time in the early afternoon just before packing up and heading for home.

Should everyone at the retreat be at the evening church service back home? By all means, if for no other reason than to report what transpired.

If the retreat lasts only two days—Friday and Saturday or Saturday and Sunday—the schedule can easily be adjusted while still retaining the essential elements.

Youth Rally

A Sunday afternoon or weeknight ninety-minute rally can go over big—particularly when it is scrupulously planned and promoted. The cabinet or planning committee should get together at least a couple of months beforehand. Planning by letter or telephone must not be attempted; that is a guaranteed way of striking out.

The size of the place for the rally is most important. Furthermore, the site can well be varied from a church to a hall or school auditorium.

The date should preferably be on a weekend, and if possible on a night or afternoon when none of the high schools have a game or other activity that would conflict with the rally.

The speaker need not be a minister, and he does not have to be young, but he should be someone the young people like and admire. He should be briefed about his subject and about the kind of crowd he will have. The committee may make suggestions that will help determine what will catch the ear of those who hear the speaker. Then the committee can work with the speaker to get an interesting title—one that will help publicize the rally. The committee must not forget to plan to cover the speaker's expenses! It should tell him exactly what financial arrangements it is able to make.

The master of ceremonies should be one who has a strong voice and a touch of humor.

Musicians should be carefully selected. A group that muddles through (or has to start over) can send a rally on the rocks. Also, there should be variety in the musical feature from rally to rally. For instance, a vocal solo and a brass quartet could be featured once, a small choir and an instrumental duet another time. Other combinations could be a musical saw and a girls' chorus, or a string trio and a male quartet.

If possible, the host pastor should train the ushers before the rally. They must be fellows who won't show up with muddy boots and T-shirts. They must understand how to work the windows, where to locate the light switches, where to find the offering plates.

Much depends upon the type of publicity used. It should notify everyone in no uncertain terms that there is going to be a rally. It will be more interesting if the committee does not depend too heavily on the usual channels; people sometimes read the church bulletin without letting the announcements settle in their minds. Unusual posters in unusual places will help. An air of mystery—"Watch for the important announcement in this place next week"—will get some response. A pep talk by a young person in Sunday school will help too. An every-young-person telephone chain is one of the best methods. Mailings and flyers and letters should sound a spritely and youthlike tone. A mature individual should be assigned the task of procuring and displaying appropriate books on a table at the back of the church or auditorium. He should also be responsible for the sale of these books.

These details must be planned step by step. But even after careful planning, remember that the rally can still be a flop if the plans are not carried out!

One capable person from each church should be responsible to recruit all the help he needs. His job is to see that the special part assigned to his church is well prepared and arrives on time; that the publicity is circulated in the church; that the transportation is rounded up. He is the key man; he can make or break the rally.

But it is everybody's job to pray—and pray specifically. Each member of the group should pray that they will think of the right ideas and people. All should pray that those having special responsibilities will carry them out conscientiously. The speaker, musicians, ushers and emcee should particularly be remembered in prayer. Also the youth will want to pray that the young people in all the cooperating churches will be able to come.

After the rally, when the committee starts thinking about the next one, it should start dreaming up ways to improve the approach. Maybe a future rally could be planned for just the junior high teens or just the high school youth. Perhaps roller skating or skiing or swimming could be planned for before or after a rally. The program should be varied in some way, because variety in rallies is important.

Graduation Event

The prom problem, a perennial headache in many churches, can be counteracted in a positive manner by getting several area churches together to sponsor a gala banquet-type gathering each May or June. There can be formals, corsages, a speaker, a grand march, a tribute to the seniors, adding up to a colorful, warm and exciting evening.

College Preparation Event

A group of churches may bring together their young people who are contemplating college in the fall. An afternoon or evening (or both) is spent briefing them on what is ahead. A college president or dean of students is often used as a speaker or workshop leader.

Singspirations

Sunday evenings after church services young people frequently have time on their hands. Why not sponsor an interchurch singspiration—or hymn sing? These sing times can be held once a month, or once every three months. When a group plans singspirations, though, it should keep them consistent with the term—plenty of music and no windy sermons.

Special Events

These can be an Easter sunrise breakfast for young people from neighboring churches, an outing not involving long distances to travel—a Saturday afternoon picnic, a steak fry, a Galilean service, a hike, a beach party, a hayride, a sunrise service, a roller skating event, or a boat ride.

Special Projects

Here are some worthwhile ventures an interchurch youth program can assume.[1] Some involve money, some do not. In deciding on a project, youth should remember that it should be something that does not duplicate what youth groups can do better on the local church level. These are some projects to consider:

1. A scholarship program for teens attending Christian colleges.
2. Partial support of a missionary, especially one who has grown up in one of the participating churches.
3. Raising funds for an improvement of the church camp grounds— a water heater, new hymnals, a projector, for instance.

---

[1]Also see chapter 17, "Youth Serving the Church."

4. Raising a designated amount within a year toward a new church in the area.

5. A team—speaker, song leader and musical groups—to travel among the churches, appearing at youth meetings and Sunday evening services, emphasizing evangelism, inspiration and information about the youth program.

6. An interchurch program of competition, challenging each church in the area to lift its level of operation. The award schould have a name fitting the particular section of the country (in Minnesota such awards are often called North Star awards, for example). The winner should be enthusiastically honored at the time of presentation.

An interchurch contest can be conducted among several youth groups. Competition could be built around bringing newcomers, improving meetings, Scripture memorization, or recruiting fellows and girls for Bible camp. Provision should be made for careful checking of performance, and the awards must be exciting.

THE NAE AND NSSA

The National Sunday School Association (the Christian education arm of the National Association of Evangelicals) has a Youth Commission which provides opportunity for cooperative witness and sharing of ideas between evangelically minded denominational youth leaders.

Membership in the Youth Commission consists of youth executives and leaders of denominational and interdenominational organizations who are in sympathy with the general program and objectives of NSSA and who agree with its doctrinal statement. This commission provides a year-round exchange center for methods, materials, procedures, and it conducts clinics and workshops at the annual spring convention of the National Association of Evangelicals and the annual convention of the National Sunday School Association each fall.

The Youth Commission also gives attention to collecting, evaluating, and communicating to the Christian public the facts and needs concerning today's younger set. The theme for the annual National Youth Week, sponsored by NSSA and scheduled annually from the last Sunday in January through the first Sunday in February, is chosen by the Youth Commission.

SUMMARY

The benefit reaped by youth groups participating in interchurch activities is incalculable. Far-reaching results are experienced and seen in the lives of numerous youth. The transforming effect on the homes and churches of the nation will be evidenced in the years ahead.

FOR FURTHER READING

CHAMBERLIN, J. GORDON. *The Church and Its Young Adults*. New York: Abingdon-Cokesbury Press, n.d.

CUMMINGS, OLIVER DE WOLF. *Guiding Youth in Christian Growth*. Philadelphia: Judson Press, 1954.

HOGLUND, GUNNAR. *Better CYF Youth Groups*. Chicago: Harvest Publications, 1960.

HUMMEL, CHARLES E. *Campus Christian Witness*. Chicago: Inter-Varsity Press, 1958.

MITCHELL, LEON. *Retreats*. Nashville: Baptist Sunday School Board, 1965.

PERSON, PETER B. *The Church and Modern Youth*. Grand Rapids: Zondervan Publishing House, 1963.

SEWELL, J. P. and SPECK, H. E. (eds.) *The Church and the Young People*. Austin, Tex.: Firm Foundation Publishing House, 1935.

WILLIAMS FORREST. "Plan a Winter Retreat," *Moody Monthly*, LXIII:52-54 (December, 1962).

Today's students are tomorrow's leaders. A college student won to Christ today will be a Christian lawyer, doctor, engineer, politician, professor, minister or missionary tomorrow. The greatest manpower pool for foreign missions today in the world is in the campuses of North America. There are thousands of entering Christian students. When we add those who will come to Christ through their witness, the potential of the missionary force coming out of the university is exciting to contemplate.

Paul E. Little

20

reaching youth in college

SIZE OF THE FIELD

The secular university campus is one of the fastest-growing mission fields in the United States today. Each year more than five million students flock to the ivy halls in small towns and the cathedrals of learning in key metropolitan areas. By 1975 it is estimated there will be more than 8 million students involved in higher education.[1] This is almost double the present enrollment and the end is not yet.

Private institutions, including evangelical Christian schools, have reached capacity and significant expansion seems unlikely. For some of these schools the problem is financial and expansion would be prohibitive in cost. For others a reluctance to expand is based on the fear of diluting the quality of education.

Within three years 95 percent of all college and university students will be on public tax-supported campuses. This means that many more evangelical Christians will be students in these secular institutions and may

[1]"Campus '65," *Newsweek*, LXVI:44 (March 22, 1965) .

Paul E. Little, M.A., is Director of Evangelism for the Inter-Varsity Christian Fellowship, Chicago, Illinois.

become a potent missionary force on these campuses. They will be strategic not only numerically but also in terms of their Christian influence.

Today's students are tomorrow's leaders. A college student won to Christ today will be a Christian lawyer, doctor, engineer, politician, professor, minister or missionary tomorrow. The greatest manpower pool for foreign missions today in the world is in the campuses of North America. There are thousands of entering Christian students. When we add those who will come to Christ through their witness, the potential of the missionary force coming out of the university is exciting to contemplate.

UNDERSTANDING THE FIELD

In reaching mission fields, whether geographical or in a particular enclave of society, there must be an understanding of the field and an identification with it before an effective approach can be made. Students are not eagerly waiting to hear the gospel any more than people on any other mission field. They need to be aroused from lethargy and indifference to realize that Jesus Christ is the only answer to life and eternity. If asked in the abstract if they are interested in Christianity, many would reply incredulously but firmly, "No!" However, when confronted with Jesus Christ in reasonable and contemporary terms, many become awakened who once thought they were not interested in the slightest. Many of these finally ask the vital question, "How can this become real to me?"

What is the typical secular university student like today? There are obvious variations and exceptions, but many of the following descriptions characterize students today.

Perhaps the most applicable generalization is that most students are without purpose and direction in their daily business. They are not quite sure why they are on the campus except that Mom and Dad have sent them. Why they are studying architecture, botany, music or physics is not clear to them. To be sure, it is to get the sheepskin denoting a degree which leads to a job, but how this relates to the whole of life and the ultimate purpose of it eludes many of them.

The rat race of study, sleep, classes, meals, sleep, study, sleep is for many students a treadmill leading nowhere. Dr. Nathan Pusey, president of Harvard University, has said that students are looking for a flag to follow, a song to sing, and a creed to believe.[2] Significantly, one of the reasons many college dropouts give for leaving is that they came to college looking for answers to life and, instead of answers, they found only more questions.

---

[2]An increasing minority are finding what they feel is short-term meaning and purpose in the civil rights movement, and in other groups such as the free speech movement at Berkeley University.

Disillusioned, they decided to try to find meaning and authenticity else-where. A staggering 40 percent of all students entering college fail to graduate.

Though we live in a so-called Christian country, the average university student is biblically illiterate. The writer frequently begins a discussion in a fraternity or dormitory by asking the students how they would define Christianity to someone from another country who had no objections to Christianity but simply was ignorant of it. Replies are shocking in that the person and work of Christ are seldom intelligently related to being and becoming a Christian.

A nonchristian student from a Pennsylvania college was riding with a Christian student. They passed a sign along the road which said, "Jesus saves." The non-Christian in all sincerity said, "That's something I've never thought of before. If Jesus was thrifty, I should be too!"

The fact of biblical illiteracy has important implications for the ways we communicate the gospel to nonchristian students. It must be in non-traditional vernacular language for the benefit of those who haven't learned "Protestant Latin," as Eugene Nida has called our traditional jargon.

Students often think they have rejected Christianity, but in conversation it soon becomes apparent that they have rejected simply a caricature of the real thing. Many students think of Christianity as essentially a nega-tion of life and its enjoyments. Christianity is thought of as a series of *don'ts* without much understanding of the *dos*. This idea must be coun-tered by the communication of the abundant life Jesus offers us in John 10:10 without in any way hiding the cost of discipleship. No man can hang onto his sin and follow Jesus Christ, but his desires change when he be-comes a new creation.

"I wish I had your faith," students often say. The implication of this wistful comment is that they just cannot be that naïve. Many college youth think of faith as the little boy defined it, "Believing something you know isn't true." To many college students, faith is just a notch above the super-stitions of primitive cultures and certainly inappropriate in the academic atmosphere of the scientific space age.

Few have ever heard the factual basis and evidence on which the Chris-tian faith is based and have not realized that in Christianity faith goes be-yond reason but not against it. They are amazed, for instance, to hear the evidence for the resurrection and the evidence for the reliability of biblical documents. Unfortunately, many Christian students are equally amazed to encounter the same evidence and are quite relieved to realize that they don't have their "heads in a bucket" after all!

This latter fact points up the painful truth that many churches have done less than a first-class job in preparing students for the intellectual climate of the thinking nonchristian world. We have tended to give them answers to the wrong questions—questions nobody is asking. This conclusion has been confirmed by an experiment the writer has conducted several times on Christian college campuses. "Let's imagine," he has said to the students, "you're a fraternity or dormitory group on a secular campus. I'll give a talk which I give on the secular campus and we'll have a question period just as we do there. You can ask anything you want and remember that we'll assume you're a nonchristian group." The questions these students ask, which they *think* the non-Christian would ask, are quite different from those the writer encounters regularly in talking to unsaved youth. They tend to be much more biblically oriented and not nearly as basic as those in Sigma Chi or Sproull Hall.

But university students, like people everywhere, have a hunger for God. It is often undefined and unrecognized, but it can be brought into focus by relating the problems of life to the source of those problems—separation from God (the result of rebellion against the Creator). Secular researchers confirm this also: "When we talked to the students about religion we found that many of them began the discussion by declaring that they felt strongly a need for some kind of a religious faith or philosophy to give meaning to their lives and to bridge the gap between the manifest occurrences of daily life and the ultimate meaning of these occurrences."[3]

The fields on the university campus are white for harvest now as perhaps at no other time in history. The advent of the bomb has given a seriousness to life which for many will never be reversed. Not that students are moping, but many are asking some serious and long, hard questions in the midst of the superficial frivolity in which many participate. Also in our time novelists and playwrights are saying what the Bible has said about human nature for 2,000 years. William Golding's bestselling *Lord of the Flies* and the subsequent movie based on the novel make the point with devastating power that human nature is corrupt. Tennessee Williams has made the point on the stage that man is sick. We as Christians believe that Christ is the answer, but if He is to be heard, we must communicate the gospel in relevant terms.

WINNING A HEARING

Getting an audience for the gospel on the university campus is the key problem. We may have the most brilliant speaker communicating the gospel dynamically, but if no one is listening but the Christians, we haven't accomplished very much in terms of evangelizing campus youth.

Effective mass evangelism in any field is based on effective personal

---

[3]R. K. Goldsen and others, *What College Students Think* (New York: D. Van Nostrand Co., Inc.) p. 156.

evangelism, both before and after the effort. However, evangelism cannot be limited to the circle of friends of the Christian student, even though it begins there. Paul says in II Corinthians 9:6, "He who sows sparingly will reap sparingly, and he who sows bountifully will reap bountifully." Our objective should be to effectively communicate the gospel over the course of a year to as many students and faculty as possible.

How we do it is as important as *that* we do it. *How* we do it will also determine *whether* we can do it in the increasingly confused climate of church-state relationships as they apply to public tax-supported institutions. For instance, not long ago students on a state university campus were denied permission to sponsor a lecture on the subject "Is the Bible true?" on the grounds that this would violate the principle of separation of church and state. Several months later, however, they were permitted to have a lecture on the subject "Are the New Testament documents reliable?"

Since students are reacting against traditional forms, one will gain a much wider hearing for the gospel by going to where they are rather than asking them to come to where he is. In other words, since they may not come to our churches, we must gain entrance to the places where they live and carry on their activities.

Evangelistic bull sessions in fraternities, sororities and dormitories are a very effective way to get a large nonchristian audience. These discussions can be arranged by contacting the fraternity, sorority or dormitory council presidents, suggesting the availability of a half-hour program consisting of a fifteen-minute talk followed by a fifteen-minute open question period.[4]

The topic should be provocative like "Does becoming a Christian mean intellectual suicide?" The more a topic expresses a question or some idea that is actually in the non-Christian's mind, the more it will attract people to the discussion.

Following the presentation the floor is opened for questions. This format has special appeal for students. They are accustomed to it and if the word gets around that the house agnostic will be there and controversy is likely to occur, this additional spice draws the otherwise disinterested student to the discussion. It is important to note here that *why* people come to such a discussion is not important. The fact that they come is all important. After hearing the gospel intelligently presented and discussed, they frequently are touched by the Holy Spirit. Interest deepens, and some

---

[4]Groups such as Campus Crusade for Christ (Arrowhead Springs, San Bernardino, Calif. 92403). Inter-Varsity Christian Fellowship (130 N. Wells, Chicago, Ill. 60606) and The Navigators (Glen Eyrie, Colorado Springs, Colo. 80901) are carrying on effective ministries on college campuses.

come to the Lord. Obviously, if they never come in the first place, this does not happen.

Answering questions is not nearly the problem it appears to be at first. The questions asked are remarkably limited in range and surprisingly predictable.[5]

The discussion should be concluded promptly at the close of the half hour with the leader suggesting he will be glad to remain to talk further with any who still have questions. Most will stay on but it will be on their time, voluntarily, rather than because they were forced to stay, out of courtesy to a speaker who kept faith with his time commitment.

Just before adjournment the speaker should offer further information to those who want it. This can be done by showing booklets like John Stott's *Becoming a Christian* and Ken Taylor's *Is Christianity Credible?* He can leave blank index cards on a table or have each person coming to the discussion receive one as he comes in. The speaker might suggest that anyone wanting a free copy of "booklet one," or "booklet two" will receive one by jotting down his name and address and the number of the booklet he wants. Giving numbers for the booklets avoids the problem of the student having to remember a long title.

This way of "drawing the net" does several things. First, it leaves the total initiative up to the individual in response to the work of the Holy Spirit. The student never feels coerced into something. This is very important in university work. If there is even the slightest touch or suggestion of emotionalism or pressure, there can be and usually is a severe reaction. If students smell even the tiniest trace of "sawdust," they revolt.

Second, this approach allows students to get the information later if, as often happens, the speaker gets tied up in an animated conversation with a vocal agnostic. If the speaker is going to be on campus the next day, he can indicate he will be available for interviews. He can name a prominent lounge or room on the campus everyone would know how to locate and then say, "I'll be there to meet you any time you indicate on your card." Christian students or the speaker can take the booklets requested to the individuals the next day. By turning in a card, spiritual interest may be indicated and further conversation may result at the time the booklet is delivered. If the student doesn't want to talk, he is not forced to and the booklet is merely left with him.

EFFECTIVE FOLLOW-UP

Evangelistic Bible studies are an effective follow-up to these discussions. They can also be started with a prior discussion. In this case, one or two students invite their friends to study the New Testament with them infor-

---

[5]Paul E. Little, "What Non-Christians Ask," *His,* XXI:1-4 (November, 1960) .

mally. This can be done by personal door-knocking or posters. It is essential to have the majority in the group non-Christians so that a free and permissive climate will be established. If the non-Christians feel outnumbered and view themselves as targets rather than participants, they will clam up and probably not return. The leader first lays down a few ground rules such as this: "The thing we want to do tonight is discover what this passage of the Bible actually says. Whether one agrees with it or not is another question and can be discussed after the study." By laying down this ground rule at the outset, a number of tangents can be avoided. By carefully prepared questions the leader enables the participants to discover for themselves what he would point out if he were lecturing to them. Several useful guides with pretested questions are available.[6]

Evangelistic Bible studies are not an end in themselves but a means to an end. In any given Bible study, seldom does the passage being studied involve a systematic or complete presentation of the gospel. Students have come to the Lord through Bible studies where there has been personal follow-up. Systematically and prayerfully each non-Christian should be visited on a friendly and informal basis. He can be drawn out as to his own understanding of the gospel, and any gaps in his information can be filled in. As the Holy Spirit leads the student, he should be invited to respond personally to the claims of Jesus Christ. This step should be carefully explained.

After several students have been won to the Lord, it is wise to establish a Bible study group to train these new converts in the basic teachings of the Scriptures and in basic principles of Christian living.[7]

In considering these group approaches, it is imperative to go through proper channels. University authorities are rightly jealous of their prerogatives. Whenever there is an existing campus Christian group which is officially recognized by the university, it will be wise to work through it. The university does not generally look with favor on uncoordinated efforts or activities which seem to duplicate those already established.

Where there is no group it is well to contact the dean of students, become acquainted with him, and explain the broad purpose and plan for the group. If any repercussion gets back to the dean before you get to him, the problem can be infinitely complicated, more so than is the case if you take the initiative first.

---

[6]See, for example, *Discussions on the Life of Jesus Christ* (Chicago: Inter-Varsity Press, 1962). The actual discussion technique is spelled out in Charles E. Hummel, *Campus Christian Witness* (Chicago: Inter-Varsity Press, 1959).

[7]For this purpose The Navigators have ten study books called *Studies in Christian Living,* Inter-Varsity has the *IVCF Guide to Campus Christian Life,* and Campus Crusade for Christ has a ten-booklet study called *Ten Basic Steps Toward Christian Maturity.* See "For Further Reading" at the end of this chapter.

Very few university administrators are prejudiced against evangelicals. The most common attitude is one of indifference. Their major concerns are *how* something will be conducted and that student interests be protected from any form of pressure. If a youth worker realizes that the dean must answer to the president, parents, and unhappy students for any reverberations, he can fully appreciate the dean's position.

THE CHURCH AND THE CAMPUS

Local churches can have a vital ministry to college youth. Churches should keep in contact with Christian students studying on the campus. Rather than pressure these Christian students to be at the church every time it opens its doors, the church should encourage them to spend time as missionaries with nonchristian students who may be reached in no other way. Christian students need training in evangelism to help them overcome the all-too-common tendency to stay in the "holy huddle."

Granted a genuine, vital relationship with Jesus Christ, apart from which no practical instruction will be of much help, there are certain definite things Christian college students must know. For instance, they need to realize that *separation* from the world is not the same thing as *isolation* from the world. They need to have practical instruction in how to live without compromise in a nonchristian world, where the behavior pattern is different from Christian circles. On the one hand, they need to avoid compromise, and on the other hand, "oddballism," which results from making minor issues major in one's Christian witness. They must know how to respond to invitations to drink, smoke and participate in other activities they will not want to be part of. How should they react in the presence of swearing and off-color stories? (For specific practical suggestions, see the writer's *Lost Audience,* Inter-Varsity Press.)

Most Christians are insecure with non-Christians because of insufficiency in one of three areas:

1. They don't know how to approach non-Christians, win their friendship, and swing the conversation from mundane things to spiritual issues.

2. They are not exactly sure what the gospel is. It is like a mathematical problem they have understood in class but are unable to explain clearly an hour later to the friend who cut class. They have believed the gospel and have been changed by it, but are unable to verbalize it clearly enough to someone else so that he too can have the same experience of personal relationship with Christ. Careful instruction in the facts of the gospel and where they can be documented in the New Testament is needed.

3. Many are afraid of being unable to answer questions asked by non-Christians. Instruction in questions and answers, as well as how not to push

the panic button when they cannot answer a particular question, is necessary vital equipment.

The Campus Crusade for Christ (Arrowhead Springs, San Bernardino, California) has been especially successful in its evangelistic ministry to college students through the use of the "Van Dusen Letter," *The Four Spiritual Laws* booklet, and a religious-census questionnaire used to introduce the subject of religion in general and then the plan of salvation. Christian collegians have appreciated the help of these tangible tools in presenting the gospel and winning others to Christ.

In addition to those whom the students and members of the church bring to services, other students can be attracted by a relevant program. Attractive, creative posters on campus are one good way a church can let students know what they are doing. The campus newspaper is also a key link in effective church and campus communication.

A separate class for college students in the Sunday school is a must. If possible a professor who can communicate with students should be asked to teach the college class. This will automatically attract some students. Whoever it is, however, he must be able to communicate effectively and to stimulate discussion. If a plumber does this better than a professor, the former should be used as a teacher. If it's a tossup, the professor should teach the college class, and the plumber should be put to work in some other key spot.

A series of Sunday evening messages on Christian evidences would be both instructive to the Christians and thought-provoking for non-Christians.

A collegiate club on Sunday evening can be very useful also. A dynamic, relevant program on topics which are really on people's minds can have a great spiritual impact. Recognized scholars in their fields can relate Christianity to their academic disciplines and comment on the relevance of the gospel to the affairs of the day. Full opportunity for questions and discussion should be a major feature of this type of program. A contemporary example of an effective program which has been greatly used of God is the Collegiate Club of the Park Street Congregational Church in Boston, Massachusetts.

Christian literature provided by a local church for its college youth can be of great spiritual help. A church library could make available books on Christian evidences, doctrine, witnessing, the Bible and science. Some churches may find it a worthy investment to subscribe to one or more Christian collegiate magazines for their older youth.[8]

The tone or atmosphere of the church itself is another factor in reach-

[8]For example, *Baptist Student* (Southern Baptist Convention, 127 Ninth Avenue, N., Nashville, Tennessee 37203) ; *Collegiate Challenge* (Campus Crusade for Christ, Arrowhead Springs, San Bernardino, California 92403) ; and *His* (Inter-Varsity Press, 130 N. Wells St., Chicago, Illinois 60606) .

ing students through a church. Are students welcomed or are they tolerated? Are they resented because they don't contribute financially and are unable to shoulder major responsibility in the church? This intangible is quickly sensed by students. A positive tone can be set by providing transportation from the campus to the church or by making an effort to arrange for students to have dinner in the homes of church members. Only those who have experienced the monotony of institutional life and food will know what a welcome relief a meal and a few hours in a home can be!

A local church should keep in touch with its students who are attending schools in other towns. This can be done through the pastor writing to the students, through the church office mailing the weekly church bulletin and other literature to the students, through adult "prayer partners" corresponding with one or more students assigned to them for prayer and correspondence. These students should also be given public recognition in church services. In a Midwest church the pastor acknowledged college students when they are home for a holiday vacation and for the summer. He also remembers the students in his pastoral prayer in a morning service just before they leave for school in the late summer or fall.

REACHING INTERNATIONAL STUDENTS

The more than 80,000 foreign students and doctors from 159 different countries who are now living in the United States are looking for friendship. A recent survey shows that 98 percent of them said that the one thing they wanted more than anything else during their time in America was one solid friendship with an American student or family. Only 15 percent of them said they had actually achieved such a friendship. No one should make an overture of friendship to a foreign student unless he is prepared to see him or her regularly until the person returns home. "One-shot" friendships are extremely frustrating to someone from overseas and often lead to disillusionment. No pressure should be put on a foreign student to attend church or become a Christian. Where there is a genuine friendship, however, it will be perfectly natural to discuss and share the Christian faith. The student will usually want to go to church with his host if he is sure the host is truly his friend, and the friendship will not hinge on what his response to the gospel is. Strategic leaders from overseas often become believers in Christ in living rooms as Christians love them, live the Christian life, and talk to them of Christ as there is opportunity.[9]

International Students, Inc. (Box 4963, Washington, D.C. 20008) is doing evangelistic work among students in the United States who are from foreign lands.

---

[9]For further specific suggestions as to dos and don'ts in contacting and developing friendships with and witnessing to foreign students, see *A Guide to International Friendship,* Inter-Varsity Press. Single copy free.

SUMMARY

The university campus in every part of the world is one of the most exciting and strategic frontiers in missions today. There is a need for more full-time student workers as well as those who in the course of other ministries will include the campus in their scope. There is opportunity for thousands of other nonprofessionals who will open their hearts, homes and local churches to those who are pursuing truth. By so doing they will be the means of many coming to know the One who is the Truth.

FOR FURTHER READING

CHAMBERLIN, JOHN GORDON. *Churches and the Campus.* Philadelphia: Westminster Press, 1963.

"Church and College." Special issue (February, 1958) of the *International Journal of Religious Education.*

Discussions on the Life of Jesus Christ. Chicago: Inter-Varsity Press, 1962.

EARNSHAW, GEORGE L. *The Campus Ministry.* Valley Forge, Pa.: Judson Press, 1964.

FLOOD, ROBERT. "Revolution on the Campus?" *Moody Monthly,* LXVII:22-25, 42-43 (September, 1966).

GOLDSEN, ROSE K., *et al. What College Students Think.* New York: D. Van Nostrand Co., 1960.

HUMMEL, CHARLES E. *Campus Christian Witness.* Chicago: Inter-Varsity Press, 1958.

LITTLE, PAUL E. *A Guide to International Friendship.* Chicago: Inter-Varsity Press, 1959.

———. *How to Give Away Your Faith.* Chicago: Inter-Varsity Press, 1966.

———. *Learn to Witness.* Chicago: Inter-Varsity Press, 1963.

———. *Lost Audience.* Chicago: Inter-Varsity Press, 1959.

PHILLIPS, J. B. *God Our Contemporary.* New York: Macmillan Co., 1960.

Ten Basic Steps Toward Christian Maturity. 10 vols. San Bernardino, Calif.: Campus Crusade for Christ.

WALSH, CHAD. *Campus Gods on Trial.* New York: Macmillan Co., 1957.

Youth programs, Sunday school lessons, sermons and personal counseling could help Christian high schoolers and college-age students learn how to face the rigors of military life with a strong Christian testimony. Too many evangelical churches have neglected this all-important matter of preparing young people for military service.

FLOYD ROBERTSON

21

youth in military service

SINCE WORLD WAR II people of all ages have become involved in the religious programs on military installations. This is largely due to the increase of families who occupy government quarters provided by the military. There is a sense in which dependent teen-agers of military personnel might be considered youth in the military and beyond the local church. However, this chapter will deal primarily with youth in uniform, those who are beyond the local church because they are on active duty in the Armed Forces. Reference to men throughout the chapter is used in the generic sense and applies equally to the many fine young women in uniform.

THE CHURCH AND THE CHRISTIAN HOME

Few things are more certain in life than that almost every young, male United States citizen in good health can expect military service. The church cannot afford to ignore this. What the church and the Christian home do

FLOYD ROBERTSON is Executive Secretary of the Commission on Chaplains and Service to Military Personnel for the National Association of Evangelicals.

to help prepare a young person going into the Armed Forces is crucial. It may well determine whether he becomes simply a statistic or a dynamic Christian witness while he is in the military.

By far the most important preparation is a personal experience of salvation through faith in Jesus Christ. The kind of faith that is essential is that wherein a young person commits his life to the person of Christ, and not merely to a church, doctrine or creed.

Almost without exception when you start to talk to a serviceman about Jesus Christ, sooner or later he will respond by telling about some religious experience he has had. These include reference to confirmation, a Christian home, an evangelical church, baptism, an office held in this or that young people's group, prizes for good attendance or memorizing Scripture. But these are not necessarily the people who are living the Christian life in the military. Only those who know Jesus Christ as personal Saviour and are walking in fellowship with Him are able to withstand the wiles of the devil in the Armed Forces.

If a person is not ready to accept Christ as Saviour and to follow Him, the next best thing the church and the Christian home can do is to make certain that he understands clearly how he may become a Christian. This may not be easy for the church and even more difficult for the Christian home, but it is in the best interest of the young person that he be made aware of this.

Both the Christian and non-Christian can be taught the great doctrines of the Christian faith: the inspiration of the Scriptures, the authority of the Word, the sovereignty of God, the deity of Jesus, the sinfulness of man and salvation by faith. There will be a difference of understanding and perception between the believer and the unbeliever. But there is a degree to which any person may be taught with profit something about the historical background of the evangelical Christian faith and its current position, in contrast with other theological and doctrinal positions. Youth in the military will need this information where, not by accident but by design, all Christendom is lumped together in one huge melting pot. Only the discerning will be able to separate the dross from the sterling.

In addition to the major doctrines which constitute the evangelical distinctives, persons going into the military should have a general knowledge about some of the differences among evangelical believers. These differences should not stand in the way of fellowship with those of like precious faith. The young person in military service should be encouraged to respect the viewpoint of other Christians regarding baptism, the second advent, the security of the believer, the gifts of the Spirit, or other beliefs and practices which may differ from his own. It is not necessary that all agree in these areas in order to enjoy Christian fellowship.

Youth programs, Sunday school lessons, sermons and personal counseling could help Christian high schoolers and college-age students learn how to face the rigors of military life with a strong Christian testimony. Too many evangelical churches have neglected this all-important matter of preparing young people for military service.

Many Christian high schoolers and older youth would welcome opportunities to discuss questions such as these: "How can I be spiritually strong in an adverse anti-Christian environment?" "What opportunities for Christian fellowship are offered in military service?" "How can I avoid feelings of loneliness and discouragement?" "How can I meet other Christian servicemen?" "Should a Christian engage in war?" "How should we feel about conscientious objectors?"

The local church should pay special recognition to the Christian young person leaving for military service. The purpose of this is to impress the young person that he is being sent out by his church as a servant of Jesus Christ, and that his mission is not unlike that of a missionary who goes to a foreign country. This should be done in one or more specific ways. A dedication service is one excellent way to do this. The young person should be assured of the faithful prayer support of the church, pastor and loved ones. He should feel that everyone will be anxiously waiting to learn how God is blessing and using him in the Armed Forces.

Certainly, similar courtesies and appropriate recognition will be extended to the nonchristian individual. It is important that those responsible for such programs will act in a way that will preclude hypocrisy or insincerity. Such interest should be expressed in simplicity with genuine love. The following suggestions on how the local church can help its servicemen was compiled by Chaplain W. A. Hutchinson:[1]

1. Provide some kind of briefing for the young man turned 17 on his military obligation and how it can be met.

2. Provide preinduction classes or counseling sessions geared to giving young men some idea on what they will face in the way of temptations such as illicit sex, gambling, profanity and liquor.

3. When a young man leaves for military service, present him with a New Testament at a morning church service. When he comes home on leave, recognize his presence publicly. When he is discharged, welcome him back publicly into the fellowship of the church.

4. Send men in uniform the weekly church bulletin.

5. Set up a correspondence schedule so that each serviceman receives at least one personal letter from the pastor each year. (One church names a

---

[1] W. A. Hutchinson, "Are Your Boys Ready?" *Moody Monthly,* LVIII:13-15 (July, 1957).

"serviceman of the week" to whom the entire congregation is urged to write or send a card that week.)

6. Give each serviceman a subscription to a Christian magazine.

7. Have a spiritually minded veteran adopt the servicemen as his personal responsibility for prayer, correspondence and counsel.

8. Teach the "how" of personal devotions so that future servicemen will learn to feed themselves spiritually.

9. Present the Christian view on such subjects as sex, vocation, marriage, parenthood and race—the latter since the servicemen will live intimately with various races.

10. Teach methods of inductive Bible study and the small group discussion study technique so the individual will know how to lead informal Bible studies.

11. From time to time, send each a helpful Christian book.

12. Above all, stress the reality of Jesus Christ and the power of Christ in the personal life. Help each one realize that he represents Christ personally even more than he represents his church.

13. Make sure he knows about the Christian servicemen's centers maintained in many cities.

A commissioning service that churches may use for military inductees is suggested by a chaplain and reported by Gunnar Hoglund.[2]

It is noteworthy that a few denominations are seeking to minister on a denominational scale to today's servicemen. For example, the Free Methodist denomination, Winona Lake, Indiana, has a Servicemen's Department. The Southern Baptist Convention encourages each of its local churches to establish a Young People Away (YPA) Department, to keep in touch with and minister to young people who have gone from their home churches to colleges or into military service.

THE CHAPLAINCY

Within the Armed Forces is a religious establishment known as the chaplaincy. The chaplaincy is owned, supported and operated by the government. Many military bases have a total population (including dependents) of forty thousand or more. They are similar to small cities, with all the self-contained facilities you would expect to find in a municipality of equal size. One distinction is the absence of competition in business enterprises and industry. Those who have the concession for business or industry enjoy a complete monopoly. This probably helps to account for the fact that the chaplaincy also maintains something approaching a monopoly over religious activities. Considerable freedom does exist, how-

---

[2]Gunnar Hoglund, "Why Not a Commissioning Service in Church for Military Inductees?" *The Standard*, LVI:27 (July 4, 1966).

ever, within the religious establishment, and there is opportunity for an effective informal Christian witness.

The military chaplaincy is not a recent innovation in military history even though there have been many recent innovations within the chaplaincy. The priests of Amon-Ra accompanied the armies of ancient Egypt into battle. The priests of the College of Augurs in ancient Rome had to be consulted before every declaration of war. In the armies of the later Christian emperors, "unit presbyters" appear as early as the fifth century.[3]

Most of the naval, military and colonial expeditions to this country brought chaplains with them. The first American chaplain in the strict sense of the term was Samuel Stone, who distinguished himself in the Pequot War of 1637.

The legal origin of the Corps of Chaplains is found in a resolution of the Continental Congress, adopted July 29, 1775. The resolution provided that the pay of chaplains should be twenty dollars per month.[4] At the time the Constitution went into effect there were no chaplains to be paid from public funds.[5] To some this seemed inconsistent with the fact that Congress had passed the First Amendment to the United States Constitution less than two years earlier. James Madison, among others, rejected the theoretical and practical arguments in favor of the United States military chaplaincy supported by the government.[6] Prior to World War I, chaplains in limited numbers were appointed, commissioned and assigned with little or no military training or instruction. During World War I, candidates for the Navy Chaplaincy were appointed "acting" chaplains. They learned their duties and functions under the supervision of the office that came to be known as the Chief of Navy Chaplains. Army chaplain candidates were enlisted as privates; sent to a chaplain school; taught the rudiments of military courtesy, close order drill and equitation; and given a smattering of instruction in Army regulations, Court-martial procedures and map reading. At the end of thirty days, each candidate was required to preach a trial sermon of ten minutes' duration on a text of his own choosing. He was then commissioned a chaplain with the rank of First Lieutenant and sent forth into the wilderness of an armed camp. His equipment included a Bible, a chaplain's flag and his native talents.[7]

---

[3]*A Brief History of the American Army Chaplaincy,* Department of the Army: PAM 165-1 (October, 1955).

[4]*The American University Law Review,* XIV, No. 1 (December, 1964).

[5]Office of the Chief of Chaplains, United States Army, American Army Chaplaincies 8 (1946).

[6]"Madison: Monopolies, Perpetuities, Corporations, Ecclesiastical Endowments," *Harper's Magazine* (March, 1914).

[7]Chaplain (Colonel) Gynther Staraasli, USA (Ret.), *United States Army Chaplain School,* docket 61-00M0100-0383, T/A, LMTC (1955).

There have been more developments in the military chaplaincy since the beginning of World War II than in all the rest of its history combined. Today more than 100 million dollars in tax funds are expended annually to support the federal chaplaincy.[8] The religious establishment in the military represents the most affluent religious operation in the United States, and the most expensive, per unit of service.

Most all faiths are represented in the military chaplaincy. The three major faith groups (Protestant, Roman Catholic and Jewish) function separately in the overall programs. Accommodations are made for some of the smaller groups. Congress authorizes the military to employ approximately one chaplain for each nine hundred servicemen in uniform on active duty. This is based on the proportionate number of ministers, rabbis and priests in the United States in relation to the total population of the country.

Protestant chaplains conduct a general worship service once a week on Sunday morning for all who care to attend. The government intends that this service will be acceptable to most Protestants and offensive to none. In addition the following programs which relate in some degree to Christian education are promoted with the official imprimatur of the chaplaincy: Sunday schools, Protestant Men of the Chapel, Protestant Women of the Chapel, Protestant Youth of the Chapel, and vacation Bible schools for children.

Any chaplain may have a diversified ministry in the military. There are certain routine requirements and demands which he must meet to satisfy his command. These do not normally impede his opportunity for a vital spiritual ministry. However, it is possible to be a successful career chaplain and yet be spiritually sterile. Many chaplains are outstanding men of God who have a dynamic witness for Christ. Also a large number of lay personnel have enjoyed a fruitful and rewarding experience working with these chaplains in one or more of the chapel programs.

The official instruction guide for the Army chaplain states:

> The chaplain has a responsibility to provide all personnel of the command the opportunity to grow in the spiritual life and to increase their knowledge of God. He does this by means of group and/or individual religious instruction. Many proved and established devices are available to assist him in this phase of this responsibility. Sabbath/Sunday or Catechism Classes, weekday study groups or prayer meetings, vacation religious schools, religious films, societies, fellowship and endeavor groups, and other allied activities provide occasions for religious instruction. The chaplain will exercise personal ingenuity and zeal to make the most of them.[9]

---

[8]National Defense Budget, Fiscal Year, 1966.
[9]*Army Field Manual FM*, 16-5 (August, 1964).

A *Unified Curriculum* has been developed by the Armed Forces Chaplains Board for use in Protestant military Sunday schools.[10] A major effort has been made to have this used exclusively by Protestant chaplains in the Armed Forces. Some have questioned the legality and practicality of this. Because many different denominational quarterlies are used to teach the Unified Curriculum, many evangelical chaplains feel that it is a hodgepodge of unrelated material. A sincere effort has been made to improve the quality of the materials but it is not easy to satisfy fifty Protestant denominations which have chaplains on active duty, and still have literature that is vital and meaningful to all. The literature may be supplemented and, depending on how liberally this is interpreted at the local level, many evangelicals have found the military Sunday schools a satisfactory program for teaching and learning.

The *Protestant Youth of the Chapel* is primarily designed for teen-agers who are dependents of military personnel.[11] The spiritual vitality of the program is dependent on the local leadership provided by the chaplain and those interested in working as sponsors. It will vary from what amounts to little more than a social outlet to groups where a positive witness for Jesus Christ is maintained. In groups such as the latter, teen-agers not only come to know Christ as Saviour but also have the opportunity to grow in grace and knowledge of Him.

The *Protestant Men of the Chapel* has as its purpose the active enlistment of every man into the chapel program. This includes the youth from our churches who are wearing the uniform. Specifically stated, the Air Force lists the following objectives of this organization:

> *Lead men* to accept Christ as Saviour and Lord.
> *Teach men* the history, the aims and the program of the chapel, all built on a solid foundation of worship and Bible study.
> *Develop men* in the skills of prayer, evangelism, friendliness, stewardship, teaching and social service—against a background of personal development.
> *Engage men* in the work of the chapel in keeping with their abilities, interests and time schedules.
> Thus, Protestant Men of the Chapel becomes a clear-cut effort on the part of local, area and theater councils to enlist, organize, train and inspire men to serve.[12]

As is true in the Protestant Youth of the Chapel and many of our church

---

[10]Joint policy statement, "How This Curriculum Came to Be" by three Chiefs of Chaplains (October, 1954).

[11]*Guidelines for Protestant Youth of the Chapel,* Armed Forces Chaplains Board (May, 1965).

[12]*Guidelines for Protestant Men of the Chapel,* United States Air Force (January, 1963).

programs, the degree to which these objectives are realized depends on the local leadership. The program often suffers for lack of interest or support by evangelicals who might be overlooking a real opportunity to serve the Lord through this avenue. Often chaplains who do not necessarily agree with or identify themselves with the evangelical position are pleased to see evangelicals assume places of leadership in the chapel programs. The reason for this is that evangelicals are generally known for their enthusiasm and leadership ability. Thus the evangelical may often be welcomed into a program even when his spiritual perspective is not fully shared.

The *Protestant Women of the Chapel* (sometimes referred to as Protestant Ladies of the Chapel) is made up primarily of dependent wives. The program varies in accordance with the interest of those in places of leadership.

Chaplains are authorized to conduct denominational programs. This includes the establishment of denominational Sunday schools or arrangement for such if they do not actually promote them. This must be done within specific limitations and according to regulations. In any case denominational activities are subordinated to the general Protestant programs which receive priority scheduling.[13]

On a large military installation, a chaplain may be assigned to primary duty as director of religious education to provide general supervision and assistance to all group functions on the base. He programs and budgets for equipment, materials and, where required, a full-time civilian religious education adviser. The duties of a civilian filling this position are very similar to those of a director of Christian education in a local church. The chaplain secures adequate facilities such as classroom space, religious-social facilities, and transportation in order to establish one or more Sunday schools. This depends on the size and geographical arrangement of the installation. It is his responsibility to recruit Sunday school teachers, to maintain an effective teacher training program. This is done in order to provide sufficient departments and teachers to meet the most up-to-date religious education standards.[14]

Whatever other deficiencies the religious education program may have on a military base, it does not suffer for lack of funds or facilities. Each branch of the Armed Forces has its own film libraries, and other teaching aids are available. An almost unlimited amount of funds are available for the purchase or rental of needed supplies or equipment, when there is reasonable justification for including them in the budget.

---

[13]*Army Field Manual FM,* 16-5 (August, 1964). The Navy and Air Force have similar regulations.

[14]Letter from United States Air Force Headquarters in Europe to European commands, dated December 14, 1964.

VITAL EXTRACURRICULAR ACTIVITIES

There are two kinds of extracurricular Christian activities provided for military servicemen. In many ways these are the most vital contribution to the Christian education of youth in the military. These may become increasingly important if the ecumenical spirit within the chaplaincy continues to demand uniformity at the expense of spiritual vitality.

1. One kind is offered by denominations and related outside organizations that provide various types of programs to assist men in uniform. The Assemblies of God, Lutherans, Southern Baptists, Campus Crusade for Christ, The Navigators, Young Life, Christian Servicemen's Centers and others provide this type of assistance in a number of ways.

In some cases a special effort is made to get military personnel into local churches through the cooperation of local pastors. The Assemblies of God have a full-time "military missionary" in Europe working with military personnel. He organizes group meetings for them on the base and provides other activities such as retreats, Bible studies and social functions. Southern Baptists, under their Home Mission Board, have established a large number of English-speaking Baptist churches adjacent to military bases overseas (as well as in the States) comprised almost entirely of military personnel and their dependents. These furnish a striking contrast between the military and civilian religious economies. In many places the combined effort of a half dozen chaplains provides a less effective program (which serves fewer people) than one Southern Baptist minister just outside the gate.

In San Diego the *Christian Servicemen's Center* developed a fine program in cooperation with several churches. A Sunday morning breakfast is provided for servicemen, after which transportation is furnished to the church of their choice. Also included are invitations to Sunday dinner in the homes of church members.

2. The other kind of activity is generated within the Armed Forces by personnel on active duty. The *Christian Servicemen's Fellowship* and the *Officers' Christian Union* are examples of these. These are both lay movements within the military composed of personnel on active duty.

Thus far in this chapter the discussion has been about opportunities for spiritual growth for youth in the military service. Now the man himself will be considered. Who is he? What are his needs? How can they be met?

First of all, the young person in uniform *is* a person. A recent research document from the *Young Men's Christian Association* reports that two-thirds of the men in the United States Armed Forces are between the ages of 17 and 30. There are currently a little less than three million military men on active duty. The young military man is faced with the same transitional problems that others his age face. Some will say that his strongest desire is to be loved, wanted, needed and appreciated. Others will analyze him in another way. However he or his needs are described, they can be met through a vital relationship with Jesus Christ.

According to a survey made at Lackland Air Force Base,[15] the shocking experience of being uprooted from the security of his home environment and thrust into a situation in the military where he must think, decide and act for himself, with virtually no counsel from loved ones and friends, makes the serviceman peculiarly receptive to the gospel. It was found that men in the military, initially at least, were more than twice as responsive to the claims of the gospel than men of the same age in civilian setting.[16] This should be a source of encouragement to those who have faithfully witnessed to a loved one only to see him leave for the military, still unsaved. *The Navigators,* the *Christian Servicemen's Fellowship* and the *Officers' Christian Union* all estimate that more than 60 percent of the men with whom they work have come to know the Lord while in the military.

In addition to using official channels of the religious establishment in the military, maximum use of the man-to-man method should be emphasized. The focal point for this ministry is the inductive-type Bible study led by laymen. This not only provides an avenue for reaching men for Christ, but is one of the most effective methods of Bible study for men in the military.[17]

Bible studies in the military follow the New Testament pattern established by the Lord Jesus: "Ye shall receive power, after that the Holy Ghost is come upon you: and ye shall be witnesses unto me both in Jerusalem, and in all Judaea, and in Samaria, and unto the uttermost part of the earth."[18]

Jerusalem is where the disciples were and the witness would logically begin there. It would spread to all Judea, the surrounding area. It would also be extended to Samaria, representing more than a national interest, and then to the uttermost part of the earth.

The pattern is interesting but not incidental. Christ speaks of "both" in reference to places. "Both" normally refers to two; yet four places are named. Both seems appropriate when we remember that we always have a "Jerusalem," our home base. We are told, "In these days came prophets from Jerusalem unto Antioch."[19] A witness was established in Antioch but the witness was not disestablished in Jerusalem. Antioch simply became

---

[15]Charles I. Carpenter, "Let Us Pray," *Army-Navy Journal* (February 25, 1950).
[16]Staff Chaplains' Conference, Washington, D.C., February 3, 1959.
[17]The Officers' Christian Union (Box 267, East Lansing, Michigan 48824) has published several "Bible Study Guides" for study groups in the military.
[18]Acts 1:8.
[19]Acts 11:27.

a new "Jerusalem" from which the pattern was repeated. It was there that "the Holy Ghost said, Separate me Barnabas and Saul for the work whereunto I have called them." So the witness spread to Asia Minor, but it was not disestablished in Antioch. Each new place became another "Jerusalem" from which the witness was extended. So, a paraphrase of the thought might be "Ye shall be witnesses unto me both in Jerusalem and all Judaea, both in Jerusalem and in Samaria, both in Jerusalem and unto the uttermost part of the earth."

This is the way it works in the military. One of the first chapters of the Christian Servicemen's Fellowship was established in Alaska. A Christian went from there to Hawaii and established a Bible study. Another went to California; a third to another base in Florida. Each Bible study group is encouraged to use Paul's instructions to Timothy: "The things that thou hast heard . . . commit thou to faithful men, who shall be able to teach others also"[20] in order that their own witness will be perpetuated, and that those who go out from the group will establish a new witness wherever they are.

These Bible studies provide a vital link in keeping Christians in contact with each other. The young person in military service needs every encouragement that can be provided. He is completely on his own, and without the influence of loved ones or Christian friends in the church. Quite often a cordial invitation to attend a Bible study is just what he needs, and is more providential than many realize.

The end product of all Christian education is to have Christians walking in close fellowship with the Lord, and this in turn will generate the right sort of fellowship with one another as John writes: "That which we have seen and heard declare we unto you, that ye may have fellowship with us: and truly our fellowship is with the Father, and with his Son Jesus Christ."[21] When Christians are rightly related to Christ, whether through Bible study groups or some other effort, anything may happen. And it does not necessarily conform to the conventional, even as it did not in the early church.

SUMMARY

Youth in the military may find the Lord's place for them through the established religious system, one of the unofficial organizations functioning within the military, or one of the programs provided by a church or group outside the military. Any number of other activities may be generated as a result: conferences, retreats, seminars, gospel teams, servicemen's centers,

---

[20]II Timothy 2:2.
[21]I John 1:3.

new churches, support for orphans, special assistance to missionaries, raising funds for students. The large number who leave the military to prepare for full-time service in the Lord's work through church-related activities are living evidence that the youth in the military can be challenged to receive Christ and to live for Him.

FOR FURTHER READING

Books

ANDERSON, STANLEY EDWIN. *Shepherds to 24,000,000 Service Men,* Butler, Ind.; Higley Press. Written by a World War II chaplain in an inspirational vein and calculated to give a good picture of what the young chaplain can expect on entering the service.

BURKHART, ROY A. *The Church and the Returning Soldier.* New York: Harper & Bros. Publishers, 1945.

DRURY, CLIFFORD M. *History of the Chaplains Corps, United States Navy.* Four volumes. Washington, D.C.: United States Government Printing Office. A voluminous account of the Navy chaplaincy written by a former Navy chaplain.

HONEYWELL, ROY J. *Chaplains of the United States Army.* Washington, D.C.: United States Government Printing Office. A well-written history of the chaplaincy by a retired Army colonel, which begins with the early concepts gleaned from the Hebrew Scriptures and ends with the Korean conflict.

JORGENSEN, DANIEL B. *Air Force Chaplains, Volume II.* Washington, D.C.: United States Government Printing Office. Written by an Air Force chaplain, this volume provides not only a history of the Air Force chaplaincy from 1947 (the beginning of the Air Force as a separate branch of the Armed Forces) to 1960, but deals extensively with the ministry of the chaplaincy, policies, administration.

Articles

BLASE, WILLIAM E. "What Military Young People Need from Their Church," *The Sunday School Builder,* XLVIII:50 (June, 1967).

CORRELL, SIDNEY. "Your Church Is Responsible for Your Servicemen," *Eternity,* XVIII:31-32 (May, 1967).

FITZGERALD, LAWRENCE. "What Can Our Churches Do for the Men in Vietnam?" *Eternity,* XVIII:30-31 (May, 1967).

Pamphlets

The American Army Chaplaincy. Department of the Army Pamphlet, PAM 165-1 (October, 1955). A brief history of the chaplaincy from its inception.

A Bibliography of Materials Related to the Military Chaplaincy. Washington, D.C.: National Association of Evangelicals.

The Chaplain. Department of the Army Field Manual, FM 16-5 (August, 1964). Basic information on the mission, status, functions and relationships of chaplains in the Army.

Christians, Stand Guard. Washington, D.C.: The General Commission on Chaplains (122 Maryland Ave., N.E.). An interesting discussion on how to meet some of the problems and temptations in the military.

Guidelines for Protestant Men of the Chapel. Department of the Air Force. Outlines programs for chaplains to encourage military men to become involved in the chapel program.

Guidelines for Protestant Youth of the Chapel. Armed Forces Chaplains Board. Philadelphia: Westminster Press. Outlines programs for chaplains working with dependent teen-agers of military personnel.

GOUGH, HUGH. *The Christian and Military Service*. Westminster, England: Officers' Christian Union. A well-documented case for Christians being in the military.

HEARTBERG, JOSEPH H. *Forward March*. Philadelphia: Judson Press. A 64-page pep talk for servicemen, covering a variety of subjects vital to them.

Opportunity of a Lifetime. Washington, D.C.: Christian Servicemen's Fellowship (1405 G Street, N.W.). Practical helps, with an evangelical emphasis, for men going on active duty.

RIGDON, RAYMOND M. *When You Are . . . the "U" in Uniform*. Nashville: The Sunday School Board of the Southern Baptist Convention. Written for men leaving for military service, encouraging high moral standards as Christians.

So You're Going into Service. Washington, D.C.: National Lutheran Council (2633 16th Street, N.W.). A preinduction training manual, this booklet covers a wide range of both philosophical and practical subjects.

WEBER, C. E. *More Than Marking Time*. Indianapolis: United Christian Missionary Society (222 S. Downy Ave.). Designed to help youth make the most of their military service.

———. *A Guide to "More Than Marking Time."* Indianapolis: United Christian Missionary Society (222 S. Downy Ave.). For use by pastors or other instructors when teaching *More Than Marking Time*.

SOURCES OF INFORMATION

Christian Servicemen's Fellowship, National Association of Evangelicals, 1405 G Street, N.W., Washington, D.C. 20005.

Officers' Christian Union (of the United States of America), Box 267, East Lansing, Michigan 48824.

The Navigators, Glen Eyrie, Colorado Springs, Colorado 80901.

Extrachurch youth movements are an evidence that God is no respecter of churches per se. These organizations are an effort to express the will of God as individuals and groups of individuals desire to witness and work. They have often sensed a vacuum in the vitality and vision of churches. The extrachurch youth movement is in a sense a peculiar phenomenon among churches in a nation that has provided a congenial setting for religious freedom.

MILFORD SHOLUND

22

extrachurch
youth movements

CHRISTIAN YOUTH WORK has grown up through the eighteenth and nineteenth centuries in the United States within the framework of denominational churches. This skein of church policy and practice has become for many ecclesiastical leaders sacred threads that should not be broken. Many leaders, locally and nationally, have committed themselves to honoring denominational lines. The inevitable result has been an institutionalizing tendency in denominational policy and practice.

The youth work of most American churches has flourished, floundered or failed in this kind of church-controlled organization. Like every other institutional effort, denominational work and life are not evil or an encumbrance in themselves. *Denominational vitality fails when it tends to neglect the purposes for which Jesus Christ created the church.* When the denominational head becomes more important than Jesus Christ who is the true Head of the church, then the churches are weakened in their witness and work for Christ.

MILFORD SHOLUND, Litt. D., is Director of Biblical and Educational Research, Gospel Light Publications, Inc., Glendale, California.

Christian youth work in America cannot be appreciated, explained or evaluated outside the context of the churches. From the beginning Jesus Christ has ordained that the local church, the local body of believers in Christ, should be the essential instrument through which He would work and witness in every generation. The norm for the ministry of these churches is described in the New Testament. But churches do not always manifest the splendor and supremacy of Christ.

It is no surprise then that in the conglomerate growth of Protestant churches in the United States there should be aberrations and some occasions when efforts to do the work of Christ effectively should occur outside of the channels of denominationally committed churches. It is a greater sin in the judgment of many leaders, however, to not serve Christ in one's generation than it is to fail one's denominational commitments. The extra-church movement is interwoven in the denominational and independent spirit of American Protestantism.

OBJECTIVES OF EXTRACHURCH MOVEMENTS

Extrachurch movements and organizations as used in this chapter refer to those efforts that are made by individuals and members of religious organizations to provide some kind of an expression of their interest and concern through an association that is not sponsored and controlled by officially delegated representatives from local and denominational bodies. "Extra" in this sense means outside of the official direction of the church and not only something additional.

Extrachurch youth movements are an evidence that God is no respecter of churches per se. These organizations are an effort to express the will of God as individuals and groups of individuals desire to witness and work. They have often sensed a vacuum in the vitality and vision of churches. The extrachurch youth movement is in a sense a peculiar phenomenon among churches in a nation that has provided a congenial setting for religious freedom.

The Sunday school was once the foremost extrachurch movement. Sunday schools, as we know them today, have not always been supported by and integrated into the denominational life of the churches.

Edwin Rice, noted authority on the Sunday school movement, states:

> The churches not being ready for such a movement, it was prac-
> tically necessary to establish it on a voluntary and union basis. Rooms
> were hired for holding its schools in rented halls. Denominational
> organizations were jealous of their prerogatives. At first, therefore, this
> new scheme was rejected by the churches, though accepted by indi-
> viduals. . . . It thus became a movement sustained by laymen.[1]

---

[1] Edwin Wilbur Rice, *The Sunday School Movement and the American Sunday School Union* (Philadelphia: American Sunday School Union), 1917), p. 45.

The Sunday schools in America in the early nineteenth century were born spontaneously in the hearts and minds of the laymen, quite distinct from the clergy. These laymen were not agitating for new organizations and groups for instruction, but they preferred agitation for teaching the Word of God to the stagnation they too often found in denominational circles.

The Sunday schools grew by leaps and bounds for forty years (1785-1825) as an extrachurch movement before the Protestant Episcopal Sunday school societies were projected as a union in 1826 in Philadelphia under the leadership of Bishop White. Shortly thereafter the Methodist Episcopal Sunday School Union began (1826).

The American Sunday School Union, founded in 1816, from the beginning has had certain marks of the extrachurch groups that were to follow and to become such mighty forces for Jesus Christ.

The American Sunday School Union was not antidenominational, for the members of the union were individual members in good standing with their respective denominations. The ASSU was not undenominational, since all its members belonged to and participated actively in local churches. The ASSU was not interdenominational in the sense of being supported and directed by representatives officially elected and recognized by denominational groups.

Another point of significance was the internal organization of the ASSU. Rice tells us, "It is significant that the managers of the Union [ASSU], in their first report, recognized their responsibility to submit a report of their proceedings not to the public, but to the members of the Society."[2]

The ASSU is one evidence that an extrachurch organization can become an asset to the churches, and that such an organization can be useful for more than one generation.

The nineteenth century witnessed the birth of a number of extrachurch organizations. The American Bible Society (1816), the YMCA (1849), and the YWCA (1855) were among those of national stature. Many notable leaders in churches were active in these organizations. The birth of these groups grew out of the need to do together what each could not do alone.

Not only was the conviction in the hearts of individuals that there should be a new association to get a job done, but the American cultural setting was fertile soil for the planting of new groups and associations for all kinds of endeavors and interests.

Alex De Tocqueville (1805-59), noted French writer, in his work *De la democratic en Amerique* wrote:

[2]*Ibid.,* p. 85.

> The Americans of all ages, all conditions and all dispositions constantly form associations. They have not only commercial and manufacturing companies in which all take part, but associations of a thousand other kinds, religious, moral, serious, futile, restricted, enormous or diminutive. The Americans make associations to give entertainments, to found establishments for education, to send missionaries to the antipodes. Wherever at the head of some new undertaking you see the government of France or a man of rank in England, in the United States you will be sure to find an association.

If De Tocqueville thought the United States was exploding with organizations in 1856, what would he exclaim today?

More than 12,500 *national* associations are listed in the *Encyclopedia of Associations.*[3] The number of associations, churches and groups organized for various purposes on regional and local levels can be estimated conservatively at more than 500,000. (There are more than 319,000 local Protestant churches in the United States today in contrast to 38,061 in 1950.)

It is no wonder that in such a milieu the extrachurch movement should grow. There was no state church to dominate and control ecclesiastical bodies. The "free church" spirit prevailed among immigrants who came to America to worship God according to the dictates of their conscience. Here they found unlimited opportunities to express themselves. They entered into the stream of religious life on the new continent with enthusiasm and vigor, and chartered their course as pioneers seeking and expressing the truth as they believed it and saw it.

At the end of the nineteenth century, the main efforts in religious work among young people were channeled through established churches and denominations. The denominations were large enough to organize, sustain and direct youth ministries which drew out the loyalty and participation of their own local church groups. The larger denominations pooled their resources for youth and related areas on an interdenominational basis in the formation of the International Council of Religious Education (1922) and the subsequent development in the organization of the United Christian Youth Movement (1934).[4] The UCYM claims to represent approximately ten million youth in forty-six constituent denominational churches in the U.S.A. The ecclesiastical setting of the UCYM has been the National Council of Churches of Christ in America.

Among liberals, youth leaders were concerned with ecumenical activities. The cutting edge of the biblical imperative was blunted by forays into economic-social-educational issues. The clear-cut appeal of worldwide mis-

---

[3]Frederick G. Ruffner (ed.), *Encyclopedia of Associations* (Detroit: Gale Research Co., 1964), p. 7.
[4]See chapter 2, "A Historical Survey of Youth Work."

sions to reach the heathen because they are lost was reduced by the liberals to concern for human welfare needs. The towering strength of the headquarters, the officialism of state councils and the impotence of countless clergy to resist the pressures from above combined to smother the incentitives for Bible study, evangelism, the Spirit-filled life, and worldwide evangelism.

In many churches tens of thousands of youth never had a chance to feel the refreshing breezes of spiritual awakening that come through powerful gospel preaching and passionate soul-winning efforts. A generation of youth scattered in the Protestant churches of America were spiritually disinherited by their parents, pastors and religious educators in reference to the vital message of salvation according to the gospel of Jesus Christ. The period of 1910-1940 was sterile for lack of energetic involvement of young people in the practical meaning of the redemptive purpose of Jesus Christ for their lives and their peers. The liberal wing of Protestantism had empty platitudes that fell on dead ears. The fundamental wing of Protestantism was torn in wretched arguments that resulted in bitter divisions and disappointments. The inability of responsible adults in church life to solve their problems and to discharge their responsibilities in religious education and training for leadership left the young generation without a solid theological foundation and without a corresponding conviction concerning the meaning of the Christian cause.

But God did not leave His church and His world without a witness. What the Lord could not get done through the formal, organized channels of Protestant church organization He was pleased to do in a measure through extrachurch movements. The scope of their activities is as broad and varied as young people themselves. There are groups designed for physical improvement, mental stimulation, social interaction, emotional growth and spiritual impact. There are groups designed for boys or for girls; some are coeducational, some local, others regional, national or international. Some groups require membership; others seek only for attendance at meetings. Many groups appeal to small group activities; others specialize on gigantic efforts. There is no way they can be strictly classified according to age, purpose or plan. The *fact* of the existence of influential extrachurch groups in American church life among youth cannot be denied. Estimates of their *value* and *significance* have varied depending on the viewpoint of the appraiser.

SPREAD OF EXTRACHURCH GROUPS

Some extrachurch groups were started as social welfare-educational groups, but have been assimilated into the programs of many local churches. *The Boy Scouts of America* (1910) and *The Girl Scouts of America* (1912) were not initiated by leaders who were trying to be competitive with existing religious groups. Through the years, however, churches have made arrangements to accommodate and use these groups in their programs.

Some groups originated abroad. The *Inter-Varsity Fellowship* (IVF) was first begun in Great Britain by Christian leaders and students on campuses and later introduced in the United States by British and Canadian students. The *Inter-Varsity Christian Fellowship* of America, organized in 1941, sponsors activities related to evangelism, Bible study, prayer, spiritual growth, and world missions.

Another extrachurch youth movement similar to IVCF but started in America is *Campus Crusade for Christ*. Founded in 1951, this movement has a strong evangelistic approach to college and university students in their sororities, fraternities and dormitories. Thousands of persons from every walk and association in life give their financial support and encouragement to these college-university extrachurch movements.

There are also groups designed to reach high school students. Two of the better-known groups are *Young Life Campaign* (1941) and *Youth for Christ International* (1944).

Young Life Campaign conducts group meetings in homes for high school youth, operates four resorts for teen-agers in the western United States and Canada, and annually directs an institute for training leaders for the movement. Youth for Christ International has expanded its ministry to include crusades, conferences, camps and projects in forty-five countries.

There are also extrachurch groups with specialized activities and objectives. The *Fellowship of Christian Athletes* (1954) directs its ministry to athletes. The FCA sponsors specialized conferences on evangelism and the Christian life. It also sends outstanding sports personalities and coaches to speak and to give Christian testimonials at youth rallies, banquets and other youth programs. The FCA encourages young people to serve the cause of Christ through the church of their choice. FCA calls attention to the priority of Jesus Christ in a person's life, stresses the importance of Christian attitudes on and off the playing field, and points out the importance of physical and spiritual fitness.

Another group with a specialized ministry is *The Navigators,* founded in 1933 by Dawson Trotman. This organization conducted an extensive ministry to men and women in military service during World War II. This was done through a program of guidance in personal Bible study, Scripture memorization, Christian witnessing, small-group Bible study and Christian fellowship. Continuing their work in this area, The Navigators have enlarged their program to include a wide variety of worldwide ministries—such as the preparation and supervision of many of the printed materials that are used in the counselor training and follow-up ministries of the Billy Graham Evangelistic Association. The Navigators also conduct a year-round program of laity leadership training at their national headquarters in Colorado. They sponsor specialized summer camps and conferences, and have representatives engaged in a broad range of Christian activities in many countries of the world.

Quite a different approach to meeting the needs of youth is shown in the *Christian Service Brigade* for boys, and the *Pioneer Girls.* These two national organizations originated in the Chicago area in 1937. Their programs include Christ-centered activities, using a club approach similar to Boy Scouts and Girl Scouts. From the beginning, each of these groups has been directed by an incorporate board of laymen. The intention and practice have been to work each club on the local church premises. In this respect these two extrachurch groups have been geared to the local church. The clubs are subject both to a local church committee and to the policies of the national extrachurch organization. Another similar church-related club organization for boys and girls is the *Awana Youth Association.*

Several independent groups are working among delinquent youth. Youth for Christ has developed a Lifeline program with camping and a year-round home for delinquent boys. *Youth Development, Inc.,* directed by Jim Vaus, a former wiretapper, works in the heart of Harlem, New York. *Youth Adventures, Inc.* (Portland, Oregon), founded by Howard Busse, ministers to teen delinquents through a rugged outdoor camping program. *Youth Guidance, Inc.* (Pittsburgh, Pennsylvania) has a rehabilitation ministry to delinquent boys through counseling, camping, recreation.

The extrachurch youth movement has not been limited to Protestant churches. The *Encyclopedia of Associations* indicates that there are 154 Catholic groups that are similar to extrachurch groups among Protestants. Ruffner also lists 206 similar groups among Jewish religious bodies. The Catholic and Jewish listings include all ages, but it is obvious that extrachurch agencies are active among their constituencies too.[5]

FUNCTION OF EXTRACHURCH GROUPS

The question naturally arises among churchmen: Why do these extrachurch groups for youth arise, and how should they be evaluated?

The answer to the first query is quite clear. Extrachurch groups arise to meet a need. If they do not meet a need, they soon dwindle or die because of the resistance and opposition of established church youth groups.

The answer to the second question depends on many factors. Some clergy and churches oppose extrachurch groups for various reasons. Some ministers and congregations merely tolerate them. Others decide to en-

---

[5]Ruffner, *op. cit.,* pp. 704-20, 731-52.

courage them and join them. The criteria for deciding what to do will obviously have to be established by the local churches and by denominational leaders.

Charges have been made by pastors, community leaders and denominational executives that the extrachurch groups were antichurch, narrow, emotional, temporary and personality-centered. After twenty-five years of experience and reputation, most of the leaders of extrachurch youth groups have been found to be responsible members and also leaders in local churches. They function on the basic conviction that Christian youth work should be related somehow to the churches. The problem as they see it, however, is that when churches fail to fulfill their trust of the gospel to the young people, then special efforts must be made to bring the gospel to them in ways that they can understand and appreciate.

Perceptive youth leaders with more than forty years of experience and observation have indicated that extrachurch organizations can and often do provide Christian leaders like no other groups have done.

The following analysis by V. Raymond Edman, Chancellor of Wheaton College (Illinois), is specifically about the development of one extrachurch organization (Youth For Christ), but his observations throw light on the strengths and weaknesses of many extrachurch youth movements.

> When Youth For Christ appeared dramatically on the religious scene in 1944, some evangelical leaders began to criticize it. Others postponed their criticism with the belief that the new "baby" was basically healthy and in time would grow up to make a large contribution to the cause of Christ. Youth For Christ is now [1959] in its 15th year, and I believe it is ready for a frank appraisal. Having worked with the organization and its leaders from the early days, but never as an official part of it, I think I have sufficient detachment to be objective, and enough knowledge to be factual. . . .
>
> The prophets of doom who announced that Youth For Christ would soon fade from the scene have, in some cases, changed their line to "The results are not lasting!" Undoubtedly in those early years many may have made a decision for Christ who were not properly nourished for Christian growth. But the fact that there are pastors, missionaries, and Christian workers today who *were* won to Christ in YFC meetings years ago is proof of fruit. . . .
>
> Whatever a local pastor or lay Christian might say about Youth For Christ, there is much that must be said for it: Youth For Christ is composed of leaders who believe unreservedly in the power of the gospel and the importance of prayer. Any secular organization with so little machinery would have collapsed in a year! Without the imposing structure of denominational prestige or financial support, Youth for Christ has made a phenomenal impact on cities and on entire nations.

It is to be commended for maturing without institutionalizing, maintaining its emphasis on youth, putting evangelism and world missions in the foreground, and depending on the power of God. . . .

One gets the impression that Youth For Christ, like Topsy, "just grew." First came the Saturday night rallies, then high school clubs, Bible quizzes, teen talent contests, a ministry to juvenile delinquents, teen films and literature, and other programs. . . .

Youth For Christ is an organization that has the program, passion, and potential for world evangelism despite all its weaknesses and past faults. . . . I am prone to agree with Youth For Christ leaders that "unless we win teen-agers today, there may be no Church tomorrow."[6]

SUMMARY

Ideally local churches around the world should be strong in Christ, magnifying His name, witnessing for Him and helping youth grow in Him. But in actuality many churches vacillate from strength to weakness. When there is a great need to fill the vacuum in the ministries of these churches, God allows what seems to some an unwarranted intrusion on the work of the churches. The ministry of extrachurch youth movements has often met a need. They have been a challenge to local churches to more effectively proclaim the gospel to young people and to prepare youth to live for Christ and to serve Him more effectively.

FOR FURTHER READING

CAILLIET, EMILE. *Young Life.* New York: Harper & Row, 1964.

CARLSON, VIOLET C. *The Christian Educator's File.* Chicago: Moody Press, 1954.

Christian Endeavor Essentials. Successor to and revision of *Expert Endeavor* by Amos R. Wells (5th revision). Columbus, Ohio: International Society of Christian Endeavor, 1965.

HAKES, J. EDWARD (ed.). *An Introduction to Evangelical Christian Education.* Chicago: Moody Press, 1964.

HARNER, NEVIN C. *Youth Work in the Church.* New York: Abingdon-Cokesbury, 1942.

LARSON, MEL. *Youth For Christ.* Grand Rapids: Zondervan Publishing Co., 1947.

NEWBY, DONALD O. "The Churches' Ministry to Youth," *Religious Education: A Comprehensive Survey,* Marvin Taylor, editor. New York: Abingdon Press, 1960.

RICE, EDWIN WILBUR. *The Sunday School Movement and the American Sunday School Union.* Philadelphia: Union Press, 1917.

RUSSELL, EUNICE. *The Development of Pioneer Girls' Philosophy.* Unpublished Master's thesis, Department of Christian Education, Wheaton College, Wheaton, Illinois, 1959.

---

[6]V. Raymond Edman, "Has Youth For Christ Grown Up?" *Christianity Today,* III:13-14 (August 31, 1959). Used by permission.

ADDRESSES OF SEVERAL EXTRACHURCH YOUTH ORGANIZATIONS

Awana Youth Association, 7511 West Belmont Avenue, Chicago, Illinois 60634.

Bible Memory Association, Box 12000, St. Louis, Missouri, 63112.

Campus Crusade for Christ, International, Arrowhead Springs, San Bernardino, California 92403.

Christian Service Brigade, 2525 North Main Street, Wheaton, Illinois 60187.

High School Evangelism Fellowship, 15 Park Row, New York, New York 10038.

Inter-Varsity Christian Fellowship, 130 North Wells Street, Chicago, Illinois 60606.

The Navigators, Glen Eyrie, Colorado Springs, Colorado 80901.

Pioneer Girls, 109 North Cross Street, Wheaton, Illinois 60187.

Rural Bible Crusade, Box 269, Wheaton, Illinois 60187.

Young Life Campaign, Box 1519, Colorado Springs, Colorado 80901.

Youth Adventures, Inc., Box 4791, Portland, Oregon 79242.

Youth Development, Inc., Box 102, Hell Gate Station, New York 10029.

Youth Guidance, Inc., 2331 Laketon Road, Pittsburgh, Pennsylvania 15221.

Youth For Christ International, North Main Street, Wheaton, Illinois 60187.

The main aim of evangelical camping is that the Holy Spirit will lead lost campers to Christ, God's Son. Godly counselors pray and teach and exemplify the Word, seeking to establish friendly beachheads in campers' heads and hearts, to help win them to Christ. Many nonchristian Sunday school students, plus many unchurched campers, receive the Saviour at camp. Camp is the strong right arm of evangelism for many churches.

LLOYD O. CORY

23

camping
and conference work

BRIEF HISTORY OF CHRISTIAN CAMPS AND
CONFERENCES

GOD'S PEOPLE have been camping for a long time. As the Todds point out, Adam and Eve had to learn survival techniques when they made their exodus from Eden.[1] Abram camped as he headed westward. For forty years Moses was director of what may have been the largest family camp that ever hit any trail. To many Old Testament people, "tenting tonight" was standard operating procedure.

Then God sent His only Son to earth. "The Word became human and lived [Greek, tented] a little while among us" (John 1:14a, C. B. Williams).

While on earth the Lord Jesus did much of His teaching outdoors— on mountain and lakeshore, in wilderness and town, on the lake, by a well. He gave up His life outside Jerusalem's walls. After Christ defeated

---

[1]Floyd and Pauline Todd, *Camping for Christian Youth* (New York: Harper & Row, 1963) , p. 3.

LLOYD O. CORY, B.A., is Editorial Director, Youth and Adult Division, Scripture Press Publications, Inc., Wheaton, Illinois.

death and returned to His Father, His followers reached large and small groups in the out-of-doors.

No one knows for sure when the first Christian camp convened. But there are a few published facts about early Christian camps and conferences in America.

The founding Pilgrim fathers wrote about their first meeting in the new land: "It was decided on the morrow that a small party would go ashore and select a campsite . . . . A campsite was selected on high ground."[2] This too was rugged survival camping.

Some trace the ancestry of Christian conference back to the old-time camp meetings. These gatherings, which consisted largely of meetings and meals, may have begun just prior to 1800. Through them many people became Christians and grew spiritually.

The first youth camps in America may have started during the Civil War. Dubbed "father of the American camping movement," Frederick Gunn was headmaster of the Gunnery School for Boys in Washington, Connecticut. Often he let his lads sleep outside so they would feel more like soldiers. In 1861 Mr. Gunn led his troops to nearby Milford-on-the-Sound, where they camped out for two weeks. His program consisted of a combination of military training, hiking, boating and fishing. He operated this first school camp each summer until 1879.

In 1880 Rev. George Hinkley took seven boys from his church out camping. According to existing records this encampment on Gardener Island, Wakefield, Rhode Island, was the first church-sponsored camp. Pastor Hinkley figured rightly that the informal living in God's great outdoors would help break down barriers so that he could get closer to his boys and win them to the Lord. His campers had Bible teaching, educational and sports activities, and evening services.

The YMCA, which started out strong evangelistically, originated organizational camping in 1885. The Y's Camp Dudley, on New York's Lake Champlain, is the oldest boys' camp still operating.

About this time D. L. Moody started a Bible conference in Northfield, Massachusetts. The Winona Lake (Indiana) Bible Conference and the Mountain Retreat Association (later Montreat, near Asheville, North Carolina) began in the 1890's. Bible conferences tried to provide a relaxing atmosphere, but their primary task was Bible study. Their founders started them because they were convinced that churches were not doing an adequate job of teaching the deeper truths of the Word.

In the 1920's and 1930's, Bible conferences switched from tents to per-

---

[2]L. B. Sharp, "The Role of Camping in Our American Heritage," *Camping*, 14:33 (February, 1942).

manent buildings. Many conferences began to sponsor boys' and girls' camps on the outskirts of their properties.

Church-sponsored permanent camping programs started taking hold after World War I. This movement has been growing ever since, except during World War II, when male leaders were scarce. The Bible conference movement, however, has seemingly reached its full growth.

In 1963 evangelical camp and conference leaders met together to form the Christian Camp and Conference Association, International. This interdenominational organization, with its conventions, magazine, field consultations and other services, is the official voice of many evangelical camp and conference groups.[3]

BIBLE CONFERENCES AND TWO TYPES OF CAMPS

Drawing lines of demarcation among the many different kinds of overlapping conference and camping agencies is hard. For no matter where the lines are traced, some will argue that they should be moved one way or another. Why? There is little uniformity in the *modus operandi* among Christian conferences and camps. Especially are there many gradations of evangelical camps, since there are more different ways to operate camps than Sunday schools, vacation Bible schools, or Sunday evening youth groups. Christian conferences and camps fall into several classifications.

Bible Conferences

By and large a Bible conference is a rather formal organization designed to accommodate whole families. Families may live together in cottages or larger buildings, though most Bible conferences also conduct children's camps on or near their grounds. Most Bible conferences have at least one large auditorium, big enough to hold a normal quota of temporary residents plus a "drive-in crowd." Outstanding Bible teachers, evangelists, missionary speakers and musicians conduct most of the meetings. Bible conferences also provide facilities for recreation and fellowship.

Conference-Type Camps

Most church camps drop into this category, or somewhere between a conference-type camp and an outdoor adventure-type camp. The basic difference between these two types of camps lies in their programming philosophies. Frequently a camp's philosophy is reflected in its building layout and its use of land. According to Gangel, "A conference [type of camp] is . . . meeting-centered . . . . The entire program—recreational, instructional, and spiritual—is superimposed upon the site so that the re-

---

[3]Christian Camp & Conference Association International, Box 3727, Van Nuys, California 91407.

sulting activities are structured very carefully and centered in the meetings of the day.[4]

Many conference-type camps are large, ranging from 150 to over 500 campers. Their large-group Bible classes often consist of lectures and written assignments. Evening meetings are less formal, frequently held around campfires. The recreational program tends to feature softball and other familiar athletic activities. As a rule the aquatic program is strong. The spiritual tone is set by capable Bible teachers and evangelists. Often camp leaders follow up the speakers' challenges by contacting their campers personally.

Outdoor Adventuring Camps

Outdoor adventuring camps are sometimes referred to as wilderness camps, primitive camps, real camps, or camping camps. This type of camp features outdoor activities that are not indulged in back home. These include camp-outs, cookouts, woodsmanship, nature lore, canoe trips—almost anything that exploits the camp's outdoor setting. Whereas nearly all activities in a conference-type camp take place in large groups, more activities in an outdoor adventuring camp are conducted in small, counselor-led groups. "Such a program presupposes thorough leadership training, for the counselor is expected to take responsibility for Bible teaching and spiritual counseling as well as assisting in activity instruction and supervision."[5]

CENTRALIZED AND DECENTRALIZED CAMP PROGRAMS

When it comes to program makeup, the two main approaches are centralized and decentralized. In a centralized program the director and his aides map out mass activities for the whole camp.

A decentralized program, which is more complex, allows small groups (as cabin units) a degree of choice in activities. The decentralized program puts more emphasis on the informal personal contacts between counselor and campers than does the centralized program's carefully planned large-group activities. Good decentralized camping calls for a crew of godly, well-trained counselors and a director who always keeps track of what each small group is doing.

As one would expect, the programs of outdoor adventuring camps are usually more decentralized than those of conference-type camps. Most

---

[4]Kenneth Gangel, "Christian Camping," *Voice*, XLIII:21 (June, 1964).

[5]*Guiding Principles for Christian Camping* (Chicago: National Sunday School Association Camp Commission, 1962), p. 3.

evangelical church-camp programs are basically centralized, with a few decentralized hours sprinkled into a week's activities.

CLASSIFICATION OF CAMPS BY DURATION AND LOCATION

Day Camping

Day camping is conducted on a daytime basis, campers going home to sleep. Especially popular with preteens, day camping has several advantages over resident camping. For one thing the cost of operating a day camp is nominal. The basic requirements are a creative director, a bus and some sports equipment. Another advantage of day camping is the absence of the emotional tension caused when younger campers are separated from their parents for a week or so. Parents see that day campers get to the church or other starting point daily, at perhaps 9:00 A.M. Campers usually bring bag lunches; the director furnishes the beverage. They bus to a park, forest preserve, lakefront or other spot. The program may consist of hiking, handcraft, Bible stories, nature study or attending a pro ball game or a museum. Campers are brought back between 3:00 and 5:00 P.M. Once a week there may be a campfire, to which parents are invited. Day camping is proving to be an excellent way to reach unconverted parents for the Lord.

Overnight Camping

Overnight camping calls for the campers sleeping out, but spending their days at home, work or school. While day camping appeals to the 8-11 age group, overnight camping has more attraction for older campers. Though generally conducted for only one night, overnight camping is sometimes repeated several nights in a row, or several times in a week or month. (Another kind of overnight camping takes place within the framework of a resident camp. This occurs when a group of resident campers and their counselor leave the main campsite for a camp-out.)

Trip Camping

As its name implies, trip campers do not settle in one location. They keep on the move, pitching camp in different spots. Trail campers travel on foot, burro, or horseback. Other trip campers slice through the water in canoes or boats. Still others cover greater distances in mechanized caravans, using cars, trailers, and "campers" (the kind that perch atop pickup trucks).

Resident Camping

The most widespread form of Christian camping, resident camping, is

conducted on a 24-hour day-and-night basis. Some say there are three
main kinds of resident camping: long-term, short-term, and weekend.

VARIOUS TYPES OF RESIDENT CAMPS

Though the following varieties of camps usually operate as resident
camps, some of them are often conducted on day camp, overnight camp,
or trip camp basis. Most of the following kinds of camps may be run either
as conference-type or outdoor adventuring-type camps. And their programs
may be veered in the direction of either centralization or decentralization.

Boys', Girls', and Coed Camps

Most Christian camping is resident camping. And most Christian resident campers are between the ages of 8 and 17. As already pointed out,
there is a wide range of camps—from platform to wilderness, from centralized to decentralized. Some children's camps are like country clubs,
with paved sidewalks, loud intercom systems, big classrooms and flood-
lighted ball fields. Others are rugged, back-to-nature, weatherbeaten, pup-
tented camps, with primitive outside facilities. Judging from apparent
spiritual results over the years, there are various valid ways to run camps.
When it comes to lasting results, what matters most are the camp's men
and women leaders, not the facilities or the methods used. Clearly the
Lord is not limited by or tied to man-made methods. When God works
in campers' lives He works through dedicated, radiant staff members who
believe, live by and teach God's Word. This does not mean that camping
know-how is unimportant. It does mean that godly zeal—a Spirit-driven
desire to win, challenge and train campers for Christ—is more important
than the camp's facilities and its leaders' knowledge of camp operations
or nature lore.

Family Camps

Family camping, in state and national parks, is increasing rapidly because (1) camping is an inexpensive way to vacation, (2) it offers many
opportunities for recreation and sports, (3) people are eager to get away
from the city's heat, noise, congestion and telephones.

Some Christian families go camping by themselves, or with other families, independently. That is, their camping is not an organized church
activity.

Others camp together in church-guided family groups. Church family
camping is on the increase because (in addition to the three reasons just
given for general family camping popularity) it is effective in bringing
about family unification and spiritual growth. In today's hectic world,
families are becoming more fragmented. In the rush of life, people do not

get to know their own children or parents—or the Lord—well. Camping out, under the stars and cloudbursts, often brings Christian family members closer to each other and to their Creator and Lord. A church family camp has a most flexible program. People spend much time in family groups. Sometimes the adults meet together while the younger set does likewise, and there are a few joint meetings. Campers of various ages share in planning, making decisions, preparing food and shelter, hiking, swimming, boating, fishing, crafts, turtle races, Bible study. Being together for days, church family campers have time to meditate, to dig deeply into the Word, to ascertain God's plans for their lives.

In addition to boys' camps, girls' camps, coed camps and family camps, there are many specialized forms of camping being carried on by evangelicals. And every year new ways to utilize camping to further the gospel are being developed.

Other Resident Camps

Youth retreats (young people think, plan, commit)
Work camps (order-of-the-towel high schoolers paint, dig, repair)
Athletic camps (many come for sports, are won for Christ)
Music camps (improve the church's music ministry
Collegiate camps (reach and train college students)
College-credit camps (outdoor education for college counselors)
Young marrieds conclaves (couples leave kids at home)
Men's retreats (fellowship with God and each other)
Camps for elderly (golden-agers love camp)
Camps for handicapped (fresh incentives for many)
Camps for retarded (happiness fosters progress)
Camps for underprivileged (appreciation runs high)
Camps for delinquents (many turn from sin to Christ)
Foreign camps (fast-growing, missionary-spurred movement)

CHRISTIAN CAMPING GOALS

Some camp directors operate with vague goals and indefinite objectives. They can be compared to an archer who hopes to score a bulls-eye but does not bother to take careful aim. His chances of hitting the mark are remote.

Fortunately the majority of Christian camp directors keep the most important goals, evangelism and Christian nurture, uppermost. Many, however, seem to forget that their campers' main goal is something different— to have fun. For a successful camp these three goals, plus others, must be attained.

Nearly all sin starts out as fun. Camp is an excellent place to teach

that a lot of fun can be had without indulging in iniquity. Camp coun-
teracts the prevalent idea among many young people that Christianity
is dull, old-fashioned, blah.

The main aim of evangelical camping is that the Holy Spirit will lead
lost campers to Christ, God's Son. Godly counselors pray and teach and
exemplify the Word, seeking to establish friendly beachheads in campers'
heads and hearts, to help win them to Christ. Many nonchristian Sunday
school students, plus many unchurched campers, receive the Saviour at
camp. Camp is the strong right arm of evangelism for many churches.

Development of Campers

Spiritually. Camp should not be a relatively unimportant tacked-on activity, merely a good opportunity for parents to get rid of their offspring
for a week or so. For a good camp is a veritable proving ground for Christianity. Leaders show Christian campers how to develop a solid faith that
keeps working, remove the "knocks" from their speech, iron wrinkles out
of their behavior, and align their lives with God's Word. In triter terms,
godly camp leaders seek to lead every camper's total life toward maturity
in Christ.

Mentally. In a properly programmed camp, campers have much more
time to be alone, to think, than they have in other parts of their church's
program. Counselors should encourage them to spend part of this alone-
time with the Word and its Author, tucking away Bible knowledge, memorizing Scriptures that can help them all their lives.

Campers also stretch their mental muscles as they learn firsthand about
flora and fauna, crafts, first aid, and perhaps work on the camp's news-
sheet.

Physically. Camp is one place in Christian education where bedlam can
be beautiful. With no TV sets around, spectatoritis is at a minimum. Campers get lots of exercise, both on land and in the water. They have plenty of
time and opportunity to expend pent-up energies. This is one reason most
campers are receptive to the gospel and Christ's claims on their lives.

Socially. Camp is a great leveling place. For instance, neither wealth
nor family prestige stand an uncooperative camper in good stead. His
peers work hard at chipping off his personality's rough edges. "Iron sharpens iron; so one [camper] sharpens the face of another" (Prov. 27:17,
Berkeley).

Thanks to the living-together setup at camp, cabin groups as a rule are
soon welded together. Campers learn to appreciate others whose abilities,
temperaments, and race are different from their own. Many camp-formed

friendships endure through the years. And in coed camps a fair percentage of campers manage to meet their future life partners.

Emotionally. Campers gain a new perspective on life by being away from home. Most of them make progress in emotional independence from their parents.

Camp should be a glad and happy time for campers, a time when they have fun and also really get to know Christ, the true Source of inner peace and joy. Their camping experience should help them develop a strong confidence in God and what He can do through them. Many parents and Sunday school teachers find camp to be a turning point; their young people come home knowing "the strength of the Spirit's inner reinforcement" (Eph. 3:16, Phillips), and are better prepared to face life's problems.

Training of Leaders

Training counselors. One reason counselor training is important is quantitative: Because evangelical camping is expanding rapidly, the need for trained leadership gets greater every year. The other reason counselor training is vital is qualitative: The counselor of a small group wields great influence over his campers. He not only *tells* but *shows* what Christ means to him. Unlike a leader at Sunday school, children's church, Sunday evening youth group, weekday club or vacation Bible school, a camp counselor cannot leave his charges after an hour or three. There is no place for a counselor to hide till the next day or week—his Christianity and knowledge of camping show both day and night. Since campers tend to pattern their actions after their counselors, an untrained or backslidden counselor can wreck a camp program. As the specialists in waterfront and cooking need training for their tasks, the counselor needs training as a specialist in spiritual matters. He also must be able to manage small-group activities, unaided.

Prospective counselors should know their camp's standards for counselors, which should be based on that camp's philosophy. Here is one list of counselor qualifications:[6]

1. Know Jesus Christ as Saviour and maintain a vital, growing relationship to Him as Lord.
2. Be able to lead a camper to Christ.
3. Radiate Christ, being a mature staff member who is worthy of emulation.
4. Understand the philosophy and aims of the camp and seek to carry them out.

[6]Adapted from Joy MacKay, "The Counselor Training Program for the Established Summer Camp" (Unpublished Master's thesis, Wheaton College, Wheaton, Ill., 1962), pp. 35-37.

5. Be loyal to the camp, its director and its policies.

6. Be able to work well with other leaders.

7. Assume responsibility cheerfully and be conscientious in performing duties.

8. See extra work to be done and do it without being told; be willing to do tasks not required in your job analysis.

9. Be familiar with the out-of-doors; feel at home there and be able to help campers feel at home too; know your way with map and compass; recognize night sounds of the woods; understand what to do when it rains on an overnight.

10. Be able to teach some camp skill.

11. Like campers and enjoy being with them, since campers quickly distinguish a counselor who really enjoys their company from one who patronizes them.

12. Understand campers, as a group and as individuals; take time to listen to each one.

13. Possess good health and vitality.

14. Know your own capabilities and limitations.

15. Be flexible and resourceful, adjusting easily to new situations.

16. Be neat in appearance and keep your belongings in good order.

17. Be at least 19 years of age, having had two years of college or its equivalent.[7] (This last qualification is omitted from many counselor qualification lists, usually because of leadership shortage.)

A counselor training schedule will vary according to the proportion of new counselors, the length of the camp, the availability of the site, the distance the staff must travel to camp and the extent to which the director believes in such training. Some phases of training can be covered by mailings and meetings in town. But a large part of the instruction, to be fully effective, must take place at the campsite.

Here is an outline of a fairly complete plan for training counselors:[8]

Counselor Training Plan

	Time	*Content*
1. *By correspondence*	Letters sent in the spring	1. Upon receipt of application send: welcome letter. counselor contract, counselor memo or challenge.

---

[7]"Standards Report of Camping Practices—Resident Camps" (Martinsville, Ind.: American Camping Association), p. 2.

[8]Joy MacKay, *Creative Counseling for Christian Camps* (Wheaton, Ill.: Scripture Press Publications, Inc., 1966), p. 113.

2. Upon receipt of signed contract send:
   job analysis,
   second memo or challenge,
   list of books to read,
   Bible study helps.

3. Then send:
   third memo or challenge,
   counselor training helps,
   cabin devotion helps,
   campfire message suggestions,
   health form.

2. *Pre-camp training* [at location near the counselors' homes]	Weekend	Discuss aims and philosophy of camp, psychology of handling campers. Pass out recommended bibliography. Discuss how to prepare Bible studies. Make activity assignments. Make cabin assignments. Go over program in general.
3. *Pre-in-camp training* [at camp, before the campers arrive]	One week or ten days	Take time to get to know each other better. Go through a daily schedule. Develop evening programs. Discuss health, morale, safety. Become familiar with site and environs. Gain experience in nature, craft, and trip programs. Make caper charts; note kitchen procedures. Practice a cookout. Discuss music in camp. Hold divisional meetings. Enlarge on the aims and philosophy of the camp's program. Allow time for counselors to prepare; get cabins ready. Impart spiritual challenge.
4. *In-service training* [while camp is in session]	30-minute counselor meeting each day; also individual interviews and evaluations.	Plan how to deal with specific problems and weak points. Give help when difficulties arise. Schedule regular interviews and evaluations with counselors. (*Note:* Give a spiritual challenge with every contact.)

Training campers to be leaders. Camp is becoming known as a prime place to develop latent leadership abilities. As mentioned earlier, most young people in good Christian camps develop spiritually, mentally, physically, socially and emotionally. Changes frequently come in campers' lives with ease and rapidity, partly because of the continuity of experience in a controlled environment.

Camp is perhaps the most logical place in the church program to develop the four *C*'s of leadership:

Confidence, not primarily in self but in God, is fostered by the campers' countless opportunities for learning by doing. Wise counselors let their charges help plan hikes, choose teams, lead song services, build a simple outdoor chapel.

Curiosity runs high, as young people come to camp expectantly, with their learning readiness revved up. Many seek adventure in the woods, on waterways, and some in exploring the Word.

Conscience is exercised and developed as the Holy Spirit speaks to individuals. He shows the camper who wrestles with his own conscience how to break loose from sin's stranglehold.

Communication of God's message is stimulated in Bible Hours, bull sessions, casual contacts, postcampfire discussions. Campers have lots of time to practice expressing the gospel clearly.

Probably most future camp leaders are now campers. There is no better place than camp for training tomorrow's staff members. The CIT (Counselor-in-Training) program and its facsimiles are spreading from camp to camp.

CIT's are older campers who work as assistants to counselors for one or two seasons. A CIT generally lives with a cabin group, takes special classes in Bible and/or camping skills, practices leadership skills, often works a few hours a day at a camp maintenance job, and sometimes takes the counselor's place so his boss may have free or study time. A CIT, like all staff members, should get a job description before camp, receive supervision during camp, and be evaluated at the close of his stint.

Widening of Everyone's Horizon

Camp spells adventure, new skills and exploration to young people who are a bit restless in their chrome-plated cities and suburbs. Counselors should make sure that camp does not disappoint them. Eunice Russell advises:

> Your example . . . is pivotal here. You can make simple hikes and stunts adventuresome just by contagious enthusiasm. Your own curiosity at a tadpole squirming in the shallow edge of the lake, or a milkweed pod ready to burst—your interest in learning to paddle a canoe or hit

the archery target—may stimulate an interest in a new field or skill. If you succeed in carrying over this same spirit of adventure into exploration of the Bible, you will help to break down the "compartmentalization" that may exist in some minds: "This is fun," and "This is spiritual" (with the implication that the latter is dull) .[9]

Compass-orienteering, ax-wielding, fire-building, horsemanship, riflery, archery, skin- and scuba-diving, conservation, and outdoor cooking are a few of the many skills campers may develop. Wise directors reserve certain privileges (as overnights) for junior highs, others(as canoe trips) for high schoolers. Such a progression program (which includes degrees of attainment in waterfront, archery, riflery, and other skills) helps get campers back year after year.

Most campers come from cities or suburbs, are used to the urban setting. They are more familiar with street lights than the lights of heaven. At camp, in the blackness of night, as they peer up toward God's sky, the world's pull is weaker, God's pull stronger (Ps. 19:1).

Eventful camp days never die. Long after a camper is harnessed with adulthood's weighty problems he occasionally relives golden days spent at camp. He recalls paddling across the still lake at sunrise, sneaking a cold frog into his buddy's bunk before lying on his own gravel-packed bed, the last night in camp—the presence of God that felt warmer than the campfire—and his promise to live for his Lord.

CAMP ORGANIZATION AND ADMINISTRATION

In simple terms organization is planning one's work; administration is working one's plan. Sad to say, camp organization and administration are sometimes viewed as necessary evils attached to Christian camping. A sizable percentage of camp overseers seem to think the more spiritual the camp the less businesslike the operation will be.

But a camp's Christian testimony is bolstered by businesslike contacts with forest rangers, deliverymen, salesmen, health and welfare inspectors, its own staff, and the campers' parents. A well-organized and administered camp usually operates so smoothly that its campers are unaware of even major problems that erupt behind the scenes.

The field of camp organization and administration is broad. There are at least as many ways to organize and administrate camps as there are different types and kinds of camps. A given camp's organizational setup and administrative activities will depend on whether it is a day camp, night camp, or 24-hour camp; a short-term or long-term camp; a conference-type camp or wilderness camp; whether its program is basically

---

[9]*How to Be a Camp Counselor* (Wheaton, Ill.: Scripture Press Foundation, 1959) , p. 5.

centralized or decentralized; the training and backgrounds of the people in charge.

Doubtless all competent camp directors would concur that good camps result from good planning. Here is a checklist[10] of a director's planning and performance duties which applies to many or most camps:

Before Camp

1. *Determine responsibility.* A committee or board should stand behind every camp, meet regularly, keep records, report to its superior organization, appoint the camp director.

2. *Decide camp location.* Choose rented or self-owned site.

3. *Determine objectives.* (See Christian Camping Goals, pages 355-58, in this chapter.)

4. *Set up organizational framework.* Depict your personnel structure on a chart, select people carefully, delegate jobs in an orderly manner.

5. *Decide camp fees.* Factors include amounts of subsidization and donated food, labor, upkeep, improvements. Determine what campers pay, what camp management gets.

6. *Be sure you're insured.* No camp should operate without medical and hospital coverage.

7. *Mark age and sexual divisions.* Decide on age groupings, whether camp will be coed or sexually segregated, whether two or more age groups will operate on the grounds simultaneously with separate programs.

8. *Get the word out.* Camp promotion includes pulpit push, posters, letters, brochures or folders, rallies, camp banks or stamp books, contests with camperships as prizes, church bulletin news releases, mock campfires at youth meetings, photos on bulletin boards, slide or movie presentations.

9. *Line up staff.* Sign up counselors, cooks, athletic director, waterfront personnel, dishwashers, nurse, *et al.*

10. *Plan daily schedule.* Base this on your goals for your campers' lives.

11. *Take care of last-minute details.* Check your staff, the campgrounds, preregistration progress, mess hall and canteen supplies, Bible study materials and visual aids, physical exams, transportation.

12. *Train your counselors.* (See Counselor Training Plan, pages 358-59, in this chapter.

During Camp

1. *Make opening day smooth.* Be efficient and friendly in orienting campers, making them feel at home.

2. *Keep praying; be enthusiastic.* These two go hand in hand.

---

[10]Condensed from *Camp Director's Handbook* (Wheaton, Ill.: Scripture Press Foundation, 1959), pp. 4-22.

3. *Insist on good records.* Over the long pull, records do much to make or break a camp. File registration information, food and equipment transactions.

4. *Play fair with campers.* Outline rules (as few as possible), orally and in writing, to campers. But don't expect 15-year-olds to act like 35-year-olds. Give each discipline case a full hearing, with love and forbearance. Lower the boom only when necessary. Be consistent.

5. *Hold daily staff meetings.* (See In-service training, page 358.)

6. *Take problems in stride.* Delegate tasks; anticipate troubles.

7. *Keep a spiritual accent.* Athletics, fun times, and the like should not become king of the hill, but should contribute toward the development of Christlike character.

8. *Give farewell counsel to campers.* Allow ample opportunity for those who have put off spiritual decisions to talk with their counselors. Warn campers about the emotional letdown they may face when they get home. Encourage them to be loyal to a Bible-believing church. Brief them on how to witness to school classmates, parents, and others.

After Camp

1. *Let churches know what happened.* Using camper evaluation forms, let the camper's Sunday school teacher (or a church visitation worker if the camper does not attend) know about his apparent spiritual, athletic and social progress.

2. *Write some letters.* Right after camp write a form letter to parents, telling how you worked to build a Christian character in their son or daughter; suggest that they write, if they have suggestions for improving camp. Also send personal thank you notes to all staff members.

3. *Evaluate.* How effective were the Bible classes, age divisions, outdoor activities, the approach to non-Christians? You might ask the campers on closing day to fill out an unsigned questionnaire, giving their opinions of camp's different activities.

4. *Lay groundwork for next year.* Report to your board or committee what transpired. Nail down the dates of next year's camp. See that next year's director (whether you or someone else) is selected before Christmas and that essential information is placed in his hands.

GEARING CAMPING INTO THE TOTAL CHURCH PROGRAM

Why Camping Belongs in the Total Church Program

Some Christian educators seem to think of camp as the dessert of their church ministry. They feel that camp makes a wholesome church diet more palatable. Though camp may do this, it ought to be more than an inducement to lure young people into liking church. For camp can be one of the most useful tools in Christian education.

More church leaders are deciding that it is not enough to reach part of their young people with part of a Christian education program. Some ask, "Can a young person have an adequate Christian education *without* going to a Christian camp?" They aver that no area of life should be ignored, that church camping is necessary. For some things can be learned better in church, others at camp.

Despite efforts to the contrary, church sessions frequently leave the impression that church meetings are separate from the rest of life: What takes place in church is holy and the rest of life is more secular. Camp offers a rare opportunity to demonstrate that all phases of a Christian's life can be Christian. Camp's hiking, cooking in the woods, warm friendships, Bible studies, campfires and swimming can all contribute toward Christlikeness.

Christian education, which deals with real life, is difficult to teach in two or three hours a week to people who may hardly know each other. Probably the two best locales for demonstrating and imparting practical Christian education are godly homes and Spirit-led camps, where elbows and dispositions rub constantly.

Responsibilities of a Camp Coordinator

A logical first step, in integrating camping into a church's overall program, is to appoint a camp coordinator to the board of Christian education. The camp coordinator may have these responsibilities:

1. He learns the present "camp score" in his church by taking a survey to find out how many, and who, are going to private secular camps, Y camps, agency Bible camps, sports camps, and the camp (if any) that his church sponsors or recommends.

2. He keeps abreast of camping trends; he finds out if a nearby Christian camp may serve his church.

3. He keeps the Christian education committee and various other church agencies informed about this camp, its schedule and program.

4. If nearby Christian resident camps are crowded (or nonexistent), he investigates the possibilities of getting together with other churches and starting a day camp or resident camp. Or he may initiate camping in his own church on a small scale by organizing a weekend church family camp, snow camp or youth retreat.

5. He encourages competent church leaders to serve as counselors at the camp their young people will attend. (It is usually good if the pastor and other leaders are with their campers when they face crucial spiritual experiences.)

6. He helps line up workers for readying and improving camp.

7. He tries to correlate (not duplicate) the camp program with his church's year-round program. He makes sure that his church is not in one corner, the camp in another, without either knowing what the other is doing. He

sees the need for continuity through the year in Bible teaching, so his campers do not study Samuel in Sunday school, vacation Bible school, weekday clubs and camp.

8. He promotes camp attendance by brochures, posters, audio-visuals, a savings plan, announcements, precamp rallies. He sees to it that camp is not pigeonholed till summer, but is talked about most of the year.

9. He submits to the Christian education committee an itemized estimate of camp-related expenses as part of the church's total Christian education budget. (This may include a camp subsidy or camperships for needy young people.)

10. He counsels with those who will soon attend camp, to help them make the most of their coming experiences.

11. After camp, he provides public opportunities for campers to share the benefits of their experiences and their enthusiasm, perhaps in a "camp echo" testimony service.

12. He helps campers fit camp learning experiences into their more mundane lives at home and school.

13. He gets ex-campers active in church agencies and perhaps Youth For Christ, The Navigators, and similar organizations that can help them continue their closer walk with God.

14. He checks to see that the pastor and the campers' Sunday school teachers read the camper evaluation forms filled out by counselors and sent to the church. (If he receives some unchurched campers' evaluation forms, he contacts the young people for his church.)

15. He finds church jobs for those whose camp experience has helped qualify them for service.

SUMMARY

Christian camping presents exciting, only partially explored opportunities for winning, challenging and training people for Christ. May thousands of additional God-directed leaders start new Christian camps. May they know what God wants them to do, and check often to see how well they are measuring up to their goals of decisions for Christ, development of campers, training of leaders, widening of everyone's horizon. As they do this, results will show up in local churches—and around the world.

FOR FURTHER READING

"Bibliography for Camp Leaders." Chicago: National Sunday School Association Camp Commission, 1962.

Camp Director's Handbook. Wheaton, Ill.: Scripture Press Foundation, 1959.

Camps & Conferences magazine. Wheaton, Ill.: Christian Life Publications.

CORY, LLOYD O. *The Pastor and Camping* (Christian Education Monograph, Pastors' Series No. 3). Glen Ellyn, Ill.: Scripture Press Foundation, 1966.

ENSIGN, JOHN and RUTH. *Camping Together as Christians.* Richmond, Va.: John Knox Press, 1958.

"Evangelical Camp Resources." Chicago: National Sunday School Association Camp Commission, 1962.

GENNÉ, ELIZABETH and WILLIAM. *Church Family Camps and Conferences*. Philadelphia: The Christian Education Press, 1962.

GOODRICH, LOIS. *Decentralized Camping*. New York: Association Press, 1959.

HAMMETT, CATHERINE, and MUSSELMAN, VIRGINIA. *The Camp Program Book*. New York: National Recreational Association, 1951.

How to Be a Camp Counselor. Wheaton, Ill.: Scripture Press Foundation, 1959.

LYNN, GORDON, *Camping and Camp Crafts*. New York: Golden Press, 1959.

MACKAY, JOY. *Creative Counseling for Christian Camps*. Wheaton, Ill.: Scripture Press Publications, Inc., 1966.

MATTSON, LLOYD. *Camping Guideposts* (Christian Camp Counselor's Handbook). Chicago: Moody Press, 1962.

REIMANN, LEWIS. *The Successful Camp*. Ann Arbor, Mich.: University of Michigan Press, 1958.

SAUNDERS, JOHN. *Nature Crafts*. New York: Golden Press, 1958.

TINNING, GRAHAM, editor. *Yearbook of Christian Camping*. Van Nuys, Calif.: Christian Camp and Conference Association, 1965.

TODD, FLOYD and PAULINE. *Camping for Christian Youth*. New York: Harper & Row, 1963.

Filmstrips: "Christian Camping." Burbank, Calif.: Cathedral Films. Color, four filmstrips and two 33⅓ rpm records.

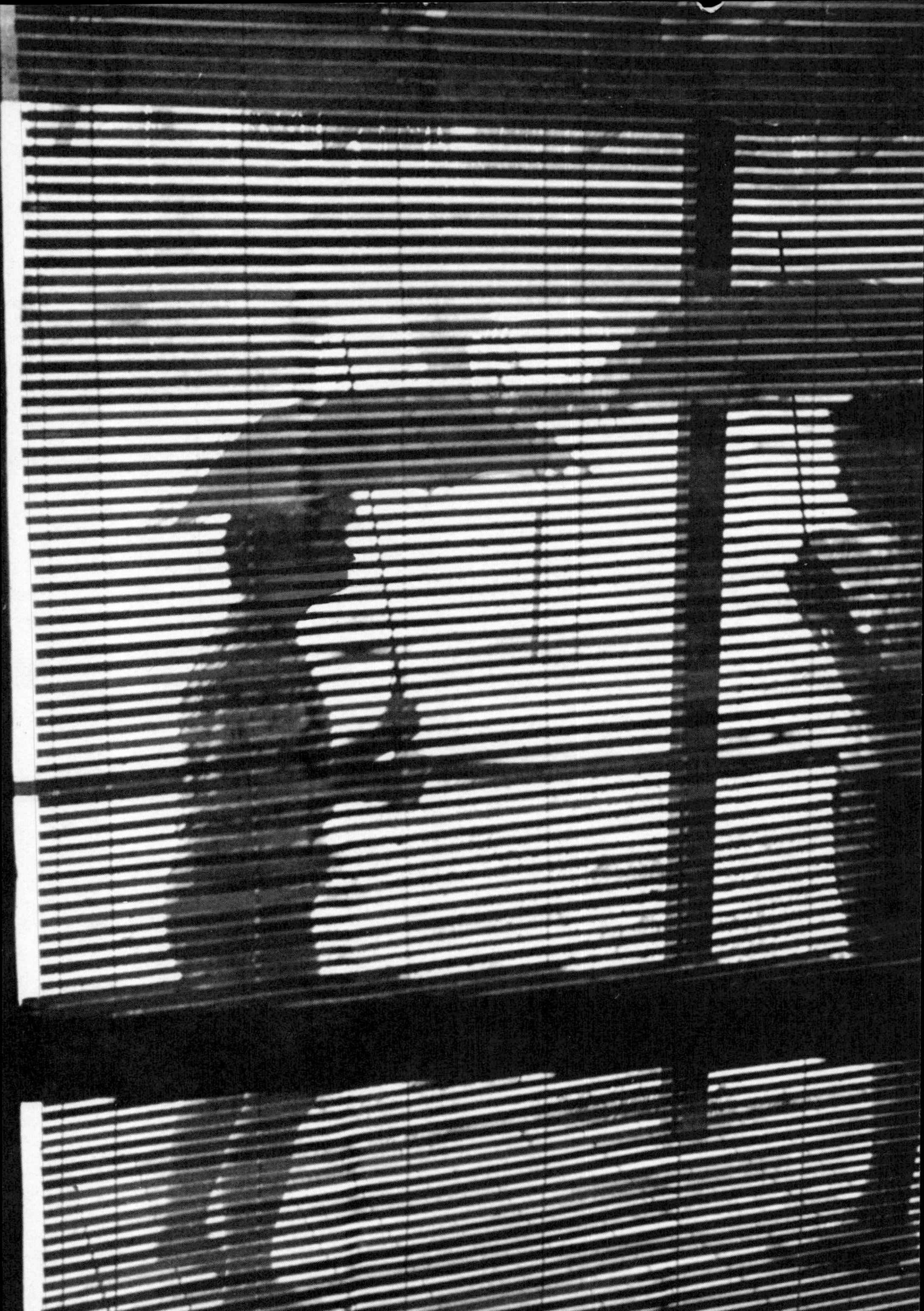

PART V

working with youth

Methods are links for uniting content and experience. They are vehicles for bringing learners into vital contact with the written Word, the Bible, and the living Word, Jesus Christ. Viewed in this light, methods are not mere gimmicks or techniques or novel approaches. Instead they are essential bridges over which the leader and his young people "walk" as they go from lack of proper knowledge, attitudes and skills to the acquiring of proper knowledge, attitudes and skills.

GENE A. GETZ

24

using creative methods

RANDOLPH CRUMP MILLER suggests that a method is "simply the means whereby Christian truth is arranged to make it effective in one's meeting and understanding of life's problems."[1]

HOW ARE METHODS RELATED TO THE LEARNING PROCESS?

Objectives Determine Methods

If a "method" is the means by which a task is accomplished or an objective is met, then a "method of teaching" is the means whereby an educational task or objective is fulfilled.

This suggests that methods used in teaching and working with youth be chosen not arbitrarily but in the light of educational objectives. A

---

[1]*Education for Christian Living* (Englewood Cliffs, N.J.: Prentice-Hall, Inc., 1956), p. 166.

GENE A. GETZ, M.A., is Director of the Evening School, The Moody Bible Institute of Chicago, Illinois.

teacher or youth worker who is concerned with meeting goals will not ask, "Which methods shall I choose this time?" but "Which methods will enable me to best meet my goals?" For example, if the goal of a unit of Bible lessons or youth programs is to help the student learn how to witness to others about Christ, the wise teacher asks, "Which methods for this teaching-learning session will best help my students learn how to witness?" Naturally some methods will more readily lend themselves to the accomplishing of that particular aim than others.

The Learning Process Determines Methods

An awareness of what learning is and how it takes place is another determining factor in the choice of methods. As youth leaders learn more about the nature of learning, they become better equipped to choose the right methods for certain desired goals. If young people best learn by listening, lecturing would be one of the methods to utilize most frequently. But if young people learn better by verbal interaction, then those methods that provide for verbal interaction with truth—such as discussions, questions and answers, problem solving—should be utilized more frequently.

This leads to the question, What constitutes learning? No attempt is made here to give a full discussion on the complex subject of the learning process, but perhaps certain basic elements essential to learning can be suggested.

1. *Learning takes place to the extent that the student is motivated.* All people have certain drives, needs, interests, incentives and motives that activate them toward goals that have meaning and significance for them.

Because of these drives, it behooves youth workers to choose those methods for lessons, programs and other activities that best relate to the students' motives, tap their incentives, meet their needs and captivate their interests. To the extent this is done, learning is aided.

According to Bowman, "Adult workers make a grave mistake if they begin imparting information or suggesting *their* solutions *before the young people have first been led to feel the grip of the problem for themselves.*"[2]

2. *Learning takes place to the extent that the student is involved.* Purposeful self-activity by the students is essential to learning. Many local church workers readily admit that they feel they learn more than their students. This is an admission that the leaders are more personally involved than the pupils! Since the teacher is to be helping *students* learn, it becomes necessary to select those methods that will *involve* the students.

Corzine points out that student involvement may be physical (writing

---

[2] Clarice M. Bowman, *Ways Youth Learn* (New York: Harper & Bros. Publishers, 1952), p. 84. Italics hers.

on the chalkboard, finding and reading a Bible passage, making a missionary map, distributing gospel tracts), or mental (discussing a question, thinking through a problem, planning a program), or emotional (worshiping the Lord, responding to a call for dedication, sensing conviction of sin or the need to correct one's ways).[3]

Since learning is essentially the *activity of the learner,* the youth worker should ask, "How can I involve the teens in this lesson [or project or program]?"

Tani mentions that active participation is the best kind of learning:

> "Ultimately the best teaching method is to project the person into the midst of the problem or subject matter. Direct experience cannot be had from film and speeches. Firsthand contact and visits, personal research and interviews, on-the-spot discussions, and face-to-face exposures to life situations are by far the most desirable learning opportunities. When a teen-ager is responsible for the presentation of a class lesson or topic discussion, for recreation or for worship, for a work project or service activity, he is on the highest learning level.[4]

3. *Learning takes place to the extent that the student interacts with appropriate content.* In Christian education the content of the curriculum is an essential element in the learning process. The Bible is at the heart of the curriculum for it is God's truth which is "able to make thee wise" (II Tim. 3:15) and to lead people into spiritual maturity.[5] Therefore it is through the learner's interaction with the principles and concepts of the Bible that he can best analyze his own life and determine to act in accordance with the truths encountered.[6]

In other words adequate living is determined by adequate concepts. Actions are affected by the understanding and appropriating of ideas.

Methods that provide for such interaction will facilitate learning.[7]

Variety and creativity in methodology help make learning interesting and appealing. Public schools and the entertainment world attract the attention and interest of youth because, for one thing, they specialize in superb methodology. If Christian leaders are content to be routine or mediocre in the way truth is presented, they tend to run the risk of losing the interest of youth.

---

[3]J. L. Corzine, *Looking at Learning* (Nashville: Sunday School Board of the Southern Baptist Convention, 1934), pp. 47-48.

[4]Henry N. Tani, *Ventures in Youth Work* (Philadelphia: Christian Press, 1957), p. 32.

[5]See Roy B. Zuck, *The Holy Spirit in Your Teaching* (Wheaton, Ill.: Scripture Press Publications, Inc., 1963), chapter 10.

[6]John T. Sisemore (ed.), *Vital Principles in Religious Education* (Nashville: Broadman Press, 1966), p. 29.

[7]For further discussion on the nature of the learning process, see chapter 6 in Lois E. LeBar, *Education That Is Christian* (Westwood, N.J.: Fleming H. Revell, 1958).

IS CONCERN FOR METHODS SCRIPTURAL?

As the Old Testament prophets taught, they verbalized, visualized, and even dramatized (consider Ezekiel, the most dramatic prophet who ever lived). Jesus Christ told stories, asked probing questions, used numerous visuals, made shocking statements, led discussions, led His disciples in projects, and used many other teaching techniques.[8] The Apostle Paul lectured, debated, illustrated, discussed, preached, wrote and counseled. Throughout the Bible God's chosen leaders used a variety of methods in communicating His message.

WHAT METHODS CAN BE USED?

There are various ways to approach the study of methods for youth. Bowman arranges methods around certain purposes[9]:

1. To stimulate interest, arouse curiosity or acquaint teens with a problem—questions, pictures, models, curios, exhibits, storytelling, field trips, group reading of a drama or Scripture.

2. To secure, arrange, or interpret information—reading, pictures, maps, charts, graphs, visits, trips, surveys, interviews, recordings.

3. To enlarge sympathies or deepen appreciations—storytelling, plays, role playing, group reading, costumes, pictures, films, curios, live or recorded music, creative writing.

4. To express thoughts, records or illustrate findings, or share with others—making posters, murals, friezes, scrapbooks, newspapers, maps, exhibits; verse speaking or group reading; poetry writing, hymn writing, script writing.

5. To solve problems—discussions, buzz groups, dialogues, field trips, surveys, interviews, films, recordings.

Lederach has a twofold division of methods: (1) teacher-to-pupil methods—lectures, questions and answers, stories, objects, programmed instruction; and (2) methods that involve the group—discussions, buzz groups, role playing, projects, creative and informal drama.[10] Edgar Dale in his "cone of experience" has distinguished between (1) methods that involve *doing*—direct experiences, contrived experiences, and dramatic participating; (2) methods that involve *observing*—demonstrations, field trips, exhibits, motion pictures, recordings, and still pictures; and (3) methods that involve *symbolizing*—visual symbols and verbal symbols.[11] Miller

---

[8]For an excellent discussion of Jesus' teaching methods, see Herman Harrell Horne, *Jesus the Master Teacher* (Grand Rapids: Kregel Publications, 1964); Lois E. LeBar, *op. cit.*, chapter 3, "The Teacher Come from God."

[9]Bowman, *op. cit.*, pp. 150-54.

[10]Paul M. Lederach, *Learning to Teach* (Scottdale, Pa.: Herald Press, 1964), pp. 38-56.

[11]Edgar Dale, *Audio-Visual Methods in Teaching* (New York: Dryden Press, 1946), pp. 37-52.

groups methods under telling (storytelling, lecturing, audio aids), showing (projected and nonprojected visuals), exchanging ideas (discussions, questions and answers, buzz groups, role playing), and group planning and activity (projects, dramatization).[12]

For the purposes of this chapter the author has chosen to group methods into two rather natural categories: teacher-centered (or leader-centered) methods and youth-centered methods. The former includes the following: lectures, storytelling, questions and answers, group discussions, audio-visuals, forums, testing, observation trips, silent thinking. The latter includes research and reports, buzz groups, two-by-two discussions, panels, brain-storming, listening teams, debates, symposiums, role playing, pageants, tableaux, pantomimes, plays, skits. Certainly this not an exhaustive list, but it does suggest more frequent utilized techniques in youth work.

Of course, all methods are in one sense teacher-controlled and directed. However certain methods, as will be explained, are more student-oriented, at least in their outworking. For example, a teacher may give a research assignment, but it is the youth who actually do the researching.

Teacher-Centered (or Leader-Centered) Methods

1. *Lectures.* One of the most commonly used teacher-oriented methods is the lecture, which is a verbal presentation of subject matter. This method is often criticized, particularly because it has been overused and used by some people almost to the exclusion of other methods. But this does not mean that the lecture method is not valid or creative. It can be used very effectively to communicate Bible truths.

What makes the lecture method creative? A good lecturer is well prepared so he does not have to read his material. He maintains eye contact as much as possible and is not note-bound. He is able to speak fluently with his thoughts well organized.

A good lecturer is able to speak with authority, convinced that he really believes what he is teaching. He speaks with feeling and sincerity, because what he is presenting means much to him. A good lecturer also presents his material with enthusiasm, revealed through the proper use of gestures, facial expressions, and voice inflection. He makes adequate use of verbal illustrations to clarify, hold interest, and apply what he is teaching.

A good lecturer also uses visuals to illustrate his material. He speaks rapidly enough to hold attention, and recapitulates periodically so that the learner sees the continuity of the material. Whenever possible he also makes good use of rhetorical questions—questions to which he expects mental response and not an oral answer.

---

[12]Miller, *op. cit.,* pp. 186-242.

The lecture method should be used when it is necessary to convey information as a foundation for discussion.

2. *Storytelling.* Storytelling is presenting an incident in story form.

Ordinarily people think of storytelling as a method to be used with children. Of course this method is used more frequently with lower age levels than with youth and adults. But this does not mean that it can *never* be used with older groups. An occasional, well-told story can serve as a main method of communication with teens. This is particularly true in worship services or even in presenting some dramatic stories from Scripture in a Sunday school class.

To use the storytelling method well, one must be prepared. Select the story carefully so that it is appropriate for the occasion. Outline the main points in the story and then practice telling it aloud.

In presenting the story, be enthusiastic, and speak naturally and with variety in your voice. When possible, use dialogue to help bring the characters to "life." Use action verbs and, when appropriate, create suspense.

Storytelling is an art. It takes effort and practice to develop the skill. Don't be discouraged if you do not feel successful the first few times. The maxim, "practice makes perfect," applies to developing good storytelling techniques.

3. *Questions and answers.* Three kinds of questions that can be used in communication are fact-seeking, thought-provoking, and rhetorical questions.

A fact-seeking question is simply a question that is asked in order to get at facts. For example, a teacher may ask a class of junior highs, "From what city were the first missionaries in the book of Acts sent out?" The factual answer is "Antioch."

A thought-provoking question is one that involves problem-solving on the part of the listener. For example, the leader might ask, "Which is more important—to witness for Christ vocally or to maintain a silent witness by your life?" In this kind of question there is no specific factual answer, for the Bible indicates that both are important. A "life" witness is probably foundational but not necessarily more important than witnessing by "lip." The two must go together. This is the kind of question that can provoke thought and lead to discussion.

A rhetorical question is a thought-provoking question but one to which you do not expect an oral response.

When should a leader use questions in working with youth? Questions may be used in many ways and at various times. They may be used as a point of contact in an approach to a story, lesson or discussion. They might be used *during* a lesson, particularly in Bible study. They are extremely effective in making applications or in reviewing or in getting students to recite. They can be used to spark a discussion or to create interest in the process of a lecture.

4. *Group discussions.* Later in the chapter several specialized forms of discussion are considered. However in group discussion the leader seeks to involve the entire group—whether Sunday school class or youth group—in interaction. Total group discussion, however, does not necessarily mean that everyone in the group will become *orally* involved, contributing verbally. But every person will be involved mentally and emotionally.

How does the discussion method differ from the question-and-answer method? In the question-and-answer method the leader specifically directs a question to one or more members of a group to get a specific response. Following the response he directs another question to the group in order to get another response. The question-and-answer method continues with this type of pattern.

But in discussion a question may be directed to the group and a student may respond. However, the answer may be directed by the leader back to the group for another individual response. Then others respond not so much to the original question as they do to what has been said by another member of the class. Before long there is interaction among members of the group. When this interaction leads toward a directed goal, profitable discussion is taking place.

It should be remembered that discussion calls for more ability, resourcefulness, and preparation on the part of the leader than many other methods. An effective discussion can only be carried on when there are provocative problems to discuss and where the individuals have sufficient background to contribute intelligently to the discussion. Young people resent being asked to discuss yes-no questions or questions to which the answers are obvious. Discussions that evoke enthusiastic response are those that challenge teens to think. Some occasions when discussion may prove stimulating are:

a. When there is a problem on which a divergence of opinion is felt.

b. When there are misunderstandings among the group members which need clearing up.

c. When group members have sufficient background of experience and information about a problem, but need now to sort and arrange their impressions into useful categories, and to formulate plans ahead.

d. When a matter is confused or not quite clear.[13]

Also, discussion must move in a specific direction. This means that a teacher must correlate and plan a discussion in order to achieve specific goals. One should not have discussion merely to consume time.

[13]Bowman, *op. cit.,* pp. 96-97.

At the conclusion of a discussion a summary by the leader helps the group grasp in succinct form the basic ideas considered. The leader can call attention to the points listed on the chalkboard during the discussion. Or someone can be taking notes during the discussion so that the material may be condensed, re-evaluated and reorganized if necessary, and possibly mimeographed and distributed to the group. With junior highs, discussion must almost always be led by an adult. Some senior highs are capable of leading discussions; but even so, many times a discussion proceeds better if an experienced adult is guiding it. Bowman mentions that young people "tend to skim the surface of questions; to take shortcuts; to base decisions on hearsay and prejudice—unless firmly guided to sturdier thinking and fact-finding and fact-facing."[14]

5. *Audio-visuals.* Some teaching aids are "audio"—they are heard. Other aids are "visual"—they are seen. Still others are "audio-visual"—they are both heard and seen.

Maps are particularly helpful in teaching the Word of God. For example, when you are discussing an epistle written by Paul, it helps to locate on a map where the letter was written and the place where the letter was received. When teaching the book of Philippians to young people, show on a map that the church of Philippi was founded on Paul's second missionary journey and that later Paul was writing from Rome to this church.

The *chalkboard* is another important tool in communicating with youth. A teacher in a Sunday school class should always have a chalkboard on hand. Use the chalkboard to outline the lesson as you develop it point by point, or to graphically illustrate some point by means of a simple

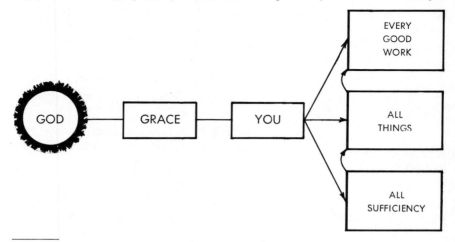

---

[14]*Ibid.,* p. 56.

visual illustration. Simple charts drawn on the chalkboard, such as the one shown on II Corinthians 9:8, help explain the meaning of Bible truths. With a little work and thought, not only verses but paragraphs, chapters, and even single books of the Bible can be illustrated with charts.

Bulletin boards are especially helpful in youth groups for publicizing meetings, announcing leadership responsibilities, as well as featuring various aspects of youth work.

Films are no longer an innovation in Christian education. But unfortunately they are often not used as well as they might be.

Additional projected visuals to use with youth are *filmstrips, slides, opaque projections* and *overhead projections*. Audio-aids include *tape recordings* and *disc recordings*. Audio-visuals, of course, should not be used alone but in conjunction with other methods, such as lectures, storytelling, discussions.[15]

6. *Forums.* In a forum, representative individuals answer questions asked by the young people. In a youth meeting on the will of God, the students would direct their questions on that subject to leaders such as a pastor, a Christian businessman, a Christian doctor, and a missionary.

7. *Testing.* Students may be asked to respond to a brief quiz in a Sunday school class. After the quiz has been given and the students have recorded their responses, the questions asked and the answers given may then become the outline for the lecture or discussion to follow. One of the advantages of this method is that it gets students thinking along certain lines so that they will be more likely to participate. Often a simple question asked by the leader and a short response put down on paper by the young people help start a meaningful discussion. Some teachers have occasionally given review quizzes or tests at the end of a series of lessons. In youth programs questionnaires, opinion polls, and quizzes may be used.

8. *Observation trips.* An observation trip is a tour to any point outside the regular classroom. If young people are discussing God's will for their lives, they may later enjoy visiting a nearby Bible school or Christian or secular college. Or after discussing opportunities for Christian service, they may take field trips to rescue missions, hospitals, jails, orphanages and rest homes.

Careful planning of a field trip is important. The place chosen should definitely correlate with some purpose or objective being pursued in the regular curriculum of the Sunday school or the young people's group.

The group should also be prepared for the trip. After the trip, have the group discuss or evaluate what they saw, did, or heard. In some instances worthwhile projects may grow out of an observation trip. A group visiting

---

[15]For tips on how to use audio-visuals effectively, see chapter 25, "Materials for Working with Youth."

a rescue mission or a jail may be challenged to organize a gospel team. A group visiting an orphanage or a needy area may become interested in providing clothing or food.

9. *Silent thinking.* In a sense this is very student-centered but it is dependent on careful direction from the teacher. Silent thinking is simply giving the group a particular question to think about and then allowing each individual to think silently about the problem for a few moments and perhaps record some of his thoughts on paper. After this period of thinking has taken place, there can then be opportunity for sharing and group discussion.

10. *Team teaching.* This is a newer approach that some teachers are using. In team teaching, a class is taught by two (sometimes three) people rather than one. But they do more than "take turns" teaching, and they do not take the class every other Sunday or so. Instead they work *together* as a team in both planning and teaching. A few churches are finding that this has added an attractive, stimulating element to the teaching of young people.

Student-Centered Methods

1. *Research and reports.* The research method can be used with young people because they have growing intellectual skills and abilities which enable them to make intelligent use of various resources. Research results from a leader assigning individuals or groups some kind of work outside of class.

Research may involve assigned reading in various sources such as magazines, newspapers, Bible versions and translations, Bible dictionaries, books. Specific assignments may be to read parallel accounts; to read and compare secular and biblical accounts; to read a book and prepare a review, an oral or written report, an outline, or a summary.

2. *Buzz groups.* Buzz groups are a form of discussion involving small groups of people from the total group simultaneously discussing the same or different problems assigned by the leader. The groups should be kept rather small—usually not more than eight—so that everyone can get involved in the discussion.

Buzz groups may be used at the beginning of an hour to get people thinking about a specific type of problem, or at the close of the hour to have the group think about implications of the material presented.

A buzz session may extend from a couple of minutes to perhaps fifteen minutes, depending on the nature of the assignment.

Usually buzz sessions are more effective when they are brief. The purpose of a buzz group is not to exhaust a subject but to get people thinking, as a basis for discussion and evaluation by the entire group.

3. *Two-by-two discussions.* The purpose of a two-by-two discussion is the same as that of a buzz group. However it is carried on in conversational style by two people sitting next to each other. The two-by-two discussion lends itself very nicely to a brief discussion of a problem. It need last no longer than three or four minutes. Then the leader suggests that the students share some of their ideas with the entire group.

Buzz groups and two-by-two discussions get people thinking. They also help allay any fear about participating. There is something therapeutic about the sound of one's own voice in talking with his neighbor or within a small group. Talking with one's neighbor helps a person develop freedom of expression, thus later he feels more free to share his thoughts with the total group.

4. *Panels.* A panel is another form of discussion, in which three to five people discuss a problem in front of the total group. Zuck and Robertson mention three kinds of panels: (1) the guided panel in which a moderator addresses previously discussed questions to panelists, (2) the planned panel in which panelists meet beforehand to decide on a specific outline and then carefully follow this outline in their presentation, and (3) the impromptu panel in which a group of young people are chosen from the group without previous notice to speak "off the cuff" about a certain problem.[16]

5. *Brainstorming.* In brainstorming, the group is encouraged to list extemporaneously as many ideas on a particular problem as possible.

Someone has said that the *ABC's* of brainstorming are as follows:

A—Accept all ideas mentioned.

B—Beware of negatives.

C—Chain your thoughts.

First, every idea that is given should be accepted and written down by a recorder on the chalkboard or on a sheet of paper. *Second,* no one during the brainstorming period should be allowed to disagree or to give reasons why an idea is unacceptable. Brainstorming is not discussion. *Third,* if one person gives a suggestion which precipitates an idea in the mind of someone else, that new idea should be stated. After the brainstorming is over, the ideas presented can be evaluated and discussed.

6. *Listening teams.* Before a talk or a film, divide the group into two or more listening teams and ask each team to listen or look for specific ideas, problems, or answers to questions during the presentation. For example, before showing a film on the Christian life, ask one team to look for the problems faced in the Christian life, and another team to look for answers

---

[16]Roy B. Zuck and Fern Robertson, *How to Be a Youth Sponsor* (Wheaton, Ill.: Scripture Press Foundation, 1960), p. 37.

to those problems. Suggest that another team listen for reference to Bible verses used in answering specific problems.

7. *Debates.* Debate teams operate in different ways, but generally a debate involves two affirmative speakers and two negative speakers. After a moderator introduces the proposition to be debated, the first affirmative speaker seeks to *support* the proposition.

The first person on the negative team would speak next, giving arguments against the proposition.

The third speaker would be the other person on the affirmative team. He would continue to build the affirmative case, telling why he thinks the resolution is correct.

The fourth person to speak—the second person on the negative team—gives arguments to further support the negative case.

At this point the debate may be over. However, if desirable, there may be a rebuttal period after a minute or two of deliberation by the two teams. This time the debaters speak in the following order: the first negative, the first affirmative, the second negative, the second affirmative.

After the debate the subject should be opened to the entire group for discussion. To be effective, the sponsor or teacher should be sure that correct impressions are left with the entire group after the debate is over. The purpose of a debate is to clarify, not to confuse; to crystallize, not to create more difficulty in understanding particular Bible truths.

The moderator should time the debaters carefully and say, "Stop!" when their time is up. Usually three or four minutes for each speaker is sufficient. Also, the proposition to be debated should be stated in positive terms.

8. *Symposiums.* The symposium is often confused with the panel. In a panel the leaders freely discuss the subject among themselves before the group, but in a symposium several people take turns addressing the group on various aspects of an assigned theme. Each person is given a specified amount of time for his presentation. After each person has spoken to a particular point, questions may be entertained from the floor.

9. *Role playing.* Role playing is extemporaneous dramatization. It does not involve a script or preplanning in the sense that those involved know beforehand what they are going to say. It enables the participants to step into the "role" of another person and thus see the situation at hand from his viewpoint. One way to use role playing is to set up a problem for two or more people and then ask them to act out the role for several minutes. A Sunday school teacher may be dealing with the subject of Christian ethics. He may call two young men to the front of the room and present the following situation:

"John is a key basketball player. He is talking in the shower room with

Mr. Smith, the coach. Mr. Smith tells John he should go out on the floor and 'get even' with one of the players on the other team because of bad conduct by the other team member in a previous game. He tells John to take every opportunity to rough him up. But John is a Christian and he feels he should not retaliate this way."

Then the teacher asks one person to play the role of the coach and the other to assume the role of John. John is to react as a Christian; the coach is to react as the one who is asking the player to engage in improper behavior.

After they have played the role for several minutes, the teacher then interrupts, and asks the class to evaluate the situation.

Several questions could be asked: "Did John react as a Christian?" "What could he have said rather than what he did say?" "How would you react if you were in this position?"

10. *Pageants.* A pageant is another kind of dramatic presentation. It involves having people go through certain actions related to a particular incident or activity. These people may be in costume. A narrator tells the story as the individuals act it out. This can be used in presenting missionary stories, Bible stories, character stories, and other interesting incidents that help communicate spiritual truths relevant to the lives of young people.

11. *Tableaux and pantomimes.* In a tableaux people are involved in presenting a scene, but there is very little motion or activity. A person speaking off the scene gives the narration. In a pantomime a scene is acted out *without* narration.

12. *Plays.* A play is a more formal dramatic presentation usually involving a script to be memorized. This type of drama involves preplanning, careful staging, and much practice.

A variation of this method is to record the script on tape. Then while the play is being presented, the tape recording is played and the players use silent lip synchronization and concentrate on gestures and other actions. This is especially helpful when it is a lengthy play and there is just a brief time to prepare the presentation.

13. *Skits.* A skit is more informal than a play. It is usually shorter though it generally calls for a written script. For example, a group of young people may present a skit in a Sunday school meeting or in a youth group on how to react in different teen situations, such as in a family discussion of the use of the family car.

14. *Creative readings and writings.* Some youth groups have occasionally given choral readings on a passage of Scripture (e.g., Psalm 23). Others have written their own modern translations of a Scripture passage in a study group, while others in the youth group are writing what they think

the passage means to them personally. Morrison and Foster suggest a number of creative projects a junior high youth group would enjoy.[17]

Ford gives an excellent summary of the values, limitations, and ways to use several of these techniques.[18]

WHAT CRITERIA SHOULD BE USED WHEN SELECTING METHODS?

The methods used in working with young people should not be chosen arbitrarily or blindly. Certain criteria should be followed when selecting methods. These are some of those guidelines:

1. Is the method suited to the age level being taught?
2. Are proper facilities available so that the method can be used successfully?
3. Is there sufficient time for preparing and using the method?
4. Will the method most effectively achieve the goal of the particular meeting or session?
5. Does the leader feel prepared and at ease in using the method?

Obviously some people have difficulty using certain methods. Usually this is because they are not familiar with the methods or they lack self-confidence in using them. Further, certain methods seem to fit certain types of personalities more naturally than other method Therefore a teacher or leader should seek to "feel at home" with the technique e is using with young people. This of course is not an excuse for omitting variety and/or for not learning to use different kinds of approaches. But it is important to consider the point of naturalness in selecting methods to be used.

As Zuck has stated, "The best method for any given occasion is the one that accomplishes the best results in the best way."[19]

SUMMARY

Methods are merely means to an end, not ends in themselves. But methods are a necessary part of any meaningful teaching-learning experience. *What* methods are used and *how* they are used are vital to effective youth work.

Youth leaders will do well to prayerfully seek the guidance of the Holy Spirit in determining the methods to choose, and will ask for His wisdom in improving their skills in using these teaching techniques.

---

[17]Eleanor Sheldon Morrison and Virgil E. Foster, *Creative Teaching in the Church* (Englewood Cliffs, N.J.: Prentice-Hall, Inc., 1963), pp. 123-25.

[18]Marjorie Ford, *Techniques for Better Teaching* (Wheaton, Ill.: Scripture Press Publications, Inc., 1963), pp. 37-40.

[19]Zuck, *The Holy Spirit in Your Teaching*, p. 138.

FOR FURTHER READING

Adkins, George H. *Tools for Teachers*. St. Louis: Bethany Press, 1962.

Barrett, Ethel. *Storytelling, It's Easy*. Los Angeles: Cowman Publications, Inc., 1960.

Burton, William H. *The Guidance of Learning Activities*. New York: Appleton-Century-Crofts, Inc., 1952.

Caldwell, Irene. *Teaching That Makes a Difference*. Anderson, Ind.: Warner Press, 1962.

Cassel, Russell N. *The Psychology of Instruction*. Boston: Christopher Publishing House, 1957.

Cornell, Alice Edson. "Ways of Involving Youth," *Baptist Leader,* XXVIII:9-10 (January, 1967).

Eavey, C. B. *Principles of Teaching for Christian Teachers*. Grand Rapids: Zondervan Publishing House, 1940.

Edge, Findley B. *Helping the Teacher*. Nashville: Broadman Press, 1959.

Getz, Gene A. *Audio-Visuals in the Church*. Chicago: Moody Press, 1960.

Gordon, Melvin A. *General Methods of Teaching*. New York: McGraw-Hill Book Co., Inc., 1952.

Hakes, J. Edward (ed.). *An Introduction to Evangelical Christian Education*. Chicago: Moody Press, 1964.

Hoffman, Randall W., and Plutchik, Robert. *Small Group Discussion in Orientation and Teaching*. New York: J. P. Putnam's Sons, 1959.

Moody Bible Institute Correspondence School, *Keys to Effective Teaching*. Chicago: Moody Bible Institute, 1964.

Morrison, Eleanor, and Foster, Virgil E. *Creative Teaching in the Church*. Englewood Cliffs, N. J.: Prentice-Hall, Inc., 1963.

Osborn, Alex F. *Applied Imagination*. New York: Charles Scribner's Sons, 1963.

Zuck, Roy B., and Robertson, Fern. *How to Be a Youth Sponsor*. Wheaton, Ill.: Scripture Press Foundation, 1960.

Youth leaders face the challenge not only of transmitting God's Word in such a way that students become familiar with its contents, but also of helping youth come to grips with God's Word in relation to their own needs, experiences and problems. Youth must do more than merely acknowledge God's truth—they need to develop Christian concepts and convictions and creatively apply them to the concerns of life.

How to teach and impart Christian truth better, in less time, is a problem which proper teaching tools or materials can help solve.

ELEANOR HANCE and RICHARD TROUP

25

materials for working with youth

Part I
Principles for Selecting and Using Youth Materials, Audio-Visuals, and Rooms and Equipment

ELEANOR HANCE

PUBLISHED YOUTH MATERIALS

But why should youth leaders be bothered with curriculum materials? Printed materials serve several purposes.

1. They give a *guide* to content to be studied and learning experiences to be imparted. They help the teacher or sponsor to avoid omitting cer-

ELEANOR HANCE, M.A., is Director of the Christian Education Department, Barrington College, Providence, Rhode Island.

RICHARD TROUP, M.R.E., is Chairman of the Christian Education Department, Southeastern Bible College, Birmingham, Alabama.

tain Bible truths needed by the age group being taught, and to avoid needless repetition.

2. They aid the youth leader, by suggesting ways the lesson or program *might* be taught or presented. They are not to be followed slavishly word for word. No printed materials can make up for the adult worker's lack of preparation.

3. They can prod thinking and stimulate creativity.

4. They can provide leadership training, giving the teacher or leader tips and ideas on how to do an even better task for the Lord.

5. They can guide and stimulate the young person to study on his own.

6. They can create learning readiness in the young person's mind and heart.

Criteria for Youth Curriculum Materials

Whether printed leaders' guides or teachers' manuals are for instructional programs for classes, Sunday evening youth meetings, or meetings for weekday clubs; whether the materials come in pocket size for one quarter, or telephone-book size for a year; whether they are printed in color or in black and white; bound in spiral or stapled; mimeographed or printed; on quality paper or on cheap stock, the curriculum materials for youth groups should follow certain criteria:

1. *The materials should be Christ-centered.* They should exalt and honor Christ, should seek to point teens to know Him as Saviour, and should lead them to desire to live wholeheartedly for Christ by making Him the center of their lives.

2. *The materials should be Bible-based.* They should be true to the Bible, should be evangelical in approach, and should faithfully impart Bible truths.

3. *The materials should take into account the interests, needs and abilities of the students.* Materials should capture the interests of teens, answer their needs, and be geared to their ability levels. Bowman cautions, "Unwittingly, adults tend to think of what *they* like; what appeals to them."[1]

4. *The materials should help teens understand Christian concepts and develop Christian convictions.* From the use of materials young people should come to understand more about God (His being and nature, His plans and purposes, His ways), man, the world, the church, Christian living. Good lesson materials help young people make these teachings their own beliefs and convictions.

5. *The materials should deal with life problems.* Since life is a continual series of decisions, major and minor, the student needs to know how to

---

[1]Clarice M. Bowman, *Ways Youth Learn* (New York: Harper & Bros. Publishers, 1952), pp. 75-76.

make creative use of God's truth in meeting his life needs. Lesson and program materials ought to guide teens in discovering God's truths for themselves and relating them to their current problems.

6. *The materials should provide adequate scope and sequence of both content and experience.* Curriculum materials are concerned primarily with determining the amount (or scope) and sequence of content and experience. The total youth curriculum must cover a certain amount of facts and understanding, and a certain range of experience. This body of content and experience must be arranged in proper order for best results.

7. *The materials should be adaptable and flexible.*

8. *The materials should be attractive in appearance.*

When choosing Sunday school lesson materials, the teacher of teens should also consider the structure of individual lessons. The following are some features to look for:

1. *The lessons should capture attention, and motivate the student to learn.*

2. *The lessons should provide for natural transitions from known truths to new truths.*

3. *The lessons should encourage student participation.*

4. *The lessons should develop student insight.*

5. *The lessons should encourage the student to respond to insights gained.*

6. *The lessons should promote carry-over into the week.*

7. The *lessons should each include these steps:*

a. *Student readiness:* Preparing the student for involvement in the lesson by capturing attention, arousing curiosity, developing a feeling of need for the new content and experience, relating the new to the old (known).

b. *Bible presentation:* Looking into the Word of God to see what He has revealed in relation to the need or problem.

c. *Bible exploration:* Exploring and analyzing Bible teaching to discover its meaning and relevance. This may include discussing the meanings of various Scripture passages and experiences to bring new insight, seeing relationships and exploring new ideas through a visual presentation of the truth, researching and engaging in activities. From this exploration should come a significant Christian concept, belief, or conviction which can be formulated as a principle to help satisfy the need or problem which sent the student on the goal-seeking quest in the first place.

d. *Bible application:* Seeing how the truth or principle relates to present-day living. Transference of new understandings and personal conviction to specific contemporary situations is not as easy as it sounds. Usually the young person has to see how the belief or principle works in many different situations before he can apply it to his own situation. Breadth precedes depth. He may "see" the truth worked out in *one* specific way through a life situation, story, or problem. He may relate its application to *many* other situations. Then through these he gains insight into his *own* situations and is better equipped to respond to the truth and appropriate it to his life.

e. *Pupil response:* Helping the pupil respond to the Christian truth or principle he has appropriated by expressing commitment to it, and assuming responsibility for carrying it out. True belief convinces and convicts to the point of change. True learning experiences bring new insights and understandings, new attitudes, new convictions, new actions.

AUDIO-VISUAL TOOLS IN YOUTH WORK

Christianity is an "audio-visual faith." God created audio-visual matter, and He created man with audio-visual receptors. The physical senses take in God's beauty and perfection through creation, His dependability through natural laws, His majesty and power through natural forces. His truth is written in word symbols so that the physical eye can read it and the physical ear can hear it. His love was made incarnate in the God-Man Christ Jesus so that the eye which saw Him and His works, so that the ear which heard Him and His words, so that the hand which touched Him, could all attest to His love, compassion and mercy.

Christ Himself leaned heavily on audio-visual teaching in a day when there was no printed curriculum or advanced mechanical equipment. He taught from material surroundings and everyday objects: the light of a lamp, the hairs of one's head, the sparrows in the market, the lilies in the field, the birds of the air, a grain of wheat, the foxes and their dens, the sheep and the wolves, pearls, grapes, figs, fish, weeds, bread.

In teaching youth we should utilize their God-given sensory receptors for these reasons:

1. Audio-visuals arouse interest and hold attention because they appeal to teen-age desire for action and adventure.

2. Audio-visuals help overcome the communication barriers of verbalism—words too far removed from experience for understanding—by building a concrete basis for abstract thinking.

3. Audio-visuals bridge the islands of individual differences by explaining things more clearly.

4. Audio-visuals make an impact on the emotions by bringing pupils into vivid contact with the real thing.

5. Audio-visuals provide a good stimulus for pupil participation in group activities, discussion, follow-up projects.

6. Audio-visuals promote effective learning by making what is taught important, clear, and practical.

7. Audio-visuals help the pupil remember more by providing experience

rich in newness, sensory stimulation, emotional tone, personal satisfaction.

8. Audio-visuals add highly useful variety.

The following facts regarding audio-visuals should be borne in mind:

1. Audio-visuals are not synonymous with films, slides, tape recorders and filmstrips. Audio-visuals also include objects, pictures, models, charts, flannelboards, chalkboards—anything audio (heard) and/or visual (seen).

2. Audio-visuals are not miracles; they are tools. Like any tool they must be handled properly. If a saw is used like an ax, the results will not be favorable to either the wood or the tool. Likewise audio-visuals must be properly used to produce the desired results.

3. Audio-visuals make certain demands on rooms and equipment, storage, finances, administration, time and ingenuity. But, to use a homely illustration, no housewife serves raw hamburger simply because it takes time, equipment and creative effort to make a meat loaf. There are as sound reasons for serving up a lesson with audio-visuals as for serving hamburger in meat loaf.

The following principles are suggested for using audio-visuals properly:

1. Plan your goals first. Decide on one overall aim or message and then plan to visualize the most important teaching points in getting across the idea.

2. Plan the audio-visual as a *part* of your total program or lesson.

3. Consider what methods and materials will best carry out the goals. Can the audio-visual experience you have in mind do the best job? Is it worth the time, effort and expense in terms of desired educational outcomes?

4. Preplan audio-visual experiences. Collect and prepare materials. Determine procedures. Make arrangements. Preview the materials. Practice presenting the material. Set up and test any equipment needed.

5. Prepare the class for the audio-visual experience. Discuss new words, phrases, or major concepts which might appear in the audio-visual, but could not be discussed during its use. Determine ahead of time what to look for during the audio-visual experience, what questions to answer.

6. Whenever possible allow the students to plan, prepare, construct and participate.

7. Prepare the room for the use of audio-visuals. Check to see that the lighting is correct. It should be shining on the material rather than coming from behind and shining into the eyes of the pupils. Arrange seating for comfort and good viewing. Check on ventilation, particularly during projected audio-visuals when windows are darkened.

8. Use the best possible techniques for the various types of audio-visual experiences:

a. When drawing or printing before the class, do it quickly, in time with verbal commentary. Prepare complicated layouts and large amounts of material in advance. Be sure what you do can be seen and is legible.

b. When displaying materials simultaneously with verbal commentary, plan for simplicity, clarity, good lighting. Avoid clutter and confusion. Display the material at proper eye level. Arrange material to appeal to the eye; watch for perspective. Keep printed material for explanation short, simple, uniform. Time the comments correctly to explain materials; do not break the continuity of the verbal commentary by turning away from the students to work with fussy details.

c. When using a silent display without verbal commentary, get variety through types and textures of material. Provide continuity for the eye through use of color, labeling and grouping. Remember that motion, sound, lighting, color attract attention. Follow the rules for good design through proper use of space, size, shape, line, texture, color. Be sure that what is displayed really communicates what is to be taught.

d. When using both nonprojected and projected visuals, be sure that the students know what to look for. When possible, allow for questions, explanations, note-taking.

9. Follow up the audio-visual experience with discussion, further reading, research, written reports, tests, other audio-visual materials to clarify certain points, or creative activities and projects to express and carry out what has been learned.

ROOMS AND EQUIPMENT FOR YOUTH WORK

Christian education is involved with people, programs and properties. Though equipment by itself does not make for education, it can facilitate the outworking of *programs* and the interaction of *people* to bring about desired goals.

Plans for rooms and equipment must take into account the *total program* for youth, which embraces more than the instructional program of Sunday morning Bible study. There must also be space for worship, fellowship and recreation. This does not mean that there need be a separate chapel, youth lounge and gymnasium (though some churches provide basketball courts, roller-skating rinks, and bowling alleys in addition), but simply that there must be space where all programs can be carried out on a scale which meets the objectives of the church.

Plans for rooms and equipment must take into account the need for *pleasant surroundings and comfort.* We cannot minimize the impact of the physical on the senses and through the senses on our mental and emotional states. Untidiness, disrepair, and violations of good decor can produce a distaste—perhaps indiscernible, but nonetheless real—which results in apathy or disorderly conduct. If a church is not concerned that its rooms and equipment be clean, orderly, attractive and in good repair, some may assume that it has little concern for the spiritual welfare of those who attend. Also, young people are not as likely to put as high a premium on what they learn if the unkempt place in which they are doing the learning denies its very worth. This does not mean that the physical surroundings must reflect affluence; but they should indicate care, not apathy; and they should engender respect, not disdain. A good rule of thumb is that physical surroundings should at least equal those of the average home of the young people who participate in the program.

Physical comfort can also contribute to learning by eliminating distractions which interfere with concentration: heat, cold, stale air, cramped positions, crowded conditions, inability to see or hear adequately, and competing noise. Measures to provide correct temperature and humidity, adequate ventilation, proper lighting, comfortable seating, and a degree of soundproofing are well worth the effort in the rewards of increased learning. Creating a sense of privacy aids concentration. If an area cannot be soundproofed, it should be screened off to eliminate the distraction of physical motion—the eye is more easily distracted than the ear. Any area in which people meet should also have adequate ventilation. It should be aired out ahead of time. Windows should be checked to be sure they can be opened without distraction during the sessions. Light should be adequate and properly directed, producing good atmosphere. Improper lighting—bare bulbs that hang from cords, light which glares directly into the eyes of the students from behind the teachers or off a chalkboard, dim or poorly diffused light—can cause fatigue and restlessness.

Plans for rooms and equipment must take into account the need for *economy*. More than one church has had to stop short of its goal because it planned too ambitiously for its financial resources. With an abundance of certain facilities and a lack of others, a balanced program cannot be attained. On the other hand planners should avoid the false economy of cheapness or shortsightedness. What is planned should (1) meet youth objectives, (2) provide for growth of youth departments, and (3) stand up under hard use.

Plans for rooms and equipment must take into account the need for *utility*. To plan well, some very practical questions must be considered. Who will use the rooms and for what purposes? What will be the largest group to use a room, the smallest? How much space should be allotted to each person? What various functions will the room need to serve? Will chairs with desk arms be needed or will folding chairs be better? How many electrical outlets will be needed—and where? How much area should be window space—for ventilation, for spaciousness, for utilization of out-door beauty? Would windows tend to distract? What storage cabinets, shelves, closets will be necessary? What space will be needed for displays and activity—bulletin boards, chalkboards, tables? Which rooms will be used for audio-visuals? Where should coats be hung? Where should lava-tories, the youth library and service facilities for refreshments be located? The aim in all this planning should be to gain maximum service from minimum space.

A well-proportioned room has a three-to-two ratio of length to width. Rooms should be ample, but not vast, producing neither a sense of over-crowding nor lostness. Young people need 15-18 square feet of floor space per person. A recommended class size for junior high groups is 10-20 pupils and for senior high, 25. A checklist of equipment would include the following items:

1. *Adult-size chairs.* Desk-arm chairs are preferred, though some folding chairs should be available. Chairs should be movable—rows for formal occasions such as worship, circles or semicircles for discussion and study, smaller circles for buzz groups and committees.

2. *Tables,* 10-12 inches higher than chairs. Folding, rectangular tables which are easily moved and stored are most popular.

3. *Chalkboards,* preferably movable and of eye-easy green with yellow chalk.

4. *Display boards and materials,* such as flannelgraph boards, magnetic boards, large flip-charts, prepared charts, tack boards—either portable or permanent wall type.

5. *Easels* to hold display boards and materials.

6. Other *audio-visual equipment and materials* such as projection equip-ment, maps, pictures.

7. *Recreational equipment.*

8. *Divider screens* to section off small groups.

Planning for economy and utility also means planning for *adaptability*. Rooms and equipment must serve a seven-day-a-week program. Adapt-ability of rooms for multipurpose use is the only practical way to meet the complex needs of a complete youth program. Teen clubs on Thurs-day evening may meet in the same rooms used for instruction on Sunday. The Saturday social may meet in the all-church lounge with its conveniently located kitchen facilities. But the adaptability principle takes into account more than multiple use of rooms. It also considers the needs for the modify-ing and enlarging of the program, and thus the rearranging of space and equipment.

Planning for rooms and equipment should take into account the need for *ingenuity.* It is easier to complain about limitations of present facilities than to see opportunities for improvement. It takes vision and brainstorming to see how present resources can be adapted to meet needs, current and future. Sometimes minor adjustments make for major improvements. Paint and draperies can create a cheerful, relaxed atmosphere. Convenient coatracks can eliminate disorder and disturbance. Portable furnishings, such as movable or foldaway worship units, a library on wheels, rolling storage units for folding chairs and tables, and cabinets on casters have the advantage of being moved to whatever room or part of the room they are needed, or removed entirely for storage. Creating one large multi-purpose room and putting it on a seven-day-a-week schedule for the whole church can do wonders for the young people. With ingenuity in planning floor and wall space, such a room can provide a movable lounge, sliding-door library, cabinet kitchenette, behind-doors worship-center unit, recreational space and equipment. With plenty of storage supplies, each group using the room can set it up for its own purpose.

SUMMARY

Though most churches do not have a bottomless reservoir of money for purchasing teaching materials, they can avail themselves of the resources of good sense, imagination, vision, and educational know-how. Top-quality curriculum materials, the most modern audio-visual tools, and a designer's dream layout of rooms and equipment cannot guarantee success with youth. But these materials combined with qualified leaders and an effective program can help provide conditions favorable to Christian faith and growth.

Part II

An Annotated Guide to Selected Youth Materials

RICHARD TROUP

THE FOLLOWING INFORMATION is based on selected materials mostly from independent sources. Additional youth materials may be secured from most leading denominations. No attempt has been made to be inclusive.

SUNDAY SCHOOL

In addition to the standard pattern of a quarterly teacher's guide, student's workbook and take-home paper, some publishers have unique approaches to the problem of maintaining teen interest in Sunday school and introducing teens to meaningful Bible study.

David C. Cook Publishing Company (Elgin, Illinois) has an eight-page student "Class-and-Home" weekly paper for each of the junior high and senior high levels. Includes discussion articles on current teen issues, Bible study features, guide for daily devotions and at-home study—all related to the weekly lesson theme. For junior highs there is an undated booklet of "pre-dawn talks." Also new curriculum-correlated teaching packets for junior high and senior high.

Gospel Light Publications, Inc. (Glendale, California) quarterlies for senior highs are pocket-size, differing from "child-type" quarterlies in both size and purpose. These manuals are reading books rather than workbooks. Visual kits accompany junior high courses on John and Acts.

Scripture Press Publications, Inc. (Wheaton, Illinois) provides for teachers of junior highs a "Teaching Aid Packet" of charts, photos, drawings. For junior highs and senior highs separate packets of lesson-related "Department Achievement Tests" are available for twenty-minute review tests on the last uSnday of each quarter.

Standard Publishing Company (Cincinnati, Ohio) has a packet of weekly four-page leaflets for senior highs with a lesson summary and daily devotions guide. For ninth graders a special "Niners" packet is available, plus a quarterly "Audio-visual Teaching Packet" for the teacher.

SUNDAY EVENING YOUTH MEETINGS

American Sunday School Union (Philadelphia, Pennsylvania). Basic manual and monthly newspaper centering on Bible activities such as memorization, personal study, quizzes. Especially designed for the ASSU's "Pioneers for Christ."

Baptist Publications, Inc. (Denver, Colorado). Introductory handbook includes how to set up a Training Union program patterned after Southern Baptist program by the same name. How to plan parties, and other related TU activities. Twelve quarterly courses are available for young people with undated manuals for each group member and each group captain.

Christian Endeavor (Columbus, Ohio). Monthly *Christian Endeavor World* includes promotional and planning articles; separate program pages for each of junior high, senior high, young people, young adult and adult levels.

Annual Planning Guides for each of junior high and senior high young people contain suggested weekly topics for the year and space to record weekly leaders. Special emphases on "Citizenship Award" and conventions ranging from local to international. Materials include a catalog of supplemental and introductory manuals and guides, promotional items such as pins, pennants, posters.

Christian Workers' Service Bureau (Redondo Beach, California). Monthly packets of program materials for three age groups: Jet Cadets (juniors),

Astronauts (junior highs), and His Teens (senior highs). Also some programs for primaries and for college-age youth. Packets include copies for program participants, party plans, "sponsor's specials," programming tips, promotion and publicity aids.

David C. Cook Publishing Company (Elgin, Illinois). Youth packets for junior highs and senior highs include introductory material and undated programs for each Sunday of the year. Programs organized in subject units of three or four programs each.

Moody Press (Chicago, Illinois). Books of youth meetings, such as *Ten Teen Programs, Here's How Youth Meetings,* and *Sparkling Youth Meetings.*

Scripture Press Publications, Inc. (Wheaton, Illinois). Training hour materials, including quarterly sponsor's guide and youth guide for junior high and senior high levels. Senior high books also include brief program ideas for college-age youth. Junior high cycle based on three-year plan, senior high on four-year plan. This makes it possible for the material to be used by groups that are divided into a two-year junior high and four-year senior high program, or by groups organized on a three-year junior high and three-year senior high basis. Fifteen areas of subject matter in the curriculum include church leadership, dating personality development, cults, missions, doctrine, vocations—presented in units of one to three programs on each subject. Includes suggestions for sponsors, parties, publicity, weekday activities, group organization. Introductory sponsor's manual.

Standard Publishing Company (Cincinnati, Ohio). Youth program books containing meeting plans for one year. Several for each of junior high and senior high levels.

WEEKDAY CLUBS[2]

Awana Youth Association (Chicago, Illinois). Introductory manual. Leaders' guides and monthly leaders' periodical. Handbooks for each age level for each of boys and girls, age 8 through junior high; separate coed senior high materials.

Christian Service Brigade (Wheaton, Illinois). Training course for men leaders plus complete leader's guide. Separate programs for ages 8 to 11, and 12 up, with a boy's manual at each level. Magazine for boys, *Venture.* Packets of leaders' helps. Related sports, camping, and leadership guidelines for boys' programs.

Pioneer Girls (Wheaton, Illinois). Parallel plan and materials to Brigade for junior-age and teen girls. Magazine for girls, *Trails for Girls.*

---

[2]Here limited to distinctively Christian programs of an activity type emphasizing achievement. Basically for boys and girls in separate groups.

CAMP BIBLE STUDY

Harvest Publications (Baptist General Conference, Chicago, Illinois). Three courses each for juniors, junior highs and senior highs. Each set contains two leaders' guides, one for an open-Bible inductive study course, the other for a larger leadership training type course. Courses include five daily sessions plus an optional sixth "overview." Two campers' souvenir notebooks of autograph-book type.

Pioneer Girls. Inductive Bible study guides provided for the leader of a two-week open-Bible discussion group in an informal setting. Highly adaptable to all such groups.

Scripture Press Publications, Inc. Cycle of three courses each for juniors, junior highs and senior highs. Instructor's manual and camper's "Do-it book" for each course of five lessons. Lesson-related devotional suggestions included. Several how-to manuals for camp counselors and directors.

Standard Publishing Company. A camper's workbook for each of several grade levels, with ten lessons in each.

YOUTH WEEK

Baptist General Conference, Board of Bible School and Youth Work. Guide for the week and/or packet of supplemental helps.

National Sunday School Association Youth Commission (Wheaton, Illinois). Leaders of some forty denominational and independent youth organizations plan an annual theme for the last week in January.

SPECIAL MATERIALS

Back to the Bible Broadcast (Lincoln, Nebraska). Booklets and individual study courses can be used by a group wanting to place inexpensive and attractive booklets in members' hands. Monthly magazine, *Young Ambassador,* especially suitable for junior highs.

Inter-Varsity Christian Fellowship (Chicago, Illinois). Inductive Bible study guides especially designed for college-level use are usable also by senior highs ready for more solid study.

Moody Press (Chicago, Illinois). Great variety of inexpensive and paperback books on missions, witnessing, vocations, doctrine. Suitable for after-school or Saturday pastor's instruction classes similar to catechism or confirmation courses.

Science Research Associates (Chicago, Illinois). Booklets on topics such as Jobs, Honesty, Smoking, Manners, Abilities, Marriage, Leisure Time, Narcotics. Written from secular viewpoint but can provide basis for discussion of the Christian approach to these issues.

The Navigators (Colorado Springs, Colorado). Course of Bible memorization and related study guides. Centers around pocket-size packets of memory course. An introductory packet of four cards includes detailed information.

Youth For Christ International (Wheaton, Illinois). Evangelistic ideas and materials including teen-level follow-up course for new Christians, adaptable to a church group. Monthly periodical, *Campus Life*.

YOUTH LEADERS' TRAINING[3]

Better CYF Groups, by Gunnar Hoglund, Harvest Publications (Baptist General Conference). Ten chapters for advisers of a CYF (Conference Youth Fellowship), highly adaptable to other groups.

The Church and the Young People, by Sewell and Speck, Firm Foundation Publishers. Originally published in 1935 as one of a "Training for Service" series for Churches of Christ. Up to date with much applicable content for any evangelical church.

"How To" Leaflets, by Baptist General Conference. On subjects such as "How to Lead Singing," "How to Conduct a Worship Service," "How to Make a Poster," "How to Be a Youth-Group President." Also available together in paperback *Youth Leader's Handbook.*

How to Be a Youth Sponsor, by Roy B. Zuck and Fern Robertson, Scripture Press Foundation. Practical how-to helps on sponsor's duties, program planning, youth-group organization, training, getting youth participation, setting and reaching goals.

Planning Better Youth Meetings. A kit of practical how-to *filmstrips* on planning for worship, study and discussion, recreation, youth projects. Complete kit of four-color artwork strips, two records and guides. Family Films, Hollywood, California.

Success with Youth, by Christian Workers' Service Bureau. A newspaper-type publication with idea articles on all phases of a youth program: meetings, decorations, promotion, parties, music.

Youth Leader's Training Course, by Christian Workers' Service Bureau. Teacher's kit of ten-lesson teacher's manual, handbooks and a pupil's (prospective adult worker with youth) workbook.

FOR FURTHER READING

Audio-Visual Resource Guide, 7th edition. New York: National Council of Churches of Christ in the U.S.A., 1965.

DALE, EDGAR. *Audio-Visual Methods in Teaching.* New York: Dryden Press, 1954.

EAST, MARJORIE. *Display for Learning.* New York: Dryden Press, 1952.

---

[3]For sponsors and/or elected youth leaders, these provide basic information on the purpose of a youth group, qualities of a leader, and related issues.

"Everyday Audio-Visuals," *International Journal of Religious Education.* Special issue (May, 1962).

GETZ, GENE A. *Audio-Visuals in the Church.* Chicago: Moody Press, 1960.

HAKES, EDWARD J. (ed.). *An Introduction to Evangelical Christian Education.* Chicago: Moody Press, 1964. Chapter 6, "Curriculum," Lois E. LeBar; chapter 8, "Audio-Visual Materials," Ruth Haycock; chapter 20, "Building and Equipment for Christian Education," Gaines S. Dobbins.

HEIM, RALPH D. *Leading a Sunday Church School.* Philadelphia: Muhlenberg Press, 1950. Chapter 10, "Providing a Pupil Program"; chapter 14, "Managing Physical Equipment."

KINDER, JAMES S. *Audio-Visual Materials and Techniques.* New York: American Book Co., 1958.

TAYLOR, MARVIN J. (ed.). *Religious Education: A Comprehensive Survey.* New York: Abingdon Press, 1960. Chapter 9, "The Curriculum and the Church," D. Campbell Wykcoff; chapter 18, "The Use of Audio-Visuals in the Church," Harold E. Tower; chapter 26, "Educational Facilities: Buildings and Equipment," C. Harry Atkinson.

TOWER, HOWARD E. *Church Use of Audio-Visuals.* New York: Abingdon Press, 1959. Revised edition.

VEITH, PAUL H. *The Church School.* Philadelphia: Christian Education Press, 1957. Chapter 5, "The Curriculum of Christian Education"; chapter 13, "Rooms and Equipment."

WITTICH, WALTER ARNO, and SCHULLER, CHARLES FRANCIS. *Audio-Visual Materials: Their Nature and Use.* New York: Harper & Bros. Publishers, 1957.

LIST OF SELECTED YOUTH ORGANIZATIONS

American Sunday School Union, 1816 Chestnut Street, Philadelphia, Pa. 19103.

Awana Youth Association, 7511 West Belmont Avenue, Chicago, Ill. 60634.

Back to the Bible Broadcast, Box 233, Lincoln, Nebr. 68501.

Baptist General Conference (see Harvest Publications).

Baptist Publications, 1732 Welton Street, Denver, Colo. 80219.

Christian Endeavor (International Society of), 1221 East Broad Street; Columbus, Ohio 43216.

Christian Service Brigade, 2525 North Main Street, Wheaton, Ill. 60187.

Christian Workers' Service Bureau, Box 413, Redondo Beach, Calif. 90277.

David C. Cook Publishing Company, 850 North Grove Avenue, Elgin, Ill. 60120.

Firm Foundation Publishing House, 3110 Guadalupe, Austin, Tex. 78705.

Gospel Light Publications, Inc., 725 Colorado Boulevard, Glendale, Calif. 91209.

Harvest Publications, 5750 North Ashland Avenue, Chicago, Ill. 60626.

Inter-Varsity Christian Fellowship, 130 North Wells Street, Chicago, Ill. 60606.

Moody Press, 820 North LaSalle Street, Chicago, Ill. 60610.

National Sunday School Association, Box 685, Wheaton, Ill. 60187.

The Navigators, Glen Eyrie, Colorado Springs, Col. 80901.

Pioneer Girls, Box 92, Wheaton, Ill. 60187.

Science Research Associates, 259 East Erie Street, Chicago, Ill. 60611 .

Scripture Press Publications, Inc., 1825 College Avenue, Wheaton, Ill. 60187.

Standard Publishing Company, 8100 Hamilton Avenue, Cincinnati, Ohio 45231.

Youth For Christ International, North Main Street, Wheaton, Ill. 60187.

SELECTED EVANGELICAL PRODUCERS OF PROJECTED VISUALS FOR YOUTH

Cathedral Films, 2921 West Alameda Avenue, Burbank, Calif. 91501.

Concordia Films, 3558 South Jefferson, St. Louis, Mo. 63118.

Family Films, 5823 Santa Monica Boulevard, Hollywood, Calif. 90038.

Films for Christ, 1204 North Elmwood, Peoria, Ill. 61606.

Gospel Films, Box 455, Muskegon, Mich. 49443.

Ken Anderson Films, Box 618, Winona Lake, Ind. 46590.

Moody Institute of Science Films, 11438 Santa Monica Boulevard, Los Angeles, Calif. 90025.

Many young people are concerned with what they should believe about spiritual matters, and why. Too many instructors, pastors and parents want youth to develop a faith that is a carbon copy of the adult's faith. Good counseling will aid a teen-ager in his struggle to develop his own faith.

GEORGE E. RIDAY

26

principles
of counseling youth

SINCE THIS VOLUME is dedicated to the total field of Christian education of youth it is assumed that the readers will be those who have not had extensive training in the area of counseling. Thus, many of the suggestions offered in this chapter will appear elementary to those readers who have formal training in this field. It is also assumed that this book will be read by lay workers in the church as well as persons formally trained in the area of Christian education. It is expected that some may turn to this volume for assistance who are teaching a class of teen-agers or sponsoring an evening youth fellowship group.

Much of the counseling with youth in churches is carried on, either effectively or ineffectively, by untrained lay persons. This comment is not intended as an indictment. This chapter is intended to be helpful to faithful and dedicated leaders of youth who, fully recognizing their limitations, nevertheless are willing to serve Christ in the best way possible.

GEORGE E. RIDAY, Ph.D., is a staff psychologist at the Patton State Hospital, San Bernardino, California.

Before getting into the specific subject of this chapter, it may be well to consider some general principles of counseling—regardless of whom it is we are attempting to counsel. It is the writer's opinion that effective counseling will employ certain methods and embrace a particular philosophy of personality growth which can be applied to practically every situation, no matter what the problem may be.

In one sense it is quite proper to speak about vocational counseling, marriage counseling, youth counseling, for proficiency in each of these areas demands particular skills. However it is not likely that a counselor who is worth his salt will be one kind of person when he counsels married couples having adjustment problems, and then adopt a different-type personality when he counsels a young person seeking help in choosing a vocation. This viewpoint concerning counseling is not meant to be interpreted as a static one. A wise counselor will observe the reactions and feelings of his client and work with him accordingly. A genuine counseling situation is a *dynamic* relationship between two persons.

WHAT IS COUNSELING?

Effective Counseling Is Not Giving Advice

One often hears an adult speak of a counseling relationship with a young person in terms of giving the youth advice. Many people feel that counseling is merely a matter of a wise and experienced adult giving advice to a naïve and inexperienced youth. If the youth were to take the advice and grow as a result, perhaps we could support this viewpoint of counseling. There is always the question, however, when a counselor gives advice, whether or not it is *good* advice. It is generally wrong for an adult to be firmly convinced that the advice he gives young people is always the best.

Another reason for going easy on advice-giving is that the one giving advice usually does not have to take the consequences that result from carrying out the advice. For example, suppose a girl is not sure whether or not she should date a certain fellow. As a counselor you may feel that he is not the right kind of young man for her. If your judgment of him is erroneous, or if he later on turns out to be a rather splendid young fellow, then you may have to share the responsibility for the disappointment the girl will feel. She gave up her relationship with the boy because of your advice, which in this instance was not good.

This warning against giving advice does not mean that the counselor may not assist the client in seeing the folly of taking certain courses of action. If a teen-ager admits that he has recently been involved with a gang that has been stealing from parked cars, the counselor is not expected to compliment the boy on his cleverness. He might handle the problem by asking the boy if he thinks he can avoid trouble for an indefinite period of time, or he may ask the youth to tell him why he feels he must associate with a group of fellows who take what does not belong to them.

It is expected that the counselor will have a set of values by which he lives. These standards will inevitably manifest themselves during the interview. One's values can hardly keep from showing. The important thing for the counselor to remember is that he cannot enforce his standards on his client. Surely there are times when a young person comes to his church school teacher or some other adult and asks for information. He has no weighty problem to discuss; he merely wants to know which of two books he should read to learn something about the church's responsibility concerning social issues. If the adult firmly believes one book is superior to the other, he simply advises the youth to read the better one. Later on in the chapter we will discuss the counselor's personality as it relates to his counseling.

Effective Counseling Is Not Moralizing

Somewhat closely related to advice-giving is the tendency to moralize. Because of the minister's role he may often feel compelled to interpret the counseling interview as a splendid opportunity to preach to a congregation of one. Good preaching is sorely needed in many of our churches today but a counseling session is not an appropriate place for it. The fact that a lay person has a position of leadership in the local church may cause him to feel that he too must preach a sermonette, or moralize in some other manner since he works with youth in the church. Some Christian workers feel they are being untrue to the faith if they do not "set their clients straight" by delivering a brief homily on some moral issue that arises in the interview.

In some instances the brief sermon really meets the needs of the counselor more realistically than it meets the needs of the client. Very often the young person who needs counseling is well aware of the wrong he has done. It does more harm than good for the counselor to start scolding and moralizing about an issue that already weighs heavily on the teen-ager. No respectable physician would treat a patient with an injured head by hitting him over the head with a stethoscope. Moralizing about an issue may help the counselor with his own feelings but it will do very little that is constructive for the client.

Counseling Is Not Manipulating People

Many individuals who come to a counselor desiring help are in an emotional state that renders them ripe for manipulation. By manipulation we mean any attempt on the part of the counselor to control the thinking and behavior of another against his will. It has to do with the imposition of one's will on another. A counselor who has a deep need to feel rather important may be tempted to manipulate a client who innocently comes looking for some kind of emotional assistance.

We have mentioned three negative aspects of counseling which should be avoided if one chooses to be helpful in his relationships. Now some positive steps that the counselor may take will be discussed.

Counseling Is a Relationship Between Two Fallible Beings

The counselor accepts himself as a person. No one should wait until he becomes perfect to do counseling. Even the best counselors, with excellent psychological training, are persons with feelings. Many psychologists and psychiatrists, who specialize in counseling and psychotherapy (a deeper type of treatment for seriously disturbed patients), submit to some kind of counseling relationship in which they are the clients. This kind of therapy is called *didactic therapy*, for it is undergone by the professional person that he might be "taught" to come to grips with his own personality, and thus better understand what the client or patient feels in a counseling situation. A person who attempts to counsel others should be rather aware of his own personality quirks and weaknesses. Let it be said again, for emphasis, that this does not mean that the counselor must be a perfectly mature person in every regard.

Good Counseling Encourages the Client to Express His True Feelings Freely

In the counseling relationship we are concerned about the feeling level of the person we are trying to help. Behavior is guided much more by our feelings and emotions than by our intelligence. Even the Apostle Paul seemed to have difficulty in this area. He claimed that what he *knew* he ought to do he frequently did not do, and that what he *knew* he should not do, he often did.

A counselor does not get his client to express his true feelings simply by saying, "Now the only way I can help you is for you to tell me openly what your true feelings are." First, the client may not know what his real feelings are. Quite often we tend to repress or disguise what we really feel. Some of our feelings are too threatening to admit, even to ourselves, so we unconsciously hide them from ourselves. Second, a client will hesitate to reveal what he truly feels about himself because he is not sure the counselor will accept him if he says what he really feels.

How then does a counselor assist his client in the sometimes painful task of expressing what he really feels?

If he knows the counselor rather well, the client has already formed some opinion about the kind of person he is. If the counselor is a minister, the client knows from the kinds of sermons he has heard how free he might be to express what is deep inside him. If the minister enjoys preaching sermons about hell and God's judgment, the client will be afraid he will be condemned if he expresses anything which appears to be contrary to what the minister holds as a conviction. A counselor must be acceptant in all of his relationships if he is to create an atmosphere in which a client does not feel threatened. In counseling youth it is particularly important to encourage free expression of feelings. Many young people are likely to be on guard in a counseling situation with a minister or some other "authority figure" in the church. For this reason understanding lay people are often more effective in their counseling than those on the church staff.

The counselor must do all he can apart from the counseling interview to establish himself as a nonjudgmental person. Someone may object that, as Christians, we have convictions we had better not give up. We are not talking about giving up convictions. Our point is that we should not use our convictions as a club. This will only force the client into a corner. He then will feel bound and determined not to let his counselor know what he really thinks. After all, when someone comes to a minister or some other person in the church, he is pretty well convinced that such a person must have Christian principles. If a teen-ager comes to confess to an adult that he and some of his high school buddies were out on an all-night drinking party, it isn't necessary for the adult to remind the boy that this kind of behavior is wrong. The teen-ager knew it wasn't right and, for that reason, confessed his wrong. He is asking for help, not more reprimanding. It is also important that the counselor refrain from making any facial gesture that reveals genuine disgust and disapproval.

Good Counseling Involves Helping the Client Help Himself

Many who come for counseling expect the counselor to supply ready-made solutions to life's problems. It is as though they are saying, "Here's my problem; I don't know what to do with it but you undoubtedly do, so what's the cure?" It is probably true that some persons have this concept of counseling. This may be because they have had an experience with a counselor who felt he had all the answers.

Helping the client help himself is both wise and reasonable. Suppose some counselor does have the insight required to solve the difficulties of others. (Remember, this is only a supposition.) What happens if the counselor is not present the next time the client has a problem? It is not the counselor's function to make the client dependent on *him*. A wholesome relationship will introduce the client to his own skills, resources and insights for dealing with personal difficulties.

Counseling Done in the Context of the Christian Faith Uses the Resources of That Faith

All of the material included in the chapter up to this juncture will be applicable, from the writer's viewpoint, to any type of counseling. The criterion we are now discussing relates specifically to the counselor who is a Christian and who feels deeply about the value of Christianity. It is not expected that an Orthodox Jew or Buddhist would subscribe to what is suggested here. For those who are Christians, however, it seems inevitable that the various advantages the Christian faith offers will become a part of the counseling process. There are times when prayer with a client will be most appropriate and helpful. However, prayer should not be used promiscuously. Rather than prescribe a definite formula concerning the use of prayer, let it suffice to stress the importance of praying at those times when speaking to God on behalf of a client will be most beneficial. Some persons may be so frightened if the counselor closes an interview with prayer that they may never return again for further help.

The counselor must be aware of his own attitudes as they relate to prayer. Does he pray as a substitute for good counseling methods and the establishment of a genuine relationship? Does he conceive of prayer as a kind of magical adjunct to the counseling session that corrects all errors made during the hour? Does he pray because the client expects him to pray and he does not have a strong enough self-concept to disappoint his client?

In addition to prayer there is the resource of the Bible. A counselor who believes the Word of God to be a revealed book will see occasion to refer to some meaningful section during an interview. Or the counselor may suggest that the client read a certain portion of the Bible between interviews. These passages should be chosen very wisely. We must not conclude that simply any section of the Bible picked at random is bound to be helpful to a person in distress. Bible passages should be chosen with the client's need in mind. There are many good books written by Christian men and women that may also be recommended as wholesome additions to the counseling sessions. Never suggest a book unless you are familiar with it. It may be that you are recommending a book that will increase the neurotic type of guilt from which your client is already suffering. On occasion it may be thought helpful to assist a client in establishing a time of private worship each day. Unless he is familiar with this type of experience he will need guidance from his counselor.

Christian doctrine is a resource which the counselor may use to advantage if he does so judiciously. A loving explanation of the forgiveness of God as revealed in Jesus Christ may be just the word that some guilt-ridden client needs to hear. Christian doctrine must be offered as a gift rather than employed as a club over an obstinate client's head. Whatever Christian aid is suggested, it must be presented to the client in an appropriate manner. If Christian resources are used unwisely, the counseling session is neither genuine counseling nor effectively Christian.

Good Counseling Often Calls for Referral

It is imperative that the counselor recognize his limitations and make proper referrals. There are times when the counselor has to admit that he is unable to help the client with his problem. When a psychotic (severely disturbed mentally and emotionally) individual comes to you for help, you should not delay in referring that person to a competent psychiatrist (or if there is no psychiatrist in the community, to a psychologist or physician). If a lay person is counseling with a client who has profound theological problems, it may be necessary to refer the client to a competent pastor who is familiar with theology. Problems relating to an engaged couple may need to be referred to a pastor for premarital counseling. Referrals may have to be made to lawyers, social workers, educators.[1] The limited scope of this chapter does not permit space to do anything other than suggest the necessity of referring a client when his problem is beyond the counselor's ability. After the client has been referred, it is a good idea to keep in touch with him. This should be done without appearing to be anything other than interested and concerned. A telephone call will often be enough to indicate concern and will help to prevent the client from feeling rejected. It should be evident that the counselor is not trying to pry into his affairs.

THE COUNSELOR'S MOTIVES

It is undoubtedly true that the kind of person the counselor is, is more important than the technical skills he possesses. The more genuine a person the counselor is, the more likely will be his success. An insincere person usually does not last very long as a good counselor.

If a person does very much counseling or is vitally interested in the subject, he may well inquire into his motivation. Does he like the feeling of manipulating people in the counseling situation? Does he enjoy prying and probing into others' lives? Is he compulsive about helping other people? Is he having some real problems with his own sexual adjustment and, therefore, looks on the counseling session as a time and place to

---

[1]One helpful book on referrals is Wayne E. Oates, *Where to Go for Help* (Philadelphia: Westminster Press, 1957).

vicariously enjoy sex by talking intimately about the subject? Some workers with youth are struggling with their own personality quirks and feel, perhaps unconsciously, that somehow youth work is the answer to their problems. This may be on an unconscious level. Fortunately, most youth workers are stable persons.

PROBLEMS IN COUNSELING YOUTH

Now let us think specifically about the young people we counsel, in an attempt to learn something about them and their problems. Let it be said again that *the material in the preceding pages, although presented in a general fashion so that it applies to the total field of counseling, can be related specifically to the counseling of youth.*

The remainder of this chapter will be devoted to some general statements about teen-agers and the problems that seem to be most crucial in the counseling of youth.

We can learn some essential truths about youth by trying an experiment with a group. Write the word *Child* at the top left-hand side of a chalkboard. On the other side of the board, write the word *Adult*. Leave space between the two words to include a third word later on. Ask the adults present to indicate types of behavior that are definitely characteristic of a little child and not characteristic of the average adult. As they are suggested, write them under the heading *Child*. You will probably include behavior such as: "has his needs cared for by adults," "cannot do very much in the way of abstract thinking," "chews bubble gum," "reads comic books." Then ask the group to mention adult behavior traits and list these under the heading *Adult*. Something like this will undoubtedly be heard: "earns his own living," "has credit cards and charge accounts," "has babies." Between those two columns which indicate child and adult behaviors write the word *Adolescent*. When we are talking about young people we usually mean adolescents. Let us say that adolescence is the period from about 12 to 24 years of age. Then look at each of the behavior traits listed under the two headings. If the group believes adolescents engage in the same behavior described as child behavior, place a plus sign beside the behavior discussed. If the group believes the adolescent does not engage in that behavior, place a minus sign beside it. If they think that adolescents sometimes do and other times do not engage in that behavior trait, place a plus and minus sign beside the behavior trait listed.

As you may well imagine, when you finish this little experiment you will find that for practically every child behavior mentioned we have not only a plus sign but a minus sign as well. The same thing applies to a comparison of adolescent behavior with adult behavior. What does this suggest? It impresses us with the fact that the adolescent is in an over-lapping situation. His predicament may be diagrammed something like this:

| CHILD | ADOLESCENT | ADULT |

The teen-ager is trying to discover his identity. What is he? Who is he? Is he still a child? The accurate answer is that sometimes his behavior is childish, but at other times quite adult. In a sense he lives in three worlds—the world of a child during some moments of his life, the world of an adult at other moments, and at still other times, he lives in the inter-mediary world peculiar to the adolescent. This means that he does not want to identify with childhood because he is trying to escape this too-juvenile world. He does not want to live all of the time in the adult world because this seems too demanding and insecure to him. He wants his own world of adolescence. This is why it is so important to the teen-ager to "belong to the gang." He does not want to be considered a child; nor does he want to associate entirely with adults; so he identifies strongly with his peer group. Perhaps this is the reason adolescent fads are so intense, if not so enduring. The adolescent *has to belong!* Anyone who counsels youth will do well to keep this in mind.

Yearning for Independence

Most of the struggles of youth center around the yearning for indepen-dence. Whether the problem has to do with sex, choosing a vocation, relationships with parents or other authority figures, finding a meaningful faith, or questions of morality, the fight for independence is surely some-where related to the problem under consideration. This struggle involves risks. We cannot solve youth's difficulties for them. We can guide them, but the choice ultimately is theirs to make.

Illustrative of other problem areas for youth are the difficulties that arise relative to sex and the task of finding a meaningful faith.

Search for Sexual Adjustment

Youth frequently seek counseling in the area of sexual adjustment. It is most natural that they are concerned about this aspect of their total development. All of them come to the age of puberty with some kind of sexual education. This information is received in their homes or whatever other type of community living that substitutes for home.

Occasionally one hears a young person object that he never had any sex education in his home. Then he immediately adds, "In our family we did not dare talk about sex. As soon as the subject was mentioned my parents would change the conversation or announce that we should not be talking about such matters." It can be seen rather quickly that refusal on the part of his parents to deal honestly with questions concerning sex created an atmosphere of tension and a feeling that sex was a taboo topic. This is a type of sex education. It is negative, but it is education.

The role of the Christian counselor is that of assisting youth to see that sex is part of God's plan for man. We must guide youth in seeing sex in its proper perspective. There are many excellent books and films on the subject. They can serve, in an ancillary manner, the whole process of counseling in the area of sexual adjustment. Youth have to be taught that thoughts about sex are not wrong. They must also be assisted in realizing that it is not proper for guilt to accompany normal sexual drives. A Christian interpretation of the role of sex in love can be a very sacred and meaningful experience under the guidance of a sensible counselor.[2]

Desire for Meaningful Convictions

Many young people are concerned with what they should believe about spiritual matters, and why. Too many instructors, pastors and parents want youth to develop a faith that is a carbon copy of the adult's faith. Good counseling will aid a teen-ager in his struggle to develop his *own* faith. Children tend to accept the beliefs of their parents and other important adults in their lives. But when they become teen-agers, it is time they start seeking to build spiritual convictions of their own. This does not mean that we permit a young person to go unassisted in his discovery of a vital faith. Nor does it mean that we say that anything goes, just so long as the teen-ager is sincere. We guide, but we do not impose our faith on another.

Concern About Science and the Bible

This is one of the real issues with which a counselor frequently must deal. There is a discrepancy in the minds of many young people between what their science professor states as truth and what the church leader claims to be true biblical teaching. Young people need a great deal of help in understanding that there is no real discrepancy between an accurate interpretation of the Bible and the findings of modern science. Unfortunately the biggest task is not always centered in the youth but in adults who cannot tolerate questions about the Bible and the Christian faith that run counter

---

[2]More pastors are recognizing the need for providing premarital counseling sessions for engaged couples. Three helpful sources on this subject are Stanley E. Anderson, *Every Pastor a Counselor* (Wheaton, Ill.: Van Kampen Press, 1952) ; Kenneth Morris, *Premarital Counseling: A Manual for Ministers* (Englewood Cliffs, N.J.: Prentice-Hall, 1960) ; and Granger Westberg, *Premarital Counseling* (New York: National Council of Churches in the U.S.A., 1958) .

to their opinions (which are often not based solidly on the Bible, or on true science).

SUMMARY

When counseling youth on the subject of faith, finding a life's work, relating to the opposite sex, or any other area of interest, it is imperative that the counselor possess an unvarnished love for youth. Teens must know that whatever they say will not be devastating enough for the counselor to reject them. They are looking for help, and the counselor can assist them by demonstrating our Lord's attitude, which assured His hearers that they were regarded as persons of infinite worth.

FOR FURTHER READING

Counseling in General

BRAMMER, LAWRENCE M., and SHOSTROM, EVERETT L. *Therapeutic Counseling.* Englewood Cliffs, N.J.: Prentice-Hall, 1960.

BRANDT, HENRY R. *The Pastor and Counseling* (Christian Education Monograph, Pastors' Series No. 17). Glen Ellyn, Ill.: Scripture Press Foundation, 1967.

MAY, ROLLO. *The Art of Counseling.* Nashville: Abingdon Press, 1939.

NARRAMORE, CLYDE M. *Encylopedia of Psychological Problems.* Grand Rapids: Zondervan Publishing House, 1966.

———. *The Psychology of Counseling.* Grand Rapids: Zondervan Publishing House, 1960.

PORTER, E. H. *An Introduction to Therapeutic Counseling.* Boston: Houghton Mifflin Co., 1950.

ROGERS, CARL R. *Client-Centered Therapy.* Boston: Houghton Mifflin Co., 1951.

———. *On Becoming a Person.* Boston: Houghton Mifflin Co., 1961.

Counseling Youth

BLEES, ROBERT A., and Staff of First Community Church. *Counseling with Teenagers.* Englewood Cliffs, N.J.: Prentice-Hall, 1965.

BRANDT, HENRY R. *When a Teen Falls in Love.* Wheaton, Ill.: Scripture Press Publications, Inc., 1965.

COLE, LUELLA. *Psychology of Adolescence.* New York: Rinehart & Co., Inc., 1948.

DUVALL, EVELYN M. *Facts of Life and Love for Teenagers.* New York: Association Press, 1956.

DUVALL, EVELYN M. and SYLVANUS M. *Sex Ways in Fact and Faith.* New York: Association Press, 1961.

KRICH, ARON (ed.). *Facts of Love and Marriage for Young People.* New York: Dell Publishing Co., 1962.

NARRAMORE, CLYDE M. *Counseling with Youth.* Grand Rapids: Zondervan Publishing House, 1966.

TOWNS, ELMER. *Successful Youth Work.* Glendale, Calif.: Gospel Light Publications, Inc., 1966.

WALSH, CHAD. *The Rough Years.* New York: Morehouse-Barlow Co., 1960.

WITTENBERG, RUDOLPH M. *Adolescence and Discipline.* New York: Association Press, 1959.

To counsel youth for the future, the youth worker must counsel youth for today. Though a young person is thinking about the future, he is living today. If he is out of the will of God today, he will have difficulty determining God's will for his future.

MARJORIE E. SODERHOLM

27

counseling youth for their future

THERE ARE SO MANY AREAS of life involved in a young person's future that it is impossible to deal with all of them in one chapter; therefore this chapter will deal primarily with counseling young people in the following areas: (1) knowing the will of God, (2) choosing a career, and (3) finding a life mate.

BASIC CONCEPTS RELATED TO THE WILL OF GOD

There are some basic concepts to be aware of in counseling young people regarding God's will.

1. God's will can be known. God is not keeping His will a secret. He has made His will known, and He wants people to know what it is. Many young people have the idea that God's will is a big secret locked somewhere and that they have to keep hunting for the "key" to find it. God has given His Word, and He gave His Holy Spirit for help in discerning the Word. The Lord is concerned that His children know His will. Young people need

MISS MARJORIE E. SODERHOLM, M.A., is Chairman of the Department of Christian Education, Trinity College, Deerfield, Illinois.

to be impressed that God did not do all of this to keep His will a secret from them.

2. God's will is for now. Young people are too often challenged to give their future to the Lord, but they continue to hang onto the present for themselves. They need to realize that God has a will for them now, that He has something to say about the way they treat their friends now, about the way they take responsibility now, about the attitudes they have toward their parents, teachers and studies now, and that He wants them to live according to His standards now.

3. God's will is not limited to location. Young people often think that the will of God has primarily to do with location, whether a person should go to Africa or to Hong Kong. They must see that God's will pertains to character and that He is concerned primarily with what a person *is* rather than with where he *goes*.

4. God's will cannot be separated from the lordship of Christ. Too many young people want to know God's will so that they can *consider* it. But God does not reveal Himself that way. He reveals His will to those who are *willing* to do His will. The Lord said, "He that hath my commandments and keepeth them, he it is that loveth me: and he that loveth me shall be loved of my Father, and I will love him, and will manifest myself to him" (John 14:21). The Lord does not promise to manifest Himself to the disobedient one who does not acknowledge His rightful place as Lord.

5. God's will is for His own purpose. Many persons live in an egocentric world rather than in a God-centered one. God's purposes go beyond what God has done for man. God redeemed man for Himself, but He wants to reveal to believers how they should live *for Him*.

6. Knowledge of God's will is not possible apart from the study of God's Word. Young people are prone to look everywhere for God's will except where it is—in the Word. They need to be directed to the Word; they need to see others, including those who would counsel them, searching the Word for answers to daily situations.

WAYS GOD GUIDES

Though much of what God wills is stated explicitly in His Word, many things, such as whom a person shall marry, what vocation a teen should pursue, and which school he should attend, are not specifically mentioned in the Bible. God supplements direct statements in His Word with other ways of guidance. The young person needs to know these ways in which God guides, and he needs to realize that if God is actually leading in these ways they will not contradict what is revealed in the Bible. Including the direct revelation of His written Word, there are at least eight ways by which God gives guidance:

1. *Through Scripture.* "All scripture is given by inspiration of God, and is profitable for doctrine, for reproof, for correction, for instruction in righteousness" (II Tim. 3:16). The young person and the counselor must recognize that the Bible is to be studied for truth, for reproof, for correction and for instruction. This seems obvious but is often overlooked.

2. *Through circumstances.* "And we know that all things work together for good to them that love God, to them that are the called according to his purpose" (Rom. 8:28). All the verse must be acknowledged, not just the first part. A person must acknowledge God's will in order to recognize His purposes; then all things work together for good.

3. *Through the inner compulsion of the Holy Spirit.* "Now we have received, not the spirit of the world, but the Spirit which is of God; that we might know the things that are freely given to us of God" (I Cor. 2:12). God's own Spirit dwells within the believer to prompt, to bring to mind God's Word, to give insight to God's way. He "will guide you into all truth" (John 16:13), and "will bring all things to your remembrance" (John 14:26).

4. *Through one's own abilities.* "Now there are diversities of gifts, but the same Spirit. But all these worketh that one and selfsame Spirit, dividing to every man severally as he will" (I Cor. 12:4, 11). The young person needs to realize that *God* has given him his abilities and that he is responsible for using them in the best way possible. He needs to face the fact that God will not force him into a situation that will demand abilities which God did not or will not give. There is much confusion on this issue and, because of it, some young people think they should be foreign missionaries in spite of the fact that it is almost impossible for them to learn a foreign language; while others who can learn the language easily are slothful in their work, wasting both their time and their God-given abilities.

5. *Through one's own mind.* This avenue of guidance includes three factors: (a) the young person's own sanctified sense of doing the right thing, (b) his desires, and (c) his peace of mind.

a. His own sanctified sense of doing right. "Judge me, O LORD; for I have walked in mine integrity: I have trusted also in the LORD; therefore I shall not slide" (Ps. 26:1). Often the way of determining God's will is simply doing what the young person knows is honest and upright. Often the problem is not his knowing what to do; it is doing what he knows. If a person knows right and does it, trusting the Lord, he can be assured that he will not go astray.

b. His desires. "Delight thyself in the LORD; and he shall give thee the desires of thine heart" (Ps. 37:4). Young people sometimes think that things are too good to be in the will of God. But God does not want His children to be miserable. He wants them to delight in Him. And if they are honestly doing this, their own desires may very well be a sense of God's guidance.

c. His peace of mind. "And let the peace of God rule in your hearts" (Col. 3:15). God says to let His peace be the umpire, the ruler, that which gives a sense of guidance. God wants His children to have peace, and having peace about a decision can be an indication of God's directive. However, this is one area in which young people can easily be misled, for it is common to have a false sense of peace. A young person may even claim to have peace when he has actually shut God out of his plans to the extent that he is insensitive to God's Word and to the leading of the Spirit in his life. If Colossians 3:16 is taken along with verse 15, this danger is eliminated: "Let the Word of Christ dwell in you richly" (v. 15). If a young person is studying the Bible so that the Word is dwelling in him richly, a false sense of peace is not likely to last very long. For he will soon come on something in the Word that will destroy that false peace.

6. *Through people who have responsibility over others.* "Obey them which have the rule over you and submit yourselves for they watch for your souls, as they must give account, that they may do it with joy and not with grief, for that is unprofitable for you" (Heb. 13:17). Young people sometimes think it is spiritual to disregard what people say and claim that they are responsible only to God. Yet God has put teachers, parents, governmental leaders and others in places of responsibility over them. Young people cannot claim to be obeying God if they disregard man, *except* when man's commands are directly opposed to something stated in the Word of God.

7. *Through other people with spiritual insight.* "Without counsel purposes are disappointed; but in the multitude of counselors they are established" (Prov. 15:22). Young people are often disappointed or frustrated when trying to define purposes or to make decisions. But through counsel with others they can become more settled and stable. Leaders should not become disturbed if young people seek counsel from several people. The Lord has not given exclusive rights of counsel for any young person to any one leader. God says that in the multitude of counselors one's purposes are established. The young person needs to be allowed to talk to several people as he is trying to make decisions. But he needs to be sure he seeks his counsel not from the ungodly (Ps. 1:1) but from the wise (Prov. 1:5).

8. *Through regulations that others make.* "Submit yourselves to every ordinance of man for the Lord's sake . . . for so is the will of God, that with well doing ye may put to silence the ignorance of foolish men: as free, and not using your liberty for a cloke of maliciousness, but as the servants

of God" (I Peter 2:13-16). Young people need to know that when they go away to college the rules governing signing in at the dormitories at night, the number of special permissions they are allowed per semester, the use of automobiles, are the will of God for them. They cannot claim that it is God's will for them to go to a certain school and then believe it is all right to break the rules of that school.

CHOOSING A CAREER

Choice of a vocation is an area in which young people often seek counsel. Young people used to think that the two full-time vocations for Christian service were the pastorate and foreign missions. With that view, people seemed to leave the work of spreading the message of salvation to those "full-time" persons. Now the pendulum has swung to the other extreme with the idea that any occupation is "full-time Christian work." Now young people choose any occupation they want, label it "full-time" and go ahead in their own pursuits. A person must be reminded that labeling a vocation full-time does not necessarily make it so. He needs to see how his vocation relates to Matthew 28:19-20: "Go ye therefore, and teach [disciple] all nations, baptizing them in the name of the Father and of the Son and of the Holy Ghost; teaching them to observe all things whatsoever I have commanded you; and, lo, I am with you alway, even unto the end of the world." A young person must determine how his vocation is related to his responsibility to make disciples, how in his vocation he can teach others to know the commands of the Lord and to do them. Perhaps questions such as these will help young people evaluate vocational interests:

1. How can I best honor the Lord with my talents and abilities?
2. How can my life be used in causing others to know God and to love Him?
3. How can I be used to teach others the Word of God?
4. Will this occupation bring honor to me or to the Lord?
5. Am I really interested in this occupation?
6. Do my grades show that I have the abilities necessary for this occupation?
7. Will my associations with people in this occupation give me opportunity to reach them for Christ? Or are they more likely to lead me astray?
8. Do I have complete peace about going into this occupation?
9. Can I enter into every aspect of this occupation in such a way that I can do it as unto the Lord?
10. Will the occupation leave me enough time to do direct Christian

work—to have personal Bible studies with others, to use my home for the purpose of reaching others for Christ? Or will I become so engrossed in the work or in the advancement that I will forget my ministry to people who need to know God?

Young people need to see the importance of relating their choice of occupation to God and His eternal purposes. Teens must use their own common sense, too, as they think about occupations. Leaders should make literature available to them. Many times young people are expected to make choices on the basis of what they do not know. Sources of vocational information are listed at the end of the chapter.

FINDING A LIFE MATE

For many a young person, relating God to marriage is limited to the prayer, "God, help me know which person I should marry." This is a self-centered approach, for the young person believes that if he marries the wrong person he will be unhappy, and if he marries the right one he will be happy. This is the sum and substance of his goal. How far short of God's purpose for marriage this concept falls! These thoughts about marriage must be communicated to young people:

1. *A person's marriage must be related to God's plan* for calling out a people to Himself, through whom *He* can live *His* life. Young people must think not only of what they are going to get out of marriage but also what God is going to get out of it. A teen should ask, "How will my marriage fit into God's purpose for Himself? If I marry this person, will our children be brought up to honor Him? Will our home be a mission station, reaching the people in our community? Will people come to know the Lord as a result of our marriage?"

2. *Marriage is God's idea.* Man did not think up marriage; God did. God made woman to be a partner and a helper to man. Sex is God's idea, too. It is not to be man's plaything. It is a holy thing as God made it, for marriage, for the home, for the future of mankind. God says that a man and his wife are to be one flesh (Gen. 2:24; Matt. 19:5-6). "Marriage is honourable" (Heb. 13:4a). It is His way of establishing Christian homes through which He manifests Himself.

3. *God has chosen the Christian home by which to illustrate His love for the church.* God chooses to use many of His people in pairs—a man and a woman living together in love and harmony, living together in a relationship that is a picture of the love God has for the church, the bride of Christ. The husband is to love his wife as Christ loved the church, and the wife is to be obedient to her husband (Eph. 5:21-33). What a ministry a truly God-centered home can have as it demonstrates the love of Christ.

Young people should be guided in direct Bible studies to search out what God has to say about marriage and the home. These passages, among others, could be used for such study: Ephesians 5:21—6:10; Mark 10:1-12; I Corinthians 7; II Corinthians 6:14—7:1.

One portion of Scripture that shows God's interest in marriage and in securing a life mate is Genesis 24, the account of finding a bride for Isaac. The following are some thoughts that could be shared in a study of this passage, suggesting guidelines for teens as they seek God's will in this all-important decision.

1. The bride was not to be just anyone; she was to be from a select group vv. 3-4).
2. She was to have a place in carrying out God's purpose for the whole world (v. 7).
3. What she had to say was to be determinative. Her response was to be significant (vv. 8, 41).
4. The servant looked for signs that she was the right girl for Isaac (vv. 14, 19).
5. Even after the servant saw the signs, he pondered as to whether she was the right one. He did not base his conclusion on signs alone (v. 21).
6. "I being in the way, the LORD led me" is the testimony of the place of the servant and the guidance of God (v. 27).
7. The servant did not divert from his purpose (v. 33).
8. Others recognized the thing as from the Lord, and they could not give their opinion for or against it (v. 50).
9. The experience was a God-conscious one, clothed in prayer and worship (vv. 12, 26-27, 48, 52).
10. The desires of the girl's family were secondary to God's plan. They recognized this; thus in her following God's plan, she was not going contrary to her parents' wishes (vv. 51, 55-58).
11. It was up to her to make the final decision (v. 58).
12. In addition to fitting into God's plan for His people and the world, she met a personal need in Isaac's life (v. 67).

This study, of course, should not be pressed to mean that this is the way God leads in detail in every instance of bringing a man and a woman together for marriage. However, it does show that God has His purpose in bringing about a marriage—that He directs, and that customs, distance and family relationships do not thwart God's will if God's children keep in His will so that He can lead them.

Young people need to see beyond the search for a partner, the excitement of an engagement ring, and the beauty of a wedding. Many unhappy marriages, including Christian marriages, have resulted from the neglect of young people to consider the danger signals which arise during their dating days.

The book *Building a Successful Marriage* includes several danger signals which young people should consider:

1. Frequent quarreling. A romance characterized by quarreling means a marriage characterized by quarreling.

2. Making up and breaking up during dating days. Doubts about the couple's relationship, especially by the girl, should not be discounted.

3. Desire to change the other person.

4. Desire to alter the course of life the other has chosen.

5. Differences about friends.[1]

Sometimes Christian young people think they can ignore all the problems of incompatibility that creep in by simply saying, "We're in love, and love takes care of everything." Or perhaps they comfort themselves by adding, "This is God's will, so everything will take care of itself." They need to be cautioned that these danger signals may be the very thing which the Lord is allowing them to see so that they may be able to discern His will against such a marriage.

Christian young people may need counsel on the hazards of marrying an unsaved person (see I Cor. 7:39*b;* II Cor. 6:14) or a person outside their faith or doctrinal persuasion.

WHERE SHALL WE START?

Anyone interested in counseling young people must start with himself. He must study the Bible in order to know the Lord and to know what He has to say. Many Christians have charged that most psychologists have put the Bible on the shelf. However, these Christians have done the same thing if they do not know where to look in the Bible for answers to young people's problems. When a person comes for help, and one cannot give it, it is not the latter that suffers though he may experience some embarrassment. The seeker suffers because he came and did not find what he needed. "A man hath joy by the answer of his mouth; and a word spoken in due season how good is it" (Prov. 15:23).

A word spoken in due season is good, and many seeking counsel are looking for just that. When a person can speak a word in due season, a word appropriate for the situation, he does experience joy by the answer of his mouth because he has the right thing to say to the seeker. This comes only out of consistent Bible study and alertness to the Holy Spirit's leading in using the right Scripture for the occasion at hand.

[1] Judson T. Landis and Mary G. Landis, *Building a Successful Marriage* (Englewood Cliffs, N.J.: Prentice-Hall, 1963), pp. 81-89.

As adults study the Bible firsthand for themselves, their own attitudes and actions before their young people can be strengthened—or corrected. Adults need to be adept in the use of the Scriptures in guiding their own children and young people. Too many adults do not know where to turn in their Bibles for answers that their children and teens need. So they turn their children and youth over to someone else who is "supposed to have the answers."

But churches ought to charge and help adults to become knowledgeable in the Word for their own sake and for the sake of their children. The Lord has given parents the responsibility for guiding their offspring in the things of the Lord, and churches should be helping parents fulfill that responsibility.

Young people must be directed in life-related Bible studies, personally and in groups. They are not likely to refer to the Bible for answers if they have never seen in their Bible studies that the Word of God really has answers to their problems. Discover what questions the young people have, and relate the study of God's Word to those questions and problems.

In your church library include books on vocational guidance. Sources for such materials are listed at the end of this chapter.

SUMMARY

Counseling young people is a grave responsibility and should be taken with diligence and seriousness. God places a high value on counseling because (1) it helps others establish their purposes ("Without counsel purposes are disappointed; but in the multitude of counselors they are established," Prov. 15:22); (2) counsel leads to wisdom ("Hear counsel, and receive instruction, that thou mayest be wise in thy latter end," Prov. 19:20); and (3) counsel provides safety from falling ("Where no counsel is, the people fall, but in the multitude of counselors there is safety," Prov. 11:14).

The Lord Himself tells where this counsel should come from. He says that His own counsel stands. "There are many devices in a man's heart; nevertheless the counsel of the LORD, that shall stand" (Prov. 19:21). He has put His counsel in His own Word. "Have I not written to thee excellent things in counsels and knowledge?" (Prov. 22:20). The Lord does not even recognize as counsel anything that is against Him. "There is no wisdom, nor understanding, nor counsel against the LORD" (Prov. 21:30). If counsel given is not in line with the Lord and His Word, He does not acknowledge it as counsel. Youth counselors must be diligent so that those they counsel may come to know the truth of these two verses:

"Blessed is the man that walketh not in the counsel of the ungodly" (Ps. 1:1).

"A wise man will hear, and will increase learning; and a man of understanding shall attain unto wise counsels" (Prov. 1:5).

FOR FURTHER READING

BRANDT, HENRY R. *When a Teen Falls in Love.* Wheaton, Ill.: Scripture Press Publications, Inc., 1965.

EAVEY, C. B. *Talks to Young People.* Grand Rapids: Baker Book House, 1958.

Family Filmstrips Catalog (from local audio-visual dealers or Family Filmstrips, 5823 Santa Monica Blvd., Hollywood, Calif. 90038). Lists a number of films and filmstrips for use with young people, dealing with family relationships, popularity problems, attitudes, dating, education, careers.

LAURIN, ROY L. *Meet Yourself in the Bible.* Findlay, Ohio: Dunham Publishing Company, 1946.

NARRAMORE, CLYDE M. *Dating.* Grand Rapids: Zondervan Publishing House, 1961.

———. *Life and Love.* Grand Rapids: Zondervan Publishing House, 1956.

———. *The Psychology of Counseling.* Grand Rapids: Zondervan Publishing House, 1960.

———. *Young Only Once.* Grand Rapids: Zondervan Publishing House, 1957.

New York Life Insurance Company. *Guide to Career Information.* New York: Harper and Bros. Publishers.

New York Life Insurance Company. "Career Information Series." Several pamphlets on various careers. Write New York Life Insurance Company, Career Information Service, Box 51, Madison Square Station, New York, N.Y. 10010.

PIKE, KENNETH L. *God's Guidance and Your Life Work.* Santa Ana, Calif.: Wycliffe Bible Translators, Inc.

PRICE, EUGENIA. *Find Out for Yourself.* Grand Rapids: Zondervan Publishing House, 1963.

REISS, WALTER. *For Your Teen-ager in Love.* St. Louis: Concordia Publishing House, 1960.

SCANZONI, LETHA. *Youth Looks at Love.* Westwood, N.J.: Fleming H. Revell Co., 1964.

Science Research Associates, Inc., 259 East Erie Street, Chicago, Ill. 60611. Publishes a list of 311 occupational booklets, each giving information on an occupation.

———. "Better Living Booklets." Written by educators, psychologists, psychiatrists and child study authorities. Some of the topics are: *When Children Start Dating, Let's Listen to Youth, Emotional Problems of Growing Up.*

———. Professional Guidance Books and Booklets. Written especially for educators. Some titles are: *Preparing Students for College, You and Your Life Work, Counseling Adolescents, Handbook of Job Facts.*

———. "Student Guidance" series booklets. For high school students, on getting along in high school, relationships to others, vocational planning, understanding and solving personal problems, solving everyday problems.

SMALL, DWIGHT HARVEY. *Design for Christian Marriage.* Westwood, N.J.: Fleming H. Revell Co., 1959.

SODERHOLM, MARJORIE E. *Understanding the Pupil, Part III, The Adolescent.* Grand Rapids: Baker Book House, 1956.

In the process of growing up, youth face a series of problems. Solving them well brings satisfaction and reward. Not solving them well brings unhappiness and social disapproval.

Henry R. Brandt

28

helping youth make wise decisions

Working with youth is a genuine challenge and a holy privilege. It gives youth leaders opportunity to participate in helping youth make their way from childhood to adulthood. Nothing drastic happens when a person enters the teen years. Yesterday he was 12 and today he is 13. He is just as much himself as he was yesterday. But he is steadily growing toward a mature, happy, useful, successful adulthood, or he is steadily inching toward an immature, unhappy, useless, unsuccessful adulthood.

DEVELOPMENTAL TASKS

Robert J. Havighurst has discussed what he calls "development tasks" in this growing-up process: "A developmental task is a task that arises at or about a certain period of the life of the individual, successful achievement of which leads to success with later tasks, while failure leads to unhappiness to the individual, disapproval of society, and difficulty with later tasks."[1]

---

[1]*Developmental Tasks in Education* (Chicago: University of Chicago Press, 1948), p. 6.

Henry R. Brandt, Ph.D., is a consulting psychologist, and a staff member of Campus Crusade for Christ, International, Arrowhead Springs, California.

What are some of the tasks necessary for Christian youth to learn if they are to become socially and spiritually mature people?

We shall here consider five of the ten tasks which Havighurst says teens should achieve:

1. Coming to terms with a changing body.
2. Establishing proper relationships with the opposite sex.
3. Preparing for marriage.
4. Moving toward new relationships with parents and other adults.
5. Developing a wholesome attitude toward work.[2]

Coming to Terms with a Changing Body

Physical. During the teen years rapid bodily changes take place. Physical growth is uneven. There can be a spurt in height, then in weight, and then in strength. Often a teen's arms and legs will grow faster than his body trunk. This alters his body proportions and gives him a gangly appearance— all arms and legs and feet. Even facial proportions can change.

In one study of a group of boys over a period of three and a half years, the change in height varied from 4 to 11 inches, and the change in weight varied from 7 to 65 pounds. Because of individual differences, the time and rate of the growth spurt may be as great as eight years. Some young people have attained the appearance of adults when others of the same age still look like children.

Says Havighurst:

> Everyone in our society goes through adolescence with a lively interest in his developing body. He constantly compares himself with his age mates. Slowness of development is almost sure to be a cause for concern. The girl asks herself why her breasts are not developing. The boy is worried because his genitals have not grown as much as those of other boys he knows. Shortness in a boy, and tallness and large feet in a girl, are often causes of concern. Both sexes are worried about crooked teeth, acne, obesity, and many other physical characteristics which they define as inferior. It is a rare youngster who is never worried during this period with the question, "Am I normal?"[3]

Youth must face the fact that they are no longer children. A boy must accept the idea of becoming a man, and a girl must accept the idea of becoming a woman. They must learn to accept the limitations and the advantages of their bodies and to appreciate the difference between them and others. Some teens are uncoordinated and clumsy, whereas others are well coordinated and athletic. People vary in strength, in looks, in size.

---

[2]For a listing of all ten of Havighurst's developmental tasks for youth see chapter 7 in this book, or see Robert J. Havighurst, *Human Development and Education* (New York: Longmans, Green & Co., 1953).

[3]Havighurst, *Developmental Tasks in Education*, p. 31.

Good grooming and physical exercise may contribute to some changes, but body type or facial features can be modified very little and must be accepted.

Mental. Along with changes in physical characteristics, there are marked changes in mental characteristics. The ability to think and to reason begins to show up differently in youth. It may be that a subject like algebra, which gave a person trouble at age 12, is grasped more easily at age 16—or vice versa. Abilities also begin to vary. One young person becomes adept in art, another in history, another in science. There are subjects that come easily and some that come with difficulty. The student who got straight B's in grade school may get some C's and some A's in high school.

Emotional. Certain emotional characteristics begin to show up during adolescence. A person's reactions to parents, family, friends and society begin to show up. There may be changing moods and varying degrees of cooperation and acceptance of responsibility.

Youth workers in the church can familiarize themselves with the details of these changes and, when necessary, talk about the growth process in youth meetings and with individual young people who may be concerned about their own development.

These changes are of interest to youth. They give teachers and parents opportunities to help their youth understand the wonder of a progressively unfolding and developing body. This process is all part of God's creation as stated in Genesis 2:31: "And God saw everything that he had made, and behold it was very good."

Establishing Proper Relationships with the Opposite Sex

"Male and female created he them" (Gen. 1:27). One very important change that occurs early in the teen years or just before is the maturing of the reproductive system, bringing with it a growing and pleasurable attraction to the opposite sex.

Youth leaders have the privilege of helping teens develop a sense of stewardship toward their own bodies, and a sense of responsibility, respect, reverence and awe about their bodies and those of the opposite sex. Whether or not the leader can handle this effectively depends on his own understanding and respect for himself, his knowledge of the growth process, and his knowledge of the resources available from God.

This awareness of the opposite sex leads to dating. This new relationship causes many teens to feel awkward and self-conscious. Teens experience new feelings and sensations. Young people have difficulty carrying on conversations, getting into groups, acquiring dates, learning proper manners, knowing what to expect of each other, handling aggressive approaches.

Sunday school and youth activities can provide opportunities for youth to meet, to work together, to associate with one another under favorable conditions. Church activities for youth should give them opportunity to discuss questions of Christian ethics, morals and proper conduct for Christians with the opposite sex.

Preparing for Marriage

Dating usually leads eventually to marriage. Most teen-agers marry within ten years after they start dating.

Young people are often concerned with the question "Whom will I marry?" But a more important question is "What kind of person will the one get who marries me?"

Ruth Strang, an authority on teen-age psychology, often addresses the following questions to teens on the subject of becoming more marriageable: "What is there about *you* that makes others like you?" "What do you lack that keeps others from being friendly toward you?" "What makes some people more likable than others?"

Many young people say they often feel "left out" of a group. There may be reasons for this feeling of being ignored. They may be selfish, critical, inconsiderate, unkind. Preparation for marriage requires that such character traits be corrected.

What does it mean to be likable? Very simply, it means to *focus attention on the other person,* to be interested in what he thinks and feels. It means saying, "Hi." It means listening to others. It means developing a sincere interest in the other person. It means losing one's life in order to find it (Matt. 10:39).

Being likable means to be *kind and thoughtful.* It requires letting the critical remark pass, or being good-natured and not hurting others. It means cooperating at home, doing chores cheerfully, carrying the groceries for mother, opening the door for someone, being alert to what can be done for others.

The Bible reminds us that "all we like sheep have gone astray. We have turned everyone to *his own way.* And the LORD hath laid on him the iniquity of us all" (Isa. 53:6). Young people need to see that to be marriageable, they must have more than reform, self-effort, or a harder try. Young people must be saved from self, from the tendency to go their "own way," to think chiefly of themselves.

Being likable means to be *tactful.* The tactless person is one who unthinkingly or deliberately says and does things that irritate or embarrass others. The tactful person thinks well of others and wants the best for them. God advises, "Never act from motives of rivalry or personal vanity, but in humility think more of one another than you do of yourselves. None of you should think only of his own affairs, but each should learn to see things from other people's point of view" (Phil. 2:3-4, Phillips).

Being likable means to be *cheerful.* Would you rather be with someone who enjoys what he is doing, or with someone who is always complaining? You can snarl at others or speak cheerfully. You can endure school and pick out all that is wrong with it, or you can look at the positive side and enjoy it. People don't like a grouch. They want to be around others who spread good cheer. "For I have learned, in whatsoever state I am, therewith to be content" (Phil. 4:11).

How can a teen-ager improve in this area of his life? He can pick out one thing in his life that needs correcting, admit it, and purpose, with God's help, to correct it. He should do this with each fault and weakness. He must want to change, and must ask God for the strength to change. He should tell God what is wrong. He should tell Him what he wants to be and depend on Him for help. Then the young person will have the satisfaction of living a purposeful life that will really count.

Youth workers, in counseling young people, need to help them face their faults, admit them, and change their ways.

Moving Toward New Relationships with Adults

Much has been written about the need for teen-agers to become independent. Many writers have stressed that teens must learn to stand alone and must emancipate themselves from their families.

In my judgment this view is unrealistic and unreasonable. Granted that teen-agers must slowly become responsible adults. But no one ever becomes *fully* independent of parents or family. No one ever becomes fully independent of demands and responsibilities.

As young people begin to make their own living and take responsibility for their decisions and eventually their own families, new relationships toward their parents and families must be developed. A healthy adult maintains a happy though changing relationship with parents, brothers and sisters. Their opinions and advice should still be considered and valued. Respect and honor for worthy parents should continue. Forgiveness and compassion for unworthy parents is basic.

Teens gradually move into a wider society. They take their place in the world of men and women. And society makes definite demands on everyone. Teens will never be independent of society's demands.

These demands can be seen when thinking about sportsmanship.

A good sportsman, in addition to possessing athletic ability, diligently practices to make the best possible use of that ability or even to improve it. He cooperates with his teammates. He doesn't "go it alone" or play against them, but with them. He doesn't try to outshine a teammate or show him up. He helps his teammates do their best. He also knows the rules of the game and obeys them. He accepts the judgment of his coach or referee. He is considerate of his opponents. If someone plays against him unfairly, he doesn't retaliate. Not that he is weak or afraid. Instead, he lives above such pettiness as getting mad at an unfair player.

These are the demands of society on the citizen and the businessman as well as the athlete. In counseling young people, youth workers should help them face up to these demands involved in being a good sport and a mature individual:

1. Make good use of one's talents.
2. Seek to improve them.
3. Cooperate with associates.
4. Don't try to outshine others.
5. Help others do their best.
6. Know and follow the rules.
7. Accept the judgment of leaders.
8. Be a friendly competitor.
9. Don't retaliate.
10. Face problems in a good, patient spirit.

In biblical terms, such ideals are stated as follows: "Whatsoever ye do, do it heartily, as to the Lord, and not unto men" (Col.3:23). "Whatsoever you would that men should do to you, do ye even so to them" (Matt. 7:12). "Now I beseech you, brethren, by the name of our Lord Jesus Christ, that ye all speak the same thing, and that there be no divisions among you; but that ye be perfectly joined together in the same mind and in the same judgment" (I Cor. 1:10). "The Lord make you to increase and abound in love one toward another, and toward all men, even as we do toward you" (I Thess. 3:12).

This is a lofty, idealistic standard, easily expounded but rarely lived. The young child can accept this quite uncritically, but as he grows in awareness, he becomes conscious of the contrast between the ideal and his own and others' reactions and conduct.

When questions, conflicts and discussions in these areas arise, youth leaders have opportunities for helping young people mature in their relationships with others.

The teens' widening world causes them to ponder some special questions. Smoking and drinking are two of them.

From coast to coast, teen-agers are debating, "Why smoke? Why not smoke?" To answer this question you need solid facts and straightforward answers. A published report of an advisory committee to the Surgeon General of the Public Health Service adds up to this conclusion: "Cigarette smoking is a health hazard of sufficient importance in the United States to warrant appropriate remedial action."[4]

4*Smoking, Health and You* (New York: Children's Bureau Publications, 1964), No. 424, p. 1.

Young people often face the temptation to use alcoholic beverages. John J. Pascuitti, Supervisor of Alcohol Education in Vermont, has stated that people who drink need alcohol as a crutch—a crutch to live with and to live by. The cocktail supposedly helps people function better in interpersonal relations. How do people prepare themselves to have a good time? In the same way they prepare for an operation—become anesthetized. In our "sore society" people must live with others, but many cannot do so without the help of alcohol.

When a young person learns to socialize in boy-girl relations or other types of tension-creating situations, he is gaining in experience and maturity. But if he must resolve these problems through alcohol, he is not developing the social and emotional arts he needs. He is not developing the resources he will need in order to function fully. This is what is meant by "arrested development."

Milton Potter, chairman of a committee for the American Medical Society on the alcoholic, says the more he studies the case histories of alcoholics, the more he is struck by the fact that the alcoholic is an individual who has never grown up emotionally. All case histories date back to childhood—improper homes, poor environment, inadequate training and guidance.

Youth workers can help young people weigh the issues in these areas of temptation. God can supply grace, joy and peace to the hearts of men. These make a "shot" of some kind unnecessary. Paul wrote, "Be not drunk with wine wherein is excess, but be filled with the Spirit" (Eph. 5:18). Everyone must tackle the future, no matter what his background. With God's help the past can be forgiven, old attitudes changed, new ones formed (Phil. 3:12-15).

Developing a Wholesome Attitude Toward Work

Developing a positive attitude toward work is a major task of the teen years. Everybody wants to advance in this world of work, to keep a job and be happy in it.

In a pamphlet entitled *So You Want a Better Job,* Paul W. Boynton, supervisor of employment for Socony Mobil Oil Company, refers to a study of seventy-six corporations aimed at learning why people do not get promoted or why they lose their jobs. It was expected that there would be a long string of reasons. Surprisingly, 76 percent of the people who failed to get promoted and 90 percent of the people who lost their jobs did so for *one* reason: *They couldn't get along with other people!*[5] The lack of specific skill or technical knowledge played a relatively small part.

---

[5]Paul W. Boynton, *So You Want a Better Job* (New York: Socony Mobil Oil Co., 1955), pp. 6-16.

Think of it! Nine out of every ten dismissals and more than three-fourths of the promotion failures were caused by unfavorable personality traits such as carelessness, lack of cooperation, laziness, tardiness, dishonesty, lack of ambition. It all boils down to the fact that the ability to keep a job and to progress in it is a matter of *attitudes*.

Teen-agers are forming their attitudes about work now. Teens are forming lasting attitudes toward work as they face schoolwork, chores around the house, working on a committee or participating on a team.

Boynton lists several traits that are vital to success in work:

1. Willingness and ability to accept responsibility.
2. Respect for authority.
3. Desire for self-improvement.
4. Personal appearance, including decent dress, table manners, and social manners.
5. Ability to get along with one's boss.
6. Ability to get along with co-workers.
7. Proper attitudes toward oneself and others.

These are all traits that youth can learn. Good work habits do not just happen. They are the result of training, experience and attitudes of children in their formative years. Work should be one of the most interesting, enjoyable, satisfying and challenging parts of life, even though someone else requires it and the task is not of particular interest. Part of developing good work habits includes learning to accept difficult and tedious tasks cheerfully.

All kinds of tasks need to be done if a family or the people of the world are to live happily. Any necessary work is worthwhile, and no work is beneath one's dignity. Work is good—to be able to work is a privilege, not an imposition.

For children and young people, *home chores, schoolwork, homework* and the *routines* of the day are their "work." Out of these comes their outlook on employment. Adults should help young people develop good work habits by directing them in the following four aspects of work:

Desirable attitudes. Cheerful acceptance of a task is half the battle. Willingness to try makes work a challenge. More difficult, but also important, is the willingness to learn from constructive criticism. Cooperation, working in terms of group purposes, can be learned whether it be the family, team, school or business.

Development of skills. Skills are learned during play and continue to be learned at school, in sports, through business and professional training, and by special study.

Acceptance of responsibility. Work involves accepting the requirements of the task, concentrating effort on the task, and persisting until the task is completed.

Feeling of security. This depends on developing in skill and knowledge, and on finding satisfaction in a job well done.

Adults teach by their interest in their own work, their cheerful acceptance of responsibility, their willingness to complete a task, their readiness to help others, their sympathetic understanding of others' limitations, and their appreciation of the accomplishments of others. All these help young people realize that work is a satisfying experience.

Adults should seek to recognize young people's abilities and fit tasks in the church to those abilities. Tasks that are too difficult may lead a young person to give up. Tasks that are too easy lead to lack of interest, carelessness, laziness. Adults can help make tasks clearly understood, so the teen knows what is required of him.

Note these thoughts about work in Scripture:

"Not slothful in business, fervent in spirit; serving the Lord" (Rom. 12:11).

"Whatsoever ye do, do it heartily, as to the Lord, and not unto men" (Col. 3:23).

"Let every soul be subject unto the higher powers. For there is no power but of God; the powers that be are ordained of God" (Rom. 13:1).

"Servants [employees], be obedient to them that are your masters according to the flesh, with fear and trembling, in singleness of your heart, as unto Christ; not with eye-service, as men-pleasers; but as the servants of Christ, doing the will of God from the heart; with good will doing service, as to the Lord, and not to men" (Eph. 6: 5-7).

SUMMARY

All teens are involved in at least five developmental tasks. These tasks provide opportunities for youth leaders to capture the natural interests of youth. All the youth activities in the Sunday school and church program—whether recreation, outings, studies, programs, or personal contacts—will be helpful to young people if centered in these areas.

For his own preparation, the wise youth leader familiarizes himself with materials that will develop his own understanding of teens' personal problems. He takes every opportunity he can to let teens know he is interested in talking with them and working with them.

The leader should form his own views on these areas, take a firm stand with regard to them, but without arguing. He will be expected to believe something and will be respected for it if he does. His effort should be to clarify his beliefs, but not to be defensive or argumentative about them. Each youth must choose the path he will follow, but should have the advantage of comparing his choices with the firm convictions of his youth group leader.

FOR FURTHER READING

ANDERSON, KEN. *Make Your Life a Miracle.* Grand Rapids: Zondervan Publishing House, 1959.

BEHLMER, REUBEN D. *From Teens to Marriage.* St. Louis: Concordia Publishing House, 1959.

BRANDT, HENRY R. *Build a Happy Home with Discipline.* Wheaton, Ill.: Scripture Press Publications, Inc., 1965.

———. *When a Teen Falls in Love.* Wheaton, Ill.: Scripture Press Publications, Inc., 1956.

CAPPER, W. MELVILLE, and WILLIAMS, H. MORGAN. *Toward Christian Marriage.* Chicago: Inter-Varsity Press, 1958.

CRAMER, RAYMOND L. *The Psychology of Jesus and Mental Health.* Los Angeles: Cowman Publications, Inc., 1959.

DUVALL, EVELYN M. *Family Development.* New York: J. B. Lippincott, 1962.

FRANK, LAWRENCE K. and MARY. *Your Adolescent at Home and in School.* New York: Viking Press, 1956.

GESELL, ARNOLD, ILG, FRANCES L., and AMES, LOUISE BATES. *Youth—The Years from Ten to Sixteen.* New York: Harper & Bros. Publishers, 1956.

HAVIGHURST, ROBERT J. *Human Development and Education.* New York: Longmans, Green & Co., 1953.

KAWIN, ETHEL. *Adolescence.* Chicago: Parent Education Project, University of Chicago, 1963.

KIRKENDALL, LESTER A. *Reading and Study Guide for Students in Marriage and Family Relations.* Dubuque, Iowa: Wm. C. Brown, 1965.

KOONCE, RAY F. *Understanding Your Teen-agers.* Nashville: Broadman Press, 1965.

LANDIS, JUDSON T. and MARY G. *Building a Successful Marriage.* Englewood Cliffs, N.J.: Prentice-Hall, Inc., 1963.

NARRAMORE, CLYDE M. *Young Only Once.* Grand Rapids: Zondervan Publishing House, 1957.

———. *This Way to Happiness.* Grand Rapids: Zondervan Publishing House, 1958.

PRICE, EUGENIA. *Never a Dull Moment.* Grand Rapids: Zondervan Publishing House, 1955.

RINKER, ROSALIND. *The Years That Count.* Grand Rapids: Zondervan Publishing House, 1958.

RYRIE, CHARLES R. *Patterns for Christian Youth.* Chicago: Moody Press, 1966.

VAN BUREN, ABIGAIL. *Dear Teen-ager.* New York: Bernard Geis Associates, 1959.

index